CW00392016

CRAVAT-A-LICIOUS

MATT PRESTON

CRAVAT-A-LICIOUS

EBURY
PRESS

An Ebury Press book
Published by Random House Australia Pty Ltd
Level 3, 100 Pacific Highway, North Sydney NSW 2060
www.randomhouse.com.au

First published by Ebury Press in 2009

Copyright © Matt Preston, 2009

The moral right of the author has been asserted.

All rights reserved. No part of this book may be reproduced or transmitted by any
person or entity, including internet search engines or retailers, in any form or by
any means, electronic or mechanical, including photocopying (except under the
statutory exceptions provisions of the Australian Copyright Act 1968), recording,
scanning or by any information storage and retrieval system without the prior
written permission of Random House Australia.

Addresses for companies within the Random House Group can be found at
www.randomhouse.com.au/offices

National Library of Australia
Cataloguing-in-Publication Entry

Preston, Matt.
Cravat-a-licious.

ISBN 978 1 74166 967 1 (pbk).

Restaurants – Anecdotes.
Food – Anecdotes.
Cookery.

647.95

Cover and internal design by Christabella Designs
Typeset by Midland Typesetters, Australia
Printed and bound by Griffin Press, South Australia

Random House Australia uses papers that are natural, renewable and recyclable
products and made from wood grown in sustainable forests. The logging and
manufacturing processes are expected to conform to the environmental regulations
of the country of origin.

10 9 8 7 6 5 4 3 2 1

CONTENTS

PART II: COOK

PART III: REVERE

For my wife, Emma,
who always puts up with me ... beautifully.
I love you.

INTRODUCTION

Does anyone ever read the introduction? Or is it like the instructions with flat pack furniture or your new mobile phone … something you put in the bottom drawer thinking you'll get to later?

So why a book? Other than a rather obvious and cynical cashing in on the success of *MasterChef*? Well, you see I've got all these retired stories sitting at my place with nothing to do and basically they need a good home. Most of them are house-trained and they require little maintenance – just an unassuming shelf somewhere. Perhaps in a forgotten corner of your study, guest room, or even in the downstairs dunny. As I've only included my least worst writing, the book shouldn't bend any shelves and it is still thin enough that it can be used for squashing blowies rather effectively.

The stories here are largely drawn from my writing for *delicious* magazine, *The Age* and *Vogue Entertaining + Travel*. If they are any good, it is thanks to my marvellous skills as a writer. If you think any of them are crap, I'd suggest blaming the editors from these fine publications, who commissioned them in the first place. They are named and shamed in the Acknowledgements section at the back of the book.

Please note that in some cases the pieces have been changed slightly from the published version because I wanted to: a) reinstate the lame jokes a generation of previous editors excised; b) correct things that I originally got wrong – yes, okay, I do now know that Rice Bubbles aren't harvested by hand; c) put back in the boring food history that was originally banished to online publication only. There are even some new pieces that no-one has seen before.

If you've been given this book as a present, then may I suggest just jumping straight into the articles that have won awards, as obviously these are the best things to read ...

'Bringing Home the Bacon' (page 20), 'Nonna Food' (page 10) and 'You're Not Going to Eat That?' (page 62) won me the 2003 Food Media Club of Australia (FMCA) biennial award for Best New Australian Food Writer.

'The Temple Kitchen' (page 92) won the 2005 FMCA award for Best Food Article and 'Preserving Knowledge' (page 204) won the 2007 FMCA award for Best Recipe Feature in a Newspaper or Supplement, beating a stellar line-up of big name TV talent.

In 2008 I won a Le Cordon Bleu World Food Media Award, naming me the World's Best Food Journalist for 'Migrant Food' (page 87), 'Refugee Catering' (page 97), 'Preserving Knowledge' (page 204) and the Mario Batali interview (page 251).

Oh, and 'A Guide to Designer Salts' (page 149) was highly commended in the 2001 FMCA awards.

I should also note that as this is a compilation of my least worst writing over the last ten years, I fear that many of the places and people mentioned in some of the older pieces may no longer be with us. To those who survive them, may I say it was a pleasure knowing them – as is witnessed by their inclusion here. They touched my life and shared their love of food with me to pass on to others. That is a rare gift to be given. I should also note that all facts and figures in the articles were correct at time of publication but beware, like my figure they too may have changed over the ensuing years.

PART I

EAT

25 THINGS YOU SHOULD NEVER DO IN THE KITCHEN

The kitchen is the most dangerous room in the house – especially in the hands of an idiot like me. For the greater public good, here is my list of the '25 Things You Should Never Do in the Kitchen'. Embarrassingly, I have done many of these. The other no-noes I have watched people do before I could scream 'No, don't!' Interestingly, when compiling this list I realised there were far more than just 25. In fact, there are 30 'don'ts' in total.

1. Don't use blunt knives. Blunt knives are more prone to slip and bounce when you use them, resulting in cuts and injuries. You'll also find you'll maul and crush whatever you are cutting.

2. Treat recently sharpened knives with the utmost respect. The improvement in performance of a properly sharpened knife means it's far more likely to do you damage if you don't concentrate when using it. And remember always to focus cutting pressure away from you, and away from your fingers.

3. Don't use the mandolin to slice vegetables thinly without the guard. It's embarrassing (and bloody) trying to pick the bit of your fingertip out of the thinly sliced carrots or fennel.

4. Don't stick fingers or cutlery in the blender when it is going. You'd think this would be obvious, but …

5. Don't wash wooden chopping boards in the dishwasher. You'll rot and ruin them.

6. Don't leave durian in the fridge, unless you want your fridge to smell like the MCG toilets after the Collingwood–Carlton game.

7. Don't lick the blades of the hand blender when it is still plugged in. Again, you'd think this would be obvious, but sometimes greedy people like me need to be reminded – especially when there's the remains of a creamy fruit fool on the head and blades of the blender.

8. Don't cook mango jam in the nude. Fibrous fruit like mango tends to bubble and spit when you mix it with sugar to turn into jam. Few things hurt more than dollops of boiling hot melted sugar hitting your skin. Well, other than peeling them off. The same rule goes for deep-frying.

9. Don't undercook chicken. Rare is fine for steak but not for chook.

10. Don't use crème de menthe in any savoury dishes. I know crazy modern cookery and culinary invention is all the rage, but certain rules like this remain for the safety and sanity of all.

11. Never serve meat without resting it. Resting meat after cooking allows it to relax and makes it seem far juicier.

12. Never overcook vegies – or undercook them. Neither squeaky or soggy should vegies be.

13. Don't use stuff bought from the supermarket when you have the time to make it yourself. Okay, there is a time and a place for short cuts, but when it only takes a few minutes of work to make soup or stock or your own biscuits, do it. The end result is usually fresher, tastier and cheaper.

14. Don't put oil in boiling pasta water. Just add a glass of cold water after you add the pasta to the boiling salted water, stir and then bring back to the boil and cook normally. *Voilà*: no sticking.

15. Don't put water in boiling oil. It will spit and sometimes flare with flames if you do.

16. Don't sift your flour. People used to do this to sift out weevils and stones – it actually won't make it any lighter.

17. Don't sear meat to hold in juices. That's a fallacy too. The reason to sear meat is to give it a nice tasty browned surface.

18. Don't keep dried spices and herbs for more than three months. They will lose their potency the older they get.

19. Don't let your idiot brother use a metal scourer on your non-stick pans. This goes for any zealous idiot who wants to raise a shine on your prized pans.

20. Don't microwave metal plates or put plastic plates in the oven. Yes, I've seen top chefs do both in moments of forgetful panic …

21. Don't put your finger in the caramel on the stove to see if it's hot. Trust me, from experience, it almost always is … very hot!

22. Don't ever put the electric kettle on the hob. So easy to do, but do it in front of the kids and they'll see it as an early sign of Alzheimer's and start visiting old people's homes for you.

23. Don't put a metal baking pan to your lips to see if the oven is hot. This leaves an ugly burn.

24. Don't put the remote control in the fridge. It makes it very hard to find when you want to change channels.

25. Don't poke the meat while it's cooking in the pan. Contrary to received barbecue wisdom, this will not help it cook faster.

26. Don't buy glass chopping boards to use with your new heavy Chinese cleaver.

27. Don't try to get toast out of a toaster with a metal fork. This can break the toaster – and you. Putting raisin toast into your toaster can also break it. Apparently those raisins can cause the elements to fritz.

28. Don't gladwrap herbs and put them in the fridge. They'll just rot.

29. Don't put hot food straight into the fridge. Wait until it stops steaming so you can maintain the fridge's cool.

30. Don't flambé on your stove unless you've cleaned out the range hood filters. The filters can hold sucked-up oil particles from when you fry. Flames from flambéing can ignite this oil. This is not good news.

31. Don't be shy with your seasoning. From pastas and meats to chocolate and caramel, a little salt brings dishes to life.

32. Don't pour your sauce over a crispy piece of fish, or any battered or fried stuff. This will destroy its crispiness, which you have worked so hard to achieve.

33. Never pour oil down the sink.

34. Don't have sex on the kitchen counter before friends come over for dinner. Invariably that will be the night they will come straight round to the back door rather than ringing the front doorbell.

35. If you're a bloke, never ever cut chilli while wearing tracksuit pants …

Originally published in 'A2', The Age, 2009

RECESSION BUSTING

Making the Cheapest Home Meal
Seem Fancy

One of my favourite stories from that last big recession back in the early nineties was how the McDonald's near Wall Street employed a swish-looking doorman, installed a baby grand piano (and someone to play it) and a chandelier. They then sat back and watched as the local brokers and bankers deserted their usual swank spots for a reassuring dose of saturated fat, sugar and calories, complete with familiar trimmings.

Now that it's official that those happy days are here again I think there is a valuable lesson that we can learn from the big clown's actions. If you can no longer afford to feast in the finest restaurants, then let's learn from them. Why not follow these simple tips for creating a dining-out experience at home?

Put a white cloth on your dining table – even at family meals. Make everyone eat together at least once a week. Combined with the tablecloth, the fact that this is such a rarity will give your meals a sense of occasion, no matter how simple the food.

Always ask your family if they have a reservation before you allow them to sit down. If they don't, ask them to wait while you see if you can fit them in – despite the fact that there are empty seats still at the table. If they do claim to have booked, still keep them waiting while you try to remember if they tipped the last time they were here. Then seat them accordingly: close to the toilet or in the carver at the end of the table with the best garden views.

Make your children take it in turns to wear black trousers, a white shirt and an apron and keep filling up everyone's water glass and offering more bread. If you refuse the bread, they must immediately whip away your side plate and never offer you bread again. They should also disappear before the end of the meal so you can't ask them for the bill. (Yes, you'll make the housekeeping go so much further if you charge your family for meals – just don't expect them to be good tippers.)

Insist on good manners. Use cutlery, but no eating off your knife. No leaving the table before everyone is finished. No jabbing brothers in the back of the thigh with forks – or even waving your cutlery around when speaking. No leaving your cutlery akimbo on the plate when you are finished – that means knife and fork together with the blade of the knife pointing towards the fork and both lying parallel on the plate at 6.30 pm (if you follow the Australian manner) or at 5.25 pm (if you want to be mistaken for being English). No elbows on the table while eating. And sit up straight. Sure, this has nothing to do with recession busting, but the great thing about the poor is that they usually have far better manners than the rich. And right now you'll need to have some reason to look down on all those insolvency lawyers and administrators who are coining it even if you aren't.

Give everything that you serve fancy French names. Then use the computer to print out a menu card for dinner. So now it's *'une grande assiette composée des oeufs brouillés, des haricots blancs cuisinés dans une sauce tomate, deux saucissons de campagne, du lard, des champignons sautés au beurre aillé et persillé et quelques tranches poêlées de tomate tous accompagnés de la sauce brune et on est servi du pain grillé'*. That's so much more high rent than 'a big breakfast with HP sauce and toast'.

Alternatively, milk the provenance of the ingredients with fulsome descriptions of 'Australian orange juice handcrafted only from the finest Brazilian concentrate, cruelty-free coffee from the southern end of aisle three at Coles, cakes of organic Australian wheat, oven-roasted in the shadow of Watagan Mountain, and hen-laid eggs sourced from the western side of battery Shed 4'.

At dinner, serve miniature versions of every dish — ideally on square or misshapen plates that are far too large for the amount of food. Repeat several times.

Remember to constantly re-offer the wine list, reminding the younger members of your family that their wineglasses are empty to justify your relentless upselling.

Buy an expensive decanter. That way you can serve your guests good but cheap red wine, like a $6 bottle of Sacred Hill cab merlot or a $15 bottle of Seppelt Heathcote shiraz and fool them into thinking they are drinking something far, far better. Especially if you leave around the kitchen the empty bottle of that expensive shiraz you drank by yourself while watching the footy last week. Your nosier friends and family will assume that's what's in the decanter. Just remember, if asked what is in the decanter, reply 'Just a nice drop from our local vintner.' Never ever use the word 'bottle-o', which will immediately have any wine snobs looking down their nose at you.

Oh, and make sure everyone wears black tie, purchased from the local op shop. It's so much cheaper than keeping up with the shifting sands of designer wear.

Originally published in 'A2', The Age, 2009

NONNA FOOD

Slow Food. Comfort Food. Soul Food. Peasant Food ... Before all these snappy nostalgia-sodden marketing concepts, many of the values they encompass could be expressed with two words – Granny's cooking.

Whether you call her Babka, Nai Nai, Bube, Ajii, Oma, Mor-Mor, Yia Yia or Grand-mère the spirit is the same. Few cultures, however, place such culinary importance on the family matriarch as the Italians.

'We grew up in the kitchen with Nonna,' says Adriana Parolin of her grandmother and Melbourne's grande dame of Italian food, Olimpia Bortolotto. 'As soon as we could stand we were helping with the gnocchi and the bolognese, but even before then my sister and I were plonked in our car seats in the middle of her kitchen.'

Today Adriana works on reception at the family's Melbourne restaurant, Cecconi's, while her twin sister, Nicoletta, is in real estate, but Olimpia still vividly remembers them standing on milk crates to lift the gnocchi out of the boiling water as soon as they rose to the surface.

While their nonna now claims that her granddaughters' gnocchi is better than hers – the secret is in the lightness of touch and using the dough immediately, Olimpia reveals – Adriana believes she learnt more than just how to cook. 'It's helped give me an understanding of where I come from,' she says.

Olimpia has also found the experience extremely rewarding. 'In an era when so many young aren't interested, it made me feel really good when they'd ring up and ask, "Are you cooking? Can we come in and watch?"' she says. 'This is how I was brought up. I learnt more from my parents and mother-in-law than I did from any cooking course. I learnt about taste and how to season and timing. But I also learnt so many of the values I have now about the importance of food and the family.'

Her own grandmothers remained in Italy when her family took the last boat out to Australia before the war, so she was deprived of their knowledge. Her mum died when she was only seven, but Olimpia still follows her secret for a good ragù. 'Brown everything thoroughly and then cook it very slowly,' she recites.

Olimpia is also a firm believer that cooking together can create bonds across the generations and keep a family together. It can also cause a few stoushes in the kitchen. Robert Castellani, chef at St Kilda's Donovans, remembers his mother, Maria, and her mother, Caterina, both being very fussy in the kitchen. 'They'd fight over the washing up because they didn't believe the other one did it properly!'

His grandmother, who came from the Aeolian Islands, off Sicily, did most of the cooking, as his parents both worked, but while he acknowledges she was a good cook he describes her as a 'pain in the neck'. She'd put stuffed squid in his lunchbox, which hardly stopped the other kids calling the seven-year-old, non-English-speaking 'Robertino' a 'wog'.

'I grew up in an alien culture,' he says. 'We were rice farmers in northern Italy and then suddenly I'm living in sixties Ballarat. There would be onions drying on the washing line above the wood-fired cooking stove, my father wanted to cultivate the median strip and we were always plucking something! At an early age I knew we were different.'

Initially, when he started cooking, Castellani rejected the background that had set him apart but now he looks back at those days as a time of 'real food', where so much family lore about food and cooking was passed down through looking and doing.

His father might have taught him the value of simplicity that's evident in his food today – 'he used to say the only accompaniment a fish needed was a lemon' – but his grandmother was just as prescriptive around the kitchen. 'Back then it was cheaper to make pasta than buy it and there were always rules and regulations on how to make it. We'd shape it around knitting needles. She'd say the hole helped trap the sauce. She always made her own stock and that had to have 'the eyes' – little pools of fat on the surface. Even today I don't like to see roasted peppers washed clean of the seeds!'

You'll find these wistful memories in lots of immigrant cultures, where the celebration of Nonna's food can be a form of melancholia for or celebration of the 'old country' and the friends and family left behind.

Newly arrived from London to take up the post of head chef at Treasury, Simon Arkless talks warmly about his childhood in Hartlepool. His 'Nanna' would come over every Saturday. She'd slip into the housecoat and slippers that were almost a uniform in England's north-east and cook breakfasts of dripping-soaked fried bread and tangles of crisped bacon rind. As much as his memories are about the good things she'd cook, like rabbit casserole or the steak and kidney pie that he still dreams about, there were also the bad dishes, like the overcooked Sunday roast of grey beef and Bisto gravy granules.

And then there were her cakes – chocolate cake, Victoria sponge, scones. 'My wife's yoyos just aren't quite the same,' he says a little mistily.

Aucklander Dee Wilson's fruitcake is also pretty darn good, according to her grandson, Blakes Cafeteria co-chef Daniel Wilson. 'I have got to get the recipe,' he says in a tone that's self-chiding and makes one wonder how many great family recipes have been lost because we just won't make the time to learn them.

He also talks of weekend visits with his sister to Dee's. Of fresh pikelets and cheese scones. Of licking the bowl and waiting impatiently by the oven. Of banana smoothies from the old Hamilton Beach milkshake maker and helping make the salad dressing. Of trips to Maccas …

There's a screech of tyres down this memory lane with the realisation that Wilson is young enough to be part of a generation where a 'happy meal with Granny' should be written with two more capitals. Are we also heading towards a time when grannies are too busy to spend time in the kitchen?

Of course, there's nothing new in the concept of the granny who can't or won't cook. Ocha's chef and co-owner Yasu Yoshida had one. 'My grandma was not a good cook. In summer holidays she'd come and stay. She cooked Japanese curry for me. I didn't like it and she was really upset,' he remembers.

Unlike Yoshida, many of France's great chefs, like Auguste Escoffier, have credited some of their skill with food to formative years spent with *Grand-mère*. In fact, it seems that Lyon's push to eclipse Paris as France's culinary epicentre was built around celebrating provincial cooking romantically dressed up as '*cuisine grand-mère*'.

This Lyonnaise influence now stretches around the world, with local lads like Daniel Boulud (of Daniel and Café Boulud) in New York and Roland Passot (of Left Bank) in San Francisco both finding success with some help from 'granny's cooking'.

Legendary Lyonnaise chefs like Fernand Point and Paul Bocuse celebrated the food of their grandmothers by showing a healthy respect for seasonality, albeit as much out of concerns about economy and availability than any sentimental notion of culinary 'rightness'.

It's easy to forget that the culture of the kitchen-bound housewife of yesteryear, slaving over the stove or the preserving bath, evolved from an age before cut-price 'convenience foods'; air-freighted avocados and motor cars and fridges for all. Peasant-based traditions like baking, jam-making or salting were about not starving through the lean months, although now a new generation is embracing them in a quest for food that tastes good rather than just shipping well and looking nice on the shelves at your local Coles.

The danger is that the warm fuzzy feelings that Granny's kitchen evokes will be appropriated by spin doctors to give the most vertical, faceless and wanky chef or soulless multinational food corporation an accessible human side. It would be interesting to know, for example, how the canteen food cooked by the mother and grandmother of Jean-Georges Vongerichten (of Jean Georges) relates to the food at his 'here-waiter-you'll-want-to-take-my-shirt-with-the-bill' Columbus Circle restaurant.

But then, it's not hard to spot those who walk the walk their grandmother taught them. Ocean Road culinary pioneer Christos Talihmanidis (of Chris's Beacon Point, Marine Café, Sea Grape) has long equally credited his grandmother alongside the French chefs who trained him for his approach to food.

Growing up in Salonika during the war and the dark times that followed, his education was at the hem of his grandmother Sofia's skirts in the family restaurant. 'I hardly went to school. The thought was that if I was in the kitchen it would keep me safe,' says the man who, aged ten, asked their chef if he could become an apprentice and twelve years later found himself cooking in Australia. 'Sofia was a widow and I had her late husband's name, so there was a special bond between us,' he recalls.

She spoilt him with food and when food was scarce took him out to forage for wild roots and greens to feed the family. 'Standing beside her in the kitchen aged nine, I'd wash potatoes and peel onions but I learnt so much more. How to choose fresh fish and ripe figs. How to spot when a sauce was off. How to be the king of the market. She taught me how to smell and touch ... how to love and respect food.'

The best of Christos' food bears Sofia's fingerprints – those simple dishes that value the primacy of the ingredients – but it is in his Greek stifado that he believes her voice is strongest. 'It's based on her recipe but while she'd use wild hare for this stew I now use rabbit.'

The deep-seated influence that our family has on who we are is self-evident, but what is more controversial is whether an aptitude at the stoves can be as much down to 'nature' as 'nurture'. Peter McLeod, the chef/co-owner behind the Hotel Spencer and the Lincoln, is often held up as excelling in food that Granny used to make – corned beef, pies, meatloaf and mash. Yet while his mother was a good home cook – her beef olives occasionally appear on Spencer's menu – he's at odds to know where his vocation to cook came from, a vocation that drove him in his twenties to swap a lucrative career in finance for the first rung on the ladder to chef – washing dishes.

When Peter recently discovered that his paternal grandmother, who died when Peter's father was three, had been one of the first Australian women to travel to France and study at the Cordon Bleu cookery school, everything seemed to click into place. 'She cooked on a big sheep and cattle station outside Terang and even though I never knew her I feel a very strong bond with her,' he says.

It was a bond made all the more vivid when, at a funeral in Terang recently, by chance and with no little surprise he happened across her grave. McLeod is now trying to find out more about this woman he never knew but whose blood runs through his veins.

For McLeod, so much of what he wants to know must now be dust. Many of us are luckier. We can still pick up the phone and call granny to see if we or the kids can come over at the weekend. To cook with her. To learn with her. To just cherish spending time with her.

It's about more than just treasured knowledge passed from generation to generation before it's too late. It's about baking bread and breaking bread. It's about the very essence of what it is to be family.

Originally published in 'Epicure', The Age, 2009

GUILTY PLEASURES

This week let us delve into the darker corners of the pantry of the soul. The place where we all harbour the things that we'd rather others didn't see. Now, I'm not talking about those foodie-scandalising short cuts that some of us sometimes find ourselves taking, like having stock cubes, lemon juice in a bottle, herbs in tubes, packet cake mix or jars of smashed garlic laced with vinegar in your cupboards. No, I want to uncover the sort of hidden culinary pleasures that take place behind closed doors. These are the pleasures that would shock and scandalise friends and family if they came out in a salacious *New Weekly* exposé.

When exploring our guiltiest food pleasures, however, we need to remember that we are not alone in our dark ways. Number two chef in the world, Heston Blumenthal, has admitted his deep and abiding love of butterscotch Angel Delight – an industrial powdered packet mousse. Jamie Oliver loves nothing more than a frozen fish finger sandwich. (For the record: both are totally delicious – especially if you cook the fish fingers in the toaster in true inner-city squatter fashion and then load the soft fake white supermarket bread for the sandwich with butter and either mayo or ketchup.)

After extensive interviews, it appears that our guiltiest food pleasures come in three distinct forms – and that they are usually taken standing up so you can take rapid evasive action if someone catches you 'in flagrante delicto' – which loosely translates as 'caught with three fingers in the peanut butter jar'.

Many expressed guilt and pleasure at grazing their way through the supermarket, whether it was pilfering cherries or handfuls of pistachios (and stashing the shells and pits behind the canned vegies). Those raised in Queensland admitted to snacking on 'cheerios' while they cruised the aisles. That's the northern name for baby saveloys or 'little boys', as they are rather stomach-turningly called down our way.

The second cluster seemed to be those with a penchant for the purest flavour hit – and a desire to avoid using cutlery. In this group we might find such sexy sins as dredging out fingerfuls of lemon curd, mango chutney, cold baked beans, canned rice or that dreadful cheap steak-in-a-can straight from the jar or tin. This seems slightly more naughty if you can get the product from the container into your mouth without digital manipulation, whether that is by squirting US aerosol-packed cheese straight into your gob, drinking cold commercial custard directly from the carton, or sucking condensed milk straight from the can.

Our final cluster of guilty pleasures revolves around junk food, whether it's a steaming bowl of 'deluxe' packet Kraft mac 'n' cheese or a cheesy crust pizza with more cheese. More complex is when this junk food becomes morning-after food: a cold chicken korma eaten straight from the plastic container, cold pizza or cold homemade rice pudding or apple crumble eaten straight from the baking dish in the fridge.

There are, of course, some guilty pleasures so outlandish that they defy categorisation. Let us call these our 'Naughty Nine'.

1) Double cream was at the heart of so many confessions. Like many, I like it whipped and dolloped on breakfast cereal, but I saw my favourite food editor in a whole new light when she admitted to mixing Horlicks, jam or Ovaltine with cream into a paste to eat neat with a teaspoon.

2) Try microwaving slices of cheap strasbourg sausage (aka 'strass') until just crispy round the edges and then serve dolloped with tomato ketchup.

3) More research is needed to find out why for so many people tinned meat pies inspire such reverence. Maybe it's just the mere idea that this crispy-puff-pastry-topped slurry of meat and gravy comes in a can and can be served in it too. Cool!

4) Licking the icing off cupcakes – and leaving the cake. It's up there with eating out the filling from biscuits. Or dunking.

5) Please indulge me if I expand on the insightful contention of culinary philosopher Dave O'Neill that everything tastes better crumbed, with my observation that popping stuff between two slices of cottonwool-soft white supermarket bread has the same effect. It doesn't matter whether it's Burger Rings, ready-salted potato chips, French fries, a meat pie or potato cakes, for a section of food sensualists, corralling them in bread and butter makes 'em better. I have to draw the line, however, at serving a sandwich filled with a great glob of chicken two-minute noodles, as one interviewee suggested, as a particularly fine hangover cure. Maybe it was the fact the bread was supposed to be lightly toasted rather than raw that put me off, but it tasted all too sludgy in the middle.

6) Naturally, Vegemite has to feature in a number of weird ways, whether spread on the top of a garlic pizza or on crepes loaded with melted butter.

7) The Flatware-Free Sundae. Shared by one of my more theatrical culinary sources, this is a clever way of saving on washing up. Tilt back your head. Open your mouth. Drop in three slices of cling peach (without swallowing or choking). Pour in a splash of evaporated milk and a handful of Coco Pops. Top with a generous squirting of whipped cream in a can. Shut mouth and chew while enjoying this textural riot of creamy slippery sweetness delivered straight to your palate.

8) Cheetos. These little cheese and bacon puffs have long been a secret love, although it's not really that secret given that they dye your fingers a vibrant nicotine orange. Come round to my place and before dinner you're likely to enjoy a little amuse-bouche

of a quenelle of snowy white Kraft processed cheese from a jar surrounded by these little orange balls. Combine on a spoon, bang it in your gob and be assailed by the creaminess of the cheese and crisp frizz of the corn puffs. Yum!

9) Hot farfalle pasta with thousand island dressing. No, I don't get it either. I've tried it – as I did all of these suggestions in the interest of culinary research – and I reckon you'd be better off just drinking the dressing straight from the bottle.

Originally published in 'A2', The Age, 2009

BRINGING HOME
THE BACON

Some families argue about politics, some about religion. I'm watching four brothers arguing about the best place to shoot a pig.

'Between the ears and an inch up.'

'No, two inches.'

'Just don't miss and shoot him in the back leg like you did three years ago!' The three brothers without the burden of the shot snicker.

Breath from the banter hangs like cigarette smoke in a dawn light that's as hard and grey as steel. Then a single shot rings out round the concrete cattle yard, followed by the sound of 160 kilos of pig collapsing onto the bed of the caged trailer.

'I'll throat 'im,' volunteers youngest brother Larry, slipping into the cage and turning his neat initial incision into a gash as he severs the jugular. 'It's quieter and easier this way,' Larry says, stepping back from the coagulating pool of claret. He remembers back to when they'd tie the pig to a post to slit its throat – and the hysterical squealing that went with it.

Once the blood would have been collected to make 'chocolate' but not any more. The lads' love of this Calabrian speciality of sweet blood pudding evaporated when they found out what went into it.

'We used to use everything but the shit,' says brother Curly, as a steaming mass of organs and guts spills from a now pristine and de-bristled carcass. These days it goes to the dogs, where once in poorer times it might have made such delights as stuffed heart or *ndugghia*, the Calabrian liver and lung sausage related to the French *andouille*. Now all the brothers save is some of the smaller intestine for use as 'bungs' (skins) for thinner sausages.

It's Curly who seems to have picked up the mantle of organiser since their dad died eight years ago. 'We had to continue or else we knew this tradition would die,' he says now. He claims his old man was much fussier than he is but brother Mo raises an eyebrow. 'Yeah but you're still worse than Mum,' he snorts. Larry and eldest brother Franco both fall about laughing.

This year there's only one pig to kill. To save time the local abattoir butchered the other three. It's a first, but Curly reckons it's the way of the future. The pigs were purchased for $2.40 a kilo from a local piggery a couple of months ago: 'Same litter, same feed. That's the secret for good salamis. You never mix your pigs,' reveals Franco, the pig expert of the brothers.

His tender care and a diet of crushed maize and wheat have seen his charges bulk up, exchanging their piggery fat for leaner meat. 'All were castrated because boar meat stinks. Also, I avoid butchering females on heat because that affects the meat. Tradition says a young sow four or five weeks pregnant with her first litter is best,' notes Franco helpfully.

Split with a chainsaw, the two halves of the cleaned carcass are driven back to hang under the eaves of their mum's garage. The 250 pounds of meat from the abattoir-killed pigs is already inside, sorted into paler meat for the big salamis and the fattier darker meat, which goes off quicker, for the faster-curing, skinnier sausages. Salt equivalent to three per cent of weight has been added to each tub of meat. Ground extra fine, it burns the hands as it's mixed in.

The flavourings are a matriarchal domain. Mum adds dried chillies, dried capsicum and 'sauce' – the fine paste of roasted capsicum that gives many Calabrian sausages their typical colour and a little sweetness. No-one questions her proportions. There's steel in those eyes and an iron will when it comes to how things should be done. 'I reckon she thinks we don't know anything, as we've only been doing this for 40 years,' jokes Larry – but only very quietly.

Mum is particular on how the sauce is mixed in: first with a rolling motion, then punching the meat until it becomes really sticky. A spoonful of the mix is fried for her approval and then one of the world's oldest production lines swings into action. There's a hierarchy on the line. The top dog fills. It's a special skill: 'The salami need to be firm. If there's air inside it kills it,' says Mo of the fat meat balloon in his hand.

As a junior, you get to refill the sausage machine and dream of working your way up to turning the handle that pushes out the meat. A third family member ties off the salami with twine and passes it on to Larry and Mum, who truss it up in the old-fashioned way.

While others have moved to artificial skins that are less prone to splitting during filling, Mum still insists on sheep's appendix for the larger casings and smaller pork intestines for the others. A bitch to clean, these also have to be soaked in acidulated water to mellow their funky flavour.

Through the morning, more help arrives until there are a couple of dozen people thronging the garage. Some clean the ears, heads and trotters that are reserved for what this Australian family with strong Calabrian roots call *souzo* – pork preserved in a sharply vinegared jelly, a dish similar to brawn or souse. 'Dad used to put the eyeballs in as well just to freak us out,' remembers Franco. The early Medieval Germanic root of the name *souzo* is just one of many signs of how old this pig-killing tradition is. The Germans ruled in southern Italy way back in the 13th century.

Calabria's famous sausages and salamis date back to when ancient Greeks colonists settled in southern Italy (according to Italy's Ministero delle Politiche Agricole, Alimentari e Forestali), but the tradition of butchering the family pig for winter food is far, far older. Pigs have lived beside us for over 9000 years, feeding on our scraps and in return feeding us. Much of what's happening in this small garage is living history.

At noon, everyone breaks for lunch. And what a lunch: Mum's small kitchen table is crowded with lasagnes, stuffed peppers, a chicken pasta bake, salads, meats and her 'famous meatballs'. Then there are pies, cakes, biscuits – all home-baked – and a bread pudding that has even the diabetic brother risking thirds.

It's one of those meals that leaves you with a warm glow on a cold day. Warm from the food; warm from the little tumblers of homemade red wine; but above all, warm from the reminiscing. Like the time Dad ran over a beehive in the field and had to be drenched in grappa to relieve the pain. Or when a cousin's pig broke loose while having its throat cut and ran squealing and bleeding through the town, the family in full cry behind. Or the brothers' bad behaviour when they were boys and the long walk to the creek to find a particularly springy switch for the beating that inevitably followed. There's much laughter, but you also suspect that these two days every year help keep those memories vivid and those who have passed on alive.

After lunch, Dad's brother arrives. Small and compact as a walnut, he trawls his fingers through the salami mix, tasting its sticky rawness. 'Not bad,' he says with studied dismissiveness. He then takes a look at that morning's carcass hanging under the eaves awaiting butchering. 'Pah, you've used a chainsaw, you lazy bastards – it would have been fine if it was sharp. I'd hate to see what you'd get up to without Mum to keep an eye on you,' he teases.

His big entrance made, he rolls up his sleeves and gets stuck in to teaching Curly how to make pancetta the old Calabrian way. Beneath the veiled jokes about how his salamis have never won gold medals like the brothers', there's no little respect for him. 'His salami are wonderful, better than ours, but don't you dare tell him,' whispers Curly.

To him also falls the honour of cutting a cross from a tile of back fat. This will be placed at the bottom of the huge stainless steel 'copper' to ensure divine help in successfully rendering the lard from the pigs' fat on an open fire overnight. Mo queries whether it's necessary and gets shot down by his mother. 'Your father did it for 50 years. I never saw him make lard without it,' she fires.

On the other side of the garage, the salamis – about 300 of them now – are boxed. Initially they'll be stored under weights in the style of the classic Calabrian sopressata. Then they'll be hung from the rafters of the garage. 'Heat and rain are the enemy of salamis. You want cold frosty weather. You don't want them to dry too quickly,' says Curly, appreciating the leaden sky.

'And you never make salamis on the new moon,' reminds Mum.

'Why?' I ask. It's a mistake. 'You just don't,' she says, fixing me with the stare she usually reserves for Mo.

Later, on selected cloudy days, a small fire will be lit to gently smoke the salamis. That's how the fire brigade got called to the farm a few years back. A neighbour saw the smoke and feared the worst.

When they are cured, the salamis can be Cryovac-ed, wrapped in foil and frozen, hung in a cold spot or stored the old way under oil.

Everything goes swimmingly until Curly sniffs at the copper, now filled with hunks of snowy pork fat. It smells bad. Curly worries that it's the strong smell of boar meat. Perhaps one of their porkers wasn't properly castrated? And then it hits. The smell's not a million miles from chlorine and it's only on the abattoir-killed skins. Their freshly killed pig smells sweet and clean. The stink makes the skin, head and trotters of the three abattoir-killed pigs useless. Luckily the meat itself is fine and the taint evaporates from the lard during the 12 hours of rendering over a slow heat. Where previously there was talk of sending all the pigs to the abattoir next year, now it looks like the ritual of the killing yard will remain at home. 'Sometimes the old ways are the best,' muses Curly.

The lard is very much Curly's own private domain. While his father was alive, the two of them would sit up through the night under the clear winter sky tending it. Topping up the water. Stoking the fire. Stirring the bubbling fat to ensure it didn't stick using the same old wooden paddle they've had for 40 years. Sometimes they'd yarn in the moonlight; sometimes they just sat there together – father and son gazing into the fire.

This year he trusts the night watch to his nephews. They do a good job – even if one of the lads gets locked in the car boot where he's sleeping and Mum finds another snuggling by her wood heater at 4 am trying to get some feeling back into his limbs. It's a cold, cold night.

The next morning more of the youngsters appear to watch bones being added to the lard along with salt to taste, and then the miracle of the lard suddenly turning clear. Their presence is a good sign for the future of the tradition. 'I reckon they know more about all this than we did at their age,' says Curly.

The lard is drained into tins, leaving a sludge at the bottom of the copper. This is the highly prized *issymolya*. Franco has been rhapsodising about it spread on his mother's *pitte* bread – a Calabrian delicacy not so removed from the cracklings served with corn bread of an Arkansas hog slaughter. The antiquity of the pig-killing tradition means you'll see many such similarities across European-based cultures where the pig is prized.

I leave with the clean smell of pig and just a whiff of jealousy in my nostrils. In this era of deconstructed families, I'm envious. My family has no tradition like this to bind us together with communal endeavour and allow us to celebrate those we love and those we've loved together. Killing the pig, you see, is about more than just bringing home the bacon.

Originally published in 'Epicure', The Age, 2002

FOODIE TRIBES

A Spotter's Field Guide

This handy spotter's field guide is the result of five years' extensive ornithological study of Melbourne's watering holes, restaurants and food stores using a cunning collection of hides, disguises and duckcall-like devices to get close to the wildlife I was studying. It is published with apologies to Harold Wesley Hall and to J. D. MacDonald, whose excellent *Birds of Australia* (Reed Books, 1973) inspired this work.

The Dollarbird

Common Name: The Food Snob.

Habitat: Suburbs where house prices end in six noughts, food stores where everything has its provenance included on the label (and is marked up by at least 200 per cent) and Melbourne's clubbier smart restaurants, where the Dollarbird knows they'll be seen by others in their flock.

Recognition: Hard to identify, as tends to blend into its chosen habitat, but has a magpie-like fascination with shiny things. Best way to identify is through its reaction to certain outside stimuli. May jump involuntarily at the mention of a new premium chocolate producer and will become excessively animated in the presence of wagyu beef, especially if there's Grand Cru in a Riedel and a Laguiole knife nearby. Also known by its Latin name, *Buyus Thermomixus*.

Mating Calls: 'I mean it was only $1849 and all the top European chefs have them'; 'I only use Peruvian pink salt'.

Habit: Lines its nest with glossy food magazines. Not the most active of birds but extremely skilled at sourcing sustenance so often plump; would be plumper without regular foraging expeditions. Known to flock with the Cashed-Up Booby (see below) but looks down on it.

Status: Increasingly common, but a tough lean winter may limit its flights.

The Golden Cashed-Up Status Booby

Common Names: 'Kevin' and 'Tanya'.

Habitat: Anywhere with valet parking, anywhere on the water or anywhere owned by a footballer (or equally a drug dealer).

Recognition: Female is gaudy, often gold at chest, claws and crown. Male has grey or dark blue plumage and dark crest with blonde variegated tips.

Mating Calls: Male: 'Splash some more of that Grange over 'ere, mate'; female: 'French, obviously'.

Habit: Invasive species moving from Templestowe, Frankston and Sydney into Brighton, South Yarra and the CBD – especially Crown. Can be identified by its imperious preening manner and its raucous calls of 'I don't know much about food or wine but I know what I like.' When immature, preyed upon by the rodents of the genus *Rapacious Sommelierus*.

Status: Increasingly common.

The Greater Coffee Geek

Common Name: The Caffeine Aficionado.

Habitat: Rwanda, Yemen, Uganda, Panama, Sulawesi, St Ali, 7 Grams, The Mailing Room and, for the more tech-obsessed, US Starbucks (only to check out their move from Verismo to the bespoke Mastrena machines).

Recognition: A twitcher's delight, spotted by its tendency to sudden, jumpy movements and peripatetic motion. Distinguishing markings include red eyes with dark rings.

Mating Calls: 'Fancy coming up for a Puerto Rican Yauco Selecto?'; 'Hmm, nice spring-loaded burr carrier action ...'

Habit: Can be spotted preening in front of the Alpenrost or a Probat Burns Probatino tabletop roaster but yearns for a Caffè Rosto Pro1500. Some of the species are known to migrate monthly as far as Canberra in search of their favourite green beans. Severe aversion to milk.

Status: Traditionally found in high-density inner-city and urban environments, but now increasingly common in and around suburban homes.

The Spangled Drongo

Common Name: The Food Blogger.

Habitat: The first service of new restaurants, obscure Asian cafeterias and out there taking wing in the ether.

Recognition: This chameleon-like bird exhibits a strange ability to morph from another species, leading some to suggest that it is a virus rather than a bona fide genus.

Mating Calls: Identified by a cacophony of calling after dark. Similar to the dawn chorus – some birds' songs function as creative expression, some are marking territory, some are just trying to impress their peers. Sadly, not many people find themselves in the right part of the forest to hear all these different songs – only other Spangled Drongos.

Habit: Usually harmless but can fly into viciousness if they feel that no-one respects their opinions.

Status: Breeding faster than bugs in a backyard Brisbane dunny.

The Greater Restaurant Tit (or Chestnut-Crowned Restaurant Babbler)

Common Name: The Restaurant Junkie.

Habitat: Any new openings, Vue de monde's chef's table and selected long-running places where tables are hard to get and the food's not too pricey, like MoVida, Rumi, Bar Lourinhã and G.A.S.

Recognition: Slightly distended belly. Often a reddening nose in the males as they mature.

Mating Calls: Likes to reply to all statements with which it disagrees with the argument-ending words, 'Well, John Lethlean says …'

Habit: A social animal, unless eating. Likes to discuss the next stop on its gastronomic odyssey, to the detriment of concentrating on the current experience. Rapacious consumer of restaurant reviews, food magazines, blogs, chef books, and anything by Gordon Ramsay. Likely to be flighty and overexcited when the *Good Food Guide* blooms each August and will be first to taste its nectar.

Status: A sudden explosion of population in the last six months thanks to the arrival on our shores of Britain's Foul-Mouthed Tern.

Common Green-backed Tree Creeper

Common Name: The Caring Foodie (aka the Organic or Political Foodie).

Habitat: Has largely migrated from its traditional St Kilda and Fitzroy coops in favour of Brunswick, Footscray and Collingwood. Usually moves to breeding grounds in Alphington, Northcote, Ormond, Yarraville or the bush when time to nest. Also found at Las Vegan, Passionfoods, The Greengrocer, farmer's markets, Macro Wholefoods (although more mature Creepers might avoid this) and any number of political rallies.

Recognition: Can be scrawny or plump. Might have dirt under its claws from scratching for its own vegetables. Most likely to be the bird inspecting its potential feed closely before selecting it. In Brunswick and regional areas like Daylesford or Nimbin, recognise it by its strange multicoloured woolly cap.

Mating Calls: Sounds like tut-tut-tutting. Especially noisy when gathered in a flock.

Habit: Invests more in nourishment than most birds. Will eat anything that is organic, 100 per cent natural and provides vital fibre, balanced protein, complex carbohydrates, essential fatty acids, antioxidants and micro-nutrients in a highly digestible form – even if it doesn't taste the best. This considerate bird is prone to nonviolent action but can be roused to violent bursts of song when its habitat is threatened. (Note: This caring and sympathetic attitude has been successfully bred out by crossing the Tree Creeper with the Dollarbird to create the Greater Greenbacked Moneyeater, which wears Armani, frequents boardrooms and isn't worried about monoculture or the planet but sees buying organic as the best because it's sooooo expensive.)

Status: Both groups are growing at a pace to raise concerns about the level of security of their food supply.

The Willoughway Swallow

Common Name: The Wine Connoisseur.

Habitat: Expensive tastings, online wine auctions, anywhere that they don't look at you funny for gargling your wine, and any restaurant where the wine list weighs more than the menu.

Recognition: Usually fair, with sleeker plumage than the Supreme Wooden Swallow whose actions it often imitates. Often exhibits a large bulge over left breast or on the hips.

Mating Calls: 'Try this, Ralph Kyte-Powell loved it'; 'Hmm, blackberries?'; 'Hmm, grapefruit?'; 'Hmm, sheep's wool and a hint of cat's wee!'

Habit: Feeding patterns similar to the hummingbird, in that it gains sustenance through sipping. Feeds on grapes, the more obscure and carefully grown the better. Loves flights. Yearns to live in a cave.

Status: As it matures, more likely to be found in areas with larger nests. The male of the species often shares a nest with the Dollarbird (see above) or The Greater Restaurant Tit.

Originally published in 'Epicure', The Age, 2009

'PEEK-A-BOO, ICU'

The sound of things going 'ping' is never one to gladden my heart. Yet the slough of despond in which I splash when I hear a microwave at a culinary establishment that mistakenly reckons reheating is cooking is nothing compared to which that ping, or more accurately the wrong ping, could force me to change the way I eat forever.

No wonder, then, that I am listening so intently as I lie on a hospital bed hooked up to enough hardware to fly a space shuttle. I'm here for an ECG and blood sugar analysis, and then to have enough blood drawn from my arm to make quite a decent *morcilla* sausage. This is so they can run a full range of 'bloods', as *All Saints'* Dr Campion would have it, for sodium and potassium levels.

This last part is the least pleasant, as it means jabbing the needle in my arm a few times and poking around a bit until they find a vein that will deliver blood. It takes several attempts. I joke about being a stone (because you can't draw blood out of that either, but now I know how my Christmas turkey feels when I wield my trusty F. Dick larding needle.

Ever since I started writing about food I've had regular heart checks at the wonderful Baker Institute at the Alfred Hospital, but getting the results has always been a nerve-racking moment. And for these tests

I'm in an unfamiliar hospital, which makes me more nervous. I run through the worst-case scenarios like Warney must have done when he had all those problems with his spinning thumb (as opposed to the trouble he had from his texting fingers).

What if my blood sugar levels are dodgy? The risk of hyperglycaemia, and the way diabetics usually find it harder to metabolise fats, would mean an end to my fantasy about going on the Atkins diet or just eating during the earlier part of the day. I think I feel hot tears rolling down my cheeks as I imagine watching a flotilla of patisserie sailing away out of reach over the horizon, along with the prospect of settling down for a night of beers with the boys at the footy. 'Mine's a mineral water, lads,' just doesn't sound right.

What if they discover hypertension or excessively high levels of sodium? Or too little potassium or calcium, which is bad news for your blood pressure? This is quite likely, as one in seven Australians have a blood-pressure reading considered at the high end of normal or above. That would mean my charcuterie plate of a life would be over, replaced by platters of celery, broccoli, carrots, garlic, onions, tomatoes and skinless chicken breast all washed down with a heady cocktail of oat bran, apple pectin, psyllium husks, dandelion root powder and guar gum.

And as for my love of sprinkling fancy salts (whether from Brittany, Maldon or country Victoria), on everything from tomatoes and avocadoes to caramel and chocolate: that would go too. A teaspoon of ordinary table salt contains about 2000 mg of sodium; the suggested range we should consume is between 1100 to 3300 mg per day. Some of the best sources of potassium, like watermelon, avocado, baked beans, almonds, cashews, peanuts and tomato sauce, all taste best with salty pork or loads of salt, further compounding the problem.

Then there's cholesterol. As about 50 per cent of Aussie adults have a blood cholesterol level over 5 mmol, that's always a worry as losing fatty meats sizzling on the barbecue, delicious creams and cheeses made with full-fat milk would be like losing a friend. I suspect that if I wasn't allowed packets of chips, deep-fried food and biscuits, I'd probably miss them too. I also remember hearing horror stories about giving up smoking cigars and binge drinking. I'm not sure I'm ready yet to give up my Dickensian lifestyle, especially when the definition of 'to binge' is seven or more standard Australian drinks. That would sound the death knell for nine-course degustation menus with matched wines – and for much of my vital research into Melbourne's cocktail and bar culture.

I feel like I've dodged five bullets when I'm told that my blood sugar, cholesterol, sodium, calcium and potassium levels are all good. In fact, interestingly, since I started reviewing restaurants a decade ago my cholesterol levels have steadily dropped from problematic high fives to the mid-threes. I'm not sure whether this is a reflection of eating less cheap pizza and fast food, or the fact that good Australian restaurants now use far less saturated fat. Perhaps it's both.

You know there are two ways to take dodging bullets. One is to think how lucky you are and just hope your run of good fortune will continue; the other is to see the results as a let-off – a warning that if you want to remain an omnivore it might be best to treat your body well.

So porridge for breakfast, more fresh fruit and nuts, fewer Snickers – and apparently there's this thing called exercise that's rather good for you, and for reducing everything, including blood pressure. I'll even stop the cigars and the second bottle of wine if it means I never have to surrender salami, *jamón* and a nice bit of brie.

When I get out of hospital there's a message asking where this week's column is. That's easy – it's there lying on the hospital gurney, wearing a very flattering white surgical gown with a back so plunging it could earn me instantaneous induction into the plumbers' hall of fame – and you've just read it.

Originally published in 'A2', The Age, 2009

SAUCY FOODS AND HOW TO USE THEM TO YOUR ADVANTAGE

Around the world certain foods have been prized and praised for their ability to stoke your ardour, and food and sex have been linked since time immemorial. Certain foods' reputation for sensual properties is usually based on one of three reasons: association, appearance or the need for a sales pitch.

Exotic and very masculine animal parts, such as cockscombs, tigers' whiskers or the *cojones* or pizzle of a bull (or any such virile animal), have long been presumed to contain aphrodisiac powers that can be transferred to the eater. By nibbling on such foods, one's virility gets a huge shot in the, er, arm. Or so the story goes. I suppose it's better than the ancient sport of hunting down rival tribes and eating them to boost your mojo.

In the Middle Ages, a popular idea known as the doctrine of signatures conferred powers to food according to their appearance – hence the sexy reputation of eels, snakes, certain roots such as licorice or ginger, bananas and the sea cucumber. Another ancient doctrine called humoral medicine – which asserted that what you ingested had a direct effect on your health – also had its two-bobs' worth, claiming that certain foods, such as spices and members of the onion family, heat the passions and improve sexual performance.

There is one other way food and drinks have achieved an aphrodisiac reputation: through the spurious claims of traders and hucksters keen to boost the popularity and price of exotic new substances, whether pineapples or chocolate.

But enough of all this theory, let's get to the practical: what's got the best reputation for seduction success?

The Big Three – Chocolate, Champagne and Oysters

While Casanova may have boosted his own reserves with 'macaroni cooked by a Neapolitan', he relied on chocolate, Champagne and oysters to aid in his conquests.

Chocolate's history as an aphrodisiac is a long one. Montezuma used to drink a frothy hot chocolate before braving his harem. More recently it's been claimed that the stimulants in chocolate (caffeine and theobromine), combined with the presence of an alleged mood enhancer (phenylethylamine), can create a heightened state. How better to test this theory than by feeding your love chocolate mousse?

Champagne is still the drink of choice for many a modern-day lothario, whether for the alluring associations with power and money it implies, or for the sexy toasty flavour and those playful, intoxicating bubbles. If you're not drinking it, I suggest pouring it over a bowl of freshly cut mango for an exciting and tumultuous reaction.

Traditionally oysters have been seen as the essence of femininity, but more recently their claim to aphrodisiac qualities has been boosted by recognition of their high mineral salt and glycogen content, essential elements in muscle contraction. They are also a lot easier to get hold of than the chipi, a tiny Venezuelan clam with supposedly miraculous sexual properties.

Spice Up Your (Love) Life

Spicing up your diet could be another way of spicing up the bedroom. Indian herbalists prescribed powdered cardamom seeds boiled with milk as an impotence cure, while their 17th-century Scandinavian brothers suggested using cloves instead. A belief in the clove's *uplifting* powers dates back to China in the 3rd century BC.

The spice road must have been a randy place. Everyone from Pliny to that Arab handbook of love, *The Perfumed Garden*, praises the effects of both ginger and pepper, while nutmeg's mild hallucinogenic powers were also credited with encouraging intimacy. Nutmeg mixed with a very soft boiled egg and honey is an old Indian recipe for prolonging performance, but I reckon that a glass of warm milk, spiked with honey and all these spices to taste, should do the trick just as well. Alternatively follow French author Rabelais's advice and mix ginger, cinnamon, cloves, vanilla and sugar with red wine for a sort of sexy mulled wine: this is similar to a draught recommended by Chaucer in 'The Merchant's Tale'.

Like almost everything 'discovered' by the Spanish conquerors in Latin America, vanilla beans were claimed as an aphrodisiac for their scent and flavour. The name even comes from the Latin word for sheath, *vagina*.

Woodland Delights

The Romans used the walnut in fertility rituals and the jellied ripeness and feminine shape of the *coco-de-mer* have earned it a saucy reputation, but it is the humble but energy-packed pine kernel that is the seduction king. Roman love poet Ovid raved about them and both the ancient Arabs and ancient Greeks suggested mixing them with almonds and honey for a restorative bedtime drink. Best apparently are the inch-long pine kernels from the Chilgoza or Noosa Pines of the north-western Himalayas. We'd suggest lightly toasting them in a dry pan, then sprinkling with salt and guzzling them with drinks – when your team of sherpas eventually returns with them.

There's also something rather sensual about mushrooms, whether they be the slippery jack, shiitake or the suggestive morel. The fungi that are most famous for bringing out the fun guy, however, are truffles. Apicius, the Roman epicurean, gives six recipes for them in the aphrodisiac section of his *Cuisine in Ten Books*, while gastronome Jean-Anthelme Brillat-Savarin believed they made 'women more affectionate and men more attentive'. If you can afford them, finely slice white truffles over hot buttered tagliatelle. The aroma alone should be enough to quicken the pulse.

Fruit and Vegetables

Their suggestive shape has earned carrots, leeks and celery a reputation, while celery seeds are particularly prized. They can be crushed and sprinkled on oysters as a delicious aphrodisiacal double whammy.

Besides its shape, the diuretic qualities of asparagus have also helped its reputation. Arab sources suggest parboiling it and then flash-frying it in fat (i.e. butter) for the best effect. Add flirtatious suggestiveness by eating it with your fingers. Use your imagination to clean up any dribbles.

Egyptian priests were forbidden by the Pharaohs to eat onions in case they got too randy and Martial, Rome's answer to Roy Chubby Brown, suggested that 'if your wife is old and your member is exhausted, eat onions in plenty'.

The Perfumed Garden tells of a man whose 30-day erection was credited to a reduction of onion juice and honey. More palatable is another Arab suggestion of scrambling fried onions with egg yolks. Alternatively, copy the old French wedding-night tradition of serving onion soup to stoke the fires of desire. Our ancestors in both the East and West were also cautioned against another member of the onion family, garlic, lest it overheat the passions. More recently, garlic has been credited with containing compounds closely related to sex hormones.

Another bulb ascribed bedroom powers by ancient Egyptians and Greeks alike is fennel. The Hindu love text the *Kama Sutra* suggests a drink of fennel juice, milk, liquorice, honey and sugar will 'enhance sexual vigour'; around the Mediterranean the same claims have been made for fennel soup.

The close relationship of the ancient Roman and Greek gods of wine and fertility (Dionysus and Bacchus) with grapes gave the fruit a powerful seal of sexual approval, even in their unfermented form. For textural sensuality, movie siren Mae West liked her grapes peeled; frozen they make an erotic alternative to ice cubes. Warmed in a pasta of goat's cheese, orange zest and spring onions, as *Intercourses: An Aphrodisiac Cookbook* (Terrace Publishing, 2007) suggests, they'll apparently plump up and explode juicily when bitten into.

Fruit has usually been perceived as having a feminine personality. The quince was a symbol of love and fertility dedicated to both the Greek and Roman gods of love (Aphrodite and Venus). Quince jelly was especially prized as a pick-me-up. Cherries, dates, avocados and, most famously, figs are also credited with amorous powers.

Although scientists scoff at these aphrodisiacal claims as nothing more than hucksterism, the pleasure from a good meal can certainly engender a state of mild euphoria perfect for encouraging sexual expression. There is also little doubt that part of the joy of indulging in aphrodisiacal foods is the license they give you to behave in a more licentious manner. So basically, if you go out for dinner on Valentine's Day and act like a slut, just blame it on the oysters.

A Recipe for Seduction

The Food

- The food should be easy to make, mainly pre-prepared and light, so the passion will not be doused by a full stomach.
- Make something the object of your affection likes. Serving something he or she is allergic to will just make the wrong bits swell up.
- Include ingredients credited with stoking the fires of desire, especially if they combine the allure of being both exotic and expensive.
- Eat with your fingers. Not only sensual, but less washing-up.

- The food should be easily transportable so it can be moved to the bedroom, lounge or the number 87 tram.
- Nothing that creates gas, please.

The Booze

- 'One more drink and I'll be under the host.' This famous saying, vastly improved by my linguistic skills from the rather turgid original by New York wit Dorothy Parker, says it all.
- In moderation, booze loosens inhibitions and encourages relaxation. It does the same thing in large quantities, but can also issue an unwanted invitation to Mr Floppy. Choose the social lubricant 'they' like – and small glasses.
- Casanova swore by Champagne and the effect of those bubbles on bare skin is fairly delicious. A bottle of Krug will do the trick, as will Champagne cocktails. Douse a sugar cube with bitters. Add a shot of brandy. Top up with Champagne. Like your date, treat them with respect or you might not make it to the bedroom – even if you do have fun trying.
- Stay away from heavy reds and ports, but a bottle of honeyed dessert wine or a crisp Gewurztraminer or Riesling is perfect.

The Setting

- The clichés work: candlelight is becoming and dim lights hide a multitude of flaws.
- A blanket under the stars – assuming there are no mozzies – is cute. A neck doused in Rid is less fun to nibble.
- Lots of cushions are good and encourage proximity for mutual feeding.
- Music is a great mood enhancer – unless it's Rammstein.
- Never underestimate the power of flowers.
- It goes without saying: take the phone off the hook and turn the television off.

The Planning

- Surprises are overrated – anticipation is so much sexier. Ring and tell them where you want them and when. Call it a 'date'.

- Tidy the bedroom – and any other scenes of seduction – even if it's just a 'boy tidy' (hiding the crap in cupboards).
- Shop early and relax, leaving yourself time to shower and dress and perfume yourself beautifully before the target of your seduction arrives.
- Buy croissants and fresh fruit for that restorative breakfast together the next morning.
- Parents should buy a new Thomas the Tank Engine/Pokémon video for the kids and a lock for the bedroom door. Far better still, farm them out for the night. The sight of parents in flagrante delicto is one of those things that can scar a child for life – remember?

Recipes

Here are three simple recipes that are easy to prepare and might get you out of a spot if you haven't been able to get a table at one of your city's more romantic spots. All recipes serve two, naturally.

FULL RIPE FIGS

There is nothing sexier than a ripe fig. This recipe is a cracker because you can assemble the figs before the evening starts. The contrast of the crispy, salty overcoat with the rich creaminess of the oozy cheese and the sweetness of the fig makes this a suitably decadent and finger-licking snack.

Ingredients

6 ripe figs
200 g mascarpone
12 slices good prosciutto

Method

Cut from the stem end of the fig to about three-quarters of the way up the length of the fruit. Using the handle of a wooden spoon, edge the fig flesh away from the centre to create a space. Stuff this space with the mascarpone. Wrap the prosciutto around the figs and refrigerate. Bang them in a warmed 180-degree oven for 15 minutes or until the prosciutto goes crispy and the figs soften. Cooked like this they will create a suitably sexy explosion in the mouth when eaten.

SEVENTIES SEDUCTION STRAWBERRIES

There's something quite daggy about them, but these strawberries seldom raise a murmur of complaint when served. I've spiced them up with a little strawberry liqueur and rosewater. They taste better if you serve them while wearing mutton-chop sideburns, a porn-star mustache and a shortie dressing gown.

Ingredients

100 g smashed slivered almonds or pistachios (depending on your loved one's taste)
250 g white chocolate
A splash of strawberry liqueur
A couple of drops of rosewater
2 punnets unhulled strawberries

Method

Toast the nuts in a dry frying pan until golden. Gently melt the chocolate, lubricated with the liqueur, in a double boiler over simmering water. Stir in a drop or two of rosewater to your taste. Dip the strawberries into the melted chocolate, then into the almonds and feed to the one you love.

It's a good idea to serve these with a Champagne cocktail made by pouring 20 ml of the strawberry liqueur into a tulip glass and then carefully topping with Champagne. Beware, as the sugariness of the liqueur will make the Champagne froth. Do this or the bottle of strawberry liqueur will just sit in your drinks cupboard getting crusty.

EBULLIENT MANGO

Ripe mango is slippery like the memories of your third teenage kiss. I reckon this texture makes it the most sensual of fruit. Add Champagne, however, and you have a simple and spectacularly dramatic dessert that foams seductively.

Ingredients

2 ripe mangoes
1 bottle Champagne

Method

Chop the mangoes into 2-cm dice. Place into a dessert glass, coupe, or similar wide-mouthed glass. Present to your date at the table (or bed or sofa or wherever you are eating it) and then pour a good slug of Champagne over the fruit. On contact the Champagne will froth up very suggestively.

Originally published in 'Epicure', The Age, 2001

RE-LIVING IN THE SEVENTIES

Sometimes we all need to give in to our inner dag, whether that means singing along to 'Jump in My Car', wearing flares and a tank top, or making a chocolate ripple cake. Throw a seventies dinner party and all this joyful dagginess can be yours in one fell swoop.

The first thing to remember when planning your menu for such a night is that no suave seventies soiree was complete without the 'hostess', as we called them back then, unveiling her canapé dexterity. Dips were all the rage – perhaps stilton whisked with Guinness or an equally exotic curry number made from a mixture of garlic powder, curry powder, ketchup and sour cream. Serve with crudités. Foremost in the canny cook's dip arsenal was the packet soup mix. Dry French onion soup was mixed ingeniously with cream cheese and milk for a dip that would have even French president Georges Pompidou (1968–1974) exclaiming, 'Ooh la la!'

If it's nibbles you're after, then the Savoy and Jatz crackers that trawled through your dips could be patriotically topped with a smoked oyster or garnished with anything as long as it was colourful. Remember, any spare oysters can be turned into smoked oyster dip as a punishment for late arrivals. Any spare dip can be piped onto lengths of celery to make 'celery boats' that no-one will eat but which look nice.

The 1973 launch of Nutri-Grain in Australia gave rise to another great nibble with drinks: 'nuts and bolts'. This combination of peanuts and Nutri-Grain again reunites us with our old friend in a packet, French onion soup, which, along with a packet of cream of chicken soup mix and optional curry powder and mustard powder, adds savour to the combination.

Pâtés survived from the sixties – often literally, it seemed – and the 'hedgehog' was still a fun way of presenting bite-size morsels of cheese and pineapple. For added style, wrap the half-grapefruit in silver foil before sticking in the cocktail sticks laden with cheese hunks or kabana. The addition of cubes of tinned Hawaiian pineapple would have Steve McGarrett, Chin Ho Kelly and the rest of the *Five-0* team salivating.

For those not afraid of the stove, the vol-au-vent is a sure-fire winner: puff pastry filled with mushrooms, chicken or ham suspended in a béchamel sauce. Use plenty of plain flour for that authentic gluggy seventies béchamel texture.

Those wives with time on their hands between tennis lessons and the spin cycle can also experience the joy of stuffing dates or wrapping things in bacon – prunes for 'devils on horseback'; oysters for 'angels on horseback'. Only the most sophisticated housewife should attempt a 'goblin on horseback', not because of the risk of teethmarks – ha ha, that's an authentic seventies joke, that is – but because the very Cantonese combination of duck livers and tinned water chestnut can be tricky to secure. Even with a toothpick.

Spicy meatballs and 'little boys' (aka 'cheerios' in Queensland) make excellent seventies cocktail-stick party fare, too. Some intensely chicken-flavoured chips would also be nice.

To drink, vodka was reaching new levels of popularity in the seventies so mix it with bottled orange juice that tastes nothing like oranges and finish with a blush of grenadine. Why not call it a 'Sunrise'? That has a nice exotic ring to it. It can be made with tequila, too.

Or follow the lead of two stars who topped the Australian charts in 1972. Harry 'Can't Live If Living Is Without You' Nilsson helped John 'Imagine' Lennon over his dumping by Yoko with the help of copious numbers of Brandy Alexanders.

Or make a large glass bowl of seventies 'tropical' punch, inspired by pictures in *New Idea* of Boney M drinking huge Tahitian cocktails at Trader Vic's. Mix a bottle of white Bacardi rum with frozen fruit juice concentrate. Add a bottle of soda water for each can and finish with a large can of fruit cocktail. Garnish with a small paper umbrella.

Australian gentlemen are expected to drink beer. This should be poured from a longneck into a glass and not ever sculled from the bottle.

Of course, 'with dinner' the choice would usually come from a cask. While Angoves claim to have invented cask wine in 1965, it only became popular in the seventies when filled with sweet fruity white wines. If it's from a bottle wine should also be sweet, fruity and look Germanic – Blue Nun or Black Tower for example – or inspire you to dress up in white and float about like you're at a party in the Hamptons with Carole King. So Ben Ean it is, then. In all cases the word 'riesling' is a sure-fire seventies recommendation, especially if preceded by the word 'Rhine'. For the early seventies look, go for a flagon or a carafe. Serve wine in brown and beige ceramic goblets with winery names on them.

When it comes to what to serve for dinner, the choice is simple. It's either a buffet or three courses. Either way, as we're in what's been called 'The Travelogue Era'(by me … just then), you should theme your food around somewhere you've just visited. The South Pacific was a popular destination, hence the proliferation of recipes for Polynesian pork saté, Tahitian appetisers like ginger chilli beef balls, Hawaiian meat roll or even Tongan Jewfish. This was 'cooked' in lemon juice in the kokoda style popular in Fiji. *Bula!*

Another option was to echo the all-conquering seventies success of suburban Chinese restaurants by serving sweet and sour pork or spare ribs with fried rice. Remember not to add any authentic flavourings like five-spice powder or shaoxing wine.

If the formality of three courses is more your style, start with prawn cocktail, avocado vinaigrette, prosciutto with melon, grapefruit and crab cocktails or vitello tonnato. Or follow Alice Waters' lead when she opened Chez Panisse for the first time in August 1971. The very first course she served was pâté maison. It is not known whether this came with Melba toasts.

Another winning entrée is one of the classic soups popular in the era: a cold Vichyssoise in summer or in winter a hearty Les Halles-style French onion soup with a thick crust of melted cheese and a crouton of bread floating on top.

Whether for a 'fork supper' or as the central element of a three-course sit-down affair, it's hard to go wrong with a European classic, whether it be chicken à la king, beef stroganoff, goulash or beef bourguignon. Remember Campbell's concentrated soup can provide a handy base for many such casserole dishes. We'll ignore the fact that despite the French name, chicken à la king was created in New York.

Cauliflower cheese, scalloped potatoes or stuffed peppers make nice side dishes. And for true seventies authenticity, never peel your broad beans.

Of course, you could always follow the advice of the seminal 1978 work, *Better Homes and Gardens' Fondue and Tabletop Cooking* (Meredith Corporation, 1978): 'Tired of working in the kitchen? Then bring the fondue to the table. You needn't wait for a party, or for family or guests to arrive. Any time is the right time to cook-at-the-table with fondue.' No surprise then that the fondue set was *the* wedding present of the seventies.

The buffet or fork supper is perhaps the simpler choice when having a large group of people over for a seventies-style wife-swapping party. All the men are expected to wear Zapata moustaches and mirrored aviator shades.

The buffet can largely be prepared in advance and thus left to dry out slightly before the guests arrive. Or you can use a chafing dish, which is a 'symbol of cooking elegance' and 'allows today's busy hostess to serve graciously with a minimum of effort', to quote the advertising of the day.

If cooking cold dishes, never forget to include seventies favourites like creamy Coronation chicken, waldorf salad and coleslaw or curly endive with orange segments.

Central of course to any buffet – or charming lunch party for that matter – is 'the ring', which gives a fine focal point to the sideboard. The ring mould reached new heights in the seventies with US-inspired moulded salads, set using sweet flavoured jellies. *The New World Encyclopedia of Cooking* (Culinary Arts Institute, 1973) offers 68 recipes for them, from 'moulded avocado and kumkquat [sic] salad' to the aptly named 'corned beef cabbage mould'. By the end of the decade, the trusty old metal form was more likely to shape prawn and cucumber mousse or a coffee and walnut cake. We were also likely to use them to form up a nice ring of salad made from day-old rice, cubed gammon, capsicum and pineapple. Alternatively, bake a meatloaf in it, but decorate the inside of the ring with red and green capsicum slices before adding the meat.

As you have just seen, presentation is vital with seventies food so garnish as though your life depends on it. Follow the helpful advice of *The Australian Book of Meat Cookery* (Paul Hamlyn, 1971), which recommended using sprigs of chopped parsley for most recipes. Also note that watercress can be used with beef, and lemon wedges can be added to the parsley for fish!

Don't forget to get busy with your butter curler or your melon baller. A trio of three chilled melons makes a refreshing end to any meal. Other desserts could include a chocolate ripple cake, pavlova, no-bake cheesecake, profiteroles or even a coffee and almond ring.

Equal care should be paid to the table settings – simple needn't be dull. Coordinated napkins and table runners or tablecloths with informal plates and beer mugs build a delightful mood. Note also that as the decade drew to a close, the earthy era of the midi skirt, homestyle soups like pea and bacon and terracotta plates gave way to a more flamboyant time, when baked Alaskas were extravagantly spiked and food was symmetrically arranged. Let your table setting match this.

End the meal with Irish coffee, Glava or Ireland's newest export, Baileys, which was launched in 1974. As you sit back sipping your Baileys, remember that the best thing about the seventies wasn't the food and drink, but the fact that most of us were younger, cuter and firmer than we are today and many of those we've lost were still alive. It helps the food taste better.

What to Wear to a Seventies Party

Hippie gear – flares – the *Shaft*/pimp look – fringing – bikie gear – turbans – maxis – the Biba look – wide-legged pants – Bay City Rollers tartan

– afros – cork wedges – mullets – rollnecks – tight-crutch pants that told you a bloke's religion – micro-minis – butterfly collars – hotpants – Glam Rocker gear – body glitter – the midi – big lapels and long cuffs – ethnic gear – Armani suits – moustachioed desperados look – Donny Osmond outfits – collarless shirts and waistcoats – tank tops – treads – Dunlop volleys – 'man' made fibres like rayon, polyester, Acrilan, Tricel and knitted Orlon – heavy metal gear – cheesecloth – halternecks – cowboy boots – Laura Ashley – disco clothes – platform shoes – ABBA – anything early punk. (Compiled with help from fashion guru Leona Edmiston)

Soundtrack to the Seventies

Gloria Gaynor, ABBA, James Brown, Barry White, The Eagles, 10CC, *Saturday Night Fever*, *Grease*, Sex Pistols, Gary Glitter, Sherbet, Skyhooks, Supertramp, post-Peter Green Pink Floyd, David Bowie, Suzi Quatro, Alvin Stardust, Paper Lace, Queen, Boney M, Dragon, The Commodores, KC and the Sunshine Band. It is enshrined in state legislation that you must play at least six novelty hits including 'Kung Fu Fighting', 'The Streak', 'Convoy', 'Popcorn' and 'Living in the Seventies'.

Significant Seventies Food Dates

1970   Health Valley Foods founded in California. The beginning of the popularisation of health foods.

1970   Melbourne International Airport opens.

1971   *The Anarchist's Cookbook* published with recipes for hash browns and pot loaf.

1971   US banker Samuel Cochran dies from botulism in a can of Vichyssoise.

1972   McDonald's introduces the Egg McMuffin.

1972   *Number 96* goes five nights a week.

1972   McDonald's Hamburger University opens in Elk Grove, Illinois.

1973   The Queen opens the Sydney Opera House.

1974   First supermarket check-out scanner installed in the Marsh Supermarket in Troy, Ohio.

1974   Soft-serve frozen yoghurt first introduced – at Bloomingdale's

Department Store, New York.

1974   Heimlich manoeuvre introduced to save those choking to death on food.

1974   Miller Lite introduced.

1975   Bob Hawke says he'll go on the wagon if he enters Parliament and becomes PM.

1976   FDA bans red no. 2 dye, suggesting it might be carcinogenic, but doesn't recall foods that are using it.

1976   Start of random breath testing in Victoria.

1976   US consumption of soft drinks passes that of milk.

1977   Slimfast launched in the US.

1978   Canadian supermarket chain introduces first cheap 'no name' house brand products.

1979   Nathan Pritikin first promotes his low-fat, low-cholestrol diet.

1979   Paris cops stop breathalysing because a restaurant claims it has been terrible for business.

Quotes

You might like to include these amusing slices of sexism as conversation starters ...

'Samantha turned to find Susan dissolved in tears, "Oh, Sam, how awful!" she wailed. "He likes skinny girls and I'm so fat! What on earth can I do?"'

(From the introduction to the diet recipe section of the 1970 *New Generation Cook Book* – a recipe book for swinging youngsters.)

'Jason looked up into her eyes, smiling. "I don't believe in working wives – especially if they happen to be good cooks too!"'

(From the end paragraph of the 1970 *New Generation Cook Book*', packed with exciting 'coffee time' recipes.)

Originally published in 'Epicure', The Age, 2003

THE PIRATES OF PURGATORY

Chapter 1 – Of Spies, Stays and a Bad Day To Be Undead

The crimson spray flicked across the walls, the floor and across Beth Bathory's cheek. 'Idiot,' she hissed, as the lifeless, pale body slid out of her arms. She stepped over the corpse and struck the shocked girl hard across the mouth, chipping one of her newly formed, bloody incisors. 'Look at this mess.' Beth wiped the black blood from her face with a scarlet velvet foulard and tucked it back into her shirt. 'Now clean it up.'

She stalked out of the room. 'Training baby vampires,' Beth spat. 'Has it come to this?

Beth Bathory, the undead, was not having a good day.

The Vampire School that she and her uncle, the Lion of Welf, had set up was under investigation for peddling illegal blood, piracy, corpse trafficking and grave robbing, all of which she flatly denied. It didn't help that she knew that the investigative noose was tightening.

Luckily for her, she had the best spies in the province: having trained with the janissaries and survivors of the siege of Malta, they were cutthroats and as cold as the grave. And they gave Beth the information that the Grand Council was watching her. Very, very carefully.

Beth got to her rooms and unlaced her stays. It was ridiculous that she was forced to wear ersatz vampire outfits to teach these tiresome children. Having been thrown out of Hagworth's School for Witches for seducing one too many students to her room late at night and for her clumsy disposal of the bodies over the side of the castle – husks of girls drained of their life-blood for Beth's sustenance – she set up a failed catering business (Bathory's Butchers: The Best Blutwursts in Bavaria!) and auditioned for the role of the brave and busty masthead in a popular pirate television series (she didn't even get a callback) before deciding that she would show those wizened hags at Hagworth's a thing or two.

But the school was not going well. Rejects from Hagworth's. That's all she had. And her mother's Iron Maiden and an eye-watering collection of corsets. Oh, and all her own teeth. She glared at herself in the mirror (as always wishing the myth were true) and sighed deeply. Money was now a serious issue.

It was last resort time. Beth had been taught the dark arts by her grandmother, the Countess of Were Welf, had learned well at the poisoner's table as well as developing a taste for expensive blood at the hands of her wasteful and squandering mother. She was also an expert hacker, having taught internet piracy to all of her students at a very high level (Beth still fondly remembered her first dux: Lars Napster). She would hack into the Grand Council's files and change history's course.

Beth heard two cars screech away from castle like bats out of hell who'd left the kettle on at home. One minute later, as she leaned out to watch the unfolding car chase, her door flew open.

'Can't you knock?' Beth spun around to see a stake chocked into a crossbow and aimed right at her heart. Apparently her spies were not the best in the province …

Original piece written by Matt Preston (honestly, it's not ghost-written by either J.K. Rowling, Stephenie Meyer, Matthew Reilly, or even Alison Urquhart, who is the publisher of this book and loves a corset and a pale scrawny night feeder). More on Beth's adventures will, I am sure, follow.

DOORSTEP RADAR

The other day I went to a restaurant that was totally without merit yet had the gall to charge over $30 for a main course. The poison pencil in my pocket started to strain and the scent of blood was in my nostrils, until the woman I love asked whether there was any point shit-canning a restaurant to which my readers are never likely to go.

'Look around,' she said. 'It's Friday night and they can't have had but four tables. This place is dying. Savaging it would be like poking a dying carthorse with a pointy stick. Why bother? Can't you use the space for something that is more "in the public interest", which is what you always tell me restaurant reviewing is all about?'

Ooh, that hurt. Grudgingly, I have to admit she has a point as sharp as my pointy stick, so this week, rather than a savaging, here are a few tips on how to spot restaurants that I reckon are worth avoiding. I hope this will help you tune your 'doorstep radar', that sixth sense that allows you to avoid places where you'd waste your money eating.

Let's start with names, which are a fine indicator of a restaurant's crapness. Establishments named after artists seldom paint a pretty picture on the plate. If they have puns in their name or funky spellings like using z's instead of s's, they often won't serve great food. The only exceptions to this punning rule are Thai restaurants, which can rival hairdressers for their linguistic ingenuity without it damaging the food too much.

These rules hold fast everywhere other than Townsville, where the two best restaurants are called – I kid you not – Wayne and Adele's Garden of Eating and Yotz, and where the town's best Thai restaurant is not called Beau Thai or even Thai Dye but just Bountiful.

Now let's peer into the restaurant and look at the room itself. If the tables sport those laminated plastic cards spruiking a 'wine of the week', that's seldom a good sign. Neither is the presence of the words 'Under New Management' painted large on the window in big pink letters, which translates to me as 'Okay, so this place used to be awful but honestly it's better now'.

Discounting can be a sign of desperation from a failing business, and you don't want to eat in one of them as there's too often the pressure to cut corners in the kitchen. So if you see home-PC-generated signs stuck to the windows for cut-price meal deals such as their 'Moo-nday Steak Night' – think carefully before approaching. Pun use in an offer exponentially increases the strength of the doorstep radar warning for me.

The presence of live music is often another sign of a last-ditch attempt to attract punters – and few things make a bad meal worse than someone murdering Karen Carpenter songs in the corner of the room. Turkish, Russian and Greek restaurants are exempt from this rule.

I also tend to avoid those places that have a plasma TV or LCD screen on the wall, unless it is serving Chinese or Vietnamese food or is a sports bar. And if the place is empty on a Friday night, this is also telling you something.

The menu can give you a wealth of warning – but first set the sensitivity of your doorstep radar based on the prices. The more expensive they are, the more concerning the following traits are. Avoid anywhere that has wacky names for dishes. The use of words like 'melange', 'mosaic', 'assiette', 'sun-dried', 'a trio of' or 'Cajun' should set the alarm bells ringing. Especially beware the presence of 'a trio of dips'. Like nachos, their presence can be a sign that the role of the chef in that establishment has been reduced to peeling the foil off tubs and waiting for the microwave to go 'ping'.

Also beware lazy words like 'Mediterranean', 'North African' or 'Asian' in dish descriptions. These suggest that the kitchen will be trying to stab at approximating the flavour of a region – this culinary generalism is seldom a success. In fact, the presence of an international selection of dishes worthy of a UN bring-a-plate party can be a worrying sign that the chef has big hotel experience, could be German, or even worse, both. I've only met three German hotel chefs who, in my opinion, could cook food I'd like to eat … and at least two of those were actually Swiss. This baffles me, as German home cooking can be marvellous stuff.

Dishes featuring cooked avocado or cream sauces – especially when made with brandy or seafood and served with steak – are other real danger signs. Unless it's one of those modern bars that thinks it's cool to serve seventies food – and that could be a danger sign all of its own. Unless you like that sort of tank-top, frizzy-perm, dinner-party tucker.

A small restaurant with lots of choices on the menu can also be a cause for concern. Likewise, be afraid if there are weird combos of ingredients on the menu. While there is a slight outside chance that a dish of lobster and caramel mousse might be edible if made by Jacques Reymond or Attica's Ben Shewry, don't expect the same success if it's on a café menu in Laverton.

And finally, never eat a place that needs to employ two 200-kilo Maori bouncers.

While these rules aren't infallible, perhaps if I'd followed them before sitting down the other night I wouldn't need to carry such a sharp pointy stick. I hope they prove to be of some vague use to you.

Originally published in delicious, *2009*

THIS GOES WITH THAT

Skipping across Australia's restaurant and café landscape reviewing, I come across some wonderful combinations of flavours and textures, from the classics like oysters Kilpatrick and calamari with rocket to the innovative − perfectly exemplified by the slice of watermelon, prawn floss and chilli sugar dreamed up by the kitchen at Attica.

But why is it that certain combinations of flavours, like Greek pastries and coffee, or roast duck and plum sauce at any number of Chinese places in our suburbs, seem to work so perfectly together?

Sometimes this can be put down to science, according to Professor Peter Barham from Bristol University. As well as being a physicist, Barham also works with top UK chef Heston Blumenthal, helping him develop radical new flavour combinations at The Fat Duck.

'There is a theory that foods that go well together often share one or two molecules in the 15 very important and 20 to 30 important molecules that make up their primary flavour profile. The more they share, the better they go together.' Barham, who was in town to work with chef Raymond Capaldi at Fenix, explains that if you analyse foods in a mass spectrometer and identify their most important flavour compounds and molecules it throws up surprising bedfellows. 'Liquorice and salmon have elements of flavour in common, as do garlic and coffee. White chocolate and caviar is one of the most surprising ones that has resulted in a dish on the menu at The Fat Duck,' explains Barham.

I've tried this dish and can attest that while it sounds weird the ingredients work together. The creaminess of the chocolate and the saltiness of the fish eggs match especially well. If you don't believe me, next time you roast a leg of lamb and stud it with slivers of garlic, rub a little instant coffee into the slits where you place the garlic. After roasting you won't taste the coffee but it will give the lamb a slightly richer caramelised flavour.

This scientific thinking also explains why a glass of good Rutherglen Muscat goes equally well with blue cheese and with chocolate. For as radically different as the cheese and the chocolate may seem, they too share similar flavour molecules. In fact, both Blumenthal and Capaldi make their chocolate mousse with a little blue cheese so it's richer but lighter.

Another fascinating facet of this research is the belief that two ingredients that have nothing in common, like garlic and chocolate, can be made to taste like they go together by the addition of a third element that 'shares' molecules with each of the two clashing flavours. In the case of chocolate and garlic, coffee is that bridging ingredient. This also accounts for why chocolate and coffee go so well together!

But Barham is quick to point out that these molecular similarities aren't the only reason things go together. Sometimes it's just the way that our base sense of taste works. Our tongue has the ability to recognise salt, sweet, bitter, sour and the recently discovered (in the West) taste of umami. Combining ingredients with contrasting characteristics (i.e. salt and sweet, or sweet and sour) can present great pairings like salty roast Peking duck with sweet plum sauce or the bitterness of coffee softening the intense sweetness of those pastries.

At other times it is the opposite – the combination of similar tastes – that creates the magic. It's suspected that the reason Parmesan cheese and tomatoes go so well together is that they are both rich in the savouriness that is characterised as 'umami'. And this strengthening of complementary tastes is seen with those oysters at Finz, where the saltiness of the bacon and Worcestershire sauce in the Kilpatrick dressing seems to make the oysters seem all the sweeter by comparison.

Originally published in Melbourne Weekly Bayside, *2006*

NO LOVE LOST IN NOOSA

It has to be one of the longest, and also most prescient, headlines that I've ever written. Three months ago I pencilled in 'Tongs at Dawn – How I Went for the Three-peat Win for the Title of "Australia's Best BBQ Cooking Food Critic" – and Finally Got Beat', and then the other weekend (May 2) it came true.

I've been involved in the Critics Cook-Off at the Noosa Food and Wine Festival since it launched in 2007 and it has provided a rare chance to sample some of the exhilaration chefs feel when they survive a particularly manic service, see the happy faces of their customers, and overall triumph as a well-oiled team. A bit like Tony Bourdain talks about in *Kitchen Confidential* – although in our case with a lot less violence, no handguns and a total absence of Class A drugs. Oh, and there were over 6000 hungry mouths to feed rather than a usual restaurant's mere 100 covers.

Winning the Cook-Off, or even selling out first, also grants bragging rights over the other critics – something I rashly exploited after my two wins. This year it seemed that the fates were conspiring to end this run after a succession of tumbles that would unsteady even the sturdiest of restaurants. The invaluably charming soapie actor turned maître d' who had fronted my barbecue stand for the previous two years was, for once, actually acting in a serious play in Sydney. And, despite his protestations, the chef who underpinned my last two campaigns was forced to help all the other participants rather than concentrating on making my stumbling recipes sing. He had previously turned sweet bread rolls filled – in the style of David Chang from NYC's superhot Momofuku – with hoisin sauce, cucumber and spring onion into an epic hangover buster with the addition of crispy strips of fried lamb belly. He had also proved how different it is to write a recipe for 1000, rather than for four, by rescuing my crystallising fish sauce caramel (to be drizzled over pork loin and a lime slaw) with little more than the judicious addition of a bit of water.

The odds were further stacked against me when Queensland critic Lizzie Loel snared the assistance of the Bailey brothers, who run festival organiser Jim Berardo's two Noosa restaurants, Berardo's and Berardo's on the Beach. It was a sad indictment on these two fine young men raised in Hamilton that they seemed to have forgotten their Victorian roots, throwing their hand in with the banana-benders. Did no-one tell them that Noosa is actually part of Victoria anyway? I think of it as Far North Brighton.

But my dish still felt like a winner. Surely poppingly fresh local Queensland prawns on a bed of crunchy golden French fries was an unassailable combination for a sunny Noosa Sunday – even if it was paired with the decadent duo of a homemade chicken salt and a bacon-fat mayonnaise inspired (okay, lifted wholesale in slavish reverence) from Melbourne-born but US-loved cook and food stylist Jennifer McLagan and her book *Fat*.

We were slammed from the get-go but there was also the ominous sign on the other side of the site – an impressive snaking queue willing to wait for a steak sanger from Tony Love, the Adelaide critic I'd narrowly bested in our previous encounters. It was building up to be a classic old-school confrontation between prawns and beef. The only other serious threat looked like coming from my colleague, cook-off novice Dani Valent from the *Sunday Age*, with her impressively zippy lamb and pineapple Asian salad.

In spite of the fact that the rest of the old team, Anita and Wendy, lifted valiantly, and despite the assistance of volunteer chefs like Julia and Matt cooking over 2000 prawns on the barbecue, Pat maintaining fry quality and one-time Pickled Sisters chef Ali McKillop lowering herself to dress plates of prawns and chips with dollops of bacon-fat mayo and sprinkles of chicken salt, I could sense our 'outs' were costing us.

No-one serving could flirt with the glam Noosa divorcees with quite the mischievous twinkle of the actor and those lost votes could cost us. This also made me realise how important a great front of house person is to the success of a café or a restaurant. They, even more than the food, create the atmosphere that makes you want to go back or recommend the restaurant to your friends. They define the place's hospitality.

The feedback on the prawns 'n' chips was good and there was a shivery thrill at seeing the likes of Gail Donovan from Donovans in St Kilda and Armando Percuoco from Sydney's Buon Riccordo enjoying this dish – which came with its own health warning and the strict instructions that you had to have nothing more than a light salad for dinner.

The choice of the day's best dish is decided by public acclamation – a bit like the crowd at the Roman circus baying for blood. Valent scored well but Love looked unassailable when the sound-level meter tipped a 105-decibel cheer for his dish. Surely my dreams of a three-peat were dead.

But I'd underestimated Queenslanders' love of a prawn – and the power of acting like a dag while corpsing for votes – dance, monkey, dance! The sound-level meter peaked at … you guessed it: 105 decibels. It sounded quieter to me, though, so I offered Love a tie, which he confidently declined. In the resulting head-to-head re-cheer his confidence was rewarded and my dream of Hall of Fame status was dashed by a mere decibel or two.

I'd like to say I was robbed – but that actually happened the night before when tinny-driving bandits broke in and stole cash from the canal-front home we were sleeping in, suggesting that it isn't just Somalia that breeds pirates. And Tony Love deserved his win for his more successful shameless pandering to the Queensland palate with a steak sanger.

I can't feel too bad – everyone knows Love conquers all.

Originally published in 'A2', The Age, 2009

YOU'RE NOT GOING TO
EAT THAT!?

Kuala Lumpur, 1989. I've eaten my way through the first bag of toffee-covered crabs – yum, salty, crunchy *and* sweet – and start on the second. Halfway through I notice these crabs have skinnier legs when one gets stuck between my teeth. Closer inspection shows, under the caramel, not crabs but plump little grasshoppers. I feel sick but don't know why.

Many odd things have passed my lips before – horse, possum, *uni* (live sea urchins) – but I have only really baulked at egg whites – either runny and clear like mucus, or set hard like slimy white marble.

There's also really not a big difference between crabs and grasshopper. They've both got lots of legs and crunchy shells; they just move on different planes. And quite frankly, they are a treat compared to the cow's foot jelly I'll breakfast on at Mandel's delicatessen in Melbourne's suburb of Balaclava a week later. At 8 am this has all the wobbly attraction of runny egg whites set with glue rather than heat. I eat it because I've been taken there, alone, by my girlfriend's father. To win the hand of the fair princess I've got to slay my own culinary dragon. It is a rite of passage. It is a gauntlet thrown down. It's something that I should probably try again.

Food is one of the great cultural definers. 'Tell me what you eat: I will tell you who you are,' wrote Brillat-Savarin. True, but perhaps more true is US academic Phyllis Pray Bober's contention that we are what we *don't* eat.

Deuteronomy might have proscribed the eating of pork in religious law in about 621 BC, but 1200 years earlier the shepherding peoples of the Near East were already banning pork as the food of their pig-farming enemies. Even before that, the pig-farming Chinese had rejected milk as the food of their Mongol rivals. 'Food taboos and food avoidance have always been supremely effective mechanisms delimiting cultural groupings,' says Pray Bober in *Art, Culture and Cuisine* (University of Chicago Press, 1999).

'Limey', 'kraut', 'eskimo' and 'frog' are pejorative names for our northern cousins drawn from their culinary predilections, proving there is nothing new in teasing others about what they eat. The ancient Greeks used to tease the Thracians about eating butter and the Boetians about eating weasels, moles and cats.

Acceptance or rejection of a food can be based on a range of factors. In the West, slippery and slimy textures are avoided as a sign of putrefaction, while these textures are praised in the Cantonese kitchen. Natural bitterness, often a sign of unripeness or, worse, poison, can also prompt food avoidance. Weird food also has a societal role to play in rites of passage to adulthood, as well as identifying friends and enemies.

Necessity, however, makes an omnivore of most people. Some weird food practices are a function of poverty. Back in a time when the diet of the poor was based on grains, pulses or rice, any extra protein was welcome, whether discarded by the rich or industry, or whether it had two, four, six or eight legs.

Man's third leg is equally as important for the acceptance of certain foods. It seems men will eat, and pay handsomely to eat, anything if it'll improve or restore their sexual vigour. 'This will make you strong' is an exhortation that accompanies everything from the genitalia of stags, tigers or deer to the still-beating heart of a cobra. Likewise, some foods have been avoided based on how they look or what that bit used to be used for.

Personification also gets in the way of eating our little furry friends. Cats, dogs, rabbits, deer, bears and horses are cute and have names like Slinki Malinki, Lassie, Fiver, Bambi, Yogi and Trigger. Guinea pigs are also quite cuddly, but they eat them in Peru where some peasants can't afford to be quite as fussy or romantic. Calvin W. Schwabe, in *Unmentionable Cuisine* (University Press of Virginia, 1979), would have it that weird animals — and the weird bits of animals — could be the difference between health and malnourishment for millions.

It's not that a lot of these foods don't taste good. Back in 1857 Peter Lund Simmonds, in his book *The Curiosities of Food* (now available again from Ten Speed Press), explained that bear tastes a bit like beef or pork (just avoid that rancid bear fat), puma tastes like veal and that very tasty bacon can be made from hippo. My dad tells me human flesh is a lot like pork — I've always been too scared to ask how he knows. He grew up in Africa.

Talk about weird foods and we are quite happy to point the finger overseas. Seldom do we look at the Australian diet with dispassionate eyes. So we don't eat bugs? Well, apart from when mum used cochineal to colour the icing red. The brilliant scarlet came from the boiled bodies of an insect that lives on the prickly pear cactus.

So you don't eat intestines? What about traditional sausage skins, let alone what they are sometimes stuffed with? Which is worse, eating a natural skin or a man-made chemical one?

The idea of rotted food is too weird? But what are fish sauce, oyster sauce and Worcestershire sauce other than delicious flavourings built around judiciously fermented or aged seafood?

And then there's our own national culinary icon, Vegemite. Kraft keeps pretty mum about where it comes from, but this yeast extract seems to owe at least a little thanks to the scrapings of beer vats. Let's not even think about the meat pie, burgers made from industrially reclaimed meat or milkshakes bolstered up with pork lard.

Even foods that are central to most Western cuisines are not universally accepted. One lactose-free Hong Kong mate reckons Westerners smell of sour milk. He's no fan of dairy and he may have a point. There is also a school of thought that suggests that man in his primeval state is naturally lactose intolerant. In dairy-free cultures, a glass of the white stuff may induce nausea or an upset stomach. Whether a slice of 'plastic cheese' counts as dairy is an interesting debate.

Even the innocuous chook isn't universally loved. Some high-caste Hindus and Tibetans look at our love for chicken weirdly. Hell, the African Walamo tribe put people to death for eating it. And then I get to thinking what a hen's egg really is and I realise that I was probably right to avoid eggs in those early years, if not the grasshoppers.

Top Six Destinations for Culinary Adventure

China

It's said the Cantonese will eat anything with four legs apart from the table. Try snake soup; deep-fried scorpion; silkworm grubs; bird's nest soup – it's the dried saliva that makes it special; every bit of the pig; live fishy things; fish eyes and cheeks; penises; thousand-year-old eggs; fish maw; jellyfish; and tendons of camel or cow.

France

Europe's true omnivores. They claim snails, frog's legs, foie gras, cockscombs and tripe as their own, although these are eaten elsewhere. The epicentre may be Lyon, where giblet salad, shaved ox nose and *rosette* sausages thrive. The guidebooks say the latter get their name from their rosy colour. I say it's got more to do with the lowest part of the intestine that forms the casing. That too ends in a tight little rosette. Sadly *Larousse Gastronomique* has now dropped its recipes for camel hump and camel foot stew but look out for the *andouille* – a smoked pork lung and tripe sausage or blood sausage. On Corsica blackbird paté and donkey sausage were once prized.

Italy

Romans taught us much about relishing weird food, whether a sow-udder stew or suckling puppy, while the Italian *cucina povera* is littered with make-do recipes like the pig's testes, Tuscan *cacciucco* or *scottiglia*

– pot-luck stews of meat and fish respectively. The Sicilians embrace delicacies of *ricci di mare* (sea urchin) and *bottarga* (the dried egg sacks of mullet, tuna or swordfish). They were once much pilloried for eating cute little songbirds, too.

Japan

If raw fish – including the risky *fugu* – is too much for you, avoid the Japanese passion for fermenting (read: rotting) soybeans into *natto* and tofu into *tempeh*. Their use of seaweed is unusual, but common elsewhere (Welsh laverbread; Canada and Ireland's dulse). They have also been known to eat crickets.

South-east Asia

So much to choose from, but their fermented fish and prawn pastes (*trassi*, *blachan*) are a good place to start. Look and you'll also find bat, dog, snakes, grasshoppers, toilet-stinky durian fruit, bull's penis soup, Laotian rat, water beetle (especially in Thailand) and fertilised and crunchy duck or chicken eggs – the dreaded *baalut* that are prized in the Philippines and Vietnam.

UK

The UK is now 20 per cent vego and there are reasons other than dodgy farming practices. Fried bread could be one, but also add blood pudding, jellied eels, brains, peacock, black and white pudding (which has all the fat and cereal but none of the blood of black pudding) or a sheep's stomach stuffed with oatmeal and the animal's pluck (haggis). The Welsh lardy cake and the use of animal fat for dumplings and puddings can also take some getting used to.

USA

One of the homes of industrial food has given us Spam; margarine (urban myth says it's the only thing that rats won't eat); chewing gum; Coca-Cola; cheese in a can; and fiddlehead ferns that can poison you if undercooked. Down south there are salads with raspberry jelly and marshmallows in them; hog maws and snouts; chitlins (pigs' intestines); opossum; squirrel (especially their brains); grits; and slimy okra. No wonder the USA is known as the home of the brave.

Originally published in 'Epicure', The Age, 2002

THE QUIET CUISINES

Vietnamese, Indian, Malaysian, Chinese, Italian, French, Lebanese, Greek, Korean, Japanese, Middle Eastern, Spanish. These are the cuisines that scream their presence from suburban shopping strips to the pages of food publications. But what of the quiet cuisines? Those notable operators who plough their own furrow for their own local community and for interested culinary adventurers?

For once let's forget the hip and fashionable food beat and listen to the song of seven of Australia's quiet cuisines – Balinese, Burmese, Cambodian, Croatian, Egyptian, Ethiopian and Iranian.

Quiet though they may be, obscure these cuisines aren't. Combined, over 200 million people eat them every day. They just tend to be lower profile in Australia for a range of reasons. Maybe they are from a culture whose people moved here in small numbers. Maybe theirs is a less established immigrant community, with less funds for members to develop their own eating houses. Maybe 'eating out' is not part of their culture. Maybe the migrants that arrived here focused on careers other than cooking. While Croatian chefs are rare, there are numerous Croatian millionaires who have made their money from eggs, chicken, tuna or engineering.

What follows is not a definitive guide, just some broad brushstrokes to encourage you to go out and find out more about these exciting cuisines, their regional variations and the customs that surround them.

Burmese

While Melbournians might discuss the weather, the Burmese are more likely to greet you with the words, 'Have you eaten?', 'We are obsessed with flavour and freshness,' says Richard Elton-Bott, who, with wife Mimi, runs Richmond's Burmese House.

'Our cooking isn't complicated. It's slow-roasting, or curries, or salads. At the heart of much of the food is the Burmese chilli paste: if that's not right you can forget the dish,' says Min Aye Tun, chef and partner at Hawthorn's Old Rangoon.

The Burmese also use a masala spice mix that's similar to but milder and more fragrant than its Indian equivalent, and loads of herbs. Min's partner, Greig Cunningham, recites an ingredient list that runs from coriander, lemongrass, lime leaf and galangal to sawleaf, mountain ebony, drumstick and calabash.

Vegetables tend to be cooked and served separately as salad, with favourite ingredients including cabbages, broccoli, beans, chokos and watercress, mixed with river fish and chicken. The yellow split pea and tamarind are crucial, Richard explains, and edible young shoots are an important part of the diet.

The Burmese eat as a family. Dinner is the main meal of the day and diners are given preference according to seniority. All dishes are served at the same time, with rice as the central element of every meal. This will be accompanied by a soup; salads; condiments like the omnipresent dried shrimp paste (*ngapi*) or pickles; and several main dishes. 'There may be three dishes on the table at the same time … one sour, one hot or salty and one sweet,' explains Richard of how the different tastes meet.

One dish that is eaten all through the day is Myanmar's national dish, a fish soup called *mohingha*. Desserts are a rarity, meals ending instead with a sugar hit in small cups of coffee or the green tea that flows all the time, possibly accompanied by a dish of pickled tea leaves. 'They have a strong flavour and like Vegemite you hate it or love it,' says Richard.

Ethiopian

Ethiopian food would be incomplete without two central elements. The first is the springy, slightly sour bread called *injera*, made from *teff* flour, which acts as both the plate and the dining implement for Ethiopian stews (*wats*). The second element is *berbere*, the spice mix that flavours these stews. This is a paste of ingredients like cloves, onion, garlic, red pepper, coriander powder and Ethiopian cardamom.

Meat – beef for everyday, chicken on special occasions – can also be sautéed, in which case the dish is called *tibs*. Lamb and goat also make the occasional appearance on the Ethiopian menu.

Besides *berbere*, flavouring also comes from a mild Ethiopian curry powder (*alicha*) and *niter kibbe*, a type of ghee filtered through spices which adds both flavour and richness.

According to Abera Ayalaw from Footscray's Cafe Lalibela, vegetables commonly used include cauliflower, spinach, cos lettuce, green chilli, beetroot, potatoes, carrots, with okra, red lentils or split peas.

Lunch tends to be the main meal, with breakfast often just griddle bread (*kita*) with butter and red pepper, porridge or *injera* with sauce (*fitfit*). Manners are simple: wash before the meal and wait for others before starting. Kids sometimes eat at a separate time and some Ethiopians pray before the meal.

Coffee originated in Ethiopia, so it's no surprise that sitting around sipping a cup of joe and chatting is big in Ethiopian village life. The coffee may be flavoured with sugar, salt or occasionally butter. The Ethiopians love their fat!

Iranian

The footprints of Iranian food stretch across the Middle East and even into India. Rich Murghal cuisine, with its sweet, creamy sauces, is Persian in origin and much of the food of Baghdad's Shi'i merchants and the Jewish community there has a Farsi accent. Heck, some academics even believe that the Croats were originally from Persia.

Given how Persian cuisine's influence has spread along the spice routes, it is a surprise when Azam Shokouhi, co-owner and chef at

Nights of Shiraz, reveals that Iranians don't use much spice: just a little cinnamon or white cardamom maybe. They do use herbs like coriander, parsley and mint, along with dried lemon, and flavourings from flowers in the form of local saffron or rosewater.

The combination of sweet and sour, and of fruit and meat, is important to Iranian food, as are casseroles. One famous casserole that encompasses all this is *fessenjoon*, chicken slowly cooked in a sauce of pounded walnuts and pomegranates. Another less desirable national favourite, *olivie*, is cold mashed potato salad flavoured with dill and peas.

'In the south they use lots of fish with herbs. Another of the south's signature dishes is Shirazy salad: tomato, cucumber and red onion dressed with verjuice, olive oil and dried mint. In the north they eat rice – Basmati – even for breakfast, and garlic because it's cold,' says Azam.

Soups also play a role, whether lamb's head, feet and tongue soup for breakfast or *ash*, a vegetable soup garnished with sour yoghurt (*kashk*), fried mint and garlic as an afternoon snack. Dinner is the main meal of the day.

Lamb and mutton are the primary meats, and beef is the second choice. All can be marinated in onion juice, lemon juice or yoghurt and saffron, then grilled over coals. They are served with bread or buttered rice and grilled tomato (*chelo kebab*). Rice may also come cooked pilau-style with fava beans or sour little barberries and Iranian pistachios.

Dessert are a rarity. Iranians get their sugar buzz from sucking spiced tea through a sugar lump clasped between their teeth and from *bamia*, sugar-syrup-soaked choux pastries.

One thing you won't see on an Iranian dinner table is a knife – or leftovers. It is polite to try everything put in front of you, using your spoon or fork.

Balinese

There's something very special about how the Balinese do their satay. Perhaps it's the way minced seafood is pressed round sticks of lemongrass or how they roast the pork in that classic Balinese style. The academic might get a thrill from explaining that satay is a legacy of the Javanese 'involvement' with the island, while a food hooverer like me might just be in raptures about discovering a culture where snacking is a way of life. Stopping off at a roadside stall for some shrimp crackers (*krupuk*) or deep-fried stuffed beancurd is an essential part of the day for many Balinese.

Agus Ida Bagus, chef/owner of West Melbourne's Warung Agus, is quick to point out that 'so long as they have rice and chilli sauce Balinese people are happy'. Remember, though, that here is a race so serious about food that the differing qualities of rice can cause arguments and that 'chilli sauce' could be any range of different sambals – although most likely it's the limey and lemongrassy sambal *matah*.

Lother Arsana, Executive Chef at the Grand Hyatt Bali and co-author of *The Food of Bali* (Periplus, 2002) explains that this interest in everyday food is carried through to a higher level by the complex rules surrounding religious, ritual and festival foods in Bali. These rules govern everything from the preparation of turtle or pork *lawar* to the sixty or so different rice cakes (*jata*) essential for festivals, and they might cover such details as the order in which food is mixed and by whom; or which herbs and spices can be used with which animals. To generalise massively, the basic rule is that spices grown underground, like turmeric and galangal, go with four-legged dinner, while two-legged protein matches flavourings grown above ground.

Ceremonial food might be tasty stuff like tamarind-water-glazed suckling pig or banana-leaf roast duck, but Agus explains even in everyday dishes, the Balinese abhor bland food. 'They want it fragrant, hot and sometimes sweet,' he says.

For Agus, the key flavours of Balinese food include lemongrass, turmeric, galangal (*laos*), ginger, the juice and leaves of kaffir limes, candlenuts, crunchy and camphorous kencur root and salaam leaf. Mild Balinese garlic and shallots, coconuts and shrimp paste (*trasi*) also feature.

While the island is 99 per cent Hindu, the people are not strictly vegetarian, eating chicken, pork and fish – the latter often in a broth. Vegetables tend to be a separate dish. Common choices include beanshoots, mung beans, *paku* (mountain ferns), starfruit leaves and unripe jackfruit or papaya. Deep-fried shallots and *krupuk* are omnipresent, and tempeh and tofu also play their part.

With all that grazing, it's perhaps not surprising to discover that the Balinese only eat two meals a day and often do so alone: Balinese families don't usually eat together. While rice is always central to the main meal, breakfast might be some strong Balinese coffee accompanying *gado gado*, a salad built around fried tofu, mung bean spouts, spinach, bean shoots, peanut sauce and a sweet chilli sauce.

Normally drinks with the meal are limited to hot water or *tuak*, a sweet wine made from coconut palm sap.

Cambodian

Cambodian food is less sweet and hot than Thai food and less salty than Vietnamese, yet Cambodians value flavour combinations like sweet and sour, sweet and bitter and sweet and salty.

Sourness comes from tamarind, lime juice, unripe fruits and pickles, while vegetables, including the pea eggplant and bitter melon, commonly supply bitterness. Cambodians use fish sauce for saltiness, much as the Chinese rely on soy sauce.

After rice, fish is the most common feature of the Cambodian diet, says Chan Uoy, who runs Yarraville's stylish Cambodian restaurant, Bopha Devi. Chan points out that Cambodia's cuisine has benefited from outside influences. 'From India, we inherited the art of blending spice pastes for stews and curries, using cardamom, ginger, cinnamon, star anise, tamarind and turmeric, to which we add garlic and shallots and our indigenous lemongrass, galangal and kaffir lime leaves.

'The Chinese introduced soy sauce and noodles, a host of new vegetables, the art of stir-frying and steaming. The Portuguese and Spanish brought chilli peppers, beans, tomatoes and corn. The French contributed valuable culinary techniques such as baking and fabulous bread.'

One thing you won't find on the menu at Bopha Devi is Cambodia's own rather unusual fermented fish paste called *prahok*. 'It is delicious,' Chan assures me, 'but often described as Cambodian cheese, and you can imagine what cheese smells like to Asians!'

Croatian

The food of Croatia splits between the Mediterranean cuisine of the coast and the continental cuisine of the interior plain. So says Dennis Valcich, who has written three Croatian cookbooks and ran the recent Croatian Food Festival at the Hilton on the Park.

Hailing from the Dalmatian Coast himself, Dennis sings the praises of the area's figs and wine; of the local scampi and crayfish; of the local lamb, fed on pastures salty from the Adriatic's spray and cooked on a spit or 'under the bell' in a sort of domed Dutch oven.

Dennis says it is important that when eating lamb from the spit, you peel the meat away with your fingers. 'The Croatian meal is very laid-back,' he says, pointing to how wine is traditionally passed round in a big communal wooden pot.

Flavourings come from oregano, thyme, bay leaves, flat leaf parsley, onions, tomato and an awful lot of garlic. Spices are seldom used. Baby spinach, shallots and Portuguese salt cod also feature.

Inland, pork is king. The table groans with suckling pig for special occasions and cured meats like *csabai* salamis, pork neck and prosciutto that's been cured for over a year – 'the way it should be done, not like how those Italians do it,' fumes Dennis.

Game dishes, sweetwater fish, cheese, cakes and a sort of savoury strudel-like pastry are also popular. Paprika is big news, too, whether colouring the *csabai* or flavouring a fish dish.

Dinner is the main meal of the day, although in summer it may instead be a late lunch starting at 4 pm. Breakfast – especially on the coast – tends to be crusty bread, dried figs and grappa. Croatians love their bread. 'A Croatian will kill you if there is not enough,' jokes Dennis.

Croatians also tend to have a sweet tooth. They'll tuck into pancakes, jams like rosehip or plum, walnut or poppy seed rolls and sultana dough-nuts with *slivovitz* (plum brandy).

Controversially, Valcich also rails that the three most readily recog-nisable Croatian dishes – skinless *cevapcici* sausage, kebabs and cabbage rolls – are all the food of the country's Turkish 'visitors' and should therefore not be classed as Croatian.

Finding Croatian food in Melbourne is a stretch, especially as those places run by Croatians, like Vlado's, Lazar's, Steve Bar's and the Ivanhoe Tavern, tend to only have a couple of Croatian dishes on the menu – maybe pancakes, *cevapcici* or cabbage rolls. For the full Croatian experience you're probably best served by pulling on your Melbourne Knights guernsey and heading out to see Marija Bacak, who cooks at the Croatian Australian Association in Footscray. Here the food's honest, home-style and huge – pork neck, walnut and jam pancakes, beef paprika and pretty legendary *sarma* (cabbage rolls). Go on a Friday when the place hums – but book and 'bring a big appetite' suggests Maria.

Egyptian

Ted Mikhail, who cooks at Bentleigh East's Valley of the Kings, patriotically swears that Egyptians make the best felafel (*ta'amaya*) and slow-stewed fava beans (*fuul medames*).

Meat is often barbecued – an approach that predates Egypt's Ottoman occupation. Lamb, chicken and pigeon are common and Egyptians also make kofta with minced lamb and beef combined. On big occasions there may be a roast that will have been marinated but never stuffed.

For flavouring, garlic, coriander seed and leaf, leek, spring onion, parsley, cumin, pepper and hot chilli predominate, says Ted. Onion is also huge, while, as in Lebanese cuisine, there is little use of lemon or mint.

Egypt is also where *dukkah* originated, a pounded mix of hazelnuts or chickpeas with seeds like coriander, sesame and cumin that can be sprinkled on bread, meats or salads.

Chef Hamada, from the unpretentious Egyptian House in Brunswick, explains that lunch is the big meal of the day, starting any time after 2 pm. Perhaps there will be an oven *tagen* – a casserole full of okra, lamb or vegetables. Another classic peasant dish is *koushary*, a combination of lentils, rice, pasta and onions with a spicy tomato sauce.

To drink, there may be a very sweet drink made from steeped carob, sweet hibiscus tea or milky spiced *sahleb*. Tea without milk and Turkish-style coffee are also popular.

Ted explains that the Egyptians also love sweet things, from rice pudding to local *baklava* or *kahak* – a date-stuffed shortbread.

Originally published in 'Epicure', The Age, 2003

HOW TO WIN A RIBBON

I want to win a ribbon – or even better, a sash. I want to bake a sponge like Mrs Croxford of Benalla or a fruitcake like Mrs Williams of Finley. I want to display my prowess in the Arts and Crafts Pavilion to a soundtrack of the woodchop and the whistles of drovers.

The trouble is, old hands tell me there's more to winning than baking a decent cake. They talk of tricks that will have the judges murmuring appreciatively and reaching for a commendation card at the very least – tales of glycerine, three-day-old eggs and baking trays lined with sand.

My search for the inside running starts in the beautiful Victorian country town of Benalla, where my interest in show cookery started, and with Lorna Croxford. This fifty-year show veteran still vividly remembers lighting the old wood stove at 3 am to bake her first entries before taking them on foot to the Arts and Crafts Pavilion at the Benalla Showground. Today she's regularly a judge of cookery sections and that Arts and Crafts Pavilion bears her name – a tribute to the long involvement of Lorna and her late husband, Frank, in the Benalla Show. She's also no stranger to winning herself, and a slice of her cream sponge shows why. I'd call it 'ethereal' but up here in Kelly Country that's 'dickhead' talk.

The most common fault she sees at shows is entries that pay no heed to 'The Schedule'. The show professionals treat with utter respect this official list of requirements for any entry in each 'class', as the individual cookery categories are called. If it says the mud cake should be no more than 21 centimetres in diameter, then 22 centimetres won't do. The Schedule may also exactly specify the recipe. Looking worryingly deep into my black soul, Mrs Croxford warns me that cheats are usually tumbled. If I use duck eggs or custard powder to improve the colour of my sponge she'll know by the smell or the telltale flecks the custard powder leaves. Using large eggs for more volume or glycerine to keep a sponge moist are legal wrinkles. As is using three-day-old eggs rather than fresh for a fruitcake – they are more relaxed and are believed to help the texture.

The show community seems divided over whether sponges or fruitcakes are the toughest classes to win. Angela Fleay, who followed her mother and grandmother into showing, is a vocal member of the latter church. 'Sponges are hardest. They are so very temperamental,' says this multiple winner of the Most Successful Exhibitor prize at the Yarra Glen Show (17 times) and the Lilydale Show (thrice).

In Fleay's experience, which also includes wins at the Royal Melbourne Show, the judges are looking for a sponge sandwich of even halves that is golden outside but paler within. Burnt bits are a no–no. The texture should be fine and light. To achieve her award-winning sponges she ensures that all ingredients are at room temperature, the oven temperature is preset and the cake tins are greased or lined before she starts. She'll even turn up the heating in the house so everything starts at the perfect warmth. That elusive texture is helped by triple sifting all the dry ingredients, but Fleay reckons the real art comes when folding the flour into the egg mixture. 'You must be very, very gentle,' she says.

Once the sponge is cooking, no-one is allowed to walk past the oven and even the slamming of a door can make it 'flop'. That's not so easy when you've got a three-year-old son and a fifteen-week-old baby in the house. Her final word of advice is to make sponges the day before, as transporting them when they aren't fully cooled can make them 'sticky'.

Fleay notes that fierce rivalry can surface at local shows, but any such small-town competition amongst the sponges and scones is nothing compared to the sniping that reportedly goes on between the cake decoration competitors. Peter Bennett is a frequent Royal Melbourne Show winner with his preserves and baking, but his foray into decorated cakes was short-lived. 'It was so bitchy,' he says with a laugh. 'They'd all be standing round just criticising each other's work.'

This year Bennett will compete in over 40 other classes, which takes no small amount of planning, and he admits that when he turns up to deliver his entries he gets a few inquiring glances. Male exhibitors remain a rarity in the cookery sections.

Ask him for tips and he'll tell you that without a good basic technique wrinkles don't count for much. He does advise leaving your cake in the tin for five minutes before turning it out and never letting it stand in a draught. He also recommends lining the tin with parchment (he uses Gladbake) rather than using butter and flour, which can leave marks on the cake's surface. His strongest advice for new entrants like me is to get to understand what the judges are looking for. He has found the live judging sessions at the Melbourne Show excellent for picking up such tips.

This year it's scones and muffins that will be judged live, and sixth-year judge and cooking lecturer Brendan Carter will be on stage openly assessing the entries for their look, texture and aroma. 'It's pretty competitive but I've never had anyone abuse me – well, not to my face,' Carter says.

Joan Graham, co-author of *Cooking for Competition* (Ercildourne, 1991), suggests volunteering as a steward for your local show's cookery section as another way to get an inside view of judging. She contends that the toughest class to win is the VASA (Victorian Agricultural Shows Ltd) Rich Fruitcake. Winning it means first triumphing at a local show and then at a regional final before duking it out with 13 others for the VASA title.

Respected Royal Melbourne Show judge Ann Marston is happy to share how she'd assess my fruitcake. First she'd appraise the outside for colour, rise and aroma. From this she can see how the lining of the cake tin has been done and spot the telltale signs of an oven that's too hot – like caramelisation, popped fruit and bad cracks. She says neat and correct insulation of the cake tin can avoid these problems. When competing herself, she favours a lining of aluminium foil and then four layers of good old-fashioned white butcher's paper. Around the tin she ties a couple of layers of greaseproof paper and newspaper rising a half-inch over the tin's edge. Other old tricks to protect the cake include standing it in a tray of sand or popping a tray of water in the oven. Any marks from a wire cooling rack will spell big trouble, so I must learn to use a tea towel when turning out a cake that's warm and impressionable from the oven.

Next she'll cut my cake in half to check for even fruit distribution and fruit and nuts that have been cut to uniform size. Scissors are best for this, apparently. Any sticks, stems or seeds still left in the raisins will cost me points, but it's more disastrous if the fruit has settled to the bottom of the cake. 'We are looking for a nice face to the cake,' she says, casually dropping in some useful competitive cake lingo. Next she'll taste my cake for texture and to see if it has been cooked through without having been overcooked. The maturity of the cake is also important as the spices mellow and mature over time. At least four weeks' maturation is advised. Six is better.

Another fault that Marston often sees on the show bench is pockets of air in the cake's texture. The causes range from clumps of sugar that have dissolved during cooking to incorrect cake tin filling. She advises sifting the sugar, packing the cake mix in carefully, dropping the filled tin on the counter to settle the mixture and then letting it rest to 'help it settle and relax'.

You can't talk about the best show fruitcakes without Jean Williams' name coming up. This Finley grandmother won the big VASA prize in 1994 and 1997 and scooped prizes in Sydney, but she's modest about her achievements. Her advice to those chasing the VASA Rich Fruitcake title is simple. 'Over-mixing may give a coarse texture but the cooking is still the most important part. You must know your oven and keep it at the right temperature,' she says.

Cook the cake too fast and it will come out dark and cracked. Too slow and it may slump in the middle. Mrs Williams' final tip is perhaps her best. 'Always bake more than one cake so you can choose the best one to submit.' They bake 'em smart up in channel country.

Eltham's Anne-Marie Primmer is a fan of Mrs Williams' fruitcake. Praise indeed from the woman who's won the McRobert Memorial Trophy for the Royal Melbourne Show's most successful cookery exhibitor for the last two years. 'I used to think that was only for exceptional cooks, then I won it,' she says disarmingly.

Primmer is now a firm believer that show victories are within reach of anyone who wants to get into the kitchen and give it a go. Besides the best ingredients, Primmer recommends stocking up on patience, a sense of humour and lots of practice. Family support is also important: 'Leading up to the show nothing gets done around the place,' she admits.

A broader adoption of this very Aussie 'have a go' attitude is vital if cookery is to survive as part of our Agricultural Shows. Show people talk of the difficulty of finding suitably qualified judges and of declining entry numbers. Royal Melbourne Show entries are down over 6 per cent since 1998 and it's worse in the bush, where there's talk of cookery sections being curtailed or even culled. That's pretty serious in a country that is identified overseas as much by its lamingtons as its leaders. The slow decline of cake, biscuit and slice entries can be blamed on packet cake mixes, urban drift and a time-poor population as much as on a generation of grannies who would rather bushwalk, bungy-jump or windsurf than bake.

So you see, my desire to win a ribbon isn't simply about self-aggrandisement. It's also a crusade to protect a unique strand of Victoria's heritage from withering on the vine. It's a noble quest and one that I hope you'll join me in by entering your own local show this year – unless you live around Benalla, in which case back off, that ribbon's mine. See you at the show bench.

Other Show Tips from the Experts

- For scones, use cream instead of melted butter or milk for a better texture. Just don't let the mixture get too wet. Roll out your scone mix to a half-inch thick for cutting. Any thicker and you risk the scones toppling when they rise during baking – a disaster. Another disaster, that of sloping-topped scones, can be avoided by always cutting your show scones from the centre of the rolled-out mixture where it is likely to be most level.

- If your cake has a nasty crack, cover it with clean, dry tea towel as soon as it comes out of the oven. That keeps the steam in and can help some cracks come back together.

- Never use a skewer to check if the cake is cooked, as it can scar the surface. You can tell if a fruitcake is cooked by listening to it – if it is singing and sizzling it needs more time.

- When joining the two sides of a sponge, always join the two cake halves bottom to bottom.

- Have a clean oven. Sunday roast splatters will affect the flavour of a delicate cake like a sponge.

Originally published in 'Epicure', The Age, 2001

IN THE BLEAK MIDWINTER

The brief was simple enough. 'Make the column about winter,' the chief told me through teeth chomped around a stogie in true J. Jonah Jameson style. (Honestly, to my mind every editor at *The Age* looks like they've stepped straight out of a *Spider-man* or *Batman* comic. They have to if I am to continue to live out my fantasies of being somewhere between Peter Parker and Clark Kent.)

Quite frankly I'd rather have been tracking down a missing shipment of kryptonite or grabbing front-page shots of Spiderman than writing this piece. At least in those cases I'd know where to start. 'Winter' is just such a wide subject. For what is the essence of winter food?

I make a list of the first things that come to mind when I think of winter. I think of cold afternoons, brisk walks and long dark nights – and the food that leaps to mind is food for those days. Food that is as comfortable as an old, stretched woollen jumper.

Birds cooked long and slow in red wine, beef braised in stout until it resembles tar, and stews of pork and cider thickened by the way the root vegetables have broken down during cooking into a sweet three-dimensional gravy. Sometimes there's the gentle hum of spices: orange peel and cinnamon; cloves; cumin and coriander seed dancing around dried fruit in a tagine. Other times the meat is forgotten so the red wine, citrus and spices make jugs of mulled wine or *vin chaud*, which almost demands aching thighs seated at a Swiss mountain bar before you drink it.

Winter, for me, is also about avoiding washing up – and the smell of cooking coming from the warmest room in the house, back when that was the only room warmed (thanks to the oven). That means a big pan of homemade soup bubbling on the stove, perhaps made with little more than pumpkin and chicken stock, or even split pea and ham hock; the sort of soup that sets thick and gelatinous when it cools.

Or perhaps one of those French one-pot wonders like *cassoulet* or an Alsatian *choucroute*, both loaded with enough expressions of pork – whether smoked, sausaged or just sliced – that they could ask for their own sties.

The *choucroute*'s sauerkraut base has its own attractions, but winter screams for beans and pulses, expressed as a *fabada* stew from the Celtic region of Spain's north, its cousins from Brazil or Madrid, or just a big dollop of molasses-sweetened Boston baked beans, stringy with more meat from trotters. (It's no coincidence that these hotch-potches of piggy extremities are linked to the traditional time of year for the annual pig kill.)

Not everything about winter is so splattered with the scent of the charnel house. Winter is also buttered crumpets and thick slices of fruitcake with a middle that's a little slumped and so moist you're thankful it wasn't cooked through, all washed down with a big pot of strong leaf tea, unadulterated by the flavour of bergamot. If alone and feeling temperate, then maybe a small pot of smoky Lapsang Souchong is an allowable monastic alternative. Perhaps to be followed by a tumbler of peaty whisky in front of a fire that has crackled and flared its way down to a glowing mound of embers, which catch in the angles of the cut-crystal glass and the amber spirit inside.

Hey, we could even talk about sushi, which my recent reading suggests originated as a winter dish – the theory being that raw fish didn't keep so well when the weather warmed in old Edo!

Winter's seasonal vegetables have an attraction all of their own, too.

Silverbeet picked straight from the garden, pan-wilted with little more than a big squoosh of lemon juice and tossed with good fetta. A big bowl of oven-roasted brussels sprouts. A large roasting tray filled with carrots or beets, their natural sweetness intensified by long, slow cooking that turns them into earthy orange and bruise-purple candies – whenever the oven's on something needs to be using that residual heat. And then there are the tubers and other roots like turnips, swedes, parsnips, plus various potatoes and yam just waiting to be roasted, mashed or thrown into a pot to stew.

But maybe winter is a pudding? The wonder of a lemon delicious, and a baking dish that goes into the oven all puffy liquid and comes out magically transformed, with golden sponge on top and gooey decadence underneath. Or jam roly-poly, or spotted dick, or rice pudding (ideally burnt slightly at the edges; perhaps left plain or flavoured in a Spanish style with lemon zest and cinnamon, or in the Indian manner with almonds and cardamom for a *payasam* or *kheer*). Or sweet, oaty rubble-topped crumbles that hide apple, rhubarb, blackberry or a mix – served with lashings of custard, of course. Or sticky date pudding with a butterscotch sauce that's worth glugging straight from the jug. What is it about the amazing alchemy that happens when you mix cream, soft brown sugar and butter together? Each of these puddings is more than worthy of its own dedicated lionising on this page.

But really, for me winter can be summed up by one concept with two executions that span both the sweet and the savoury worlds – that puffy-light expression which is a dumpling. Whether swollen in the steam to cover the surface of a stew, its base dyed a rusty meat-hued orange by the gravy and its texture rich from the use of suet; or cooked bobbing in golden syrup so each takes on the burnished colour of an orb from the coronation of some particularly sweet-toothed royal potentate. The golden syrup dumpling is the Australian answer to India's *gulab jamen*, Greece's *loukamades* or the US's sugar-glazed commercial quoit of yeast and fat. A noble expression of a baking past, a pride in the Queensland sugar trade and the heritage of a time when an honest day's labour gave you the sort of appetite that could do justice to a bowl of golden syrup dumplings with a splash of milk – or even cream – after a hard day in the fields or the foundry.

Laziness, rather than the desire to reduce fat, has seen me remove suet from my dumplings, but the use of self-raising flour gives suitably cloud-like nuggets that lighten in the heat. The ratios of the recipe are simple: 20 g of butter rubbed into a cup of self-raising flour. Add one beaten egg and a splash of milk to moisten and make a dough. Then drop the 'dumps' – the word means a 'misshapen lump' – into a solution of golden syrup and water, or into your stew. Now just add winter for the perfect supper.

Originally published in 'A2', The Age, *2009*

MIGRANT FOOD

Chan Uoy was six when he left Cambodia. He and his parents were among the first of the 12,000 refugees that fled the country, and Pol Pot's regime, between 1976 and 1986. He remembers it well: 'The Australian government sent a Qantas plane to get us out and we were even greeted by a minister when we arrived. That was in March 1976. The country collapsed the next month. It was quite unusual compared to these days,' he observes wryly. Now Chan Uoy runs the modern Cambodian restaurants Bopha Devi in Yarraville and Docklands.

In the same year, the Talj family arrived from the Lebanon – Walid was eighteen, his brother Bilal was sixteen and their little sister Dahouk was fifteen. With their mum, they were among the 16,000 Lebanese who fled to Australia between 1975 to 1981 to avoid the civil war. They joined their aunt, one of the 3000 Lebanese who had moved to Australia in the years after the 1967 Arab–Israeli War, and soon after arriving the two families were asked to run a restaurant for a friend who was heading overseas.

They made Abdul's in Malvern a big success and went on to run Almazett in Caulfield. Today, Walid Talj has Dunyazad in Balwyn, Bilal Talj owns Richmond's Kanzaman and Dahouk White has Carlton's Zum Zum, while alumni of their restaurants run The Cedar Tree in Brighton, Mount Waverley's Samsara and Maroush in Eltham.

These are just two examples of how waves of settlers and refugees from different cultures helped create the rich multicultural tapestry of our food. Such stories stretch back to Australia's earliest days.

In the first Australian census, in 1861, Chinese-born settlers were the second-biggest ethnic group after those born in the UK. Many were escaping famine, floods and disorder in southern China, and worked in the diggings or feeding the miners. It could be argued that it was in the goldfields that the Australian tradition of a national cuisine based on culinary cross-pollination was born, with groups like the Swiss-Italian miners of Jim Crow, as the goldfields round Daylesford were known, leaving the Australian kitchen the bullboar sausage as their legacy.

The 1901 Australian census recorded 878 Greeks in Australia, many of whom ran or worked in restaurants or tilled the soil to grow food. In the same period Italian migrants, along with the Chinese, contributed greatly to the emerging fishing fleets and market gardens.

The biggest waves of migration from these countries came in the postwar years, with the launch of the assisted passage scheme in 1952. The Italians mainly came from Calabria, Sicily and the Veneto. Visit the Italian butchers of Melbourne's north or a salami competition in Myrtleford and you'll see this reflected in the fat mild Veneto, spicy Sicilian or capsicum-sweet Calabrian salamis proudly displaying the maker's heritage.

It was in 1957 that Gilbert Lau of Flower Drum fame arrived, almost 100 years after his grandfather and great-grandfather had walked from Robe to Bendigo to join the gold rush. Along with Lau, this post-war poly-ethnic migration delivered into our kitchens a host of chefs like Hermann Schneider, who was brought in for the 1956 Olympics and stayed, much to the benefit of Melbourne's culinary culture.

Of course, there are no hard and fast rules about how quickly migrants' culinary culture impacts on a city. Take the case of the Moras and the Zeleznikows, for example. Both couples arrived from post-Holocaust Eastern Europe via Paris in 1951. Three years later, Georges and Mirka Mora opened the Mirka Café in Exhibition Street with one of the city's first Gaggia espresso machines hissing and spluttering on the counter. The second machine was round the corner in a café established the same year by Tuscan brothers Leo and Vildo Pelligrini.

Mora defied council by-laws by putting tables and chairs on the sidewalk and pushed for the right to serve wine. The Pellegrinis made beautiful coffee. Together these two establishments, opened by migrants from radically different backgrounds, sowed the seeds for today's vibrant café culture in Melbourne.

As a newsreel announcer of the time put it in clipped Anglo tones, 'Perhaps for the continental migrant, there's a touch of home in the picturesque sidewalk cafés at the top end of Collins Street.'

Of course this scene around Lonsdale, Exhibition and Bourke streets had already been shaped between the wars by the great Italian restaurant families – names like Codognotto, Triaca, Massoni, Molina and Vigano. The impact of these migrants in helping create a restaurant culture for Melbourne cannot be underestimated and would need a book, or two, to do it justice.

It took Avram and Masha Zeleznikow four years longer to scrape together enough from their menial jobs to buy a run-down milk bar in Acland Street and name it after the Parisian café that had been their rendezvous point after they separately fled Poland. Scheherazade opened in 1958 and became a home away from home for the generations of Eastern Europeans who had fled Nazism, Communism or the Russian tanks that had rolled through Hungary.

In fact, the *Yellow Pages'* restaurant and café listings pay testament to man's inhumanity to man. Flick through and you can see the impact of political and economic upheaval around the world. That Iraqi bakery run by Samira and Amir Kalash bakes the bread the way Amir's father taught him as a boy back in Baghdad. They fled Iraq after the war in 1992 and opened the wonderful Amir Bakery in Brunswick in 1996.

Other waves of migration to Australia inspired by these pressures are reflected in the many listings for Italian, Vietnamese and Chinese restaurants. Many of the 49,000 Vietnamese who fled their country between 1975 and 1985 would end up either setting up or, almost more importantly, patronising the Vietnamese restaurants and supermarkets that sprang up in Footscray and Richmond.

And surely the massive boom in Malaysian-style hawker restaurants, led by Danny Ko's Penang Coffee House in the late eighties, must be connected with the Malaysian-born Chinese who fled oppression in Malaysia and the Malaysian students who came thanks to the push of Australian education institutions into Asian markets, prompted by the Colombo Plan. This boom, which saw about 100 Malaysian cafés and restaurants open over those years, helped make ingredients like galangal, screwpine and lemongrass both more readily available and cheaper, as other migrants set up businesses to supply the restaurants.

More recently, the rise of restaurants in areas like Footscray and Kensington serving food from the Horn of Africa can be linked to the arrival of Somalians, Eritreans and Ethiopians, a huge proportion of whom settled in Victoria. In 2001, 67 per cent of Somalians, 56 per cent of Ethiopians and 62 per cent of Eritrean-born settlers – a total of about 5000 people – were living here.

Likewise, it is easy to surmise a connection between the recent boom in Indian migration – India is now Victoria's largest source of settlers – and the huge growth in the number of Indian restaurants and cook shops (canteens) that have opened over the past five years.

There is naturally a difference between migrants and refugees – and not just in the eyes of John Howard. According to Pablo Gimenez from the Asylum Seeker Resource Centre, the bulk of refugees to Australia can be divided into two groups: those 1000 to 2000 a year who come on tourist or student visas and seek protection once they are here, and another 9000 who have arrived by boat over the last three years. The majority of these have an Iraqi or Afghani background and tend to be based in Victoria or Sydney – although, like the rabbitohs and cameleers before them, many of the Afghanis have headed to the bush to find employment picking fruit or in meatworks. There are also a number from the Congo, Sierra Leone and Sri Lanka – many of whom head to Clayton and Pakenham in Victoria.

Julie Shiels curated the evocative and moving 'Cooking Stories' exhibition at Melbourne's Immigration Museum, interviewing fifty refugees to discover the role food played in their departures and their lives. 'Listening to their stories you are struck by three things: the resilience of the tellers, their humour in adversity and how something as ordinary as sitting down to a meal has become extraordinary,' she says. Shiels believes the role of food transcends the mere recipe or the assemblage of the ingredients: 'Food is how we provide comfort and a reassurance of our identity.'

It seems that through the ritual of 'breaking bread' we confirm our place within our community, our family. No wonder Christians call it 'communion' and built a religion about it. And those rituals at which food is so often central are surrounded by stories. The smells and sounds from the kitchen, the anticipation, the preparation and the gathering are all part of the experience. There is a sense of occasion.

Julie Shiels feels that another way refugees impact on our culinary culture is pretty immediate: once they become settled a market arises for ingredients new to Australia, ingredients that connect them with the home country. For the Australian cook and the chef, this can be like discovering a whole new spectrum of colour. 'Some shopping centres are transformed,' explains Shiels. 'West Heidelberg used to be an area of huge poverty. Now there are lots of Somalians living there and this is reflected in the ingredients and services you can find there. I can travel to some areas around Melbourne and feel I am in another country.'

Shiels knows she is not alone – she discovered that people came to the exhibition because they were fascinated by the food as much as by the refugees' stories. They wanted to find out more about their 'exotic' dishes.

And that's the beauty about our food in Victoria. Thanks to the contribution of a rainbow of migrants, many dishes that were once deemed exotic rarities are now very much part of the fabric of what we eat. It is what makes this such a wonderfully cosmopolitan place to live. If that's not a reason to seek out your local Lebanese, Ethiopian, Chinese, Indian, Italian or Cambodian chef and give them a hug just for being here, then I don't know what is.

Originally published in 'Epicure', The Age, 2007

THE TEMPLE KITCHEN

The ritual sharing of food is central to many of the world's great religions – and the youngest, Sikhism, in no exception. An important element of Sikh religious services is the *langgar* – a devotional vegetarian meal shared by the congregation. Introduced by Sri Guru Nanak, on whose teachings the religion was founded, and later institutionalised by the third Sikh Guru, Sri Guru Amar Das, the *langgar* is the perfect expression of some of Sri Guru Nanak's central tenets, such as the rejection of the caste system and the rather radical belief, for the 16th century, that all men and women are equal.

The idea of the *langgar* is simple. All must sit down to eat together, regardless of social position, gender or religious persuasion, and all are welcome.

At Blackburn's Sikh temple, where many of Victoria's 8000 to 10,000 Sikhs come to worship, there is a massive mess hall lined with eleven long runners of carpet. Here the devout will sit to eat the *langgar* from little round stainless steel trays after the service, which takes place in another simple, unadorned hall that houses the Sikh's scripture – the venerated Sri Guru Granth Sahib.

Out back of this sprawling old mail centre is a gleaming stainless steel kitchen, where volunteers prepare the *langgar* for every Sunday lunch and Wednesday dinner. But today is extra special. This is the holy day marking the birth of Sri Guru Nanak. Rather than the usual hundreds, today the temple is expecting over a thousand worshippers.

Given those numbers, ten families have banded together, for not only will they prepare the meal but they'll also donate all the ingredients for the raita, curries, salads, breads and Indian sweets.

Only one of their number is a chef: Amarjit Wahi, owner of Malvern's Indian Harvest. The rest of this motley crew includes a bank teller, a teacher, an industrial chemist, an electrical engineer and a computer programmer.

I arrive expecting chaos. This is a huge task to attempt with a team of hardened professionals, let alone amateurs, and while undoubtedly there are some good home chefs among them, at least one of the husbands admits his kitchen skills are limited to 'making chai' (Indian spiced tea).

Instead I walk into the calmest commercial kitchen I have ever visited. In fact it's so calm that Amarjit Wahi wanders over to say hello and share a cup of milky chai. The air is heavy with the smell of spices – cumin, coriander powder, cloves and green cardamom. The kitchen's six hefty wok burners are already loaded with huge 100-litre stockpots, bubbling away. A family member stands at each pot, huge paddle in hand, turning the contents to stop them sticking. A couple of pots are filled with the beginnings of the vegetable curry – peas and potatoes cooking down in thick gravy. Beside the burners, a long line of buckets filled with cauliflower florets to be added later give a sense of quite how many people will be fed today. Another couple of burners heat more cauldrons, this time filled with a dark, aromatic *dhal* full of black lentils and kidney beans.

Amarjit has been here since 5 am; the night before, other volunteers from his group cut up the vegetables and helped Gurpreet Singh, who is sort of like the temple's verger, soak the 30 kilos of pulses for the *dhal*.

Planning for today's meal started a couple of weeks ago when the families met to assign duties. What would they cook? Who would shop? Who would chop the vegetables for the curry? Who would hand-make the thousands of little balls of chickpea flour, or *boondi*, for the yoghurt raita?

'It's a matter of the system,' says Amarjit, explaining how everything stays so calm.

There's a quiet confidence that everything will be all right. Today is, as I am constantly and rather reassuringly reminded, 'an auspicious day' for me to visit. Sri Guru Nanak was born on this day. It's a bit like a Sikh version of Christmas but without the turkey or the fights and with everyone working together.

The most labour-intensive – and largest – job is making the bread. About 3000 *parshadaas* (flat breads like *rotis* or *chapattis*) have to be made and cooked by hand. Here the families have help from Jasmail Singh Khaira from Richmond's Curry Club restaurant. He is the master of the dough at the temple and has been coming in most Sundays for fourteen years to help out the volunteer families. Today he's worked an impressive 110 kilos of flour into a fat mound of dough.

At two tables, women, men and children turn this dough into *parshadaas*. There is no gender delineation here, as you'd expect given the first Guru's teachings on equality. The women are dressed in traditional Sikh dress of *salwar* (trousers) and *kameez* (shirt) in soft lime, pale salmon, rusty brown, shy blue or purple. They work the bread by hand into small balls and flatten them with small rolling pins. As the dough is slapped from hand to hand, their *chunnis*, a sort of gossamer shawl, billow rhythmically with the activity.

At the temple, all must cover their heads in respect to the Sri Guru Granth Sahib. The women use their *chunnis* for this. Some of the older men wear turbans, but for the younger lads the headwear ranges from traditional saffron *patkas* (cloths) tied around their heads to those with a swoosh or even the logo of Harry Kewell's Liverpool soccer club.

All have bare or stockinged feet that slap on the kitchen's tiled floor. That's another sign of deep respect.

Once flattened, cooked on a griddle and then toasted over an open flame for speed, the *parshadaas* are brushed with *ghee* (Indian clarified butter) and stored in eskies lined with tea towels. It's a finely oiled production line and by 9 am it's in full swing, with over thirty people making bread – the room is full of the smell of toasting flour. As other members of the congregation arrive they roll up their sleeves to help. Interestingly, no-one ever seems to need to be asked to do anything here.

Help just miraculously appears, but then *seva* — selfless and voluntary community service — is another central tenet of Sikh theology.

It's the two 100-litre pots of rice that offer one of the biggest challenges for Amarjit and the families. 'Too much water and it will become gooey,' he says, adding just enough. It's also physically tough turning the rice to prevent it from burning. He places a large, flat metal *tawa* cooking plate under the huge pots of steaming rice to help diffuse the heat and covers the rice with wet cloths, to make the steam 'more efficient'.

The salad is an essential but easier part of the meal. Today it's a special one of white radish, cucumber and onion dressed with lime and mango pickle with mustard oil. The dessert is much more problematic. The group are making *kheer* — an Indian rice pudding flavoured with almonds, cardamom, ginger, cloves and sugar. It needs to be kept moving constantly. 'Milk burns so quickly,' says Amarjit. 'You can't even have a cup of tea while it is cooking.'

There is, however, time for the group to stop for a mid-morning snack of *pakoras*. These are slices of fluffy white bread dipped into a *besan* (chickpea flour) batter spiced with coriander and red chilli powder and then fried in hefty metal woks of bubbling oil. They're sort of like Indian French toast — egg-free but delicious.

All through the day the kitchen is filled with the wafting sounds of prayers and *kirtan*, the singing of devotional hymns from the Sri Guru Granth Sahib, which is piped from the main part of the temple. Also throughout the day other donations appear. Cases of bananas. Endless boxes of Indian sweets. Or small things like the delicious fudge-like *burfi* sweets one of the women has made.

Before the service comes to an end, in the kitchen the food the group has cooked is blessed by the recitation of *Ardas*, a Sikh congregational prayer often said at the conclusion of significant endeavours. This act makes it a ritual offering and therefore holy — for the *langgar* is in essence a devotional meal. 'Everything we are cooking is an offering,' says Amarjit respectfully.

Suddenly, as if by magic, an army of young men arrives and grasps silver *balti* (serving buckets) filled with *dhal* or curry. They walk the line between each carpet runner, now filled with a hubbub of worshippers sitting cross-legged and shoulder to shoulder, offering *raita*, vegetable curry, salad, *dhal* and bread. Each member of the congregation signals whatever they want with a subtle hand movement reminiscent of twisting or sticking at the blackjack table. Seconds are offered and then, on the same plate, the *kheer*. The repeated offering of food is an important element of the *langgar*. In fact, the idea of the *langgar* is that the food should feel unlimited, that it should never end and always be sufficient.

As one person leaves another takes their vacated place and still the food keeps coming. Some use those arduously handmade roti to scoop up handfuls of curry. Others use spoons. But one thing is universal: the plates come back cleaned of food. It's just not the done thing to throw away food that is blessed.

Then just as suddenly as the servers appeared, there is a legion up to their armpits in soapsuds, washing up those used metal trays and cups. Again, there is no call to the sinks – it just happens.

Over an hour later the swell has subsided and Amarjit finds himself a vacant place on the carpet. He picks a spot by the wall so he can lean against it. After nine hours on his feet, his back welcomes a rest. Steel trays are laid before us and filled by the servers, who still patrol the aisles doling out more food.

Slowly, and with dignity, together we eat this simple food, which to me tastes better than much of what I've eaten in Melbourne's Indian restaurants. Amarjit says it's a credit to the teamwork of the ten families and to the whole congregation who have, each in their way, helped.

But for me something else keeps coming back. Another reason why this meal might taste so special. Something one of the women had said earlier in the day – that the meal was bound to taste good because it was made with love and given with an open heart. Now that's the sort of recipe advice we can all take note of in these electric-can-opener days.

And perhaps that's why mum's Christmas turkey always tastes so good – even if she is still working on the miraculous unprompted apparition of family members to do the washing up.

Originally published in 'Epicure', The Age, 2003

REFUGEE CATERING

In these days of $2 million fit-outs and $10,000 a week rent, is it any wonder that so many migrants and refugees find themselves driving cabs or cleaning offices rather than opening restaurants?

It's a problem all too familiar to Pablo Gimenez, who coordinates the Asylum Seeker Resource Centre's (ASRC) social enterprise and small business unit. 'A lot of people are interested in starting up food businesses,' he says, 'but often the capital costs make it impracticable.' Even if their costs would be only a tiny fraction of what it takes to open a Comme or an SOS.

That's why Pablo's unit has concentrated on helping those 25 per cent of refugees who are allowed to work by setting up a catering operation that runs out of the centre. The ASRC Catering Service was launched in May 2005 and directly employs asylum seekers. Currently the team includes workers from Sudanese, Indonesian, Sri Lankan, Afghani, Iraqi and Congolese backgrounds and is specialising in organic produce, where possible, and vegan meals, which makes it much easier for Hindus, Muslims and Buddhists to all work on these jobs together. 'We are mainly doing finger food for the arts community events and openings, although we have just done our first wedding,' explains Gimenez.

Serafina Wodhoomall is one of the women working for this initiative.

She fled East Timor because of the political situation and arrived by plane as a refugee seeking protection in 1996. After an eight–year wait she was granted a humanitarian visa. In East Timor she was a housewife, cooking recipes passed on from her Chinese mum and the Indian side of her family. She explains the food that the ASRC Catering Service is putting out is a multicultural blend. 'We each come up with recipes; taste them and work out what to put on the menu,' she says.

Working with the project has helped her English, which she feels will be invaluable when it comes to finding a job, and it has also given her valuable experience that is often denied unless you are a teenager. 'Age can be a problem when it comes to getting a catering job,' she agrees, pointing out that the lack of Australian qualification requirements makes catering jobs an attractive option to refugees.

Perhaps the most high-profile of a crop of new catering businesses set up as social enterprise initiatives is the Sorghum Sisters. This group of Eritrean, Somali and Ethiopian women came together to make spongy, tangy *injera* bread and they now run a successful catering business built around staples from the Horn of Africa like *chapattis*, spicy stews, vegetable *wats* and, of course, *injera*.

Munira Mahmoud co-ordinates the project, which works out of the Carlton Primary School. She arrived from Eritrea in 1994 and noticed that the different cultural groups from the Horn of Africa didn't tend to socialise, in part because of language differences. 'They seemed divided and isolated, so bringing them together in a food business seemed a good idea,' explains Mahmoud.

'As well as the social aspect – and there is a lot of laughter in the kitchen – they got to learn English and received training in everything from food preparation and handling from their dedicated chef-trainer to marketing and production. Basically everything they needed so they could become owners of a successful business and start to employ others.'

One year on and the business is going well enough that they can recruit six new 'sisters' of similar geographic backgrounds to help cope with the demand for events feeding up to 500 and a client list that includes John Thwaites, whose fiftieth birthday party they catered.

The Sorghum Sisters project is one of several community social catering enterprises funded in part by the Adult Multicultural Education Services (AMES), as part of their brief to provide training, development and employment pathways for segments of the community affected by systemic unemployment. 'They receive on-the-job training, learn English and at the same time use their cooking skills,' explains AMES' Felicity Reynolds.

The programme specifically targets unemployed refugees and migrants. Its success can be gauged by the fact that at the end of 2006, AMES will support training at three more of these social enterprise catering businesses. They currently back four. Besides the Sorghum Sisters, these include Babouska's Delight, which was set up by three (female) Russian engineers who were unable to find engineering work here; a group called Spicy Girls, which is run by women from Iraq, Syria, Lebanon and Argentina; and SMART Cuisine. This grew out of the Oakes Mothers Club and combines women from Eritrea, India, Bangladesh and the Cook Islands. Spicy Girls run a canteen and do catering out of what was once the Chisholm TAFE, while SMART Cuisine has taken over and reopened the Westhall Primary School canteen.

The appropriately named Lucinda McCook looks after the training for both the Spicy Girls and SMART Cuisine. She's helped the former develop a menu that takes in aspects of all the women's different cultures. There are those savoury Argentine pastries called *empanadas*, pungent *chimichurri* sauce served with roast meats and a host of Lebanese dishes like lamb *kibbeh* and *kofte*. The menu is all halal.

'A lot of the women involved in these projects have been in Australia for years but have been stuck at home looking after the kids. In the case of SMART Cuisine, the founders joined a school sewing circle and from that came the catering business,' says McCook. 'They all know how to cook; I just train them in a more commercial capacity – like how to juggle twenty jobs at the same time and get the food out. How to think commercially as a caterer does. Also, we put a lot of emphasis on the correct processes, hygiene procedures and achieving all the required certification that they have to have.'

But this isn't all. McCook has also noticed that the impact of these projects goes far beyond the training and earning a little money. 'It has given them another boost to their lives; they've become more confident,' she says. She's also learnt heaps: and not just the recipes passed down orally from mother to daughter for generations or tips like how feeding your kids *tabbouleh* keeps them 'regular', but also life-affirming lessons. 'They talk about their pasts and it makes you appreciate life. It also makes you appreciate their strong ethics and values, which Australians have largely thrown away. Like not putting old people in nursing homes,' she says.

Rashmi Chaubal is one of the women behind SMART cuisine. She arrived in Australia from Mumbai in 2005 but felt she needed to know and understand Australian culture before entering the workforce or undertaking the required post-grad certification to allow her to continue her Indian career of coaching English. She first volunteered for the Salvation Army and now she's with SMART. 'We all have a good time trying to understand each other's foods and culture,' she says, talking from the kitchens of Westhall Primary School, which SMART have reopened for two days a week after twenty years of closure with a new healthy menu.

'I think we all learn new things from each other, including that Australian type of food, which is quite challenging,' she says. 'But I'm not sad to leave my own country. If you want to learn something new that is what you have to do. I think of it as a great challenge.'

At home Chaubal cooks *chapattis* to serve with curries of lentils, vegetables or chicken. 'These are made spicier than most Australians might like it,' she says.

She also shares that very Indian love of super-sweet things like *halwa* and syrupy *gulab jamen*. So what exotica greets the children of Westhall Primary each Wednesday and Friday? How is the food of these migrant cultures impacting on this next generation?

'No, no,' says Chaubal, 'we are making beef pies, chicken sausage rolls and Anzac cookies ...'

After forty hours of research that often dipped into loss and displacement, hardship and vulnerability, it was strangely uplifting to hear this prosaic answer.

But then it is an answer that speaks of both integration and culinary exchange without loss of your own culture – just a few of the glittering facets of the jewel that is culinary multiculturalism, arguably the gem of greatest value in Melbourne's culinary crown.

Originally published in 'Epicure', The Age, 2007

THE FIVE WORST THINGS
I'VE EVER EATEN

We all have our envelopes. No, not the ones we keep in the top drawer beneath the broken fax in the mistaken belief that one day we might actually send someone a letter, but the envelopes that envelop us. Those invisible barriers that constrain us and what we do, and in doing so define who we are culturally, spiritually and emotionally.

From the earliest age we spend our lives accumulating information about what is and isn't good; where our culinary boundaries lie that define that envelope. At three I learnt that kitchen bleach wasn't cordial to be supped straight from the bottle; at eleven I learnt that two litres of alcoholic cider could do similar damage. I cannot recall drinking either since.

The boundaries of food are far more complex, entwined as they are with a Gordian knot of taboos. I have found myself eating crickets, scorpions and a sweet coconut milk soup filled with frog ovaries, as you do, and none have appalled me, as they actually tasted okay. The crickets came in a thick sticky caramel and were reminiscent of eating unshelled prawns, thanks to all the spindly legs. Scorpions were bland but crunchy.

This has also given me the understanding that some stuff that culturally should repel me doesn't – at least, assuming I don't think about what I am eating. Supermarket sausages, doner kebabs, foie gras and meat still warm from the slaughter are all far, far easier to eat if you don't know the facts of their provenance.

I have also learnt from bitter experience that if I am enjoying eating something in Hong Kong, France or Shanghai I should not ask what it is until after I've consumed it. Only then, after I've made my unbiased assessment of its culinary deliciousness, can I feel appalled or nauseous.

The exception to this rule is when the answer is reassuring. The fact that durian is a healthy, sweet, juicy fruit makes it far easier to stomach, even though it smells like really bad Singapore drains, and knowing that the grey sludge in front of me that stank like six-day-old garbage left on the summer streets of Naples was actually preserved tofu made it far easier to dull the gag reflex as I swallowed it. It actually tasted strangely like very ripe blue cheese. Yum!

Some foods I can appreciate for their value to other people's culture but they leave me cold, other than as a vehicle to transport magnificent sauces or soups. In this category I'd place such luxuries as shark fin, fish maw, abalone, jellyfish, bird's nest and chicken feet, which are all appreciated in Chinese cuisine for their texture. I'll acknowledge the moral issues that come with some of these luxuries but save delving into them for another day, and for other, wiser voices. I like eggs and bacon for breakfast, so I already have enough ethical and intellectual problems! I mean what's weirder to eat? A scorpion or an egg?

There are certain foods, however, that I have tried that are firmly outside my comfort zone, and have firmly stayed there.

SAVOURY JELLY

It started with me having a throw-down aged six over the congealed jellied meat juices in a school lunch Scotch egg. Cold cubed consommé and whole fish covered in a skin of aspic confirmed the aversion. Savoury jelly just seemed wrong – especially as it wasn't served with whipped cream. In the last few years, as jellification has become the cause célèbre of Spain's modernist chefs and their followers, I've tried to get around it by forcing myself to eat jellyfish and the cow's foot jelly from a deli in Carlisle Street. But, try as I might, neither has replaced Peking duck or chopped liver in my list of favourites. My aversion to savoury jelly reached its apotheosis with a Calabrian version of brawn or headcheese called *sudso*. It is mixture of the leftover bits of pig from salami-making that has been boiled down until the mix of eyes, ears, snouts and trotters release enough gelatine to create a sort of firm squelch when you spoon it from the jar. If you are lucky you get an eyeball in your serve.

GUTS AND OTHER BITS

Okay, I love sweetbreads, tripe, livers and steak and kidney pudding. I even like brains, especially when they are all creamy and in a crunchy crumbed crust served with an acidic sauce. I have even enjoyed sheep's eyeballs done the same way: they tasted to me a little like brains. Intellectually I can deal with other variety meats, but my body revolts when asked to eat toilet-stinky *andouillette*, giblet salad or pig's lung soup. I still crack a sweat at the memory of a perfect set of spongy lungs being lifted, fully intact and joined, from a tureen of almond soup. Instinctively my throat prepares to rebel against swallowing a slice of lung; it seems to close involuntarily against it. No matter how I reason with myself, I cannot overcome this visceral reaction.

MOBY DICK

Whale – I tried it raw. It popped up, unwelcome, on a sashimi platter. Don't bother. Venison carpaccio would be similar, and seasoned with far less guilt.

STINKY SKIPPY

Shopping at a central Australian community's store was an eye-opener, not for the shelves of luminous-coloured junk food in packaging of matching luridity, but for the chest freezer full of frozen roo tails. That night, much to my excitement, the friend I was staying with cooked one under coals for us. It was horrid. The tail was so sinewy it was hard to chew the meat off it and it seemed to be covered in a rancid fat that had a palate-clagging impact similar to cold mutton fat. To make matters worse, it was a dry town, so there wasn't even a can of VB to help wash it down.

PRESERVED CRAB

Imagine taking a freshwater crab and salting it so the flesh inside preserves, turning to a grey industrial sludge. What is really scary is that it is actually worse than it sounds.

A bit like a sandwich I was served recently by the charming hoofer Todd McKenney, which mixed lemon and lime Starburst jellies with Vegemite. It was a magnificently revolting combination. It would be hard to find something that worked worse with the yeasty salty spread.

Originally published in 'A2', The Age, 2009

EAT YOURSELF HORSE

It is an innocuous-enough looking plate of thinly sliced meat. Two piles of wafer-thin parings with the ruddy congealed-blood colour of an old claret. The meat's dense texture gives it the look of *bresaola*, that Italian air-dried beef claimed to have originated in Valtellina on the other side of the Alps, but here in this French-speaking part of Switzerland they call it *viande séchée* – literally 'dried meat' – and it is the perfect precursor to a fondue.

Nothing too remarkable about that, but there's an unusual nervous tension in the air as half a dozen forks circle the plate of charcuterie hesitantly. The reason is that one side of the plate has *viande séchée* made from beef, the other *viande séchée* made from horse. And no-one knows which is which.

There is a pretty hefty taboo about eating horse in the English-speaking world, but intellectually it's hard to argue there's much difference between eating a good-natured lumbering Daisy and the great-grandson of Phar Lap. If cows posed a greater threat to our self-preservation or were less useful it might make sense targeting them for dinner, but the argument for not eating horse usually revolves round how we lack the same emotional connection with cows as we have with horses. This argument tends to crumble when you think of those huge, trusting, heavy-lashed bovine eyes and then think of a bolt popping between them.

Yet even the most committed and analytical carnivores at the table – happy to eat cow, pig or sheep – are wavering about the horse. Sure, horse is deemed unsuitable for Jewish consumption and was once banned by the Vatican because of its connection with pagan worship – especially of Odin – in Northern Europe, but this isn't the issue.

The only logic seems to be that in the English-speaking world it is taboo for carnivores to eat animals that might be pets – even if dogs, guinea pigs and horses are delicacies elsewhere. And it seems that when Winston Churchill claimed that there was something about the outside of a horse that was good for the inside of a man, he wasn't thinking about eating Makybe Diva for dinner.

I've eaten horse before – both knowingly and unknowingly. In my opinion, pan-fried or grilled it is often a preferable alternative to cheap tough beef in a dodgy French bistro. Often the meat is likened to beef, but it also has a soft looseness that is reminiscent of the most tender kangaroo. It's lean like roo, too, and higher in protein than beef apparently, but while eating the bearer of our coat of arms is acceptable to many, eating horse generally is not. Even if it is slathered in a rich sauce of morel mushrooms and served with excellent crunchy *frites*.

Not everyone around the world feels that way. Some 4.7 million horses are slaughtered each year by the ten leading countries producing horse meat – and in 2008 the *Sun Herald* revealed that Australia exported a further 2000 tonnes of horse and donkey meat to markets like Japan, Russia, Belgium and France. Outbreaks of BSE and foot and mouth disease overseas have given horsemeat sales a fillip in the recent past, but now it is the soaring cost of cow that is making the cheaper horse more attractive. This year it is expected that France's consumption of horse (rated at 25,380 tonnes in 2006, according to figures quoted in a report in the *International Herald Tribune*) will rise.

Interestingly, in France it was poverty that first championed the eating of horse, which was legalised in 1866, although its popularity seems to have first arisen after the French revolution, when eating horse

– a potent symbol of the deposed ruling elite – took on the mantle of a revolutionary act.

Back round our table, everyone eventually tries both piles of dried meats. The horse is declared slightly sweeter, a bit more metallic in taste; but there's no denying that many will think twice next time before rashly blurting out, 'I'm so hungry I could eat a horse.'

Originally published in 'A2', The Age, 2009

20 CULINARY CRIMES

We are gathered in this place to rip aside the veil of silence that allows the most foul of practices to continue. We are here to punish the evildoers and point the searchlight of truth into the dim recesses of culinary crime with all the foaming-mouthed fury of a *Current Affair* cub reporter. First let us turn to the most serious of transgressions, which threaten to overthrow the very natural order itself.

The Capital Offences

Caeser that Ain't

There is a simple elegance about Caesar Cardini's salad, created in Tijuana in 1924. So why slash this *Mona Lisa* by using chopped hard-boiled egg rather than poached; iceberg rather than cos; or adding chicken – a crime compounded by the presence of the word 'Cajun'?

Sentence: Off with his head.

Waiters with Bad Body Odour or Blue Plasters on Their Fingers

'Nuff said.

Sentence: Pass the black cap for both the waiter and the restaurant owner.

Bad Pizza

Another example of culinary vandalism, carried out in shopfronts and supermarket freezer cabinets across Australia. Rather than spray cans, the culprits use olive slices that look and taste like black rubber washers, dried herbs and strange pink matchsticks that scream 'reclaimed meat' at me. Really, what is so hard about cooking topped dough? It is only because the core idea of pizza is so beautiful that these aberrations don't have ordinary Aussies reaching for the pitchforks and flaming torches to chase Mr P. Zerhut and Mr Mick Cain out of town.

Sentence: Form a lynch mob, boys. Curly, get the rope.

Fecking Up Spaghetti

While Antonio Carluccio might claim that there are ten essential rules for cooking pasta, really it isn't that hard. So there's no excuse when eating out for the spag arriving in a clump stuck together like a witch's switch. And even though this carb is beautifully forgiving, there's no excuse either for insulting it with rubbery green-lipped mussels or, some might suggest, chicken.

Sentence: To be dropped into boiling salted water and cooked till 'al dente'.

Warm Avocado

Cooking the alligator pear in any form – on pizza, in a creamy pasta sauce (with chicken), grilled – is a cardinal sin punishable by the severest penalty. The only exception is if it has been topped with lots of dolcelatte and then toasted on top of ciabatta. Yum.

Sentence: Either way is a death sentence, one is just swifter …

Badly Done Fusion Food

While most of the judiciary is rather conservative, we don't mind a bit of innovation in the kitchen – as long as it works. Stumbling into the pantry blindfold and grabbing the first three ingredients – or however these dishes have been devised – tends to lead to horrors. Prawns cooked with coffee beans and cream. Risotto with smoked salmon, banana, coriander and semi-dried tomatoes. Steak with a banana and Malibu sauce. These are just plain wrong in a 'lions copulating with monkeys' sort of way. (Yes, these dishes are real examples!) Some might also suggest that meat is not a natural partner to sorbet, nor fish to chocolate. And that foams are for shaving with. But then, one man's *spuma* is another man's thirds of *zabaglione*, *sabayon* or 'wild mushroom cappuccino'. One man's blackcurrant sorbet with lamb is another's redcurrant jelly – albeit 12 degrees cooler. And so forth. Thus the crime is actually in failing to fuse different foods into a coherent and cohesive whole.

Sentence: Get it wrong and it's a lifetime cooking in a tourist motel in Cairns or an aptly termed 'gastro pub' in Adelaide. Although, win your appeal and you might get a job with Ferran Adria at El Bulli. Eggplant, yoghurt and Fishermen's Friend, anyone?

Felonies

Dressing the Plate

There are loads of different offences here. We are prepared to give five years for each of the following: presenting fish, a baked potato or anything else at the table in silver paper; paper doilies (unless under little pinwheel or finger sandwiches); stacking food in architectural towers; and any combination of two of the following on a dessert: fanned strawberry, sprig of mint or a dusting of icing sugar. All three together is a capital offence.

Sentence: Five years in a daggy hotel in southern Tasmania.

Inane Floor Staff

'Enjoy'; 'How are your meals?' … and, worst of all, the staff member who saunters over a few minutes after the red-hot electric wall heater has fallen onto your table, spilling cocktails and dust into your meal, and asks, 'Is everything okay here?' Well obviously not – unless the fajitas are supposed to come with a Dimplex garnish.

Sentence: Six months' community service in a call centre, speaking only from a script.

Chefs Trying It On

Pancakes served burnt side down, overcooked steak presented without comment, or worst, the Greek salad where the fetta has been substituted with look-alike tofu because 'the chef thought you wouldn't notice'.

Sentence: Into the stocks with a large sign saying, 'He tried to cheat his customers.'

Flowery Menus

It might have been okay in the eighties when excess was allowed, but now 'symphonies', 'mosaics' and 'melanges' belong in an art precinct rather than a menu.

Sentence: Five years without access to a thesaurus.

Not Checking Your Butter

There are a few things worse than rancid butter – nuclear war, testicular cancer and a Manly premiership being three that spring readily to mind. But nothing starts off a meal worse than a mouthful of bread slathered with the stuff.

Sentence: Life in a hot country without any refrigeration.

Talking Over Breakfast

All you should hear is the crunch of the toast, a mellow snap, crackle and pop and the occasional page turn. When breakfasting out, muted conversation is allowable to show that you still get on with the person on the other side of the table – always assuming that conversation isn't on a mobile phone and/or about deals, babies sleeping through and who you slept with last night. Unless it was me. That would be cause for an instant acquittal – although forgiving yourself might take a little longer.

Sentence: Ten years in solitary confinement but with time off for good behaviour.

Seasoning

Perhaps the most critical skill in the kitchen and one that is too often flawed.

Sentence: Not seasoning enough – five years. Seasoning too much – seven years. Arguing with a customer over whether a dish is too salty – off to the Siberian salt mines with you.

Using Flour to Thicken a Sauce
Instead use heat and time, gentlemen, please.
Sentence: Twelve months or until the sauce has reduced by half.

Exporting Our Best Produce
National art treasures are often protected from export. So should it be with our best produce. With that sort of protectionist legislation in place, not only would we keep our best seafood here, but also seafood generally would become much cheaper – and our deputy editor would stop getting all misty-eyed about those days way back when 'a dollar down Victor Harbor would buy you a bag of crayfish' (with thruppence left over for the bullock cart ride home, one suspects). Only one downside: there might be fewer multimillionaire fishermen.
Sentence: None until we change the law. Then we'll export their children for profit.

The Devil's Food
While it was well known in medieval times that garlic and onions grew in the footsteps of the Devil, today we know that it is actually crème de menthe and those desiccated ears called sun-dried tomatoes that are the devil's own ingredients. Neither should ever be seen in food.
Sentence: We follow our medieval antecedents and declare both 'nithing' and banish them from our land, along with all that use them.

Misdemeanours

Crimes of the Table
While rancid butter is by far and away the worst of these, I'd still like to issue fines for the following: terracotta wine coolers, bread baked in flowerpots, wet salt, too-soft butter, jugs of water with three-day-old

mint or lemon in them, stupid window frames where the view should be, side dishes arriving 15 minutes after the main and wine lists with no choice by the glass, a crap choice by the bottle and no BYO policy. Wineglasses upside down on tables is another no-no.

Sentence: A three-month subscription to *Donna Hay* magazine for rehabilitation help.

Bundy and Coke with Fish

Now, the customer may be always right, and my wine-writing colleagues may tell us there are no longer any rules about what you should drink with fish, but this pairing I spotted at Brisbane's lovely Pier 9 (now closed) is just plain wrong. If it had been a crisp gin and tonic with a slice of lemon we'd have been acquitting, but as it is the gavel must fall.

Sentence: Attendance at a drinker re-education course led by a wine expert. This may seem rather harsh, but desperate issues call for desperate measures.

Oakleaf Lettuce

Coral and oakleaf lettuce leaves not only look like something a New Romantic Adam might have worn, but they taste – I think the professional term is 'cack'. Lettuce should be green, not red, yellow or brown. The only exception is radicchio.

Sentence: One month for every leaf in the salad.

Making a Fuss About Being on the Atkins Diet

The carb-free call is a loud clamour these days. That's fine, but stop making such a fuss about it.

Sentence: Life – but can I have it without the bread, fruit, rice, potatoes, pasta and polenta, please? Plus another three years on the side.

Using Dried Herbs

Allowable only if you are Greek, Mexican or Calabrian. Otherwise there's no excuse for ruining food with their overly pungent flavour.

Sentence: Three years, but you will get to work in the prison garden to see how easy fresh herbs are to grow at home. A longer sentence for using herbs in a tube.

Plea Bargains

Pineapple on Your Pizza or Your Hamburger

We'd be willing to accept a plea-bargain on this case, because the counterpoint of sweet or acidic fruit against a salty or savoury ingredient like ham is a fundamental of many cuisines – especially of those 'bleeding dish' nations of Northern Europe. With the hamburger, the pineapple MUST be cooked so it adds a caramelised edge to the burger and doesn't make the bun sodden. We have also dismissed charges brought for serving hamburgers without beetroot, which is undesirable but inevitable as our Australian culture becomes swamped by culinary globalisation.

Hairy Fish

Okay, so you wouldn't want to look too closely at them, but cheap anchovies have their role in adding stinky big hits of salt to pizza or breaking down to form the invisible and untastable backbone of many a decent *sugo* or stew. They must be handled judiciously, however, to avoid the wrath of the court. Too much is a crime. Presenting any other hairy fish is instant death … probably for all concerned.

Indian, Cajun or Thai Food on a Pub Menu

Caveat emptor, as those Roman legal brains used to say. You should always stick to unadorned protein and chips unless the chef is called Singh, Prudhomme or Saraphee Paranort.

Thinking Too Much or Too Little About What You Put Into Your Mouth

Food fadism is the latest manifestation of excessive self-obsession and vanity – so beware, double-decaf-skinny-soy-latte brigade, for the eyes of the law are upon you. Why drink coffee if you are going to denature it to such an extent? Likewise, the reckless and rather nihilistic pursuit of nachos with sour cream, extra cheese and bacon (or similar) also has a distasteful reek of self-obsession in that McAdvertising 'yes it may harden your arteries but hell, you deserve it' way. Not to mention the fact you'll leave behind a widow(er) and two children to struggle on without you.

The court would like to recognise and thank the following members of our jury for their tireless work in unmasking culinary criminals everywhere: Teage Ezard, Ros Grundy, Michael Harden, Stuart Gregor, Michael Lambie, Sally Lewis, John Lethlean, Kylie Walker and Necia Wilden.

Originally published in 'Epicure', The Age, 2004

PART II

COOK

HOME-COOKING EASY BISCUITS

Life's too short to stuff a mushroom or ice a VoVo. That's why I love these quick and easy biscuit recipes – five minutes on the worktop is all it takes to be impressing drop-ins and depriving Arnotts' US shareholders of a few more of our dollars.

And frankly, dry, mass-market biscuits seldom compare with the homemade alternative. There's the way the smell of freshly baked biscuits wafts through the house and the great honest rush of satisfaction that comes with eating a moist, chewy biscuit, warm from the oven.

Baking is also good therapy. The process of mixing and kneading is so very calming. It teaches patience, too. And there's more than a little alchemy about putting claggy scoops of gloop on a baking tray only to remove delicious fresh-baked bikkies minutes later.

These recipes are the simplest sure-fire winners from those I've collected (okay, stolen) from friends and family over the past ten years. As much souvenirs as recipes, there are few better ways of reigniting memories of people you've met. Like any collection of recipes, together these make up a map of my life.

Recipes are threads that flow through the fabric of our society – passed from hand to hand and generation to generation. Each of these is linked inextricably to people I've met and places I've been, but they all also have a deeper past and futures that will stretch beyond the time when I am dust. We are never owners of recipes, just their stewards and propagators for a short time.

COCONUT BISCUITS

This easy to remember and never-fail recipe arrived with the wife as a sort of dowry. It could almost be the perfect biscuit, with a good friable crunch. Pull some out of the oven a little earlier and they'll be deliciously chewier.

Ingredients

1 cup coconut
1 cup self-raising flour
1 cup sugar
1 egg
125 g / 4 oz butter, melted

Method

Preheat oven to 180 degrees C. Mix the dry ingredients together. Stir in the egg and then the butter. Work everything together with your fingers. Form walnut-sized nuggets with your hands. They'll feel a little greasy but resist the temptation to add more flour. Arrange on an ungreased tray with lots of room to spread. Bake for ten minutes.

CRUNCHIES

This brown-sugar shortbread recipe comes from one of those wonderful charity collections of country women's cookery and is credited to a K. MacGregor. It is my favourite biscuit for its firmer crunch. It's also really, really simple and yet to play up and give me a disaster. Use an unrefined muscovado brown sugar for a more intricate flavour.

Ingredients

185 g / 6 oz butter
¾ cup soft or light brown sugar
2 cups plain flour
pinch of salt
extra brown sugar

Method

Preheat oven to 180 degrees C. Cream butter and sugar together, ideally in a mixer. Add flour and salt and mix into a firm dough. Knead dough together and then form into two rolls about 4 cm in diameter. Sprinkle brown sugar on two squares of greaseproof paper and roll the dough up in the paper so it gets coated in the sugar. Rest it in the fridge until it has become firm. Unwrap and slice into 5-mm-thick discs. Arrange on a baking tray and cook until the brown sugar around the edges colours up – around 15 to 25 minutes depending on how cool the dough is.

STORING BISCUITS

When my grandfather died he left me the family cookbook that was hand-written in 1765. Among the 'receipts' for everything from oyster ketchup to worming powder is this peculiarity for 'storing biscuits'. The sugar-coriander combination is intriguing and the cakey texture shows where the US got their use of the word 'biscuit' for their scone-like creations.

Ingredients

4 eggs
250 g / ½ lb sugar
60 g / 2 oz coriander seed
155 g / 5 oz plain flour
sugar for sifting

Method (with original 18th-century spelling)

'Take 4 eggs and beat them an hour, strewing in sugar till you have put in half a pound. Put in 2 ounces of coriander seed. Stir in five oz of flower. Put in buttered paper pans. Sift a little sugar on the top. Cook in ovan rather quick.'

The recipe is reproduced word for word, but I'd suggest using an electric whisk for 10 minutes rather than a hand one for an hour. I use a muffin tin rather than 'paper pans' and bake in a moderate (180-degree C) oven until a skewer comes out clean. You can also toast and crush the coriander seed if you like.

TARA'S MACAROONS

When my friend Tara was having trouble sleeping she turned to baking biscuits to overcome her insomnia. There is certainly something very calming about shaping these balls.

Ingredients

2 egg whites
100 g / 3½ oz caster sugar
160 g / 5 oz desiccated coconut

Method

Preheat oven to 180 degrees C. Whisk the egg whites, sugar and coconut in a bowl until they lightly come together. With wet hands, press the mixture into small rough balls the size of walnuts but slightly peaked on top. Place on a lightly greased baking tray and bake in the centre of the oven for 15 minutes, until very lightly golden. Transfer to a wire tray to cool. Store in an airtight container for up to one week.

I reckon that whisking the egg whites to firm peaks, then folding in the sugar and coconut, makes for a less dense and marshmallow-chewy biscuit, but you'll need to shape the mixture with two spoons prior to dropping it onto the baking tray.

VICTORIAN COUNTRY SHORTBREAD

Of course I am bound to say that my mother-in-law makes the lightest, crumbliest shortbread I've ever had, but more interestingly it is possible to recreate at home without any strange secret Country Women's Association business. She claims she stole this recipe from her friend Jane.

Ingredients

250 g / 8 oz butter
125 g / 4½ oz granulated sugar
375 g / 13 oz plain flour
60 g / 2 oz cornflour
pinch of salt
¼ cup caster sugar

Method

Preheat the oven to 170 degrees C. Cream butter and sugar well (in a big mixer if possible). Sift together all dry ingredients except sugar. Add to the butter and sugar combo and mix to combine. Turn onto lightly floured surface and knead lightly until smooth. Roll out to 8 mm thick and cut into about 6-cm circles. Pour the caster sugar into a bowl and dredge one side of each biscuit in it, then prick them twice with a fork. Bake for 20 to 25 minutes or until very faintly golden. Cool on a cake rack after resting for a minute.

JEN'S YOYOS

I only started baking biscuits nine years ago: greed drove me to it. My flatmate Jen was courting a farmer so inept in the kitchen he'd burn hard-boiled eggs. Every Friday I'd awake to the smell of freshly baked yoyos and afghans, only to find that Jen and the biscuits had already legged it to the farm. After four weeks of torture I exchanged my frustration (that she never left me more than four biscuits) for the recipes and self-sufficiency. And, dear reader, she married him.

Ingredients

Biscuits

250 g / 8 oz butter

4 tablespoons icing sugar

4 tablespoons cornflour

1½ cups plain flour

pinch of salt

Filling

¾ cup icing sugar

2 tablespoons butter

1 teaspoon vanilla extract

Preheat oven to 180 degrees C. Combine biscuit ingredients in order in mixer. Mix until a dough forms. Roll into balls and put on lined baking trays, squashing with a fork to mark the tops. Bake for 15 minutes, until biscuits are coloured slightly at the edge. Remove and cool on a wire rack. They must be completely cool before filling.

For the filling, whizz everything together in a food processer, and use to sandwich biscuits together. Let the finished yoyos stand one hour before storing. This makes 'short' and golden biscuits that really benefit from the filling.

JEN'S CHOCOLATE AFGHANS

A little bit more effort, but well worth it. Great texture, a simple chocolate fix and always a winner.

Ingredients

Biscuits

220 g / 7½ oz butter

½ cup caster sugar

1 teaspoon vanilla extract

1 cup self-raising flour

½ cup plain flour

3 tablespoons cocoa

2 cups cornflakes

2 tablespoons desiccated coconut

Icing

2 heaped teaspoons butter

1 cup icing sugar

1½ tablespoons cocoa

a few drops vanilla extract

1 tablespoon boiling water

Preheat oven to 180 degrees C. Using a rolling pin or other blunt instrument, lightly crush the cornflakes in a clean plastic bag. Cream butter, sugar and vanilla together until light. Sift in the flours and cocoa together and add the lightly crushed cornflakes and coconut. Now add the butter and sugar mixture and mix thoroughly. Place heaped teaspoons onto baking trays lined with silicon or greaseproof paper, squeezing mixture down lightly with the back of a spoon. It may be a little crumbly but it holds when baked. Bake for 15 to 20 minutes. Remove from trays and leave to cool on a wire rack. Ice when cool.

To make the icing, first melt the butter. Sift the icing sugar together with the cocoa, then add the melted butter, a few drops of vanilla and then the boiling water. Beat well. Use while still warm.

THE ULTIMATE CHOCOLATE CHIP COOKIE

Blame the Dutch for the way Americans call biscuits 'cookies' – the word comes from the Dutch word for cupcake, *koekje*. 'Biscuit' comes from the Latin for 'twice cooked': *bis coctum*. Thank American Ruth Wakefield for, in the thirties, inventing the world's best cookie – the toll house cookie, precursor of the chocolate chip cookie.

My search for the perfect chocolate chip recipe took me through versions made with condensed milk and those that use various combinations of sugars, but ended after reading the US edition of Jeffrey Steingarten's *It Must've Been Something I Ate* (Knopf, 2002). He's the food writer I want to be when I grow up and so I was delighted to discover that his ultimate choc chip recipe had all the gooey buttery decadence of those sold by warm cookie concessions in shopping centres. I have adapted it subtly. While Steingarten uses Nestlé Toll House Real Semi-Sweet Chocolate Morsels, I'd rather make like Wakefield's original and use hand-cut chocolate chunks so I can get bigger lumps. I've also increased the amount of salt, which helps the chocolate flavour shine through and cuts against all that sugar.

Ingredients

500 g / 1 lb chocolate of your choice (dark, white or milk)

1½ cups plain flour

1 teaspoon salt

½ teaspoon baking powder

250 g / ½ lb unsalted butter, softened

⅔ cup light brown sugar

¼ cup dark brown sugar

⅔ cup granulated white sugar

1 teaspoon vanilla extract

2 tablespoons water

1 egg

Method

Preheat the oven to 190 degrees C. Chop the chocolate into 1-cm hunks or bigger. After natural wastage during the chopping process you'll have 400 g of choc hunks left. Reserve. Sift together the flour, salt and baking powder into a bowl. In a mixer, cream the butter and mix in the three types of sugar. Add the vanilla extract, water and egg. Beat together. Beat in the flour mixture. Stir in the chocolate hunks. Drop heavily heaped teaspoons of the mixture, well spaced, onto non-stick baking paper on baking trays. Bake for about 10 minutes or until golden. Eat some immediately. Let the rest, um, err, rest and then cool on a wire rack. You could also try replacing some of the chocolate with nuts, like quartered macadamias.

Coda: Some people found there was too much butter in this recipe and the biscuit became sludgy. If you are a baking novice you might want to follow the revamped recipe below.

Six weeks on and the dust has settled after my story on easy-to-bake biscuits. I've been delighted to discover the Yarraville mothers' group, who take turns to bake Tara's Macaroons, and was even stunned by an email praising the '1765 Storing Biscuits' from Cape Town.

Controversy still simmers, however, over my recipe for the Ultimate Chocolate Chip Cookie. For every email of praise there was another claiming they came out a 'buttery sludge'. 'Too thin' said another young baker. One misguided youth even called them 'too buttery', which is not a concept that I am familiar with, or that I think even exists.

Still, as I have learnt in endless corporate training sessions, criticism is a tool for improvement, and so I went back to kitchen and developed this recipe, which produces a thicker biscuit that is less buttery thanks to more flour. I also dramatically increased the number and size of hunks of choc and added nuts because, well, I felt like it and it just seemed like the right thing to do.

I have also included a choc chip recipe from my Western District baking guru Jen Ryan. This produces a crisp, firm and quite high-sided biscuit that isn't 'too buttery' and is a good dunker.

Also note that the new Betty Crocker choc chip cookie mix makes a mean cookie if you like them a little cakey.

MY ULTIMATE CHOP CHIP COOKIES
REVISED – WITH ADDED NUTS

Ingredients

600 g chocolate of your choice (dark, white, milk or any combination)

2 cups flour (75 per cent wholemeal gives an earthier texture – not that I'd actually advise it, but hey, this is a more democratic biscuit so you decide)

1 teaspoon salt

1 teaspoon baking powder

250 g unsalted butter, well softened

⅔ cup light brown sugar

¼ cup dark brown sugar

⅔ cup granulated white sugar

1 teaspoon vanilla extract

2 tablespoons water

1 egg

125 g almonds

125 g macadamias

125 g skinless hazelnuts (if you leave the nuts out, replace with the same quantity of chocolate)

Method

Preheat the oven to 180 degrees C. Break the choc into 2–cm squares. You want the milk or dark choc hunks to be bigger than the white ones, because they'll melt more when cooked and if too small they will disappear. Reserve. Sift together the flour, salt and baking powder into a bowl. In a mixer, cream the butter and mix in the three types of sugar. Add the vanilla extract, water and egg. Beat together. Beat in the flour mixture.

Stir in the chocolate hunks and the nuts. The mixture should come away from the sides of the bowl and form a ball. If the mixture is still 'sticky', add a little more flour.

Drop balls of the mixture, well spaced, onto non-stick baking paper on a baking tray. Use a dessert spoon for big bikkies and a teaspoon for smaller ones. Bake for about ten minutes or until almost golden. Eat some immediately. Let the rest, um, err, rest and then cool on a wire rack.

JEN'S CHOC CHIP BISCUITS

This quantity makes over 50 biscuits, so if you think that is too much (i.e. you haven't got a big enough bowl or have strange ideas about the value of a full biscuit tin), you can halve it. They also freeze very well.

Ingredients

500 g butter
1¼ cups caster sugar
400 g condensed milk
5 cups self-raising flour
250 g white choc chips
250 g dark choc chips

Method

Preheat oven to 180 degrees C. Cream butter, sugar and condensed milk until well combined. Fold in flour and choc chips. Using about 1 tablespoon of mixture at a time, roll into balls and place on lined baking trays, leaving room for spreading. Squash flat with a fork. Bake for 15 minutes until golden. Cool on wire racks.

GENERAL BISCUIT TIPS

'Creaming' is beating together butter and sugar to create a sort of whipped consistency. This is easiest done with softened butter in a bowl mixer – assuming you use a large enough bowl for all the subsequent ingredients. This also makes these biscuits a one-bowl operation, reducing washing up. Creaming can be done with a hand mixer but the butter can get stuck in between the beaters and will need to be scraped out a few times during the process.

Remember, your biscuits will keep cooking once they are removed from the oven – especially if left on the hot baking tray – so bang them on a wire cooling rack first. It's often best to let them firm up for a minute or so before attempting this transfer.

Ovens are peculiar beasts. Some run hotter than others, so always check your biscuits during cooking. I often remove half the biscuits a little underdone – in part as an insurance policy, in part as a constant experimentation in baking the perfect biscuit.

I reckon butter is better but the shortbread and coconut biscuits are both very fine made with marge.

Always use vanilla extract not vanilla essence, which is something created by the Devil in his lab of fake tastes from everything from wood to petrol.

Originally published in 'Epicure', The Age, 2003

FIVE FORGOTTEN
INGREDIENTS

Visit continental Europe and one of the first things you'll notice – if you are a foodie tragic like me, trotting the globe looking for a feed – is how the range of ingredients used by many top chefs is limited. It's as if 90 per cent of these restaurants are cooking with the same 10 per cent of ingredients, largely ignoring foods so readily available here – even in suburban supermarkets – such as fish sauce, hoisin sauce, dukkah, mirin and Shaoxing wine. These rarely feature outside ethnic restaurants.

In Spain – and in those high-end places that follow the ideas of *la nueva cocina* espoused by the likes of El Bulli's Ferran Adria and Juan Mari Arzak – it sometimes appears as if finding new techniques, often with the help of technology, has been more important than finding new ingredients. Reworking old flavours into new forms is the main game, whether it's creating a virtual olive or dehydrating horseradish into a dust or freezing it into snow.

But things are shifting. Now some of Europe's most innovative chefs are concentrating on finding unique flavours for their menus. Arzak has a growing obsession with the ingredients of Peru, and El Bulli alumnus

Rene Redzepi of Copenhagen's Noma is making heroes of under-appreciated indigenous Scandinavian ingredients such as musk ox steak, rare wild berries and native grasses. It's something we've seen here in Australia, too, at George Biron's Sunnybrae; with Patrizia Simone collecting wild greens for her Bright restaurant; or with Attica's Ben Shewry foraging on bay beaches for purslane and seaweeds.

All good stuff, but I'd also like to make a quiet plea for the re-institution into our shopping baskets of five ingredients that these days seem overlooked and deserving of more attention.

Forgotten Fish

Nannygai, also known as 'red fish', is an inexpensive big-eyed beauty that is delicious whether grilled, fried or braised. Nannygai are, however, notoriously hard to scale, so take the time to check for any missed scales before cooking. This is apparently why this excellent table fish dropped off restaurant menus a decade or so ago. There were also concerns about over-fishing, but if you catch one, they're well worth making the effort over. Also look out for the humble rock cod, which, while not quite as delicate, is another forgotten feed. With juicy, fresh, fat petals of white flesh, it's perfect for frying, grilling on the barbecue or in stews, curries and braises. The smaller the fish, the sweeter the flesh, but remember that there are more sustainable fish you could buy instead like mullet, ling or tailor.

A Hot Swede

Now is the time to cosy up with a hot swede. Forget that the English used to tease the Scots about their love of what was known as cattle fodder. This cabbage/turnip cross, with its gentle sweet orange flesh, is known as rutabaga in the US and a neep in Scotland. Boil them and mash with carrots; or with potatoes to make the Welsh delicacy of potch; or just serve with 'tatties' (potatoes) and haggis on Burns night. Soup 'em, stew 'em or roast 'em in butter but remember that swedes also love other root vegies, bacon, lamb and barley. Buy the firm and heavy ones, and remember excessive consumption can be associated with hypothyroidism, which leads us to …

Glands

Sweetbreads struggle to gain the audience they deserve, mainly due to people getting freaked out at the concept of eating thymus and pancreas glands from sheep, pigs or cows. It's a pity, because fried and crunchy, but still creamy-centred, they are as delicious as brains. So delicious, in fact, that they were the hottest ingredient in New York 18 months ago.

They are, however, a pain to prep thanks to having to soak and peel them, so splash out on veal sweetbreads. These are generally less funky-tasting than glands from older, stinkier animals, too. Sweetbreads go well with mushrooms, caramelised onions, peas, lemon, cream, capers and sauces based on sweet wines such as madeira or a sweet-sour gastrique. But not all at once!

A Nice Pear

Certain fruit and veg seem destined to be one-trick ponies or just a plain conundrum to cook. In this group number the choko, the bitter melon and, often, the nashi pear – even though they are far more versatile, with a flavour and texture halfway between an apple and a pear. Juice 'em, bake 'em splashed with verjuice, serve them as you would apples, caramelise 'em to serve with pork or your breakfast French toast, or use them in a winter salad to add sweetness, freshness and crunch, perhaps partnering a little blue cheese and sliced fennel.

I like 8-millimetre-thick slices, topped with an oyster and a squeeze of lime just like the bloke at Jamon Sushi once showed me.

Lovable Liver

While retro chicken liver parfaits were the ubiquitous Melbourne appetiser in 2008, the livers themselves still remain in limbo. This is despite the fact that chicken livers are a sensual delight when fried in foaming butter and finished with a splash of port and then cream. Calves' liver, too, was once big on restaurant menus and while it might be high in saturated fat, it's a great treat. Just dust it with flour, fry it in butter and serve on creamy mash dressed with buttery pan juices. One request: please don't perpetrate the crime of overcooking liver, which has put so many people off eating these satiny delights. Also, always remember to clean and trim liver before cooking it. Serve with pan-fried apples, figs, sage, caramelised onions or bacon.

So, to paraphrase a beautiful saying of Pearl's Geoff Lindsay, if finding new ingredients is a bit like suddenly being given a pack of 80 Caran d'Ache pencils when you've previously been used to creating with just 40, then please enjoy playing with these forgotten pencils.

Originally published in 'A2', The Age, 2009

IN SEARCH OF THE
PERFECT TOMATO SAUCE

It isn't just the Colonel who jealously guards the secret of his herbs and spices. There's a particular patrician matriarch of my acquaintance who's just as stubborn about her tomato sauce recipe. For years I have tried to wheedle this ancient Spanish family recipe out of her. I've offered money ... flattery ... fame ... even my own family secret – no, not the one about Grandpapa running off with that dancer from the Tivoli but my 250-year-old recipe for oyster ketchup – but this woman's not for turning.

I'm not willing to sink as low as my two increasingly desperate rivals for the recipe. I've caught one rifling through her kitchen files, and the other offered to marry her son. Me, I've made like Johnny Cash, taking it one piece at a time.

The matriarch's greengrocer tells me he boxes up any fruit that's too ripe to sell and keeps it for her until there's enough for a sauce batch. Like Margaret Fulton, she then cooks up all the tomato sauce ingredients at once rather than cooking the tomatoes first and sieving them into a pulp before combining with the other ingredients. She cooks her sauce slowly for over three hours in a wide-topped copper pot and then moulis the lot at the end of cooking for a slightly coarse body.

Until I can get the remaining pieces of the puzzle, I've embarked on a quest to assemble a suitable alternative, filling in the gaps from 200 years of tomato sauce and ketchup recipes.

The earliest recorded recipes for tomato ketchup were published in Canada in 1812 by an American, Dr James Mease, and by another physician, William Kitchiner, in London in 1816. While Mease doesn't strain his, Kitchiner does. The presence of anchovies in Kitchiner's recipe also hints at ketchup's past. The original 'catchups' were anchovy or oyster interpretations of the fishy 'ke-tsiap' sauces from the Chinese island of Amoy, first encountered by European seamen and traders two centuries earlier. I've found an anchovy fillet or two adds an unfathomable depth to a tomato sauce.

The popularity of tomato ketchup grew alongside the acceptance of the tomato, which initially was widely regarded as poisonous or, worse, only fit for the poor. Likewise, the growth of canning in the second half of the 19th century boosted the commercial production of tomato ketchup, with ketchup pioneers like Jonas Yerkes using skins, cores and green tomatoes discarded in the tomato canning process. His is an ingredient list that, while unappetising, at least omits the coal tar that was sometimes used to give a bright red colour to early commercial ketchups. This I'll leave out of my stand-by recipe.

What you will need is spices, vinegar to inhibit the growth of yeasts or bacteria, sugar to correct the taste and tomatoes.

The better the tomato, the better the sauce. Follow Heinz's lead for their ketchup (which they've been making since 1876) and only use tomatoes that have ripened and developed their flavour on the vine. Many cheap supermarket tomatoes have been picked green and then gassed to redness. It doesn't matter if the toms are a little soft but the redder they are the better the colour of the sauce.

Heinz favours common or roma tomatoes, generally from Northern Victoria or New South Wales, grown from seed developed from their own 40-year Australian seed programme, while SPC uses mainly Victorian tomatoes for their Dick Smith's tomato sauce.

The spice mix is a matter of personal taste. The usual flavour palette covers cinnamon, cassia, cloves, pepper, garlic, ginger, nutmeg, mace, mustard, allspice, paprika and cayenne. The last three are especially common in American tomato sauces. My tight-lipped maestro at least admits to following the common practice of tying her spices in muslin to avoid spices spotting the sauce, and regards 'Ezy Sauce' as another name for the Devil. The contents of her muslin bundle are still a mystery but I'm plumping for cinnamon, cloves, nutmeg, allspice and, given the recipe's Spanish provenance, a little paprika and some garlic.

She says she omits the common addition of onion and shares the widely regarded view that adding apples to give your sauce more bulk is heretical. But then she's a wily coot and not above supplying misinformation.

When it comes to creating the perfect sauce, award-winning sauce maker Peter Bennett advises slow cooking to help avoid burnt sauce disasters. 'This lets the flavours combine and gives you more control,' he says.

Another aim of cooking is to reduce the sauce. He advises a wide-topped pan rather than a saucepan, for a greater area of evaporation. The issue of consistency is one of personal taste, but central to the difference between a ketchup and its thinner brother tomato sauce.

Using your Bostwick consistometer (what do you mean you don't have one – how serious are you about this ketchup-making lark?), you'll find that perfect ketchup will ooze between three and seven centimetres within 30 seconds at 20 degrees Celsius. If by some amazing fluke you don't have a consistometer, just cook it until no liquid separates from the pulp when you dump a teaspoon of the sauce onto a flat plate. A small amount of 'weeping' when a dollop is poured cold from the bottle is acceptable.

Ingredients

5 kg ripe tomatoes
1 whole small onion, peeled
8 cloves
2 small anchovy fillets

3 cloves garlic

2 tablespoons rock salt

1 stick cinnamon

1 teaspoon allspice berries

1 teaspoon black peppercorns

½ teaspoon grated nutmeg

2 teaspoons paprika

3 cups cider vinegar

2½ cups soft brown sugar

Method

Wash, dry and slice the tomatoes. Stud the onion with the cloves. Using a mortar and pestle, mash the anchovy fillets and garlic into a paste with the salt. Bundle up the cinnamon, allspice berries, peppercorns, nutmeg and paprika inside muslin. Throw all the above, along with the vinegar and the sugar, into a heavy-bottomed, wide-topped pan and slowly bring to the boil while stirring.

Turn down the heat and let simmer very gently for between three and four hours or until the ingredients have combined, reduced by well over half and come to the desired consistency. Stir regularly to prevent burning. Remove the muslin spice bundle and onion.

Pass the sauce through a Mouli (or a fine sieve if a fine consistency is required) and discard the waste pulp left behind. Put sauce into sterilised bottles and seal. Always keep your sauce in a dark place and out of direct sunlight, as light may make it darken. Heat may make it ferment. It's not a bad idea to wrap silver foil round the bottles to protect the sauce from light until use.

Experiment with spices and flavourings until you reach the perfect blend for your palate, then try the same sauce-making approach with apples, plums, peaches, mangoes or mushrooms, but leave previously recorded historical catsup disasters (shaved tree bark, pig parts or dust) to the likes of Ferran Adria.

Originally published in 'Epicure', The Age, 2002

PERFECT RISOTTO

In life we all occasionally come across people who fundamentally change the way we cook at home. These aren't the people who just supply us with a favourite recipe or two but those chefs, writers and friends who cause us to alter the very core of how we cook something.

My rollcall of those who have inspired such paradigm shifts reads McGee, Batali, Hay, Ryan and Ezard. The only name missing from that list is Simon Humble, who changed the way I cook risotto forever.

Humble, who plies his trade at Tutto Bene in Melbourne's Southgate, has perfected a failsafe risotto that requires minimal stirring during the cooking process but still delivers a risotto so unctuous, so creamily delicious, that each week he uses 100 kilograms of premium risotto rice to keep up with demand.

Humble's secret is in that rice. He only his uses vialone nano, an Italian rice with a far higher starch content than the arborio usually recommended for risotto. (It's the starch from the rice grains that gives a good risotto that lovely creamy texture, and gently stirring or jostling the arborio while cooking helps free that starch). The beauty of vialone nano is that freeing the starch is much easier and makes me think that with all that stirring arborio should really be called *laborio*.

This higher starch content means you can cook the rice in the oven pilaf-style, but when you vigorously stir in the butter and Parmesan at the end of cooking it still creams up a treat. 'Voila' (or more appropriately 'Eccola!') – risotto without 20 minutes of dull laborious stirring.

I drop in to Tutto Bene for a refresher course from the master and he bombards me with some basic tips for an impeccable risotto. Back home I follow advice about using a 'suitably sized pan' which seems to mean selecting a very heavy-based pot where your uncooked rice will just cover the bottom when poured in. In olive oil gently fry a quarter of a medium-sized onion and half a small clove of crushed garlic per person but just so they don't colour. When soft, I add rice measured so it fills my kitchen ladle: one ladle for each person. I toast the rice in the oily pan until it starts to go a little golden and moves like wet sand.

Then I add two ladles of – and this is important – *hot* stock for each ladle of rice. Humble has explained that cold stock risks shocking the rice – and it's already looking a little pale after seeing the dreadful state of my car on the drive back from the yuppie food emporium. Humble feels measuring the rice by volume compared to the stock – rather than by weight – ensure the ratio of rice to stock is always perfect.

Humble also believes that a good risotto is about the rice and the hero ingredients; not about the stock. He suggests using neutral stocks, like a light vegetable stock, to ensure that, say, your mushroom risotto tastes of mushrooms and not that reduced, slightly heavy, gelatinous chicken stock flavour, although he doesn't go as far as Italy's grandfather of gastronomy Gualtiero Marchesi, who took to using no more than salted boiling water for his signature *risotto Milanese*.

His advice to put a lid on the pan and turn the heat down low to let the stock absorb still sounds a bit weird and it takes all my willpower not to give the gently cooking rice a little stir or two over its 12 to 14 minutes cooking time.

To take your mind off this unnatural act, bring a plum-sized knob of unsalted butter up to room temperature while you wait and grind up a toddler's-fist-sized lump of decent Parmesan (ideally not the stuff sold entombed in plastic – and certainly not one of those shaker packs that smells uncommonly like the time someone smuggled moonshine into the Year 10 formal with unfortunate results).

Now comes the clever bit – as you get near the end of the twelve-minute cooking time, take up your trusty wooden spoon and lift a grain of rice from the risotto on to the clean back of the spoon and, using your thumb, press down on the grain. As if by magic the cooked outer edges squidge out, leaving a tiny star of hard rice at its core. One large white spot like this means it needs to absorb more stock but when you press and three tiny white dots appear the rice is perfectly cooked.

Now comes the energetic part. Vigorously stir in some of the Parmesan and some of the butter with your wooden spoon. This is not a time for reticence so give it some welly and you'll start seeing the rice go all creamy and gooey. When it resembles the texture of an oozy Camembert – so that it will very slowly spread out on the plate – it is ready to serve. If it is too thick you adjust the viscosity by adding a little hot stock to loosen things up.

Then stir in, or garnish with, the hero ingredients. Never cook them in with the rice. Stirring in cooked peas and sprinkling each plate with crispy bits of pancetta is a fine starting risotto and a resounding success – albeit thanks to Mr Humble's fine technique rather than any cooking skill on my part.

MR HUMBLE'S PERFECT RISOTTO

Quantities per person

One ladle vialone nano rice (about 85 g)

Two ladles stock

20 g unsalted room temperature butter

25 g grated quality Parmesan

2 teaspoons extra-virgin olive oil

¼ onion (diced)

½ clove of garlic (chopped)

Plus what ever flavouring you desire. Artichoke heart pieces in the rice and a few grilled butterflied prawns on top of the rice are a fine combination, currently starring at Tutto Bene. Other favourites of Humble's are duck and porcini mushrooms, or asparagus and truffle oil. If choosing your own flavouring, follow his advice and take the very Italian approach of less being more when it comes to what to use in risotto.

Originally published in 'A2', The Age, 2009

PIADINA

A year ago I suggested that piadina would be the next big thing to follow the pizza. Next thing we know, our sister food section in Sydney is hanging on to the running boards of our bandwagon, raving about Melbourne's piadina craze and publishing a huge picture of Piadina Slowfood off Lonsdale Street.

Twelve months on from our first prediction and this thin flatbread folded over a range of fillings is on the verge of becoming the city's next 'wrap'.

Peter Zorzi is one of the Melbourne's piadina pioneers – they were on the menu of his café Holy Cannoli when he opened two years ago. Now he sells up to 300 of the eight or so piadinas on his menu every week. The hot flatbread is cooked to order and filled with scrambled egg, bacon and tomato or chorizo for breakfast; perhaps prosciutto, pear and rocket or tuna niçoise for lunch. 'Back when we started a few people knew what they were, but it's amazing how many different names they knew the bread by,' remembers Zorzi.

Whether as *piadina*, *pie*, *pijda*, *pieda*, *pida* or *pita*, this flatbread has connections back to the Estruscans of 1200 BC, who cooked unleavened bread on the hearth of their fires, and also to the ancient Greeks. Yet piadina's true home is claimed by people of the Italian region of

Emilia-Romagna, where it has become the emblem for the working class of this left-leaning Italian region, even praised by poets as the region's perfect low-cost peasant food. It was only in the 1970s, however, that the piadina rose to commercial popularity in Romagna, when little shacks sprang up along the region's Adriatic coast serving piping hot folded flatbread sandwiches to the beachgoers.

Tony Nicolini, who turns out impeccable razor-thin and lightly crispy piadinas at Carlton Espresso, takes the Romagnan piadina of the region's *adzore* or mammas as his archetype, although like Zorzi he has had people claim he's doing them wrong. 'In Liguria, they roll the bread up like a wrap, but for me the Adriatic coast is home to the piadinas I make,' says the man who originally built his reputation at Pizza Espresso in Templestowe as one of the city's best new wave *pizzaioli*.

Down Lygon Street, Stuzzichino chef Jamie Gibaldi is making about 400 piadinas a week. Their menu offers nine or so choices, with fillings like smoked salmon, cream cheese, red onion and capers, or bresaola and rocket, alongside sweet choices filled with nutella and banana, strawberry or ricotta. He reckons they've been going gangbusters because they are such a quick lunch. 'It's something different. We've had wraps and all those franchises but the piadina is a bit more traditional and – my dad who's got a pizza shop will kill me for saying this – it's a bit like a new form of pizza.'

At the Spiga bar in Menzies Alley, owner Adam Keyte has had to put piadinas back on the menu because of public demand. He puts some of the new-found popularity of the piadina down to the low-carb trend, as they offer less bread than a foccacia, roll or pide. 'They like them because it is a very balanced meal and you don't feel stuffed and tired after eating them,' he says.

Spiga usually buy in their bread, and are not alone in this. Down at the Orrong Park Kiosk in Prahran East they make a pretty creditable piadina using *chapattis*, an Indian flatbread that's a sort of cousin to the piadina.

That's not the way for Stuzzichino's Gibaldi. He is a purist about his piadina, making the 2-millimetre-thick bread at the start of every service and toasting to order. For him the dough has to be no more than baker's flour, lard and water with no raising agent at all. 'The secret is to keep the dough flexible. If it is too flaky or dry it'll crack,' he says.

'The true piadina has got to be lard and no yeast,' agrees Zorzi, who rolls 70-gram balls of dough into thin, 11-inch discs before toasting them in a super-hot cast-iron pan for 20 seconds on each side.'The secrets to a great piadina are the timing in the pan and how you make the dough,' he explains.

While traditionally back in Romagna the piadina was cooked on a terracotta tile over hot coals, here most people opt for a heavy cast-iron pan. At Piadina Slowfood they use large, round cast-iron camp trays, which cost about $50 from Barbeques Galore. 'The tiles can break when you wash them and are pretty expensive as they have to be imported,' explains Dan Zeidan, one of the two guys behind the tiny café.

Zeidan and Zorzi also believe that a hot metal pan adds a bit of smokiness to the piadinas, compared to using a tile.

Having been open only four months, Piadina Slowfood are still pretty coy about the composition of the dough for the fifteen piadinas on their menu, but co-owner and chef David Morant does admit it is yeast free. 'The dough is actually better on the second day,' he says, but goes on to explain that measurements or a recipe are pretty irrelevant, because the exact proportions for the perfect piadina dough vary depending on the temperature and weather. Touch his dough raw, however, and it has a soft, silky feeling.

He also cooks their soft, chewy piadina fresh to order, which we reckon is certainly the way to go if making piadina at home. He explains that for the best results the dough needs to be at room temperature when you roll and cook it. 'Also, to ensure the fillings are warmed through without the bread burning I'll turn down the flame to complete the cooking process, letting the residual heat in the pan finish things off,' he says.

That's a little funny, for when it comes to piadina in Melbourne, one thing is for certain: with an increasing number of cafés offering piadinas on their menus each week, this is one trend where the heat is only starting to be turned up.

Making Piadina at Home

While fresh piadinas are easy to make at home, there is a wealth of tips and customisations that the home cook can use in the search for the perfect dough.

The first decision to make is the flour. Holy Cannoli's Peter Zorzi and Stuzzichino's Jamie Gibaldi use plain flour, while the guys at Piadina Slowfood and Tony Nicolini use a pizza flour like the finer '00' flour. Nicolini is looking for a dough that is soft and velvety but suggests a three-to-one ratio of flour to water is a good place to start with both piadina and pizza doughs. As for leavening agents, he prefers to take a sourdough approach, adding a little of yesterday's dough to today's batch to give it some lift. Most people, however, use a little baking powder to make the bread more digestible.

Using Nicolini's advice, and that of the other *piadaroli* we talked to, here is a lard-free modern piadina recipe that I've found works pretty well. The milk seems to make the dough sweeter and lighter, while the baking powder provides lift. The other recipe is more traditional and for the carnivore with access to a source of good rendered pig fat. The latter result tends to be a bit denser but not as dense as some of the old recipes we tried that recommended double the lard quantities!

Modern

250 g fine '00' flour
250 g bread flour
½ teaspoon baking powder
Salt
150 ml warm water
150 ml milk
60 ml good olive oil

Sift the flours, baking powder and salt together. Add the liquids and knead until a smooth, pliable dough is achieved. This will take about 15 minutes of vigorous activity. Add a little extra water until you achieve a moist, light but not sticky dough. If you are lazy, use a breadmaker on the pizza dough setting or a dough mixer to do the hard work. Let the dough rest for 30 minutes to an hour – or longer. Chop, cook or prepare your fillings while this is happening.

Split dough into 70-gram balls. On a floured surface, roll out into very thin discs about 1 mm thick or thinner. Heat a cast-iron frying pan, *tawa, teggia* or heavy-bottomed non-stick frying pan. When the pan is very hot add the thin dough disc, having first shaken off any excess flour. The dough will bubble slightly and lift off the pan when the bottom is cooked. Using a palette knife, rotate the dough clockwise until it has tanned spots. (Some *adzore* like to burst the bubbles as they rise, but I reckon they add texture.) Then flip the piadina and turn the heat down.

Add your choice of filling, fold the dough disc over and cook on each side. The dough should still be a little pliable and the filling melted or warm. After cooking a few piadinas, a residue of browned flour will build up in the pan, which will need to be wiped out.

Serve in quarters immediately with a glass of sangiovese and a lightly dressed green salad.

Traditional

500 g white bread flour
30 g salt
5 g baking powder
80 g lard
Water as needed

Sift the flour, salt and baking powder together. Chop up the lard and work into the flour with your fingers. When you have a bowl of crumbs and no lumpy lardy bits, gradually work in water until you have a moist dough. This will be a ratio of about 3:1 flour to water. When the dough has been fully kneaded and is springy, leave to rest. Cook as above.

Fillings

Piadina can be a little dry, so a cheese that melts moistly is a good start.

Think fontina, fior di latte, taleggio, asiago or stracchino, which is a very traditional piadina cheese. Or Romagnan squaquarone, if you can get it.

Bitter leaves like *cicoria* or *rape* (chicory leaf or broccolini), perhaps cooked with garlic, are traditional in piadinas, as are rocket, silverbeet and Italian cured or cooked meats like prosciutto, salami or ham.

Seven Favourite Piadina Fillings

Asiago and asparagus	Carlton Espresso
Avocado, flake salt and lime juice	Piadina Slowfood
Mushroom and taleggio	Piadina Slowfood
Stracchino, rocket and prosciutto	Enoteca Vino
Eggplant, zucchini, provolone and pesto	Stuzzichino
Rocket, tuna mayo and roast veal	Donnini's
Chicken, avocado, mayo and rocket	Holy Cannoli

Originally published in 'Epicure', The Age, 2007

A GUIDE TO DESIGNER SALTS

S alt. Strange to say, but never has this most basic of all condiments been more hip. In New York, top chefs are vying to outdo each other with the obscurity of their choice. Hawaiian black lava salt, Maltan red clay salt, pink Peruvian lake salt carried out of the Andes on llamas – the more remote the location, the more highly prized the salt.

Used as much for colour as flavouring, the salts' prices also encourage judicious use. At $60 a pound, alae – a red clay salt from the Hawaiian islands – is cheap compared to the $160 asked for the smoked Danish salt used to cure gravalax at Manhattan's hip organic, dairy-free restaurant, Heartbeat.

It's not just a nutty New York thing either. Across in California's Napa Valley, French Laundry pastry chef Stephen Durfee sprinkles choice sea salt on bittersweet chocolate to enhance the flavour and add texture. In the UK, wonderchef Michel Roux, at whose feet many of our chefs have learnt their trade, sprinkles expensive French *fleur de sel* on his fois gras to bring out its delicate flavour. In Boston, they are even using sea salt spiked with gold leaf to cure gravalax. The salt helps the precious metal permeate the fish, adding an alluring glister.

While the desire for character-giving impurities may be a 'new thing' for salt – a reaction perhaps to Western society's push for over-refinement and standardisation – paying top dollar for salt is not. Known as 'white gold', salt was once used as money in Africa and China and at times exchanged on a parity with precious metal.

The high value put on salt is a reflection of its life-preserving role. Once our ancestors moved away from their nomadic existence and a diet of raw or roast meat, their daily supply of salt dropped. Without it, regulating electrolytes, controlling the body's fluid balance and potassium absorption, regulating blood pressure, sparking nerve communications and activating muscle contractions become tricky. Heck, chloride even supplies the essence of digestive stomach acid, and enhances the ability of the blood to carry carbon dioxide from respiring tissues to the lungs. Fairly crucial stuff.

According to salt authority M. K. Bloch, it is thus no fluke that early civilisations sprang up alongside salt deposits. There's also evidence that man was producing salt by evaporation well before historical records begin.

The importance of salt to our ancestors can be seen in the words it has given to our language. Salary, salvation, hale, hall, hallelujah, hallmark, hallow, halo, *salaam* and safety all derive from words for salt. From Hawaii to Tibet and across the Middle East and the Mediterranean, salt played a role in both purification and religious ceremonies.

The quest for salt drove the first trade routes into Asia and Africa and gave birth to empires. Rome was founded on the site of a salt market; the first twitches of the Romans' imperial aspirations were the conquests of the Etruscan salt pans. Later both Gaul and Palestine were annexed, in part for their salt. Not that fighting over salt was anything new – one of the first ever wars was fought over the Jordanian city of Essalt's salt supplies. The preserving power of salt allowed armies to roam and settlements to wait out the inhospitable months, allowing towns to grow.

Later, the first European settlements of the New World were those of the French and English salt-cod fleets. Back home, the Catholic church's control of salt helped define borders, while the numerous meat-free holy days ensured a ready market for fish – and the salt to preserve it.

Controlling salt was power and from as early as 2000 BC Chinese rulers were using their monopoly on it for taxation purposes – a trend that continued in Europe. The French Revolution was in part sparked by anger over the French *gabelle* or salt tax, and Gandhi chose to challenge British authority in India with his march to the sea to make illegal free salt.

It's a mark of the value that Forest Hill's own Luke Mangan puts on the mineral that he named his luminary Sydney restaurant Salt. He wanted a name that symbolised hospitality and friendship, values long associated with salt in Hebrew and Bedouin culture and exhibited in the Biblical phrase 'salt of the earth'.

Salt is either won from the sea (sea salt) or mined from the earth's deposits (rock salt). Much rock salt is refined to remove mineral 'impurities' and has iodine and/or anti-caking agents added. The presence of iodine is a legacy of the US campaign to combat the problem midwestern farmers had with goitres from iodine deficiencies

Sel Gris

Sel Gris is coarse sea salt made from the natural evaporation of seawater. Mainly from Brittany – look for salt from locations like Ile de Re, Ile de Noirmoutier and the marshes of Guerande – but some from Normandy. It has a fresh 'sea breeze' flavour. It gets its colour from magnesium, iron, calcium, potassium and other minerals found in the water along France's Atlantic coast, and can come complete with algae for an even more seaside flavour. Enjoyed a revival in the eighties when the art of the wooden paddle wielding *sauniers*, or salt collectors, looked like dying out. Also known as *gros sel* (thick salt) or Celtic sea salt. The moist, rough granules are milder, with a lower sodium content than rock salts and a slower release of flavour. Good for baking, roasting, seasoning, marinating or finishing a dish. They can also be used to add a surprising crunch to a chocolate tart as well as intensifying the flavour.

Fleur de Sel

Called the 'caviar of salt', this fragile sea salt of small lacy white flakes only appears as a wispy crust on *sel gris* pans on warm breezy days with no rain. Low yields and hand harvesting help account for the price. It's also the least salty, purest part of the saline. Some believe they can taste a hint of violets among the iron, magnesium, calcium, potassium, manganese, zinc and iodine of this delicate crunchy salt. Best used sparingly as a finishing salt. Sprinkle it on ready-cooked foods to appreciate its texture and flavour. Works wonderfully on ripe tomatoes and scallops. I prefer that from the Ile de Re, which seems more delicate.

Maldon Sea Salt

Very hip sea salt that comes from the unlikely location of Essex, just north of the Thames estuary in England. Its large opaque and fine flakes have a lacy quality and fairly intense flavour. Wonderful as a salad dressing.

Murray River Pink Salt

Australian flake salt from northern Victoria. Salt is solution mined, the brine then evaporated and treated to create a flake. Less lacy than Maldon but still with a bright flavour and a fine crisp flake. This is my salt of choice, thanks to its delicate pink hue.

Hawaiian Alae Salt

Originally this salt was found on the shores of Molokai and Kauai, where local clay coloured it pale orange. Now salt from oceanside drying ponds (pans) is mixed with red clay (*alae*) for flavour and colour. Clay and salt tend to separate in water, so it's best used as a finishing salt. Used for island rituals and for *poke*, the Hawaiian delicacy of cubed raw fish.

Sicilian Salt

As sharp, bright sea salt from this Mediterranean island. The coastal plains around Trepani are dotted with pans and old-fashioned windmills to grind the salt. Great on seafood or as a general cooking salt.

Kala Namak

A staple of Ayurvedic medicine, this Indian black salt is actually pink when crushed and a hard purple when in rock form. It's a staple of Indian cooking and often used sprinkled on salad, but its pungent, sulphurous bouquet can be off-putting.

Pink Salt

The colour usually comes from salt-loving bacteria that produce a red carotenoid pigment that's a source of beta-carotene. They are unwelcome in most commercial salt production, where a pure white salt is preferred, and because they can occasionally cause spoilage when used in the preservation process. They can also cause 'pinkeye', a pinkish discolouration of pickled foods.

Other Salts to Drop Annoyingly into Conversation with New York Chefs

Korean roast salt with a milder nutty flavour; rare black Japanese sea salt; Tibetan holy salt from the salt pans of Changtang; Saharan rock salt from Timbuktu or Mopti in Mali.

Out of this World Salt

Possibly the oldest and rarest salt landed within a meteor in Texas. The 3-millimetre crystals of blue and purple halite were estimated to be 4.5 billion years old.

Originally published in 'Epicure', The Age, 2000

THE ULTIMATE CHEESE
SANDWICH

I t's way past deadline and I am listlessly cruising the web, as is my wont
when editors are screaming for my copy. It's strange how only now
do I find compelling stuff to read. Like the piece on the famous New
York food author who went to London and said that the best thing she
ate was not from the fancy kitchens of Gordon Ramsay or Eric Chavot
but a toastie from Jamie Oliver's favourite shopping spot, Borough
Market.

Made by a gentleman with the rather Dickensian name of Bill
Oglethorpe, it's a toasted cheese and onion sandwich full of gooey,
stringy melted Montgomery Somerset cheddar cosied up to leek, red
onion, shallots and a little garlic. Oh my goodness, how much my mouth
is watering.

I call Qantas for a mercy flight, but $2600 is a lot to pay for a cheese
toastie. Far better to make it myself. I've got a Breville toasted sandwich
maker like Bill uses, so next I need the cheese.

I harass cheese importer Will Studd at his Port Melbourne warehouse.
Will used to import Montgomery Somerset Cheddar, but can't any more
thanks to our draconian raw milk cheese laws. Instead, he suggests I opt
for Quick's Devon-made cheddar as an alternative, as that's available

from Richmond Hill Café and Larder's cheese room.

I toy with the idea of substituting brie or mozzarella mixed with parmesan but that just seems plain wrong. While these are perfect in their own native baguette, piadina or pizza, I reckon there is something earthily honest and smock-wearingly, Englishly yeoman about a toastie. This makes cheddar the perfect choice – especially as it has the punch to stand up to the onions: its saltiness matching their sweetness.

Will also shares with me what he reckons is the mother of Bill's cheese toastie recipe – cheesemaker Jamie Montgomery's family recipe. Oh my, this is feeling like being a real investigative journalist now. Or it did until Will tells me it's included in his TV series *Cheese Slices*.

Jamie Montgomery's version is simpler. Buttered brown bread is filled with his grated cheddar, blanched leeks and chopped brown onion. The secret here is to keep the filling chunky and rather rustic. He cooks his toastie on the top of an Aga between two metal trays. I trial it by using my tabletop pizza oven for a similarly tasty effect. While it is certainly an improvement on a couple of Kraft cheese slices and shaved slices of onion slapped between the fluffiest white Tip Top you can find, I feel the brown bread is a distraction. It's not perfection.

Instead I go in search of something more fitting to enshroud my ultimate toastie. Oglethorpe uses slices of Lionel Poilâne's chewy dark French bread imported from Paris. I can't afford the Fedex bill, so opt for a white sourdough that'll toast up nicely, hold together and also add an extra tang to match the bitey piquancy of the cheddar. I collect admirably suitable loaves from Baker D. Chirico in St Kilda and from Ludo Foodstore in Sandringham, where they sell the excellent sourdough from the La Madre bakery in Geelong. After much trial and error (well, I told the wife it was trial and error, it was actually just me being greedy), I alighted on the following recipe, which seems to offer the right balance between the onions.

MATT'S ULTIMATE CHEESE TOASTIE
(WITH APOLOGIES TO BILL OGLETHORPE AND JAMIE MONTGOMERY)

Serves one

Ingredients

1 small leek, trimmed and sliced into 5 mm rounds

1 medium red onion, diced

1 perky spring onion, sliced up until just before the green end gets floppy

2 shallots, finely diced

1 clove garlic, very finely diced

1 kg best quality English cheddar

butter, at room temperature

a loaf of good artisan-baked sourdough bread

Method

Warm up your sandwich-maker or sandwich press. Pop the leek slices in a bowl and cover with just boiled water. Let them sit for a minute, then drain thoroughly and place the leek on sheets of kitchen paper to dry out. When dry, mix the leeks up together with the diced onion, spring onion, shallot and garlic. Grate the cheese. Butter one side of four 1.5-centimetre-thick slices of bread.

Lay slices on the bottom plate on either side of the sandwich-maker, butter side down. Push your fist into the bread to make a small depression. Sprinkle the depression with a little of the leek mixture. Add a generous handful of grated cheese, then top with some more leek mixture. The ratio is up to personal taste but I like the cheese to outnumber the leek mix at least two parts to one. Add the second slice of bread, butter side up. Close up the sandwich-maker and toast until gooey.

Repeat until either a) the cheese, bread or leek mix runs out; b) you are full; c) you find the perfect ratio between leek mix and cheese for your taste, then get a pen and cross out my name in the recipe title and write yours over the top.

Originally published in Melbourne Weekly Bayside, *2007*

TACKLING AN OCTOPUS

An octopus's long slimy tentacle has curled itself around my forearm a couple of times. It's as if this 5-kilogram beast from the deep is a seer and knows its future: a future that holds nothing but the prospect of a long recline on a sizzling metal grill over hot coals.

Admittedly that sounds far more rugged than the situation actually is. The octopus is dead and we've picked it up from the Lorne Fisherman's Co-op after it was caught raiding craypots that morning. 'We' is me and Kosta Talihmanidis from A La Greque restaurant in Airey's Inlet – a man with a reputation for cooking very good 'Henry'. Yet, dead or not, still those tentacles cling.

We are standing, trousers rolled up, in the frothing surf by a large outcrop of rocks on the beach near the co-op, as Kosta teaches me the Greek way how to make perfect octopus. The secret, apparently, is to bash it on the rocks 40 times; 100 times if it's one this big. The aim is to tenderise the flesh by beating it, otherwise it will be rubbery. This also helps remove that slime and loosen the membrane around the legs, which needs to be slipped off before cooking.

The head of the beast has been removed and Kosta grabs the fat end of the remaining legs and, with the action of a miner swinging a heavy pick, sweeps them over his shoulder and back onto a flat rock in front of him with a loud 'thwhack'. He does it again, the suckered legs flailing in a smooth arc across a cloudless sky of Cycladian blue.

After each couple of lashing strokes, Kosta swirls the mass of tentacles anticlockwise a few times on the rough surface of the rock. He explains that this helps remove the sliminess and that when the rock surface starts to look foamy the octopus will be ready to cook.

I step in and take over. The legs are still slippery and the first time I flail them against the rock they almost slip from my grasp, but soon I'm in the rhythm and channelling my inner *pau pao* or *yia yia*. I instantly feel my back getting hairier and I have the intense desire to smoke, drink strong coffee and click worry beads. A passer-by asks where my black dress, black headscarf and walking stick are and Kosta laughs and offers to call me a donkey to take me home. I quieten my inner Spartan and ignore these insulting comments, taking them instead as a back-handedly flattering comment on the assured manner with which I'm now dealing with the cephalopod.

After about five minutes pretending to be wielding a cat o' nine tails on the back of a particularly mutinous crew member, the tentacles are starting to feel soft – almost squeezy. Occasionally a piece flies off. Three minutes later and the speckled pink and brown skin of the octopus peels away easily and the legs are cut into 10-centimetre lengths, tossed in a partially emulsified mix of oil, lemon juice and torn oregano and then laid with a fizzing sound on the hot grill. The meatier pieces contract like they are writhing and after a while they start to leach a milky liquid. The smell of the charring is delicious, but I get a slapped wrist and a 'not yet' when I reach in to grab a fat piece. Instead, Kosta hands me a little crispy squiggle that was once the end of the tentacle that curled around my arm. It looks, for all the world, like a piece of browned and crispy bacon rind. Even weirder, it tastes a bit like it too – that smokiness from the coals and saltiness from the sea.

So it is with the fatter pieces, which seem to have an almost porky stickiness when cooked this way, though inside is firm but sweet and salty flesh. They taste a bit like someone has wrapped sweet bacon around a hunk of lobster. It is, in short, delicious and better than any

I've had before. 'This is the best octopus you'll ever have,' Kosta declares with typical Greek pride and a raised shot of ouzo. It's the perfect, and traditional Hellenic, match for the octopus.

He's probably right. What I'm not sure about is whether this is due to the octopus, Kosta's skill at cooking it, or the ancient ritual of beating, cleaning and then eating it by the waters from whence it came. Perhaps it's all those reasons, but one thing is certain: sitting on those rocks where the work was done, with the tide coming in round our ankles and the octopus hot from the grill burning our fingers, it is surely among the best lunches I, or anyone, could have. *Yiamas!*

Originally published in 'A2', The Age, 2009

THE CHOWDER
RESURGENCE

It started as a whisper, but over the last three years there have been increasingly frequent signs that this will be the winter that chowder returns to its rightful place as one of the 'great meals in a bowl'.

So long a staple of seafood restaurants like the late Watergrill restaurant in South Yarra and on hearty pub menus at places like the Hotel Spencer, slowly the creamy white chowder, and its companionable flavours such as potato and smoky bacon with corn or clams, has eased themselves back onto café menus at places such as The Commoner in Fitzroy or Cafeteria in Black Rock, and into restaurant degustation line-ups from Avenel to Brisbane. It has appeared on the menus of Asian restaurants such as Man Mo in Docklands and Fitzroy's Viet Rose, and even modernist chef Robin Wickens has deconstructed the flavours for a dish. Stokehouse's Anthony Musarra chose a chowder of blue swimmer crab with *pangrattato*, chives and Spanish pepper crème fraiche to represent the restaurant as one of his feature dishes at Taste of Melbourne. I even hear news that there's a café in Robe where chowder can't come off the menu, such is the love some cray-fishermen have for it. The signs are there, so surely the time is right for one of the world's great soups to reassert itself.

Chowder has a long and illustrious history. While some Victorian cookbooks attributed its invention to China (perhaps given its similarity to Cantonese crab and sweetcorn soup and the name's slang Chinese connections), it is known that chowder was popular amongst the French-speaking settlers of Acadia (Nova Scotia) in the 1750s, actually deriving its name from the large cauldron (*chaudière*) it was cooked in on sea voyages across the Atlantic. This stew used fish (or salt cod) and other ship's provisions like salted pork and hardtack (a type of biscuit). Potatoes were a later addition, and crackers were introduced to replace the hardtack in some recipes.

According to James Tracer in *The Food Chronology*, once the British took Acadia they also adopted some of the recipes and thus chowder spread south to New England. Eighty-five years later, the menu of the restaurant above Boston's seafood market cited chowder alongside fried cod tongues and apple pandowdy. Interestingly, in his book *Cod* Mark Kurlansky cites a 16th-century recipe for chowder written in the Celtic tongue of Cornwall and remarks on reports that the Native Americans were already making a fish chowder before European settlement. With other examples of chowder existing, such as the Andalusian *gazpachuelo*, it seems that success once again has many fathers.

One thing that is certain is that the image of chowder took a terminal blow in the seventies, when cookbooks picked up on the San Francisco folly of serving chowder in a hollowed-out cobb loaf rather than in a bowl. Overnight, chowder became one of the poster boys for outdated seventies food. A leading Kiwi food editor reports that there's still an awful lot of chowder on the menu of New Zealand restaurants.

For me, however, true chowder is anchored on the fishing coast of New England, which covers the states from Connecticut up to the Canadian border. And it was in the Massachusetts town of Taunton, just south of Boston, that Shane Phillips was raised.

If the chowder is this winter's soup, then Phillips is its evangelist. Three years ago he and partner Gary Cooke upped sticks from their groovy little café Gas Milk Bar in Brighton and opened a chowder shack in the unlikely surrounds of Hepburn Springs. Their slightly kitschily decorated Chowder House Café has become an unlikely hit with tourists and locals alike.

The guys always have six chowders on the menu and these might include a Boston-style clam chowder, a prawn, a chicken and corn, a smoked cod, a plain corn chowder and, the most popular, the seafood combination chowder. All are made from the same base and are served with cornbread which, along with Boston molasses bread, is a traditional partner to chowder.

'Eighty per cent of people who come in for lunch have a chowder,' says Gary. 'Locals seem to want white creamy chowder. These make up 90 per cent of our sales at weekends, but then we can also sell a tomato-based Manhattan chowder which we won't shift during the week.'

Phillips might come from a family stock that includes Sicilian, Ukrainian, Native American and African-American antecedents but chowder was still a huge part of his family life. 'I grew up with my grandparents' soul food – chitterlings and collard greens – but Thursday night was spaghetti bolognese and chowder was Friday,' he recalls.

'All my aunts made chowder and they all made it differently. You bet they argued over who made it best. The one thing they all agreed on was who made it worst: my mum. She'd just boil milk with potatoes and add a couple of cans of clams,' he says with a laugh.

His Aunt Marjie even ran a crab shack selling corn dogs and quahogs (local clams) on the I-495, with a big pot of chowder always bubbling away though summer. 'It was so thick you could stand your spoon up in it. I like it thinner though,' he recalls.

For Shane and his aunties, the secret of a great chowder is all in the first few stages. 'It's like Indian food: everything is about the masala at the beginning,' he says. 'Oh, and cooking it slow so the flavour develops!'

Traditionally a chowder would start with slices of fat back bacon or speck, but Shane's Hepburn Springs customers are more health-conscious than those on the I-495, so adding a little smoked salmon to his seafood chowder helps get that smoky flavour. He adds further flavour to his corn-based chowders by adding not only the corn, but also the cobs for a while so they can add their savour to the brew.

He advises using vongole rather than pipis, because they can be too metallic, and counsels using blue eye as the closest fish to what they'd use back in New England – sweet, fleshy but not too oily fish like sea bass, or 'striper', as the locals call striped bass.

Travel writer and chowder aficionado Susan King grew up in Maryland, which is famous for its Chesapeake Bay crabs, but snowy winters meant they looked to their northern cousins for warming recipes. 'We'd always make chowder in the winter,' she recalls.

'Mum would pull out her copy of Rombauer and Becker's *The Joy of Cooking* and start from there. Chowder is the kind of dish that families have their own versions of. It's very folksy. It can be made with fresh or tinned clams. The creamy New England clam chowder is far more common in the US than the tomato-based Manhattan version.'

If using fresh clams, or pipis, Susan suggests it is best to prepare the chowder 24 hours in advance, as the flavours will develop in the fridge overnight. Just remember to reheat it gently for serving as the clams cook very quickly.

She also has a canny solution for what to use instead of the oyster crackers that are the traditional accompaniment for chowder in the US but which aren't easily available here. She uses 1-centimetre-long pieces of broken-up grissini.

Originally published in 'Epicure', The Age, 2009

CHOCOLATE OR VANILLA?

So you're shipwrecked, right, and as you load your raft with that last pannier of chickens, sack of flour and loaf of sugar, you realise that there's now only space for your jar of vanilla beans or for your bucket of chocolate. Which do you take? The chocolate or the vanilla?

While this dilemma might stump our leading ethicists, who'd probably say something along the lines of 'I think a professional ethicist can show that in any situation there is a range of possible and defensible views', Victoria's chefs are not so wishy-washy.

I asked a baker's dozen of them to pick their favourite and in almost every case their response was immediate – but first, the history.

Vanilla is the seedpod of an orchid vine native to Central America. Fresh, these pale yellow and green pods have no flavour: they must be cured so an enzymic reaction can produce the 300 naturally occurring flavour compounds in the vanilla bean. A good vanilla bean should be moist to the touch, pliable and have a distinct aroma.

The beans that give chocolate its texture and flavour grow in large pods on the cacao tree. They are fermented to develop their flavour, dried in the sun and then roasted until their thin shells fall away. The beans are then crushed to create cocoa paste and from this fatty substance cocoa butter is derived. Remove the fat and you end up with a cocoa cake that can be ground into powder – a trick not discovered until 1828. In fact, it was only in the 19th century that chocolate was developed for eating and names like Nestlé, Lindt, Cadbury and Rowntree were born.

Prior to that, chocolate was a fashionable beverage to rival tea and coffee. It was as a drink that chocolate was first offered to Columbus in 1502 off Honduras. The bean had ritual religious significance and was extracted as tribute by the Aztec rulers. It was drunk spiked with honey and vanilla or with ground annatto, anise, red peppers and cinnamon.

The local Mexican custom of using chocolate in savoury cooking was adapted for the creation, in a Puebla nunnery, of the *mole* sauce for fowl, and spread through the Spanish world. Hence the chocolate sauces served with calf's tongue in Aragon and with hare in Sicily.

Vanilla and chocolate rode into the European culinary consciousness hand in hand. Both were brought back to Europe from the New World by the Spanish conquistadors in 1524, and chocolate's popularity spread from Spain via its colonies, like Sicily. Chocolate became all the rage at the French court after the Spanish princess Anne of Austria married Louis XIV in 1615.

The English drank chocolate made with milk. Queen Elizabeth I's apothecary, Hugh Morgan, is credited with suggesting in 1602 that vanilla could be used as a flavouring by itself. While chocolate was subsequently credited with medicinal properties, vanilla was praised as a nerve stimulant and aphrodisiac.

Both vanilla and chocolate are costly to produce. Hand pollination, the long and laborious curing process and the fact that only 50 per cent of flowers produce beans account for some of the savage cost of vanilla. In the last ten years, storms have also ravaged the most highly prized plantations of Mexico and Madagascar. This destruction, combined with fungal rot attacks and political turmoil in Madagascar, has drastically reduced the vanilla harvest and increased prices. According to spice expert Ian Hemphill, prices rose over 500 per cent between 1997 and 2002, although it should be noted that 'farm gate' prices bottomed in 1997 at under US$20 a kilo after the 1995 deregulation of exports of Madagascan vanilla.

The current price of prized Bourbon vanilla beans from islands like

Reunion and Madagascar makes them out of the question for most Melbourne chefs, according to the Essential Ingredient's Syd Weddell. Much of the vanilla he imports now is the comparatively less expensive Indonesian variety, which still sells at between $550 and $770 a kilo at retail. He says the problem is that the supply from Bali has become erratic, in part due to climatic problems, and reports that it is hard to develop trusting relationships with wholesalers, as the quality of Indonesian vanilla can vary dramatically.

Today, chocolate production in three of the four major producers – Ivory Coast, Ghana and Nigeria – is under attack for using child labour and child slaves to meet the low cost expectations of the multinational chocolate manufacturers. In 2000, the U.S. State Department's *Human Rights Report* estimated that there were 15,000 child slaves working on cocoa, cotton and coffee farms in Ivory Coast alone. Stung by these allegations, chocolate manufacturers signed the Harkin-Engel Protocol and the International Cocoa Initiative (ICI) to banish child labour and slavery from cocoa production in West Africa by 2005. This has helped injected further volatility into the world price for cocoa, which Syd Weddell describes as 'always fluctuating'.

The first person I ask to choose between vanilla and chocolate is Jacques Reymond. His answer is thoughtful to the point of almost being philosophical. 'Oh, vanilla,' he tells me. 'For with vanilla I can scent the chocolate, but with chocolate I cannot scent vanilla. By the osmosis principle you can give the vanilla to the chocolate but you can never give the chocolate to the vanilla.'

Okay, so it sounded much deeper with a sexy French accent, but the dashing Burgundian has a point when he says that vanilla can be used for many, many purposes, like desserts, ice-cream, dressings and syrups. Jacques also believes it also adds 'another dimension of flavour outside the normal vocab of savoury'.

He suggests that parsnips candied very slowly with vanilla pods are fantastic served with fish. In fact, using vanilla-scented sauces for seafood, especially lobster, has been advised by everyone from many-starred nouvelle French chefs to Rick Stein.

The two pastry chefs to whom I posed this dilemma also came down on the side of vanilla. Freelance pastry chef Loretta Sartori isn't crazy about chocolate herself. 'Sure, it's luscious but it tends to overpower, while vanilla enhances,' says the queen of cakes. 'Vanilla makes so much taste better, like fruit, cake batters and pastries. It also helps promote flavours like orange and lemon zest, adds depth and dimension and behaves differently when used with fat, sugar syrup or alcohol. I'm hopeless, I put it in everything.'

Danish-born Khristina Dock, Victorian Wine Precinct head pastry chef, does love chocolate but sees vanilla as too important to lose. 'I use it like a spice. It gives life to dishes. You can even use it in syrups or sauces for meat, but it works best with white meat as they need something that light.'

The savoury use of vanilla is something dismissed by Middle Brighton Baths executive chef Paul Raynor, who remembers tasting a Gordon Ramsay barramundi dish using vanilla that failed to impress. He's still firmly in the vanilla camp though. 'I'm a traditionalist. Vanilla is so adaptable and the flavour that comes out of that pod for brûlées and ice-cream is amazing,' he says.

In fact, Raynor is such a fan that he admits to stockpiling vanilla after the price went through the roof seven months ago. 'I'll get my money's worth. After using the pods I wash them and put them in sugar, which they'll infuse with their flavour.'

Koots's Patrice Repellin lines up alongside Raynor – he's not 100 per cent sure that a vanilla risotto he once served with a confit rabbit leg worked but he gets quite rhapsodic when remembering a vanilla soufflé he used to make at the Richmond Hotel in Geneva. 'Chocolate is great to work with but I love vanilla. I love poaching fruit with a vanilla bean and you can't do a crème anglaise without it.'

When the subject moves to chocolate, the conversation quickly becomes saucy. Talking about chocolate, Brigitte Hafner, executive chef for Stefanos, Bistro 1 and the Avoca in Mildura, sounds like she's describing a bloke she fancies, using words like 'interesting', 'deep and dark' and 'complex'.

Guy Grossi shares that appreciation of chocolate's naughtiness. 'It instantly gives me a feeling of decadence and richness and I like that kind of feeling when I'm cooking,' says the man who rules the kitchens at Grossi Florentino. 'It gives me flashes to the early Venetians and their chocolate rooms. They thought it was almost like a naughty thing to do. I love to use it in savoury food too. We finish off a hare casserole with dark chocolate melted down with some cognac. It darkens and enriches the sauce.'

Grossi is also excited by the new chocolate choices that exhibit distinct flavour differences in the plantations' terroir.

Even Tom Stevens of Mexicali Rose has a reaction that links chocolate to the bedroom, as he claims that only chocolate can be eaten in bed. He reveals that Mexican cuisine still uses chocolate more extensively that vanilla. Given the small role desserts play in a Mexican meal, chocolate is mainly used in the traditional way as a drink or as a subtle spice in moles.

Sean Donovan, head chef of radii, Toey's Pierre Barelier and Stephen Mercer of Mercer's Restaurant in Eltham all cite the value of chocolate in adding a bittersweet complexity and a glossiness normally associated with butter to sauces intended for game. However, the three of them all primarily base chocolate's indispensability in its dessert performance, 'You always have to have a chocolate dessert on the menu,' says Barelier.

While Donovan praises the flexibility of chocolate as a raw ingredient that works well with everything from flour and butter to eggs and nuts, for Mercer that flexibility runs to the range of products from the cocoa bean. He uses cocoa mass to screen-print the outside of sponges, adds cocoa butter to liquid chocolate for spraying and also uses cocoa powder.

Melly Beilby, who cooks at Spoonful, sees the value of chocolate as lying in its versatility, yet she feels that familiarity with its use in cakes, ice-cream or brownies means that sometimes we forget how good these, if well made, can be. It is an attitude closely related to that of Bluestone Restaurant head chef Mickael Gaultier, who sees chocolate as irreplaceable in recipes like these. 'It's easy to substitute vanilla, even in a dish like crème brûlée or crème caramel, with another flavour but a chocolate fondant has to be chocolate. Coffee or caramel just won't work!' he claims.

On a straight count it's chocolate by eight votes to five, but that's a lot closer than I thought it might be. And just as intriguing is what each chef's opinion reveals about how they approach core ingredients. Like my old maths teacher used to say, 'It's not the answer that matters but how that answer is reached.' Unsurprisingly, he was a member of the old Labor party.

For the record, Matt Preston is a vanilla man.

Originally published in 'Epicure', The Age, 2003

BOTTLING THE SEASON

In orchards across the state, the fruit is ripening. Cherries, peaches, nectarines, apricots, plums, apples, pears ... for a couple of months not only will they be in their prime but they'll also be at their cheapest. But how best to capture these little drops of Aussie sunshine for the dark months ahead? The choices are myriad – drying, candying, glazing or jellying – but none of these methods of home fruit preserving has quite the same resonance, taste or healthiness as bottling.

Talk to grandparents about home fruit bottling and many will reminisce about ranks of rainbow jars in the pantry or that hiss as mum opened another bottle of last summer's fruit. They might also mention a name that's every inch as much an Aussie icon as the Victa Mower and the Hills Hoist – a combination of metal clips, rubber seals, glass bottles and a processing bath that together comprise a name nigh synonymous with home bottling, the Fowler's Vacola preserving kit.

Howard Everard is one of Victoria's most experienced home bottlers. It's now 82 years since he first learnt the art at his mother's skirts and he still uses a Fowler's Vacola, but while loquacious and knowledgeable Howard has been the star of radio, TV and press interviews, it's his wife, Mary, who does much of the best work in the kitchen. Early on she pulls me to one side and with a smile whispers, 'I could do this more efficiently. You know the secret is good preparation.'

When the preserving process starts you can see this is no idle boast. Her nimble fingers deftly slip new rubber ring seals on three jars while Howard's still struggling with one that's as twisted as the Marquis de Sade's love life. The secret, she explains, is softening the rings first in a bowl of hot water for 10 minutes.

Today cherries are the fruit of choice, the first of the 350 or so bottles that will make it into the Everards' store cupboard over the summer months. Howard checks each empty jar for cracks. Next he carefully washes the cherries, picking through the fruit and discarding any that are bruised, split or turning. Bad fruit can discolour the finished product or, even worse, help induce fermentation. He de-stalks the good ones and rolls them into thick-lipped glass bottles. Mary picks out the stalks that he's missed. Later Howard admits Mary seldom gets the credit she deserves for the success of his preserving. 'I couldn't do it without her,' he says, just out of her earshot.

Mary half-fills the bottles with a light syrup (one part sugar, three parts boiling water) that she's mixed in a jug for easy pouring. Howard fills them with fruit to about half an inch from the top, packing it tightly and occasionally shaking the jar to help it settle so no airlocks are created which could lead to spoiling later. Mary then fills the jars to the brim with the syrup, as any uncovered fruit can discolour. A lacquered tin or stainless steel lid is then retained on each jar with a metal clip – Howard uses two for extra safety. The completed bottles are submerged in what looks like a squat tea urn and the water in it is slowly brought up to the boil. The heat not only kills off any gribblies, it also, when the fruit cools, creates a vacuum that sucks the lid firmly to the jar, creating the air-tight seal that is the essence of the Fowler's Vacola system of fruit preserving.

The Everards use an electric Vacola rather than an old stove-top model, and Howard advises using it next to the sink so it's easier to drain once you've finished. While the Fowler's Vacola may have become an Aussie icon, there is nothing new in hermetically sealing food to preserve it. The Romans did it by adding everything from honey and sugar syrups to brine and alcohol under the sealed lids to keep food-spoiling bacteria at bay. The first recipes for preserving fruit without these heavy solutions appeared at the start of the 18th century. This process of slowly boiling cork-stoppered glass bottles of fruit, most notably gooseberries, allowed for sterile preserving without sugar.

Home bottling became easier with the US introduction of the Mason jar (1858), which replaced sealing with corks and wax with clips, screwtops and rubber rings. The wire 'lightening seal' (1882) and the Ball Mason jars (1887) followed.

Englishman George Fowler introduced his first bottling kit in 1889, targeted at sportsmen who wished to vacuum-preserve game birds they'd shot. In 1912 his nephew, Joseph Fowler, emigrated to Australia and three years later launched his own fruit-bottling outfit from the cellar of his Camberwell home.

Fowler's Vacola boomed for over 50 years, helping sustain Australians through the lean years of war and Depression, but with the death of Joseph's son Ron, the company passed out of family ownership and into the hands of plastics and brushware manufacturer Sabco. When Sabco went into receivership, John Roy bought the brand and since 1993 it's been a family-run company again.

Daughter Nicole Roy, who works as a product manager, explains that Fowler's Vacola is now benefiting from the renewed interest in home preserving. The way she tells it, bottling's booming, driven by everything from food scares and the popularity of organic produce to nostalgia and the seachange phenomenon. Nicole also sees a lot mums who are keen to preserve because they can regulate the cleanliness of the production process, the quality of the fruit and what goes into it – especially sugar. 'This way they can be sure that the peaches that they are feeding their children have been peeled by hand and not with caustic soda or acid,' she says.

The challenge from the Roys is to get more young people, like East Doncaster's Julie D'Amore, into preserving. Julie may be a novice compared to the Everards but she's already had her bottled fruit commended at the Royal Melbourne Show. It was her mother's old Fowler's Vacola kit that she sought out when she wanted a new hobby. The main beneficiaries have been her three boys. 'It's fantastic for the kids and unlike canned fruit I know what's gone into it,' she says.

She's even used clear apple juice for her pears as a healthier alternative to syrup, which she reports didn't adversely affect the peariness of the finished product.

Julie is full of sensible advice for would-be preservers, although is quick to point out that so long as you get the water level and temperature right, bottling is a fairly simple operation. 'I thought it would be so hard but it really isn't,' she admits.

She first sterilises her bottles by boiling them then drying them off in the oven. 'This also means the bottles won't crack when hot sugar syrup is poured into them,' she says.

To avoid having fruit like pears or apples discolour during bottling, she advises dousing them in salted water (acidulated water could also be used) followed by a thorough rinse. She also suggests bottling in small batches (i.e. three jars) to minimise the time the fruit is exposed to the air.

While Julie's found fruit preserving a fairly easy process, there have been some disasters — but now she can laugh about the strawberries that went brown and a mango sauce that went mouldy.

Generally, Bentleigh's Wendy Dunlevie describes preserving with her 30-year-old kit as 'easy, easy, easy', but her worst preserving moment came when she checked a jar of red and green grapes that she'd taken hours to artistically arrange. 'The colours had run and I was left with a very dreary-looking jar,' she remembers ruefully.

That's not all Wendy's had to suffer for her love of preserving. Workmates rib her mercilessly because 'they think it's such a daggy thing to do' and now even her sons have joined in on the act. 'When I told my son that I'd been highly commended for my preserved pears at this year's Royal Melbourne Show he told me it sounded like "something you'd get on a chance card at Monopoly".'

While Wendy gets her fruit from the local greengrocer, both Julie D'Amore and the Everards have developed relationships with growers, buying from the farm gate and U-pick operations. While firm ripe fruit is seen as best for showing, most agree that for home use, fruit that's ready to eat right now is the best buy, especially if you can get it in the bottle quickly. Howard Everard even picks raspberries straight into preserving bottles to speed up the process.

Overripe fruit can not only cause preserving problems, but it can also contribute to the fruit rising in the bottle. According to prize-winning preserver Peter Bennett, this problem can also be caused by too little fruit or packing the fruit in so tightly that the syrup can't bubble up freely during the sterilisation process. If this happens, Bennett advises that turning the bottle upside down while it cools might help.

Bennett learnt to preserve on a stove-top Fowler's Vacola and is about to return to it after an unsuccessful run with one of their new-style $120 electric plastic preserving units. He likes the better control his gas stove gives him to bring the unit slowly to the boil and to ensure it doesn't boil too long. He's also not game to spend a little under 400 bucks on the metal electric version. He's not alone, but others complain about the cheaper model's tendency to steam up the place.

He's a big stone fruit fan but Bennett shies away from bottling berries, as he feels it can make them mushy compared to freezing. He also avoids adding alcohol or spices until he breaks the seal. While he strains his syrup through muslin for improved clarity, there are some processes, like extracting and adding the apricot kernels for their added flavour, that Bennett sees as just too much of a hassle.

Bennett also suggests bottling a range of sizes so you can open just the amount of fruit you need through the year and recommends leaving the processed bottles for 24 hours before removing the clips to ensure the best possible vacuum seal.

All preserves should then be stored in a cool, dark spot – ideally at between 12 and 15 degrees C. Julie D'Amore also advises leaving the fruit to temper for six weeks before opening.

Back at the Everards', the cherries have finished their 75-minute bath and Howard is describing the future fate of each bottle as he removes the steaming jars one at a time. 'On a plate with a big dollop of cream' seems to be the most common destination. Mary just quietly looks on as Howard takes the limelight. She's got the look of contentment of someone who knows that it's not important how the battle is won but just that you get to share in the spoils.

Other Fruit Preserving Methods

As suggested by Joan M Graham in *The Show Bench* (Ercildourne, 1994).

Crystallised

Heat sugar syrup to 105 degrees C (strong thread stage) and soak fruit for 10 hours, then cool in oven.

Glazed

Heat sugar syrup to 150 degrees C (hard crack stage) and dip the fruit. Drain and cool in oven.

Candied

Heat sugar syrup to 110 degrees C. Remove from heat and stir gently over a basin of warm water until it becomes cloudy. Dip and drain fruit, then cool in the oven. Use sugar cubes or granulated sugar for the best results. *Larousse Gastronomique* (Paul Hamlyn, 1966) recommends no more than 300 ml of water to every 2 kilos of sugar – this means it is barely moistened – but experiment for the best results. Shake the pot but do not stir the sugar during cooking.

Dried

Leaving fruit on hurdles to dry in the sun or threading it on strings in the open air is fraught with problems. If your oven is sensitive enough, it's safer in our climate to dry fruit very slowly at around 80 degrees C. The best results will come from thin and well spaced out slices. The fruit can be treated with a stock syrup first if required. Make this by bringing 550g of sugar and a litre of water to the boil for five minutes.

Handy types could make a dehydrator with a box and a light bulb of a wattage to heat the box to between 63 and 71 degrees C, but the rest of us might find spending about $150 on a dehydrator easier and will probably give better results.

Jams, Jellies and Conserves

Fruit can also be turned into jam (see page 204) or jellies. Chose ripe but not overripe fruit, as this tends to have less pectin, the essential element for setting. To boost pectin levels add 250 g of tart apples or quinces, or two tablespoons of lemon juice, for every 1.5 kg of fruit.

Remember to check for the correct pectin levels for setting before adding sugar and that too much sugar will inhibit setting. The pectin level can be checked by adding a tablespoon of metho to a glass containing a teaspoon of the cooled cooked fruit liquid. If the fruit forms a single lump, the pectin level is good and will take up to 1 cup of sugar for each cup of fruit.

The secret for clear jellies is to strain the fruit slowly and without squeezing after bringing it to the boil slowly with enough water so the fruit just floats, and simmering it very gently.

When To Look For The Fruit – A Rough Guide

Apples	Feb–Dec	Pineapples	Dec–April
Cherries	Nov–Dec	Apricots	Dec–early Feb
Mangoes	Nov –Dec	Nectarines	Jan–March
Strawberries	Nov–Feb	Plums	Dec–March
Blackberries	Dec–Jan	Figs	Mar–April
Blueberries	Dec–Jan	Kiwi fruit	May–Oct
Raspberries	Dec–Mar	Pears	Mar–Dec
Peaches	Dec–April		

Always check with your local grower, market or greengrocer to find out what's best this season and whether each fruit is early or late.

Originally published in 'Epicure', The Age, 2001

SOME THOUGHTS ON
EATING BURGERS

This year marks an important anniversary: the centenary of the hamburger. According to fast-food lore, the hamburger made its first public appearance at the St. Louis World's Fair in 1904 at 'Old Dave's Hamburger Stand'. Texan Fletch Davis sold a simple grilled ground beef patty served between two slices of freshly baked bread, with mustard-flavoured mayonnaise, sliced onion and cucumber pickles. This is surely the perfect excuse to rush out and order 'one with the lot'.

Dig a little deeper, and you'll find that the hamburger's provenance is somewhat muddier.

The good people of Hamburg have been frying up patties of pounded or minced beef since before the 1800s, and with the waves of German immigration to the US it is no surprise that the dish of hamburger steak was known in the US well before 1904. In fact, New York's Delmonico's restaurant had patties of fried minced 'hamburger steak' on the menu in 1826.

Old Dave's claim to having the first true hamburger because it was the first served between toasted bread or a bun is also hotly disputed by the likes of US hamburger researcher Linda Stradley. She reveals claims of hamburgers served on the transatlantic voyage from Hamburg to New

York in the 1850s. There are also reports of hamburger sandwiches sold with a fried egg on top at the Hamburg docks in 1860s.

In the US, there are incidents of ground beef patties being sold between bread in 1885 at both the Outagamie County Fair and the Erie County Fair in Hamburg, New York. The latter was apparently flavoured with spices, brown sugar and coffee. Oklahoma lays claims to the first burgers served in a bun – sold there by Oscar Weber Bilby on Independence Day, 1891.

Whatever the truth, one thing is beyond dispute: Melbourne is in the grip of burger fever with a new generation of 'healthy' burger joints seeking to become the next mega franchise success to rival juice bars.

Some Thoughts (Okay, Rules) on Burgers 'With the Lot'

The Master Rule of a burger is that YOU must think it tastes great. Nothing else really matters. This may change depending on your mood, your biorhythms or the time of day, but a truly great burger reconfirms its greatness whenever you try it.

Having said that, here are the guidelines I have drawn up by analysing some of the best burgers:

1. The ratio of meat to bun and filling is vital. Each bite should have meat and bun in it.
2. The meat must be beef, obviously (a veggie or chicken burger with the lot is acceptable but these are not real 'burgers with the lot'). This is not a semantic issue. The patty itself is a totally personal issue in terms of how lean it is, whether it's thick or thin, how it has been flavoured (herbs, spices and seasoning should always accentuate the taste of the meat), and the coarseness of the grind. I prefer a roughly minced burger.
3. A slight smokiness from bacon or the cooking process is welcome.
4. A burger has a toasted bun. With no top and bottom bun it is not a burger but a 'fuckarcher' or a sandwich.
5. Onions add savour but should provide sweetness, whether they

are slightly caramelised brown or red onions. Sweetness can also come from pickles, fried tomato, beetroot or sauce – also assuming rule 9 is observed.

6. The contrast of textures is important: the crunch of lettuce, the bun's toasted surface and hot plate-tanned edges of meat against the gooiness of cheese and egg, with the yielding fleshiness of the tomato.

7. The presence of freshness to balance the richness of meat, cheese and bacon is vital, whether it's through the crunch of lettuce or the sour edge of pickled beetroot. Slices of dill pickle can do both jobs.

8. The tomato can be thick and cooked or sliced thinly (but only if it is a good tomato). A bad tomato should always be grilled and never there for its crunchy texture.

9. Beetroot is un-Victorian. It's sort of thing they do where they play league, but I am not against it in your larger, two-patty burger. Pineapple is the sort of thing Queenslanders – maybe – do, but admittedly some Victorians do like Noosa for a holiday.

10. The sauce should subtly accentuate the burger, not dominate the taste. Sauce smeared on a bun not properly toasted can lead to an unwelcome sliminess as the bread breaks down with the moisture. The bacon is the same: it must be well cooked.

11. The egg is a tricky one given the exploding-yolk risk. Less confident places 'wreck 'em' so the yolk smears into the white; the more confident use a egg ring or pan and time things perfectly.

12. Leaving the bacon and tomato slices whole may look great but you are going to be eating this, not taking photos of it. There is an interesting trend in non-gourmet places to cut up the bacon, and less commonly the tomatoes, so that when you take a bite the whole rasher of bacon doesn't come out, destroying the stability of the burger and bringing the rest of the filling with it.

There could be a whole chapter on the rules of how a burger should be properly layered, but suffice to say that those choices significantly impact on the burger's performance. Personally I like the salad under the meat and the onions, cheese, bacon, sauce, egg, etc. on top.

If you don't agree with any of these criteria please send your irate comments to someone in Iceland.

Parts of this piece originally published in 'Epicure', The Age, *and* Melbourne Weekly Bayside, *2004–2008*

IN SEARCH OF THE PERFECT SLICE

There are few things more proudly Australian than the slice. England's Elizabeth David ignores them and they don't feature in Delia Smith's books. There's nothing between 'slash' and 'slivovitz' in the *Larousse Gastronomique* or between 'skyr' and 'slipcote' in *The Oxford Companion to Food*. Mrs Beeton doesn't even mention them in the 'new edition' of her *All About Cookery* and Tish Boyle's US cookie bible *The Good Cookie* has recipes for springerle cookies, snickerdoodles, and stroopwafels but not one for slices.

Yet turn to those arks of the Australian culinary spirit, the spiral-bound cookery books produced by CWAs, church groups or country charities, and treasured family recipes for slices abound.

It's no surprise then that the humble slice can also be read as a culinary, or even cultural, identifier of Australia's Anglo-Celtic heritage. It is the *spanokopita* or homemade salami of generations of Smiths, Jones and O'Briens, if you will. This is perhaps part of the reason that many Australians find there is something rather reassuring about a slice.

The beauty about a slice is that it is not as ostentatious as baking a cake for visitors, yet it says you've made so much more of an effort than just knocking up a batch of biscuits.

What makes slices even better is that they needn't be that much more work – or so my brains trust tells me. As with most brains trusts, this one relies on the wisdom of experience. And to search out great slice recipes one must consult with one's elders. They alone know which recipes are sure-fire winners and which have been passed on with flaws – booby traps to derail the unwary slice novice. So over the last year and a half, like *The Producers*' disreputable Max Bialystock, I have ventured out not in search of 'checkies' but something much more valuable: recipes for great slices. Here is a selection of the less lurid and best received ones that I've found. These are not fancy or highfalutin recipes – just slices that go perfectly with a cup of tea and an open fire.

JEANETTE'S COCONUT DATE SLICE

It's very simple, but this unbaked slice is so good it started this slice quest almost two years ago when Epicure's editor, baking guru Kylie Walker, first tasted it. The main thing to remember is to cook the dates slowly and not boil them or their sugar will turn into a binding agent strong enough to crack the teeth of a carthorse.

Ingredients
1 cup / 125 g dates
½ cup / 125 g sugar
90 g butter
4 cups Rice Bubbles
2 cups coconut

Method
In a large, heavy-bottomed saucepan, slowly simmer together the dates, sugar and butter until the dates are soft and mushy (about 15 minutes). You can chop the dates first but it is not necessary. When it is done, the cooked mush will taste fudgy. Do not cook too long or too hot or else the caramel may burn, become bitter or set rock hard. Add the Rice Bubbles and stir in well. Press the mixture into a small Swiss roll tin so

the mixture is about 4 centimetres thick. Put in refrigerator for 2 hours. Cut into cubes and roll in coconut.

I know it's a bit cheesy but another great version of this slice is to melt four Mars Bars with 125 g / 4 oz of butter and then mix that through four cups of Rice Bubbles. Press the mixture into a pan, set and when cold finish by drizzling lines of melted chocolate over – if you can be bothered.

JUDY'S GINGER SLICE

Ingredients

Slice

250 g / 8 oz butter

125 g / 4 oz caster sugar

250 g / 8 oz plain flour

2 teaspoons baking powder

2 teaspoons ground ginger

1 teaspoon finely grated lemon rind

Ginger Icing

2 teaspoons golden syrup

2 tablespoons butter

1 teaspoon ground ginger

6 tablespoons icing sugar

Method

Preheat oven to 170 degrees C. Cream together butter and sugar. Add dry ingredients and mix to a dry dough. Press into a 23 cm × 23 cm (9″ × 9″) lamington tin. Bake until risen and cooked through. Top with ginger icing when cold. To make the icing, mix all the ingredients together and spread on slice.

For a zingier ginger taste you could add a little juice extracted from grated and squeezed ginger, but be careful. Too much will make the slice unpleasantly bitter.

THE BUS DRIVER'S MOTHER-IN-LAW'S ALMOND HONEY SLICE

One of the perks of taking a bus up the Hume Highway is a certain bus driver on the Euroa line and the slices that her mother-in-law makes. This recipe, recently shared, has been making the rounds and it's a cracker.

Ingredients

Base

90 g / 3⅛ oz melted butter
½ cup / 121 g firmly packed brown sugar
1 cup / 155 g plain flour
½ cup / 70 g ground almonds

Almond Topping

125 g / 4 oz butter, chopped
¼ cup / 94 g honey
1½ cups / 200 g slivered almonds

Method

Preheat oven to 170 degrees C. Combine the base ingredients and mix well. Press into a 20 cm × 30 cm (8″ × 12″) greased lamington tray and bake for 12 minutes until browned. While the slice is cooling, make the almond topping. Combine butter and honey in a small heavy-based saucepan. Stir over heat until butter is melted, then simmer uncovered for about 3 minutes or until mixture is a light caramel colour. Stir in nuts.

Spread base with hot topping and return to the oven for about 15 minutes or until golden brown. Cool in the pan.

COCONUT ROUGH SLICE

Our old neighbour used to talk wistfully about her memories of this slice and eventually I chased down this recipe from an early seventies cookbook. The use of coconut makes this a quintessentially Australian slice.

Ingredients

Base

3 teaspoons cocoa (something nice and rich and Dutch)

1 cup self-raising flour

good pinch of salt

⅓ cup / 85 g / 3 oz caster sugar

¼ cup / 28 g / 1 oz dessicated coconut

115 g / 4 oz butter, melted

Topping

3 tablespoons condensed milk

1 tablespoon cocoa

1 cup / 125 g / 4⅜ oz icing sugar

30 g / 1 oz butter

1 cup / 110 g / 4 oz dessicated coconut

1 teaspoon vanilla extract

Method

Preheat oven to 160 degrees C. Sift cocoa, flour and salt for the base into a bowl. Add sugar and coconut, followed by the melted butter. Mix together. Press into an 18 cm × 28 cm (7″ × 11″) greased lamington tin and bake for 25 minutes. Cool on a wire rack but add the topping while the slice is still warm. To make the topping, mix all the ingredients together and spread the mixture all over the base. Dust with icing sugar or drizzle with melted chocolate, and cut into long fingers.

THE GARIBALDI

This fruity slice, apparently originally baked as hard rations for Giuseppe Garibaldi's Red Shirts in 1860 while they were unifying Italy, blurs the line between a biscuit and a slice. Even blurrier is the name. Some suggest that the Garibaldi actually got its name because it looked as pitted as Garibaldi's complexion, while by 1909 H. G. Wells was writing about them as 'squashed flies' – the name by which they are more commonly known today. My friend food writer Necia Wilden tells me that in Adelaide, Garibaldi biscuits are known as 'fly cemeteries'.

Ingredients

½ cup / 76 g currants

½ cup / 100 g raisins

1½ cups / 250 g sultanas

1 tablespoon muscat (or sherry)

2 sheets frozen shortcrust pastry (24.5 cm × 24.5 cm)

¼ cup / 68 g / 2 oz sugar, for sprinkling

1 egg

Method

Preheat the oven to 180 degrees C. Chop the fruit. If you use a food processor, add the muscat at this stage. Lay the pastry onto a greased and lined baking tray or Swiss roll tin, say 26 cm × 32 cm (10″ × 12″). (You can roll it out longer if you want a high fruit ratio with each bite.) Spread the dried fruit evenly spread across the pastry and splash with muscat (if you haven't added it already). Place another sheet of pastry over the top. Using your hand, press down on the pastry to eliminate air pockets. Crimp the edges of the pastry together, then score the top of pastry sheet into separate tiles, prick with a fork and brush with a roughly beaten egg. Sprinkle with sugar. Blast in the oven for about ten minutes, then reduce the temperature to 160 degrees C for about 20 minutes or until the biscuits have browned up. Cool on a wire rack.

MATRIMONIALS

While the concept of the slice appears unknown in the US and the UK, there are some recipes from those parts that are too fancy for a biscuit and still not a cake. The American chocolate brownie is one example. This old English recipe is another. It draws inspiration from a classic crumble topping but can be a little dusty, so I've increased the amount of butter used. In Canada they replace the jam with a mush of stewed dates, while Australian recipes for matrimonials often add coconut. A far better idea is to substitute 70 g of the oats with a similar weight (i.e. four) Weetbix instead. The name is supposed to have been inspired by the roughness of this slice with the occasional splash of sweetness. Like any marriage, success of these matrimonials is based on the exacting balance of all the ingredients.

Ingredients

355 g / 12½ oz plain flour
250 g / 8 oz cold butter, cubed
295 g /10½ oz rolled oats
240 g / 8½ oz soft brown sugar
355 g / 12½ oz jam (blackberry, raspberry or strawberry)

Preheat oven to 170 degrees C. Sift the flour into a mixing bowl. Add the cold butter, and using the tips of the fingers work it into the flour until you have a crumble-like texture. Stir in the oats, sugar and, if you are using them, the broken-up Weetbix. Press about half the mixture into a 28 cm × 18 cm (11″ × 7″) pan that's at least 4 cm (2″) deep. Spread the jam over the base. (Warming the jam slightly will make it easier to spread evenly.) Top with the remaining mixture so it completely covers the jam and press down lightly. Bake for half an hour – or until they are browned. Cool in the pan before cutting into squares.

JENNIFER'S FLAPJACKS

Here's a family recipe that eclipses the version espoused by the Sassenachs and proves the Australian slice's link to its Celtic antecedents. We know it is originally a Scottish recipe, because the English use to tease Scots that their staple grain, the oat, was only fit for English horse feed. The secret of this flapjack recipe lies in using demerara sugar, rather than brown sugar, for its less molassesey flavour. Oh, and in not adding any sultanas, as some philistines do. These flapjacks are no relation to the US dish of the same name, which are thick fluffy breakfast pancakes.

Ingredients

115 g / 4 oz demerara sugar

170 g / 6 oz butter

1 rounded teaspoon golden syrup (preferably a pale one like
    Tate and Lyle)

230 g / 8 oz rolled oats

Method

Preheat oven to 170 degrees C. Over a medium heat, combine the sugar, butter and golden syrup. Stir in the oats. Press into a greased 18 cm × 28 cm (11″ × 7″) slice tin.

Bake for about 20 minutes or until it's golden brown. Let it cool and then cut tiles.

Must Do's When Baking Slice

- Always have a pot of tea on the go.
- Warm the oven to the correct temperature before popping in the slice.
- Grease the pan with butter and line it with greaseproof baking paper.
- All spoon measurements are for a spoon levelled off with a knife, not a heaped spoon – unless specified.

- Cup measurements are for loosely filled cups rather than 'packed' cups.
- You'll note that all the recipes use different tin sizes, which is undoubtedly a conspiracy by cake tin manufacturers. Generally, though, so long as the surface area of your tin is about the same you should be right. Just keep an eye on the slice when it is cooking, because the different dimensions can alter your cooking times slightly.
- When in doubt, cool in the pan.
- If you like any of these recipes, pass them on to your friends.

Originally published in 'Epicure', The Age, 2004

SWEET SURRENDER

In the boiling house we found a Negro at each copper attending to the boiling and skimming of the cane juice. What with the steam and the ladling and splashing and the calling of the firemen outside to regulate the fire it recalled the preacher's vision of hell.

Visitor to Mount Healthy, a Tortolan Sugar
Refinery in the Caribbean, 1830

The Caribbean

Through thickets and barbed vines I've pushed to find this pile of rubble. Here in the shadow of Mount Healthy I stand among the wreckage of an old boiling house, hidden amongst broken palm fronds and rotting coconuts. Here is the succession of raised copper bowls, still snugly housed in brick, beneath which the fires once burned. The coppers are rotten now, palms growing up through the rusty metal. In the surrounding jungle lie old rum stills, toppled like elephants that have reached their end. It's an eerie place, but then the story of sugar is home to many, many ghosts.

Sugar reached the Caribbean with the Spanish. It is recorded that Columbus, whose mother-in-law owned cane fields in the Madeiran Archipelago, first planted cane on Santo Domingo in 1493.

Sugar was the ideal crop, as it thrived in the tropics and could be grown by unskilled labour on the same spot over and over without exhausting the soil. More importantly, it was high yielding, high priced and growing in European popularity.

Its position was secured when other leading powers, like England and France, who were jostling for control of the Americas, were supplied with the stolen secrets of sugar production by the Dutch, who hoped to stimulate trade. The Dutch even offered some settlers credit against their first crop to buy rollers and coppers.

The trade, however, wasn't just in industrial products. It was also in souls. Sugar production was labour intensive, and slavery, which had long existed in West Africa for prisoners and debtors, provided a cruel solution. Over three centuries 10 million Africans were landed alive in the Americas as slaves. Many were destined for the cane field and the boiling house. Yet as many again may have died en route or in the slave *barracoons*, or trading forts, along Africa's west coast.

Slavery had many long-reaching implications, but culinarily the desire to feed slaves cheaply saw Captain William Bligh dispatched to search for the breadfruit and achee that are still staples in Caribbean cuisine today. The plantations also provided a market for low-grade salt cod from New England and Canada. The steel barrels it arrived in, when not turned into drums, returned full of molasses – hence the growth of New England's rum trade and the prevalence of molasses in dishes like Boston Baked Beans.

The slave trade had helped foster sugar, yet sugar provided one of the most persuasive arguments for slavery's abolition. In 1792, Abolitionists – and the East India Company, which was using hired labour for its rival Indian sugar production – pointed out that a family consuming five pounds of Caribbean sugar a week would kill a slave every 21 months. In 1833, emancipation was declared and came into force a year later.

Europe's dependence on the tropics for sugar had already started to wane with the discovery of a European-grown source of sugar. In 1811, starved of Caribbean cane sugar due to the blockades from the Napoleonic War, the French discovered sugar could be refined from beets. As both sugars were pretty much pure sucrose, any differences were indistinguishable to the human palate.

The story of sugar began some 11,000 years earlier, when the sweet grass now known as sugar cane first grew on the rich volcanic coastal plains of New Guinea. Its sweetness was one attraction; another was its ease of propagation. Stick a short-cut length of cane in the ground and it will grow. This helped sugar spread north-west to India, where it appears to have been widely grown and its juice reduced into sticky balls of *gur* by 500 BC. Sugar experts like Peter Macinnis suggest, however, that the Indians might have learnt these basic refining techniques from the Indonesians. One thing is not in doubt: that it is from the Sanskrit word for 'grain' – *carkara* or *shakkara* – that sugar gets its European and African names.

From India, sugar and sugar cane reached China and the Middle East. It became a high-priced commodity traded alongside pepper, ginger and cinnamon, and provided an alternative to traditional sweeteners like honey or syrups made from sorghum, figs or dates. Its sweet beguiling message then rode on the back of the spread of Islam and was finally taken home by the Crusaders, who created a ready market throughout Europe.

Back then, rollers driven by wind, water or draught animals crushed the cane. The resulting juice was boiled down, clarified to remove impurities and boiled some more until crystals started to form. Then it was left to dry out.

Yarraville

A month later I'm standing in Sugar Australia's refinery in Yarraville, which has been processing sugar for 130 years. Where once a thousand people worked, automation has taken over, and a team of only six now oversees all the sugar refining.

According to Sugar Australia's general manager of operations, Glenn Cohen, the process has changed quite a bit over the years. They no longer purify the sugar with char – burnt animal bones – and those pans are under vacuum so the evaporation of water and the crystallisation of the sucrose can happen at a lower temperature.

South African sugar cane arrived in Australia with the First Fleet in 1788. Initially it was a failure, according to sugar historian Robert F. McKillop, but by 1885 there were 102 mills in New South Wales and 166 in Queensland. This growth had been fuelled by legislation like the 1862 Coolie Act, which allowed plantation owners to recruit cheap indentured labour. This practice was commonplace globally after emancipation and accounts in part for the Indian populations in Fiji and Natal, as well as the Japanese in Hawaii. In Queensland it was Melanesian workers who were 'recruited'.

Australia's warm and temperate climate produces some of the finest sugar cane on earth, but it needs to be processed with 24 hours of harvesting or it 'goes off'. Sugar Australia's general manager of sales and marketing, Ed Leibel, explains that's why you'll find over 26 mills in Queensland operating during a harvest season that runs from June to November, crushing the cane from Queensland's 6500 or so cane farms. The resulting liquid, which is 67 per cent solids and 33 per cent water, is heated and centrifuged to evaporate away the water and separate out the majority of the impurities. These 'impurities' take the form of molasses, which goes into animal feed or is fermented to make rum.

The majority of the output from the mills is an industrial-grade raw sugar that is 98.5 per cent sucrose but still includes some impurities like molasses. The sugar destined for further purification is stored in silos at ports like Mackay until needed by the refineries down south.

Some is processed under food-grade conditions and sold under the 'raw sugar' label. The majority of other brown sugars on the Australian market are made from re-adding syrup (molasses or caramel) to caster sugar at a final processing stage.

The tradition of having the final refining stage close to the end consumer rather than to the fields is one that dates back to the Middle Ages. Traditionally, this helped to ensure the quality of the product at the point of purchase and it also allowed colonial masters to ensure that the major profits from sugar resided with them.

The process of refining sugar is simple. The raw sugar is melted, washed and filtered, and then the water is evaporated off until the right size of crystals are formed following the addition of tiny seed sugar crystals. This process is monitored remotely from the Yarraville refinery's control room. It results in pure white sugar that's 99.85 per cent sucrose. The sugar is then sieved: the larger particles are bagged as white sugar, the smaller crystals are labelled caster sugar. This name dates back to the 'caster' or sugar shaker that this finer sugar was served in at the table.

London

Globally, the sugar market is in decline, but there is a trend towards unrefined sugars, says Billington's Export Manager Caroline Hemming over a London pint that's as brown as their dark muscovado. The British company is the world's biggest importer and exporter of unrefined sugars, which retain impurities like molasses rather than removing and later re-adding them.

Unrefined sugars may only represent 10 to 16 per cent of the UK retail market, but Hemming still sees this as a sign of an awakening food culture. 'It's a natural product. We keep the molasses in our sugars and this carries a lot of vitamins and minerals like calcium, potassium and iron. I think a lot of people feel cheated when they realise their sugar has been sprayed brown.'

While sugar refineries in Australia, the US and Europe strive for consistent purity, Billington's welcomes a product that changes from year to year, depending on the climate. 'After a dry season our golden granulated will be darker, while the density and the taste of our light muscovado will change from year to year,' Hemming explains.

Listening to Hemming talk, it is perhaps surprising that sugar marketeers haven't gone down the salt road and created more boutique brands. Where's the 'fleur du sucre' or the vintage date on every pack? That's something to ponder as you lift a spoonful of sugar, whether it be Mauritius demerara, Yarraville white or Barbados muscovado, to sprinkle on your Wheaties.

The Sweet Facts and Figures

According to Sugar Australia, we produce about 1 million tonnes of sugar a year. Of this, 20 per cent is exported, 50 per cent finds its way into food and drink production, 10 per cent goes to the food service industry and 20 per cent – with a street value of about $153 million – goes to retail. Over the last five years, white sugar's share of retail sales has dropped to 64.3 per cent, down 1.6 per cent in favour of specialty sugars (14.3 per cent) and raw sugar (21.4 per cent), according to AC Nielsen figures.

Sugars are soluble carbohydrates produced by many living things as a method of energy storage. They come in many forms and can be made of a single molecule or two; the disaccharides include maltose and lactose (milk sugar). The most culinarily common is sucrose, a molecule of glucose combined with a molecule of fructose. Polysaccharides are usually molecules of glucose bound together and found as starch in some root vegetables.

Sugars have differing levels of sweetness. Lactose and galactose, which is hydrolysed from lactose, are less sweet than sucrose. Fructose or laevulose, which is found in fruit or honey, is about 75 per cent sweeter.

The average Australian consumes 46 kg of sugar a year. The majority is not naturally occurring in foods but added by us or by food processors. While sugars may be absorbed differently, all sugars eventually break down in the body and end up as glucose.

Originally published in 'Epicure', The Age, 2003

THE SECRET LIFE OF
PANCAKES

It's a frightful shame that our history and our pagan past mean that it's only around Easter that pancakes have been afforded their rightful position in the pantheon of Great Things To Eat.

Of course it is fitting that the noble pancake should be the celebratory food for Shrove Tuesday in England, at Candlemass in France or during Maslensita festivities in Russia. The idea that something so silken, so delicious, could come from no more than a batter of eggs, flour and milk is the sort of magical transubstantiation that everyone can believe in, no matter what their religious position.

Not that this whole pancake thing is the invention of a contemporary belief system. Once again, the connection with Christian holydays is thanks to the smarts of the earliest clerics, who overlaid their religion onto existing pagan beliefs. In this case, they rebadged the old pagan celebrations of mid-winter (such as the Celtic Imbolc or Oimelc, or Maslenitsa), when sacrifices were made and feasts were held to ensure there would be a good crop in the coming year and that the current supplies would last until that next harvest. The rebirth of the earth and the return of the sun were also heralded. Surely it is more than just a coincidence that the perfect pancakes or blintzes we eat at this time of year are golden circles.

The versatility of the batter means it can take many forms. The Dutch turn it into those little *pooojoofferpooffeers*, or whatever those little pancakes sold at every Australian country fair are called. The New Zealanders have pikelets, the Moroccans their *beghrirs* and the Welsh have their *crempog* or *ffroes*, which some etymologists suggest might show that this version of pan- or griddle-fried, flour-and-egg-thickened batter might have inspired the first crumpet.

Of course the pancake is not only a Northern European thing – it's just that other cultures are far happier to eat them through the year. In Eastern Europe, *blintzes* and *palatschinken* vie for the title of the most famous pancake cousin – the Austrian *palatschinken* distinguishing itself by often being made with beaten egg whites for a lighter texture. *Blintzes* also share religious connections, featuring as treats at *Chanukah* or *Shavuot*.

In the US and Canada, a stack of thick fluffy pancakes made with buttermilk and served with maple syrup is a common breakfast, whether with bananas or berries, or best of all fried eggs and crispy bacon interlaced between the layers. In Japan, the savoury *okonomiyaki* is known as Osaka soul food, while the Swedes eat pancakes with pea soup and the Italians wrap them round spinach and ricotta to make cannelloni. And where would Peking duck be without those pancakes – other that bouncing down your shirt-front coated in that sticky brown sauce!

In fact, the pancake is the one dish that binds the world's people, even if they might omit or substitute one of those three key ingredients. There's the Vietnamese *Banh Xeo*, the South Indian *dosa* made with ground lentil and rice flour rather than wheat, or that Ethiopian staple *injera*, traditionally made with millet flour, which acts as their bread to scoop up curries. Just like the best pancakes, the batter for *injera* and *dosai* is left to stand to allow the flavour and texture to develop.

And anyone who has settled down to a plate of *papusas* in El Salvador will feel their relationship to the pikelet or the thick pancake, if not to France's thinner and more lacy *crêpe* or Brittany's *galette*.

For me, however, is in this thinner and more delicate *crêpe* form that I worship at the griddle one Saturday a month. It's only once a month because good family pancake-making is a furiously messy business where as much of the flour and batter ends up on me and my three small children as it does in the pan. This makes the clean-up a good three-week process.

The most reliable recipe I've found comes from Margaret Fulton's *Encyclopaedia of Food and Cookery*. It's just one egg, one cup of flour, one teaspoon of baking powder, one and half cups of milk, and a little salt and melted butter.

Just sift all the dry ingredients into a bowl, then drop the wet ingredients into a well made in the middle of them. Mix the ingredients together, slowly at first but then with increasing vigour. Then let the batter stand for an hour (if you can wait that long).

Transfer the batter to a jug and pour enough into a hot, heavy and oiled skillet to coat. Cook on both sides.

Remember, the first pancake you make will be rubbish. This is a universal truth that has resulted in the good people of Brie in France always giving the first pancake to the hen who laid the eggs for it.

Serve and eat each one straight from the pan rather than keeping them warm on top of each together They are never as good that way and tend to get flannelly. Frankly, pancakes are best eaten as a solitary delight – even when eating as a group.

For a perfect savoury pancake breakfast, there's loads of inspiration out there, whether it's a Vietnamese pork and shrimp combination, a fresh Asian herb salad, or even cauliflower. In the Lazio region outside Rome they have a cauliflower pancake festival each year. If you are looking for something more epic, serve your pancakes wrapped around good beef or pork sausage and then drizzle them with maple syrup and a goodly twist of black pepper.

But for me it has to be folding the pancake, once it is cooked on one side, over a filling of spinach and a gooey melting cheese like fontina, stracchino or a little gruyère.

For something sweet, you could once again play on an Italian theme and roll your pancakes around a filling of ricotta spiked with a little lemon zest, then dust with icing sugar. Or make like the English and drizzle them with jam or marmalade that you've warmed until it's runny. Add some Drambuie or Cointreau and a squeeze of lemon juice or orange juice while melting the marmalade for a breakfast take on *crèpes Suzette*. I'd dollop cream on too, because it is safe to say that if you are eating these pancakes for breakfast that's the day the diet's gone out the window anyway.

For all this, it's still hard to beat a fresh pancake out of the pan squeezed with lemon juice and sprinkled with a little caster sugar. Now that's perfect.

Originally published in 'A2', The Age, 2009

TRAILER-TRASH
COCKTAILS

Fast food, sticky fizzy drinks and bad parenting are the trinity most often cited for the crime of Australia's growing childhood obesity 'epidemic'. Quite frankly, I'd happily support a ban on all of them, even though, for the sake of full disclosure, I'd better admit that I am guilty of indulging in all of them on occasion.

The fast food and bad parenting both usually tend to be cases of momentary weakness, but I have to admit that my indulging in 'pop' is far more regular and far more considered. The thing is, I have a bit of a yen for the way sweet fizzy drinks have been incorporated in to boozing cultures around the world.

While the birth of alcopops has been largely, and quite rightly, derided in Australia, there is a long and valiant history of adding fizzy drinks to alcohol to create a refreshing libation. It's a tradition that goes far further, and into far more exotic locations, than the true Aussie talent of splashing Bundy or bourbon with Coke – a combination that owes much to the classic Cuba Libre.

The inhabitants of the south of England are derided by northerners as 'softy southern shandy drinkers' for their habit of adding lemonade to their lager. In France, adding white wine to your lemonade creates a *blanc lime*, which is a bit like one of those lemon Ruskies minus the vodka – a drink that was itself inspired by a refreshing cocktail popular in the cafés of south-west France last century, made with herbs, lime juice and soda added to white wine.

The French also have a strong tradition in their more basic bars of adulterating their beer with sweet syrups in the same way that a shot of raspberry cordial might be added to a pint of lager in England or to the vodka lemonades of young women in Gold Coast nightclubs. The addition of grenadine makes *un tango*; lemonade makes *un panache* (a Gallic shandy) and most frightening of all is *un valse*, which is the ugly combination of beer and a mint syrup that brings back awful teenage memories of beer with crème de menthe depth charges.

It is the Spanish, however, who are the experts at adding soft drinks to wine to create some truly unique combinations. I've spent long, hot nights in the docks of Barcelona when 50-cent local red rot-gut has been rendered almost drinkable by the addition of lemonade to create a sort of low-rent *sangria*. In the Basque country there's also a variation made by mixing red wine and fizzy orangeade in equal quantities, which brings to mind the habit in some Chilean families of serving children a little red wine mixed with orange juice. Yet all of these seem quite normal combinations when compared with the daddy of all red wine and fizzy drink combos – the *kalimotxo*.

I discovered this oddly alluring combination of red wine and cola over a particularly long and hot summer with a Spanish school friend. It was perfect to drink while mooching around beachside car parks with cool, stolen, all-white Ducados dangling from our lips. The harsh black tobacco might have clawed at our teenage throats, but the sweet mix of cask red and supermarket cola soothed them. Little did we know back then that we were pre-empting the Spanish teenage trend of gathering for impromptu open-air parties, or *botellones*, which grew up as a sort of 'mobbing' phenomenon in the nineties. *Kali* – how fitting that the diminutive for *kalimotxo* is the same as the name for the Hindu goddess of destruction – was the drink of choice at these gatherings, too, because it's cheap, easy to drink, easy to procure and, of course, alcoholic. The traditional way to drink *kali* at such parties is to buy a two-litre bottle of Coke, pour half of it away, fill the empty space with cheap red wine and mix.

I'd never advise drinking this, given the pain of the ensuing bonce-crunching hangover, as well as the acts of gross sugar-rush-and-red-wine-fuelled stupidity that you might commit and then have to face up to in the morning. Having said that, next time you are rustling up a few dishes from Frank Camorra's MoVida cookbook for friends, why not treat your guests to this most trailer-trash of cocktails? Just serve it in small glasses with crushed ice. Add a slice of lime, or even a splash of blackberry liqueur (such as a cassis like *crème de mure*), if you want to be unnecessarily fancy.

You'll find it's actually a surprisingly refreshing tipple: the acidity of the cheap red is mellowed by the sweetness of the cola and it all slips down rather well. You might also note how flavour notes in the cola such as lavender, cinnamon or vanilla may well echo in the wine – especially if the wine has been treated with new American oak. Or at least that's the justification you can give your wine snob friends for making them drink it!

If your guests are more cultural, then point out that *kali* reached mainstream popularity in Spain during the late seventies but reportedly originated at a street festival in Getxo outside Bilbao in 1972. Now it has spread across Europe and on into Latin America; it is known in Chile as the 'black-headed vulture', as 'mushroom' in the Czech Republic and as 'bamboo' in Croatia.

Oh, and then you can initiate a discussion about which came first – the alcopop or the binge-drinking teenager. And if it was the latter, then whether this makes the act of big business launching sweetened booze for the young a more, or a less, cynical act.

Originally published in 'A2', The Age, 2009

PRESERVING KNOWLEDGE

My mother made jam. My grandmother made jam. And so it stretches back. My memories of preserving are the distant impressions of fingers and lips stained from blackberries that would never make it to the bramble jelly pot and of the grazes from scrabbling up fruit trees to pick Victoria and Damson plums, their burgundy coats dusted with the faintest white bloom. Oh, and digging the spoon into a shimmering jar that had captured the soul of the season to spread it, a glossy blue-red carpet, across a thick underlay of butter melting on bread warm from the oven.

It is to my eternal regret, however, that I never paid much attention to the bit in between the gathering and the eating. The bit where the jam was actually made.

Now I have children of my own, and I want to know that what they eat is free from preservatives and processing. I want to make my own jam. I want to pass that knowledge on to them. So I enlist the help of three of Australia's best jam-makers to teach me – Amanda Cunliffe of Cunliffe and Waters, Sarah Locke from Bellbrae Harvest and Jam Lady Jam's Lisa O'Connor.

I pick them because none of the 20 jams, conserves and preserves lingering at the back of my fridge bears their names – perfect proof that their jams are so delicious that they never hang around long.

With a generosity of spirit common amongst custodians of a traditional craft, they open their kitchens to me. What follows is an amalgamation of their wisdom, a sort of idiot's guide to how to make your first jam. How this idiot fared follows later.

Both Lisa and Sarah start my education with a pep talk. 'Jam-making is a lovely therapeutic thing to do, and when you've finished the whole house smells like fruit,' extols Sarah above the noise of the birdsong at the pretty café she runs in the bush north of Bell's Beach.

In front of four bubbling preserving pans at her commercial kitchen in the Yarra Valley, one time botanical artist Amanda Cunliffe tells me that jam-making is not as tricky as one might suspect – assuming you follow the basic steps.

Ex-opera singer Lisa looks me straight in the eye outside the Healesville garage she's converted into a commercial kitchen and gets serious: 'You should be well rested and in a good mood. Set aside a morning to make jam. Buy the fruit and do it that day. The process should happen all at once and very quickly. Don't forget to stir through the edges as the jam often catches there, and remember jam cannot be left alone. It needs constant attention. And most importantly, make sure you have no interruptions, because that is when disasters happen.'

Later, as she tries to stop me stealing her fig jam recipe, her strawberry jam boils over and I realise that teaching me might class as one of those interruptions.

The Background

Jam is fruit preserved with sugar in a gel-like state. The name comes from the old Arabic word for preserved fruit, *jamad*, but the process is comparatively recent.

Originally fruit was preserved in solid paste conserves, preserves and marmalades. The first preserves were bought back to Europe from the Middle East by Crusaders in the Middle Ages – it was the Arab world that had first secured the use of cane sugar from India.

Not that preserving fruit was unknown in the West. The Romans used honey to keep, and to cook, quinces for preserving. However, recipes for jam as we know it today only appear in cookbooks in the 18th century and jam only gained mass popularity when the price of sugar dropped in the 19th century.

The Basics

To make the simplest jam, you cook fruit in a big pot until it has broken down and released its moisture, stirring to ensure the fruit doesn't stick while this is happening. Then traditionally you add the same weight of sugar to the pot (i.e. 1 kilo of sugar for each kilo of raw fruit) and bring it back to a rolling boil, stirring occasionally, in order to thicken the jam without stewing it and thus help it set.

How it sets is dependent on the levels of pectin in the fruit – different fruits contain different levels of pectin. Adding extra acid in the form of lemon juice balances the sugar's sweetness and also aids setting by reducing the pectin molecules' negative charge, so they are keener to attach to each other and create a gel. Lemons are also high in their own pectin.

The jam is ready for bottling when it reaches the gel stage. This is identified by either watching for when the jam mixture drips in pearls from your spoon after cooling, or by putting a large drop of the jam on a cold saucer and placing it in the fridge to cool. If the surface of the drop wrinkles up when you push your finger through it, or the jam resists filling the channel your finger has made, then it is done and should set once bottled in a sealed sterilised jar. If not, cook it a little more, re-testing as you go until the gel or setting stage is achieved. Simple!

Choosing Your First Jam

Raspberries are easy because they need no preparation, but according to Lisa O'Connor fig is the sure-fire winner. 'It seems to set no matter what,' she says.

She counsels avoiding blueberry or apricot first up. 'Blueberries behave like no other fruit. I reckon you have to undercook the jam to get it to set right. Apricots rise quickly but are prone to sticking on the bottom of the pan because they are fibrous, so you have to stir them a lot, otherwise they burn.'

Apricot jam like fig, rhubarb and mango, tends to splatter so Lisa advises wearing long sleeves when making these jams. Also, turn them down before stirring – and use a bigger pot than usual if you can, or less fruit. 'If you get spattered and go to wipe off the jam, the skin comes with it!' she cautions.

Blood plums, like apricots and strawberries, take time to prepare but Amanda Cunliffe reckons they are a great jam to start on. You just need to de-stone and cut up the fruit and then boil it (with the equal weight of sugar) until it starts to feel viscous. Often it doesn't need any added pectin or lemon juice.

Also note that there is no need to cook up great quantities of jam. The biggest batch of fruit that Sarah Locke or Amanda Cunliffe cooks is 4 kilos. In fact, all three jam-makers praise the notion of making even smaller batches at home. 'Two kilos of fruit will give you about ten jars of jam, and there's nothing wrong with doing as little as a one-kilo batch,' Lisa says.

Amanda points out that with larger batches the longer cooking times can give the jam a stewed flavour; Sarah points out that the smaller the quantities, the quicker the fruit will cook and thus the better the colour you'll get. 'Your strawberry jam will be pinky-red and not burgundy red,' she says.

So start simple and start small.

The Fruit

The whole point of making jam was always to preserve the seasons' excess bounty; to make sure that you had some of that fruity joy for the cold barren months of winter. In short, jam-making is all about the fruit.

For this reason Lisa O'Connor suggests using the best you can afford if you want to make great jam. 'All the money I can get goes on Pam Vroland's berries,' she jokes, name-checking Silvan Estate's legendary berry grower.

When it comes to preparing the fruit before cooking, both Lisa and Amanda prefer not to wash it if it comes in clean. As Lisa says, 'Boiling the jam should kill off any nasties' but all our jam-makers use local produce from growers they trust not to spray anything scary on their fruit.

If you do want to wash your fruit, Sarah advises doing it just before you make the jam so you don't risk it going soggy. While some recipes panic about making jam with wet fruit, none of my brains trust were unduly worried. Lisa even adds a little water to her fruit to help it break down and to ensure it doesn't stick.

Amanda also suggests picking firm fruit with good colour and, if making strawberry jam, picking the smallest strawberries you can find. As for raspberries, she prefers to use Serpell's Willamette raspberries because they tend to hold more flesh around the seeds. Lisa, who is a Bogong raspberry fan, suggests mixing different strawberry varieties, like a Pajero for sweetness with a white-fleshed variety that has higher acidity. She is also a fan of adding the fruit in two batches to give some extra body to the final jam.

Pectin

Pectin is what makes your jam set. It is released from the fruits' cell walls in cooking, but not all fruit are created equal in the pectin stakes.

Citrus fuits are high in pectin, as are redcurrants and blackcurrants, tart apples, guava, cranberries and quinces. Most berries (except strawberries) have reasonable levels of pectin – certainly more than apricots, peaches and rhubarb. Cherries and nectarines usually need the most help in setting due to their low pectin levels.

Pectin levels decline as fruit ripens – it's the pectin that actually helps ripe fruit soften – but Amanda Cunliffe has found that they can decline after picking too, especially with strawberries. It's a concern as this is a notoriously fickle jam when it comes to setting. That's why she tries to get fruit picked in the morning and the jam made as soon after that as possible.

The pectin levels of any fruit also fluctuate during the season and from season to season. 'All this makes it very hard to have a recipe and so you have to be flexible and embrace the fact that your jam will seldom be exactly the same season to season,' laughs Lisa.

Sarah Locke suggests picking a mixture of ripe and firmer semi-ripe fruit when making a jam like apricot. 'The softer fruit has less pectin but gives a rich flavour, while the greener fruit tends to have a higher pectin level and adds a little tartness,' she says.

While Lisa O'Connor and Sarah Locke both rely on the pectins in the fruit, Amanda is not averse to the helping hand that dried powdered pectin (refined from fruit high in pectin, like apples) can provide.

'Adding pectin stops a lot of mucking around. We love pectin. Adding pectin means the jams don't have to be reduced for so long to achieve the setting point. Shorter cooking times mean you don't lose that wonderful colour and the fresh flavour of the fruit.'

She initially uses about 35 g of pectin for each kilo of raspberries, added near the end of cooking, but with a low-pectin fruit like blueberries or Morello cherries she'd use twice that amount. 'Stir the jam while adding pectin powder to stop it clumping and don't add too much or you'll end up with a gritty tasting paste,' she advises.

While powdered pectin or jam setters (containing pectin, acid and sugar) are a safety net for the jam maker, Sarah Locke recommends adding a high-pectin fruit like grated apple to your jam to help it set, especially for stone fruit low in pectin. 'It will break down and you won't notice it is there,' she reveals.

Otherwise, just take Lisa O'Connor's rather healthy attitude and don't stress about how firmly your jam sets. 'There is too much emphasis put on setting. I've had criticism because my jam is sometimes runny, but I'd rather a runny jam that tastes of the fruit than those commercial jams that are almost unspreadable and overloaded with sugar.'

She even dismisses the cold saucer test as an old wives' tale. 'Look, you won't be setting your jam in the fridge. I've made jams that passed that setting test but never set in the jar. It's a feeling in the thighs. It is how the paddle moves through the fruit. It's the smell. The way the bubbles move and burst that, after a while, tells you when your jam is ready.'

And if your jam doesn't set, you've still got a beautiful ice-cream topping or a fruit-based glaze or sauce for meat or game!

The Sugar

Sugar is an essential element in any jam because it preserves the fruit. Add your sugar once the fruit has broken down and released much of its juice.

The amount of sugar you use will be affected by various factors, including taste and the jam's ability to set. The traditional ratio for most jams, like plum, apricot and berries like raspberry, is a kilo of fruit to a kilo of sugar. Use less sugar for fruit like pears and strawberries, which are sweeter and have less pectin – Delia Smith suggests a 4:3 fruit to sugar ratio for her strawberry jam.

'Pectin can only hold a limited amount of sugar,' explains O'Connor. 'Too much sugar makes for a terribly sweet jam and one that is runny, so the general rule is match sugar levels to the pectin content of the fruit. For low-pectin fruits like strawberries and pear, use less sugar.'

Lisa suggests that if you are making small batches at home that will be consumed quickly, you should use less sugar so the fruit's flavour comes to the fore. But remember, less sugar will impact on the jam's lifespan, so eat it quickly and keep it in the fridge once opened.

None of our three experts follow the old adage about warming your sugar before adding it to the fruit, citing the power of modern burners as overcoming any issues about the sugar cooling down the cooking jam.

The Equipment

You'll need a pot that is both good at dissipating heat evenly, to help cooking without burning, and that is designed to maximise evaporation during cooking. Driving off the liquid from the fruit helps it set.

Amanda uses slope-sided aluminum French preserving pans. Sarah prefers copper pots. These are more expensive, but she explains that she's found she gets a better, brighter colour cooking the jam in copper.

You can also use any wide saucepan, but remember that your jam will rise up while boiling, so make sure you pick a big pan and leave plenty of headspace.

Lisa also suggests not using your pot for anything other than jam-making and cleaning it without detergent until it shines. 'Just like your fruit, your pot and your utensils must be bright and clean,' says Lisa.

To stir, use a long-handled wooden spoon or paddle, as this can be safely left in the jam during cooking for constant stirring, whereas metal will become dangerously hot. It is also possible to make jam in the microwave or your breadmaker, but it might be sacrilegious. Heretics can find tips on the internet.

The Jars and Filling

While the jam is cooking you'll need to sterilise your jars. You can use a solution with a long chemical name, but less worrisome is the age-old method of heat. Lisa O'Connor pops her jars in the oven, brings the temperature up to 130 degrees C and keeps the jars in there for ten minutes. Sarah immerses all her lids and jars in water, which she then boils for five minutes.

If using the oven, rest the jars on their sides on the oven racks or stand them on a baking tray to make them easier to remove from the oven when hot without contaminating them with your dirty oven glove. Let them rest on a dry bench for a short while before filling. The baking tray will catch the jam drips during filling, but leave enough space on the tray so you can get in between to put the lids on.

Lisa recommends bottling while both jam and jars are hot, not only for the purposes of sterility but also to ensure the savagely hot jam does not crack cold jars. Just let the jam rest off the heat before pouring and if you are really obsessive about clear jam remove any scum from the surface.

Fill past the shoulder of the jar and up the neck, as the jam may shrink back a bit as it cools. Leave the smaller jars until last so you can avoid half-filled jars.

Tighten the lids by hand, always remembering that if the metal jar lid is hot it will contract and tighten further when it cools. If you are really concerned about mould you might want to wipe around the lip of the jar and the inside of the lid with white vinegar first. Sealing when hot should also mean that a vacuum forms in the jar, further helping to protect against spoilage.

For a more old-fashioned look, the jams can be sealed with a layer of wax or waxed paper on the surface and then lidded or covered with a square of cellophane secured by a fine elastic band.

Wipe down the jars and leave them to cool slowly, then store in a cool dark place until needed. After opening, store in the fridge.

When it comes to choosing jars, Amanda Cunliffe favours using smaller jars so the jam spends less time in contact with the air before being eaten and is thus less likely to get 'juicy' (when liquid leaches out) or grow things. Another good tip if making a lot of jam is to pick a square or bevelled-edged jar that will take up less shelf space when stored.

You'll often find cheap collections of jars at op shops but for new jars try glass wholesalers. Alternatively, you could always do what I've done: scrape all those unfinished jams cluttering up the fridge into the bin and use the jars for your own beautiful jams!

How I Fared

The advice of experts is all very well, but when I read in *The Oxford Companion to Food* that perfectly set jam contains 60–65 per cent sugar, between 0.5 and 1 per cent pectin and has a ph level of 2.8–3.4, I get scared. It's a tiny window of opportunity, especially as the sugar, acid and pectin levels of fruit differ not only between species but also from season to season and during the season!

So I ring Mandy Lunney, who a year ago was a novice jam-maker. Together with Marcia Annois, Mary Carter, Di Roderick, Kia Wittner, Bernadette Fenton and Jenny Rapke, she spent a year studying, making and selling jam leading up to the biennial Malvern Central school fête, a huge weekend when they made $6000 clear profit for the school by selling their jam. 'We did it because of each other. If we didn't get on we wouldn't do it,' says Mandy modestly.

Her tips are simple. Do not overcook the jam. Cooking times vary so you have to pay attention. Have patience. And raspberry jam always sells. 'Also, people think any old fruit will do but you must have good produce to make good jam,' Mandy shares.

So I go to the market and buy the best strawberries, raspberries and apricots I can find. I decided to be brave and reduce the traditional sugar quantities as I've watched Lisa O'Connor do.

My Apricot Jams
Recipe
1 kg apricots (some ripe and some slightly green, stones removed)
750 g sugar
75 ml lemon juice

The apricots do spit like buggery and they also stick to the side of the copper as they break down. This means they burn. I have to keep swapping pots to wash off the burnt bits so it doesn't taint the jam. This ceases to be a problem once I add the sugar, and what results is a good firm jam with loads of tartness, thanks to following Sarah's advice on fruit selection.

I also make another apricot jam using the same quantities but the technique of covering the fruit overnight with most of the sugar. The next day I remove the fruit, boil the syrup with the rest of the sugar and then add the fruit, lemon juice and little chunks of preserved ginger. The macerating means the apricot pieces hold their shape and the result is an interesting jam. This macerating technique also works well for strawberries.

My Strawberry Jam
Recipe
2 kg hulled strawberries
750 g sugar
juice of one large lemon (about 75 ml) – I threw the juiced halves in as well to help the set and removed them before bottling

My strawberry jam is a disaster. I panic that I've used too much sugar and that the jam will never set, so I add too much powdered French pectin and cook it for too long. As Amanda promised, I get a strawberry jam that sets like a paste and tastes gritty. Next time I'll take Lisa's attitude and not panic about the setting — a loose syrupy strawberry jam would be far preferable. And I reckon it would have set okay without the extra pectin, dag nab it. I suspect that fear is the enemy of good jam-making.

My Raspberry Jam

Recipe

2 kg raspberries

750 g sugar

juice of one large lemon (about 75 ml) — again I threw the juiced halves in as well

Perfection. Finally I make a jam to make my mentors proud. Clear, sparkling and with a bright colour, it tastes tart and bursts with the flavour of the berries. It is also perfectly set — easy to spread but sitting up on the plate if spooned out. Mission accomplished. Now I want to make loads more and see if I can reduce the sugar quantity further!

Originally published in 'Epicure', The Age, 2007

JAMMING: THREE
YEARS ON

I think Bob Marley said it best in his paean to one of Australia's country pastimes, his song 'Jamming!' Who would have thunk that beneath all those dreadlocks and that pall of ganja smoke beat the heart of a kindred spirit of many a CWA member? Yet jam-making is alive and well, thriving in many a suburban, as well as country, kitchen.

So it is last Saturday. I'm standing in one of the former about to lead a jam-making boot camp for many of the dozen mums from the local primary school who have bravely taken on the responsibility of running the jam stall for the biennial fête.

They are a far more wholesome bunch than those I helped out for the last fair – this lot don't crack the sparkling until after the jam's made – but their aims are as lofty: to make a 1000 jars of jam in the next five months.

It is a situation that Bob was obviously familiar with – just witness his line from 'Jamming' about how there aren't any rules but that you can still 'jam'.

How right he was about no rules. Jam making is about applying basic principles of cooking fruit with sugar to achieve a thick gel-like set, thanks to the formation of chains of pectin that bind the sugared fruit juice together. In turn, the highly sweet environment, when encased in a sterile jar, helps the jam fight off the bugs that would turn the fruit bad in normal circumstances. Hey, that's why they call 'em preserves.

The challenge, however, is that fruit is capricious. Variations in pectin levels, acidity, sugar and ripeness, not only in differing varieties but also from apricot to apricot or strawberry to strawberry, mean that each batch can behave differently. So jam-making is more about feel and smell than following the stone-set rules of a recipe.

But standing here in front of all these expectant, up-turned faces, the only thing I can smell is fear. My fear. Their leader has told me that they want to make strawberry jam. Strawberry jam ... oh dear.

You see, raspberry, apricot, blackberry, mango and lime ... these are jams that I am very comfortable with, but strawberry is my nemesis. It is the only jam I have ever made that was a total, unmitigated disaster. See, I lost my bottle thinking it would never set and so added powdered pectin. The result was inedible – like a strawberry jam sanger that had been dropped on the beach. The added pectin gave the jam an unpleasant granular texture. Scarred, I've not made strawberry jam since.

Now I have to advise, to show confidence and pray that I won't see my reputation crashing in flames in front of some of the school's most important opinion formers with a strawberry jam that refuses to gel by itself.

The girls hull, clean and dry kilos and kilos of that most deceitful of fruit. They've decided they want to liquidise some of it to help those dangerous first few minutes when the hard dry fruit and the sugar hit the heat and it can stick, ruining the batch. It's not a purist's approach, but it seems like a safe one that will still get a decent result. We talk about how cooking the fruit in smaller batches tends to mean you get to the setting point quicker, resulting in a brighter, less 'cooked'-tasting jam. We discuss how adding a little grated fruit high in pectin, such as apple or quince, can help jam set, but instead decide to add lemon juice and the juiced lemon halves, as their acidity helps the pectin to form the long chains that 'set' the jam.

Soon there's a steady rhythm in the kitchen, with two stirring pots on the stoves, two on the fruit, one washing up and two filling the jars, marshalling the sugar and ensuring the jars are properly sterilised. A safe distance from this picture of industry roars a tornado of random small children who belong to the assembled women. Their screams and laughs are the backing track to easy conversation between a group of women who don't all know each other but who are bonding over manual work. For jam-making is one of those great rituals, like making salami or the bottling of tomato sauce, that acts as a social glue between communities and families. As one mum remarks (with the sort of concise encapsulation that would exhilarate anyone making a jam-making documentary), 'We might all have different accents and cultural backgrounds, but look how jam-making unites us.'

This really is social networking in its purest form. Pure because there is an altruistic intent; a common but concrete goal to achieve, and perhaps even more importantly, they are doing something that is actually social – in all the meanings of the word.

We make jam for about three hours and in the end process about 20 kilograms of fruit. It seems to leave us with a pathetically small number of jars, but 'the set' is good and by the end the women (and I!) can identify when the strawberry jam has reached the correct gelling point by its 'strawberry shortbread' aroma, the way it starts to resist the wooden stirring spoon more forcefully, and the way the cooked jam hangs and falls in droplets from the raised spoon.

We aren't even a tenth of the way to the total yet, but my small contribution is done (and quite frankly they were probably all more than capable of doing it without me). That's good news because in the coming months they will need push on alone. At least they'll always have Robert Nesta Marley's words to inspire them. As he put it so succinctly 'We're jamming, jamming. And I hope you like jamming too.'

I think they do … and I think you will too!

Originally published in 'A2', The Age, 2009

THE SEARCH FOR THE
PERFECT ICE-CREAM

George Washington got into debt over it, Nero sent slaves across his empire because of it, and the success of the café owes a huge debt to it. Not sex, but just about the next best thing – ice-cream.

Through the ages, ice-cream has captivated the hearts, minds and stomachs of chefs and diners alike. Legendary chef Georges Auguste Escoffier claimed that no other area of cookery offered 'more opportunity for culinary fantasies and masterly presentation'. He went on to prove it with 192 recipes for sorbets, ice-creams, iced mousses, parfaits and granitas, alongside less well known ice concoctions like marquises and spooms, in his *Complete Guide to the Art of Modern Cookery*. That list doesn't even include his ice-cream dishes like Peach Melba, named after our own, operatic dame.

Those who doubt Escoffier need only to look at the menus of ice-cream parlours and restaurants. The motto today seems to be 'if you can infuse it, you can use it'. Herbs and spices are now joining more traditional flavourings like fruit, chocolate and cheeses in ice-creams. Australia's restaurants and ice-cream parlours offer everything from chocolate-chilli and lemon delicious to basil and blue cheese flavours, alongside the traditional chocolate, vanilla and lemon sorbet. We've still got a long way to go, however, to match the invention of Manuel Da Silva Oliveira at his ice-cream parlour in Merida, Venezuela. He has over 700 varieties including squid, fried pork rind, trout and tuna ice-creams.

Many cultures claim ice-cream as their own, but it is the Chinese who are credited with first adding salt and saltpetre to snow or pounded ice to lower its freezing temperature through evaporation in order to make a frozen dairy dish. Some experts claim the process may have started as early as the Harn Dynasty (206 BC–AD 220) but ace ice-cream researchers Robin Weir and Caroline Liddell only present hard evidence from the T'ang period (AD 618–907) in their hyperbolically but deservedly named *Ices – The Definitive Guide*. Back then the dynasty's founder had 94 dedicated 'ice men', with the court enjoying dishes using cow, goat, buffalo and even fermented mare's milk.

The love of iced desserts and drinks dates back much further; the earliest ice-house (2250 BC) was unearthed in Iraq in the Sumerian city of Ur. Nero loved his 'slushees' of snow flavoured with honey, fruit and wine. The Arab world had their *charabs*, the Turks their *chorbets* and, after his conquest of Egypt in 345 BC, Alexander the Great had fifteen trenches dug and filled with snow for his cooled 'punches'.

While that old fraud Marco Polo might have claimed that it was he who introduced iced creams to Europe from China, it seems much more likely that their popularity had spread West earlier. There are reports of the endothermic effect of salt on ice in Indian writings of the 4th century and Arab writings of the 12th century, while according to Weir the Mogul Court of North India was enjoying kulfi as early as the 1400s.

Initially the food of royalty, it wasn't until the 17th century that the craze for ices filtered down from the top tables of Europe. The 1660s saw water ices in South Italy, Spain, Vienna and Paris, while Venice had its iced creams, but it took the birth of the café to make them a popular fashion. When a Sicilian named Procope opened Paris's first café in 1686, it was the sorbets and ice-creams that entranced Parisian society as much as the coffee or the ornate mirrors and chandeliers.

Within 100 years, iced desserts had incorporated eggs, captivated diners from the US to Scandinavia and were being sold by itinerant

Italian *garzones* as a salient attraction for the promenaders at the 'pleasure parks' that had sprung up around London.

In the 1850s, an editor of *The Age* newspaper in Melbourne, James Harrison, invented the icemaker and the fridge, thus making ice more readily available all through the year. But a fair degree of chemistry was still needed to make ice-cream. In the turn of the century *Encyclopaedia of Practical Cookery*, ice and ice-making expert Theodore Garrett listed 15 different freezing mixes, adding such fun ingredients as hydrochloric and sulphuric acid to reduce the temperature of snow or pounded ice for freezing.

The US's obsession with ice-cream started with Washington, who ran up a $200 bill for the stuff in the summer of 1790. By the time Escoffier first served Dame Nellie Melba her eponymous dessert (vanilla ice-cream, peaches and raspberry puree), industrial ice-cream production was underway, ice-cream sodas and sundaes were common and the portable hand-cranked ice-cream freezer had been making smoother, lighter ice-creams for forty years. It was also in the US, at the St Louis World's Fair of 1904, that the recently patented ice-cream cone, or cornucopia, became a hit – replacing paper cups and glass dishes.

Prohibition gave ice-cream another boost as bars turned into ice-cream parlours, while competition and immense consumption between the wars saw the birth of ice-creams and ices on a stick, the eskimo pie, and rocky road ice-cream. Clarence Vogt's continuous freezer made large-scale commercial production economical and the democratisation of domestic refrigeration in the 1930s assured ice-cream's success.

In more recent times we have seen the sixties boom of 'odd' flavours, the arrival of super-rich premium ice-creams and a move away from ice-creams towards lower-fat alternatives like sorbets and frozen yoghurts. With the invention of the pre-frozen canister style of ice-cream machine, making smooth and quick-churned ice-cream at home became much easier.

The Boring but Crucial 'Definition of Ices' Bit

Iced desserts vary in two main ways – by their fat content and whether they are agitated or churned while being frozen. Fat, in the form of cream or milk, gives richness and smoothness to ice-cream, parfaits and semi-freddos. Sorbets, spooms and granitas usually don't have any cream or milk but may use the emulsification properties of egg whites to bind the mix. The smaller the number of fat globules, the larger and more populous the ice crystals. That's why many people find sorbets colder-tasting and more refreshing than ice-creams.

The issue of churning is important because it introduces air during freezing, which makes the ice lighter and easier to bite into. Generally sorbets, sherbets and ice-creams tend to be churned, while parfaits, semi-freddos and *kulfis* aren't and thus will be denser. At home this air added by churning, also called 'overrun', is unlikely to be more than 25 per cent of volume, whereas commercial ice-cream can have as much as 50 per cent. That's why it's a good idea to buy ice-creams by weight rather than carton size. It's also why your ice-cream-maker overflows onto the bench top in a sticky mess when you overfill your machine.

Making the Perfect Ice-Cream

While I'd recommend using an ice-cream-maker for the smoothest results, you can make great ice-cream without one. The process is just slightly more laborious, as you'll need to scrape away the frozen mixture from the sides of the bowl and beat this through the rest of the chilling mix at least twice during the freezing process. If you are using this manual process, put your ice-cream or sorbet in a shallow bowl in the coldest part of your freezer to encourage freezing.

The cheapest motorised ice-cream-makers use a pre-frozen canister in which you churn the ice-cream. As the mix touches the side of the canister it freezes and is scraped away by a motorised rotating paddle (dasher), to be replaced by more runny mix. The dasher keeps the mixture moving so that air is incorporated for lightness and so the ice crystals stay small and don't have time to gang up. As it can take up to 24 hours for the canister to pre-freeze, it's worth investing in an additional canister for making larger quantities or a second flavour. A saccharometer to help you measure and achieve the right viscosity in your sorbet and granita mixes is also a wise investment.

The most common ice-cream is made in the French style from a cooked custard (*crème anglaise*) base, which is cooled and then churned either with or without the addition of whipped cream. To avoid tears this custard must be cooked slowly – a heat diffuser mat is a good idea – and stirred constantly to stop the egg yolks cooking, or you'll end up with scrambled egg ice-cream. I always keep a whisk and large bowl of iced water on hand when making the custard, but that is because some of us can only cook on high. Plunge the pot into the water if things get too heated and whisk frantically to dissipate the lumps and reduce the temperature more quickly. You can also use the bowl for cooling your custard later if it's a success.

Tips from The Best

Don't be afraid to fail. Even the experts do

Val Gaskell, the cool brains behind Rickett's Point Fine Foods and one of Melbourne's ice-cream gurus, says accepting 'cock-ups' is part of the joy of making ices and shouldn't stand in the way of experimentation. She suggests starting out by trying high-fat-content ice-creams at home for their smoother results and their winning richer mouthfeel.

Freshly made ice-cream is the best ice-cream

Fernando Rodriguez is a third-generation ice-cream-maker of Spanish descent. With his father, John, he won three gold and three silver awards at the National Dairy Products Awards for 2000 with what they describe as their Spanish-style ice-creams. Their range of ice-creams and sorbets, Lick Me, is made at The Gourmet Ice-cream Factory in Camberwell. The colder taste that results from a high proportion of ice to fat alerts you that these are almost more iced milks than iced creams. In keeping with the company's mantra to 'churn, cool and consume quickly', they pack them in 500 ml tubs. Rodriguez senior suggests that if attempting this style at home, the lower freezing point of milk-based ices means that they need an extra hour in the freezer to harden.

Freshness is one of the keys to great ice-cream, which is why Ian Curley, food supremo for The Point, Beaumaris Pavilion and the Mentone Hotel, insists on churning theirs as close to serving time as possible. Old ice-cream can taste flannelly and is often betrayed by ice crystals on its surface. Freshness is also the reason why Paul Moser, a part owner of Charmaine's before he opened Richmond's Sorbayze, steers away from too many weird flavours in his store. 'Ice-cream is best fresh and flavours like a rose ice-cream just don't turn over fast enough,' he says.

Only the best ingredients give the best results

For Moser, another secret for great ice-cream is not skimping on the quality and quantity of ingredients. For his best-selling honey crunch ice-cream he adds crumbled Violet Crumble at the start of the custard process and bigger chunks at the end of the churn. And when his much-missed chocolate chip ice-cream returns this summer that'll be Cadbury's flavouring the frozen moussiness of this Italian meringue and cream confection.

Experiment with infusions

As a custard base is at the heart of so many ice-creams, it's easy to introduce flavours through infusing the milk used to make it. David Wilson, who runs Charmaine's with partner Anthea Holmes, suggests ice-cream novices try a ginger ice-cream using this approach. 'Infuse the milk for the *crème anglaise* with ginger powder and some fresh ginger, and then re-highlight the flavour by adding hunks of glacé ginger at the end of the churning process,' he says. The same principle can be used with anything from cinnamon or herbs.

To draw out the flavour of your ingredients when infusing them, Wilson recommends heating the milk almost to boiling point and then placing it aside to cool and let the flavour permeate. Tasting the milk to keep track of how the taste develops is important, but remember that once frozen and diluted with eggs and/or cream the flavours will be less prominent.

This is the approach he uses for their vanilla ice-cream, and he recommends using Madagascan bourbon vanilla beans and scraping the seeds into the milk so everyone knows you are using the real thing! And remember that a pinch of salt will perfect your chocolate ice-cream.

Don't over-churn your ice-cream

Il Bacaro chef Jason Jujnovich learnt to make his ice-cream when working at the River Café in London. There he reached the conclusion that the secret to making great ice-cream was to 'have a nice little machine to make it in!' The only danger, says Jujnovich, is that over-churning can turn ice-cream turn into a 'horrible buttery blob'. Experience now tells him to check the mix every ten minutes. He praises strawberries, hazelnuts and dessert wine, especially vin santo, as excellent flavourings to experiment with.

Ice-cream-makers is a subject that Dianne Kerry at Red Orange knows something about. When she was at Blakes she had a $15,000 Carpigianni at her disposal. 'It made a litre in six minutes, and at that speed the ice-cream was smoother, richer and more emulsified.' At Red Orange she uses a $600 Spanish Simac machine and achieves better results by only churning a small amount of ice-cream at a time – a tip she highly recommends when using any home ice-cream machine.

She now rejects the custard approach, which she feels is prone to lumps and splitting, in favour of what she calls an idiot-proof Italian meringue approach that delivers a very creamy ice-cream. For this she heats 250 g of sugar and 250 ml of water until the solution reaches 114 degrees C (the soft ball stage), then she slowly beats a drizzle of this boiling syrup into 10 well-whisked free-range egg yolks. When the mix has chilled to lukewarm she mixes in a litre of pure cream (45 per cent butterfat). Once cooled she churns it.

There is no one way to make the perfect ice-cream. Try them all and pick your favourite.

The basic rules for ice-cream, according to both Robin Weir and food scientist Harold McGee, is that any ice-cream under 30 per cent in solids (sugar, fat and non-fat milk solids) will be icy. Some flavourings with a high water content, like raspberries, will affect this balance, so US ice-cream maker Jerry Greenfield, of Ben and Jerry's, recommends using a high-fat-content base to maintain smoothness. Too many non-fat milk solids and not enough water can lead to lactic crystallisation, which gives ice-creams a gritty or sandy texture.

The Perfect Sorbet – Maybe

On the whole, ice-creams can be a doddle compared to sorbets. There's somewhat more that can go wrong with this seemingly simple combination of sugar, water and flavouring.

If the syrup is more than 22 per cent sugar the sorbet will stay mushy and won't freeze – tricky when the sugar content of fruit alters depending on how ripe it is. Some of these problems can be overcome with a saccharometer, which measures the density of syrup to get an inkling of its sugar content. Even more accurate – and about twenty-five times the price – is a refractometer, the perfect gift for the cook who has everything.

Over-churn a sorbet in an ice-cream maker and you can end up with texture somewhere between cottonwool and snow. This problem at least can be overcome by not churning for much more than 15 minutes or by using the manual agitation – or forking method of freezing.

While ice-creams and sorbets flavoured with booze might be all the rage, making them can be tricky as alcohol retards freezing. Get round this problem with liqueur essence concentrates made by the liqueur makers.

Val Gaskell adds that the mix for a sorbet should be slightly sweeter to taste so the flavour comes through to tastebuds numbed by cold. Both Gaskell and John Rodriguez use the old trick of adding egg white to lighten and stabilise sorbets where the pureed fruit lacks the body or the pectin to do so itself. Fruit high in pectin, like strawberries or quinces, shouldn't need this addition, says Gaskell. He also suggests always using caster sugar in sorbets as it dissolves quicker. Dianne Kerry reveals she uses liquid glucose to make sorbet smoother and 'sloshey'.

ICE-CREAM GLOSSARY

GELATO

Italian word for ice-cream. Churned, but tends to be less airy so it's more intense in flavour. A lower cream content in the custard base means it can also be less rich and have a colder mouthfeel than French ice-cream.

GLACE

French word for ice-cream. This is usually a rich, high-fat-content version of a cooked custard (*crème anglaise*) agitated/churned while freezing.

GRANITA (aka an ice or, in French, *granité*)

More granular than a sorbet, thanks to a higher proportion of water to sugar. Traditionally will not contain eggs. Debate rages on whether a granita should be stirred during freezing and whether the ice should be scraped from the hard frozen mix or allowed to thaw slightly first.

ICED KACHANG

Malaysian dessert of shaved ice drizzled with rose syrup and coffee on top of hunks of jelly, corn kernels, lychees and palm seeds.

ICED MILK

Higher water content from more milk than cream means a colder mouthfeel and less smoothness, unless made very quickly. Lighter, less creamy ice, often with a correspondingly lower calorie count.

KULFI

Dense Indian ice-cream made from milk that has been reduced by slow cooking for hours. A shortcut is to boil up cans of evaporated milk. The longer you boil the milk the nuttier and richer tasting the ice-cream. The same process, but with cans of condensed milk, is the basis for South American *dulce de leche* ice-cream.

MELLORINE

Official name for ice-creams that contain no butterfat but vegetable oils instead. Illegal in much of the US and the EEC. Also known as pareve.

PARFAIT

Light, unchurned, cream-based frozen custard dessert, often served sliced.

SEMI FREDDO (aka *perfetti* or, in Spain, *semifrio*)

Moulded, partially frozen Italian dessert similar to parfait but often served slightly less cold.

SHERBET

Lighter than ice-cream, richer than an ice, basically this is a sorbet that contains some milk but is still under 5 per cent fat. Can contain gelatine or egg whites. Related to India's *sharbat* and the Middle Eastern *charbat* – traditionally both drinks thick enough to eat with a spoon.

SORBET (aka *sorbetto* in Italy)

Iced flavoured sugar syrup that contains neither fat nor egg yolks but can contain egg whites for textural improvement. Often served as a palate refresher.

SPOOM

Add whipped uncooked meringue to the above flavoured sugar syrup and you get spoom. A light, mousse-like iced dessert that's frozen un-agitated.

EMERGENCY SUPER-FAST
ICE-CREAM RECIPE

Using the freshest cool ingredients straight from the fridge and a good ice-cream-maker you can have soft scoops of ice-cream in less than 20 minutes. The trick is to follow the lead of the US's grooviest ice-cream makers, Ben Cohen and Jerry Greenfield, of Ben and Jerry's fame. They use an uncooked sweet cream base similar to the one first made famous by the good ladies of Philadelphia. This recipe is the richest of several sweet cream bases in their excellent *Ben and Jerry's Homemade Ice-cream and Dessert Book*. It's the recipe I use at home when churning ice-cream for personal consumption.

Ingredients

2 large eggs
¾ cup sugar
1 cup milk
3 cups heavy or whipping cream

Method

Whisk the eggs until light and fluffy, which takes a couple of minutes. Whisk in the sugar a little at a time until it is all blended in. Whisk in the milk and cream. Pour into your ice-cream-maker and churn. For a true sense of the Ben and Jerry's experience, add too many large hunks of something delicious in the final minutes of the churn. Homemade macadamia nut brittle, bits of Cherry Ripe, chocolate-coated toasted almonds or M&Ms are among my favourite choices. Don't serve to pregnant women or other people worried about uncooked eggs.

Originally published in 'Epicure', The Age, *2002*

PART III

REVERE

MARGARET FULTON:
THE COOK

I have eaten great meals at Europe's great tables, but neither Bocuse in Lyon nor Restaurant Gordon Ramsay in Chelsea could match the thrill I feel right now. I'm sitting at the simplest of long thin wooden tables, but it was here, in this narrow kitchen in Sydney's Balmain, that some of Australia's most influential recipes were written. And the small strong hands passing me a plate of little Sydney rock oysters wrote them. I'm about to eat oysters and drink champagne with Margaret Fulton and I'm pretty much beside myself with excitement.

Margaret Fulton has been a hero of mine since I 'discovered' her *Encyclopedia of Food and Cookery* (Reid Books, 1983), which is still the most used book in my kitchen. It's small, compact and a font of knowledge that never runs dry – not unlike Margaret herself.

For almost 50 years Fulton has been shaping the way Australians eat and entertain through her 19 books and many columns in women's magazines like *Woman's Day* and most recently *New Idea*.

Fulton was born outside Inverness in Scotland, the youngest of six children. Her parents, both tailors, immigrated to Australia when Margaret was four. It was in the Glen Innes, New South Wales, kitchen of her mother that young Margaret learnt to cook. She still remembers stirring the custard pot while her mother watched her – catching curry if she lost concentration and the custard skinned, stuck or ended up lumpy. 'When a mother has to feed six children, you are always seeing food being done and always doing it,' says Margaret dismissively of this apprenticeship.

Her parents, however, never expected cooking to be a career choice. 'Nice girls didn't do what I was doing. Nobody did it. They thought I should have gone to university,' Margaret remembers. 'I wasn't considered a rebel. I was just considered a bit odd.'

In fact her first job – as a cooking teacher with the Overseas Corporation – which she started in 1947, also took Margaret by surprise. 'I didn't want to be a cook, I wanted to be a showgirl, but my little five-foot Scottish frame didn't say much for that.'

Promoted to sales manager and partially responsible for the introduction of the pressure cooker to Australia, she then moved to the pages of *Woman* magazine in 1954. This later folded into *Woman's Day* but kept Margaret on. 'They used to say, "Join *Woman's Day* and see the world." It was that era of expansion so countries and airlines were inviting you around the world. I had five or six two-month visits to some amazing locations.'

'It was a tremendous learning curve but when I had to do "365 Ways With Mincemeat" I could remember what they were doing in Mexico, and how the Lebanese women handled it. I actually brought these things to Australia straight from the horse's mouth, so to speak.'

An army of housewives sick of cooking meat and three veg every night embraced Fulton's exotica, but she remembers husbands being less keen. 'When I first discovered and wrote recipes for spaghetti, men would tell their wives, "That was very nice dear, but what's for dinner?" Men were very reluctant to cross that border. Of course once they did, they crossed it like a horde of marauding monkeys. They even got into the kitchen once they discovered how good it can be.'

Twenty-four years with *New Idea* followed, but it was the 1958 publication of Margaret's first book, the *Margaret Fulton Cookbook*, that really cemented her position. An instant hit, the book brought a little security for Margaret and her daughter, whom she was bringing up alone.

The combination of Margaret's food and publisher Paul Hamlyn's books, which were cheap, bulky and designed with lots of colour, created a string of hits. Her 19 titles have sold a total of almost four million copies. 'Unlike today, there wasn't a lot of competition for cookbooks. There was the *Australian Women's Weekly* doing what they've always done but most books were imported from Canada, the US and the UK.'

Fulton remembers Hamlyn as a sharp business operator but also a socialist and a bit of a larrikin like herself. As the first publisher to print *Larousse Gastronomique* in English, it was no surprise to Margaret when he suggested she embark on the 18 months of work that resulted in the *Encyclopedia of Food and Cookery*. It is another period she remembers fondly – for the trips to London to liaise with publishers, editors and designers, but also for what Hamlyn told her. 'Paul said it was the best book he ever published,' she says, flushing slightly with pride.

The *Encyclopedia of Food and Cookery* is now out of print and while Margaret has retained the rights she reckons it's probably too big a task for her to revise and reprint. She is now 78, although she points out that her food hero, the great Scottish food writer Elizabeth Craig, was still writing at 90. 'There's a wonderful story from near the end of her lying in a hospital bed with, I think, a broken hip and her publishers suggesting that someone else should finish her next book. She told them they were being ridiculous, had her filing cabinets wheeled in and finished the book herself.'

This sort of dour determination is particularly Scottish and resonates with Margaret. Like so many separated from the Highlands by the tyranny of distance, it is as a Scot that she fundamentally identifies. 'The minute I go back I feel absolutely at home,' she says.

Elizabeth David is another writer she respects, although meeting her near the end of her life was a depressing episode. 'Basically drinking got her. Her teeth were stained, she had little bits of food down here,' she says, pointing to the front of her shirt.

Margaret no longer drinks wine and doesn't smoke but she does have the occasional malt whisky, putting down the length of her success to her parents' longevity and their stable influence.

Margaret's own family life has been slightly more fractured. Ask her if she was as wild in her youth as her contempories say she was and a twinkle returns to her eye. 'I had my times,' she says. She laughs when reminded that she once claimed to have had more husbands than jobs. She's been married twice but it is her second husband, actor Michael McKeas, whom she describes wistfully as the great love in her life.

'Michael and I lived together since the eighties. We had a wonderful time; every year we'd go and visit his friends in the US and UK. The only thing about Michael was that always before a photograph he had to have a lit cigarette in his cigarette holder …' she trails off.

It was lung cancer that eventually he took him.

Fulton's only daughter, Suzanne (Gibbs), was born in 1950, from the first marriage. Fulton bought up her alone. 'What happened was I had a sister who was married to an author and they lived out in the bush. When it was quite hopeless with Suzanne, when she was ten months old, we went and lived with them up on the Hawkesbury River. They had goats. We grew corn and artichokes. It was lovely living in an author's household.'

When the bright lights of the city called she'd head to the highway and thumb a lift down to Sydney. 'Yes, 50 years ago it was a bit unusual – but I knew it was a means to an end,' she says, pre-empting my next question with a direct and very Margaret statement.

With Fulton no longer writing regularly for a magazine, I'm interested in who she sees as picking up the culinary torch she carried. Jill Dupleix? Donna Hay? *Women's Weekly's* Lyndey Milan?

She dismisses them all somewhat sharply, as if the loss of her *New Idea* role still stings. 'A lot of those people don't do what I did, which was be the cooking person. A lot of these people rely on a team to work with them … I entertained 13 prime ministers [for the Commonwealth Heads of Government Regional Meeting hosted by the Australian Government in 1978].'

It's Stephanie Alexander whom she anoints. 'Stephanie has done an awful lot and is still doing things. She's also done her own thing in her own way — she's encouraged young people and she's also got in there and cooked.'

She also gives TV chefs short shrift. 'I think it is a terrible fiasco. It is entertainment but they all get so terribly serious about it. It's all malarky.'

One of the problems as Fulton sees it is that food today is often about assembly, not cooking. She's also no fan of ready-meals, believing it's better to go to the market and get a nice bit of fish, although the trouble, as she points out, is that to do this people have to know how to cook.

Fulton is no less busy now that she's no longer writing a weekly cookery column. There's her work as the patron of the Australian Native Dog Conservation Society and the time she spends at the gym — weight-lifting. I'm even more incredulous when she tells me that 'these little legs can lift 600 pounds'. I'm still a little stunned to be discussing weight-lifting with the 'women who taught Australia to cook', but it is part of her fitness regime and helps in strengthening an arm whose tendons have been damaged by all those years of chopping and slicing.

My ageism takes another knock when we start talking about the politics of food. Margaret Fulton is no sponge-baking grandma with a lightweight mind to match. She as mad as hell about genetically modified food and appalled that so few of Australia's food writers have taken up the issue. 'It's so big. If genetic modification gets its way we can never fix it. We can clean up the rivers eventually and we can fix up the forests even if it takes centuries, but basically if this happens we will never be the same again,' she storms. She feels so passionately about this issue that she helped Greenpeace promote their 'True Foods' guide to GM products and wants to write more about the subject.

She's also none too happy about the globalisation of food and the relentless quest for profits over taste and morality. 'There are good thing happening, like farmers' markets and the Slow Food movement, which are "people power", but the forces ranged against them are daunting. But I like to recount an old African saying: "If you think you are too small to make a difference, just spend a night in a dark bedroom with a mosquito." We have to realise the enormity of the battle but be prepared to be mosquitos.'

She even uses the f-word and, reeling, I stagger back to safer ground – so what's her favourite recipe, I ask. Interestingly, she cites not her much-vaunted one for beef Wellington, which launched a thousand dinner parties, but one for roast shoulder of lamb, acquired from an English writer. 'It has all the elements of a great recipe – beautiful ingredients, simply and intelligently cooked. There are layers of sliced potato and onions, strewn with anchovies, then more potatoes. The shoulder of lamb rests on top and everything is doused with vinegar, stock and some white wine. The intelligence of that recipe is it is something that everyone can afford. It is something that shows the skill – the anchovies you can't taste but they are catalysts of flavour. The vinegar cuts back the fat from the lamb. In the end you get meat that is both crispy and moist. To me that is what really thinking about food is all about, rather than the dishes we are getting with little squirts of this and overly complex flavours.'

Her secret for a great meal? When it is made by someone who has really cared about it.

With my pulse rate approaching normal again, I ask her to describe herself. Snatches like 'bossy', 'a realist' and 'I like being in charge' come out eventually. She has less difficulty describing what she hopes her legacy will be. 'I hope I have shown that cooking is fun and that it's a good thing to do. It's the real melding together of family relationships.'

But judging by the fire that's burning fiercely in her belly these days, it should be a long, long time before that's a legacy that we will have to assess.

Originally published in 'Epicure', The Age, 2003

Due in part to the interest generated by this article, *The Encyclopedia of Food and Cookery* was updated and reprinted by Hardie Grant Books in 2005.

SKYE GYNGELL:
THE SPRITE

It's been a watershed 18 months for Skye Gyngell. Last year, the Petersham Nurseries Café, her establishment that she describes as somewhere you can put your elbows on the table, won 'Most Original Restaurant' at *The Tatler* Restaurant Awards. Then her first book, *A Year in My Kitchen*, took top gong at the Le Cordon Bleu World Food Media Awards. And, of course, she started writing for *Delicious*.

Writing exclusively for an Australian audience greatly appeals to this 44–year-old cook, who doesn't own a chef's jacket or even travel with her knives, in spite of an apprenticeship served in Michelin-starred fine diners in Europe. In fact she puts her London success down to her unique Australianness. 'It's that sense of being a magpie thanks to our migrant culture. In London, Indian and West Indian food hasn't really integrated. Also I think Australians have a confidence about food, so much so that if I am being really honest I think if I'd tried to do this [Petersham Nurseries Café] back here I'd be one of many,' she says.

Confidence is very much a watchword for Skye these days. She talks of the confidence needed to take ego out of what she's doing and just let the produce shine. Of having the confidence to pare back her food even further than when she started. It's an aim that dates back to one of her finest food memories – eating with her father in a little trattoria outside Florence and tasting an immaculately ripe summer peach on ice. 'I've never forgotten that beauty of perfect produce,' she says. 'I love the strength of *less*. The result is that we are now much punchier in terms of flavour than we were three years ago.'

Not that confidence was always Skye's long suit. We talk about her childhood. It's not a comfortable memory. Now hailed in the UK as a great beauty, with her pale skin and freckles she admits she didn't fit into Sydney's beach culture. Having a crooked nose and a black tooth from a car crash back then didn't help either. 'Guys on the beach at Bondi would call out "On your way or on your back",' she recalls, still smarting a little.

'I've never had any confidence at all. I think that is because I grew up in the beach culture of Sydney. I also had a famously beautiful mother and everybody knew our dad [Bruce Gyngell – Channel Nine head honcho and the first man on Aussie TV]. None of us kids fitted the grade. That was quite hard.'

Hard enough for Skye to look for solace in alcohol and substance abuse. It was an addiction that led to her eventual estrangement from her mother and brother. One of the joys of being clean, and of the success of opening Petersham, has been their subsequent reconciliation.

Even in more recent years the road hasn't all been smooth tarmac. There was the 'terrible scandal' of her writing Nigella Lawson's recipes when the Domestic Goddess was exhausted after husband John Diamond's death from cancer. 'Nigella just did what a lot of people do,' says Skye. 'At the time I got paid quite a lot and I was very grateful.'

With a famous father and a beautiful socialite mother, Nigella's childhood echoes Skye's, but that is where the similarities stop, believes Skye. 'Her personality has been so formed by the tragedy in her life that it is very hard to get through that. She's a bit of an ice queen. I'm not.'

Skye's own personal life has been no bed of roses, either. She's been married twice and recently separated again. 'I am a disaster in relationships,' she confesses. 'I'm very driven. I'm a very reckless human being and not particularly happy.' She cites her focus on Petersham as part of the cause of the latest separation. Ask her whether the obsession with Petersham has shades of an addiction and she'll think on it and then say 'probably', but it's also been her saviour.

'If I am being honest, Petersham has led to a huge growth of self-esteem in that I was acknowledged. I never thought that would happen. I was always the fuck-up in my family,' she says. 'Then the other day I went to lunch at the Australian embassy. I was sitting next to the ambassador and had "a moment". I thought how proud my father would have been – and that I had got here on my own merits.'

Originally published in delicious, *2008*

ROSE AND RUTH: THE BELLADONNAS

This is one of those unlikely stories. A tale of two housewives who decided to open a canteen at a husband's business, only to see it rocket them to the sort of household fame where foodies know them by their first names alone.

Now after seventeen years, the restaurant that the canteen became, The River Café, and the associated cookbooks, have earned Rose Gray and Ruth Rogers the mantle of the champions of real Italian food. Italian food served with style, sophistication and, above all, simplicity.

Sure, it helped that the canteen was in Sir Richard Rogers' globally recognised London riverside architectural practice. Rogers designed such strikingly famous buildings as the Pompidou Centre in Paris and the new Lloyds building in London. But perhaps more important was the fact that both Rose and Ruth, or Ruthie as everyone at the restaurant seems to call her, had an unflinching vision of what they wanted to achieve. 'We knew we wanted a small restaurant serving home-cooked Italian food. We worked out how to run it from the point of view of the domestic cook and we didn't want to do it any other way,' recalls Rose.

Rose and Ruth had no formal training apart from their experience of being in Italian kitchens in Italy. 'We learnt as we went along,' Rose says.

The freedom of not being hidebound by a chef's typical classical French training is one reason Rose points to for their success. 'Not being Italian also helps enormously,' she says. 'When you are Italian, you are only from one region. It is so interesting when we have Italian cooks coming to work with us: they just think you are doing everything wrong because you aren't doing it the way their mothers did it in the region they come from. It's quite a narrow view.'

It is the excitement of constantly discovering new gems from different regions that helps sustains Ruth's passion for Italy. 'What is so exciting for us about Italy is that it is so regional,' she says. 'You can be in Florence and they won't know about something that they do 150 miles away in Bologna. Last June we went to Puglia for five days and came back with an enormous amount of learning and recipes.'

As we speak Ruth is in the process of proofreading their latest book, *River Café Two Easy*, which mainly contains recipes from this trip and those sourced and inspired from the kitchens around Verona and Milan. She is quick to point out that while these 'Easy' books were designed for busy modern lives, the recipes are, as she calls them, 'ethical'.

'We are not dumbing down the recipes,' she says and points to a soup of bread, water and olive oil that she currently loves as an example of how wonderfully simple food can be in Italy.

These trips and producing the books are when Rose and Ruth work closest together; for in the kitchen they each tend to run their own shifts. 'We respect the space around each other,' says Rose. 'We have a sense of independence. When we do books and tours and demos we work together and really work at being together. And we really enjoy that too.'

Ruth likens their relationship to a marriage and suggests that while they have both have different approaches and are different people, their partnership has survived because they respect these differences and let each other go their own way.

Rose and Ruth first met when Ruth, a young graphic designer from New York, was invited to dinner at Rose's just after arriving in London. 'She brought a little potato gratin, which I always remember because it was so delicious,' says Rose.

The friendship developed further when Ruth married Richard Rogers, with whom Rose had been at art school, and as their mutual love affair with Italy deepened.

Ruth moved to Paris while Rogers was working on the Pompidou Centre, but spent increasing amounts of time in Italy chasing up long-lost family in Tuscany. 'It was a complete revelation to go to Italy,' she explains. 'I loved French food and their sauces but suddenly to go to Italy and have the realisation that if you have a wonderful ingredient – something so delicious and perfect – what you want to do is complement it with something simple like lemon and olive oil.'

Her understanding of Italian food was further developed by lessons from her mother-in-law, a talented cook from Trieste, who introduced Ruth to the northern Italian kitchen rather than the tomato-sauce-smothered cuisine of the south that she knew from the US. Now Ruth says, 'When the plane lands and I put my foot down on Italian soil I feel better.'

Rose, on the other hand, had fallen in love with Italian food when she was an art student making annual pilgrimages to Florence, Venice and Rome. The dream of writing a book on pasta saw her relocate to the walled Italian city of Lucca for five years in the eighties.

A home counties girl who grew up in the wartime Britain of rationing, Rose's family had dabbled in subsistence farming and when she arrived in Lucca she planted a vegetable plot. 'It wasn't long before all the women in the local village started to teach me things that were specific to that little bit of Italy,' she remembers.

Interestingly, while Tuscany is still close to Ruth's heart – she and Richard take a place each summer between Piacenza and Montepulciano – Lucca is not Rose's favourite region of Italy.

'My favourite is usually the last place I have had a good meal,' she laughs. 'At the moment I love the food around Verona. The wine. The borlotti beans. The cured meats. They are great with risottos. There is also the influence of all the fish from the Adriatic. They are always surprising you with combinations like a pasta with vongole, white asparagus and cinnamon and you think, "Oh my God, what a concoction!" It just sounds too wacky but eat it and suddenly the whole thing clicks.'

Talk to those who have worked at the River Café and a clear picture emerges of how very different a place it can be for a chef to work. Darren Simpson worked there for two and a half years. He describes landing in Rose and Ruth's kitchen as a breath of fresh air. 'They are like chalk and cheese, but they gave me the passion for the food I want to cook. Rose has such a passion for food. She's like my long lost auntie but she can also scare the shit out of you.'

Philip Johnson, chef and owner of E'cco in Brisbane, agrees that Rose can be quite intimidating. 'She has very forthright views but just spending two weeks with her changed the way I looked at food,' he says.

Scary, yes, but also generous with her knowledge. Tobie Puttock, who ran the kitchen at Jamie Oliver's Fifteen in London, reckons he learnt more in his first month at the River Café than in his first six years working in Australia. And he'll also never forget his first day in the kitchen. 'I walked in and the chefs were sitting around a big table. Rose said, "Hey, babe, come and sit down and help write us the menu together." They wanted my opinion. I was shocked. It was unlike anywhere else I had ever worked.'

What impressed Nathan Hoeksema the most was the produce. Raspberries from Scotland and turbot and Dover sole straight off the boat from Devon; seasonal and organic produce sourced from suppliers all over Europe; and borage flowers and dandelion leaves taken straight from the vegetable garden outside the restaurant.

The River Café can also be a radical eye-opener for floor staff. While Nathan was working in the kitchen, his partner, Jaclyn Treloar, was working on the floor. 'As a waitress part of your job is to prepare food for the kitchen before each service – you might be depitting Ligurian olives, de-salting Spanish anchovies, picking herbs or peeling garlic. That is the most amazing insight into a restaurant for a waiter.'

Originally published in delicious, *2005*

ROSE GRAY:
BELLADONNA ALONE

Trailing through Melbourne's Prahran Market after Rose Gray is a fascinating insight into the philosophy of London's River Café, her successful Italian restaurant that spawned a million cookbook sales.

She's searching for ingredients for a lunch she's preparing for chef Guy Grossi and his family to mark the end of her time in Australia for the Melbourne Food and Wine Festival. It's a spring menu but the vagaries of magazine deadlines mean we're shooting it in late autumn, and this poses a bit of a challenge for a woman whose whole food ethos revolves around seasonality.

Her pace picks up when she sees some baby zucchini that will be perfect for adding to the *fretteda* – an Italian braise of asparagus, broad beans, peas and waxy potatoes. 'This is the perfect Italian dish because you can alter it to use the veg that looks best in the market – artichokes, fennel, cabbage,' she shouts over her shoulder as she careens off to an organic stall to fossick for dandelion leaves, or maybe sorrel, to accompany the bruschetta.

Strewn in her wake are gems of culinary lore that she's let fly as we amble round the market – like how the redder the rhubarb the better the taste, and how the real secret of that *fretteda* is to cut the veg into slightly uneven sizes so they cook at different rates and give textural variety.

Later she talks of her horror of spag bol, a hatred that appears to date back to a particularly bad pasta restaurant she frequented during her art school days. Something else you'll never see on the River Café menu is chicken. 'The chickens are just not good enough in our country except for using for stock,' Rose explains.

Looking for a whole red snapper to cook with potatoes, capers and olives, she sniffs at the amount of fish being sold as fillets rather than whole. 'Without gills to check for redness and eyes to check for clarity it is so much harder to gauge how fresh it is,' she explains. She loves the little black olives we find in a deli, though.

It is this energy and genuine excitement about ingredients that Rose and River Café co-founder Ruth Rogers share that has helped their restaurant reach the milestone of its twentieth anniversary. It's an amazing achievement for any restaurant, let alone one that started out in an unfashionable corner of Fulham as a sort of de facto canteen for Ruth's partner's architecture business.

'We are also both older ladies – it's our second career. That alone gave us a massive amount of confidence,' says Rose. 'It also helped that we are both obsessive about what we do and that, as we have only one restaurant, we are always there.'

Rose also credits the steady stream of Australians in the kitchen with helping make the restaurant such a success. 'We love Australian chefs because they are very well trained and tend to have an open mind when it comes to learning our approach to Italian food. They've taught us a huge amount, too – I even think it was an Aussie who showed us how to grate pastry for our almond tart, which is now very much a River Café technique,' she laughs. (It minimises the handling of the pastry.)

For Rose, however, the most important other chef in the River Café kitchen has always been 'Ruthie', whom she obviously misses on her Australian adventure. (Ruth, having fracturing her pelvis in a skiing accident, was unable to come with her.) 'We are pretty good at keeping each other company. We talk all the time and spark ideas off each other.

Whatever you do in life it's good to listen to another person and have them to bounce ideas off, as you tend to get a better result.'

But like any long-term relationship, they both have foibles that can confound the other. Rose reckons Ruth thinks her obsession with the veggie garden outside the restaurant is a bit crazy – especially when Rose heads out there to dig the garden after doing a whole shift at the River Café. And for Rose, it's Ruth's use of her mobile. 'It's constant!' she laughs, 'because there is always something else going on.'

Originally published in delicious, *2007*

NOBU: THE BLADE

Nobu is holding a small ball of rice up to the sunlight streaming through the kitchen window. 'You see, this is perfect. See how the light can still glow through – this shows that the rice has not been packed too tight. When you eat sushi, the grains of the rice should be just lightly pressed together but still separate.'

We are standing in a typical Australian kitchen as the most famous Japanese chef in the world explains his simple rules for making perfect sushi and sashimi at home. 'The thickness I cut the fish depends on how fresh it is; the fresher the fish, the thinner I cut it. Fresh fish can be a little tough, so if you cut it too thick it will be chewy,' Nobu explains.

Knowing how fresh it is – well, that's a far trickier skill to pass on in these pages and something that Nobu largely puts down to his experience of growing up in Japan. 'For us, we have oceans around [so] we know how to choose fish, how to prep fish and eat fish. I can close my eyes and touch the fish and tell how fresh it is. This is the Japanese experience.

'As with all Japanese cookery the produce must be number one [quality]. Then the Japanese way is to treat it simply. The best product doesn't need much processing. I want to keep the natural flavour, so the dressings and sauces are background flavours. It's like a painting – mountains, the greenery – everything has to be in balance.'

Nobu explains that for him, besides great ingredients, cooking is the melding of skill, experience, technique and passion. There's also something more. When he lays his hand on a fish that he is about to work, he always tries to treat it gently and with respect. 'The fish is like my girlfriend,' he laughs.

While he talks, his hands move with a practiced ease and almost artistic rhythm as he smoothly draws his knife first through kingfish and then salmon with fluid strokes reminiscent of a Japanese *Shodo* master wielding his calligrapher's brush.

Next the knife is down and in a succession of deft hand movements, he applies just enough pressure to bind another ball of the warm rice together, apply a tick of mustard-hot wasabi and place a slice of fish on top. Suddenly, out of thin air, like a magician's conjuring trick, a perfect piece of *nigiri-zushi* appears in front of me – a small sushi-shaped rabbit.

'Sushi should also be eaten at body temperature and only ever dip the *fish* in the soy sauce – never ever dip the rice,' he instructs firmly.

'This is really very simple cooking. When I wasn't busy like I am now I would make sushi for my kids at home. Now – even though I have a fully fitted out sushi bar at my houses in both Japan and Los Angeles – this only happens once a year. Me making sushi, now it's a New Year's Day tradition.'

And to finish? Nobu explains it is increasingly common to find meals in Japanese homes ending in a Western style with cake or ice-creams, but he'll still do the more Japanese way: 'Not chocolate, not cream; just very simple, very seasonal fruit,' he advises.

While Nobu's manner is easy and relaxed in front of the camera, there's no little steel there below the surface. You see it reflected in the equal measures of respect and fear that he commands in his chefs. Some chefs have even likened working for Nobu to joining a religion: things are either 'Nobu style' or they are not.

Nobuyuki Matsuhisa, or Nobu to his Hollywood chums and as the rest of the world knows him, runs a restaurant empire of over 22 establishments spanning from Melbourne to London by way of Los Angeles, Dubai, Milan and Mykonos.

He's so famous that he's made Hollywood movie cameos in roles as diverse as a kimono artist in *Memoirs of a Geisha*, as the evil Mr Roboto in the third Austin Powers movie, and in *Casino* with his business partner and friend Robert de Niro. That's the sort of luminary status that not even Gordon or Jamie has achieved!

Nobu was born in Saitama Prefecture, Japan, in 1947; the third son of a lumber merchant who was killed in a road accident when Nobu was just seven. To his father is attributed his wanderlust, but it was his older brother who began Nobu's obsession with sushi, when he took the young boy to a local restaurant. Nobu was captivated and after high school he joined Matsuei Zushi in Tokyo's Shinjuku district as the apprentice. He lived with the owner's family doing chores and carrying fish back from Tsukiji market. Such was the strict training and hierarchy in those days that it was three years before he was allowed behind the sushi counter!

Once there, and after a couple of years perfecting his skills, a customer lured Nobu to Peru to open a restaurant with him. Aged 24, Nobu, with his new bride, Yoko, took up the offer and opened his first restaurant, named Matsuei Sushi in honour of his mentor. It's still stands in the Lima suburb of San Isidro today.

Nobu spent three years in Lima and then a year in Buenos Aires developing an interest and knowledge of South American and European techniques and flavours such as jalapeño, coriander and garlic. His marrying of them with traditional Japanese techniques and dishes would become a huge hit when Nobu opened his first restaurant in Los Angeles in 1987.

But getting to this point was not without its trials. After South America the couple, now with a young daughter and another on the way, returned to Japan with little money. Next Nobu was enticed to join a venture opening a Japanese restaurant in Anchorage, Alaska. After building the sushi bar himself and then working 50 nights in a row he took a night off for Thanksgiving, only for the uninsured restaurant to burn to the ground in his absence, leaving Nobu penniless and without a sponsor to allow him to stay in the States.

Again he returned to Japan to lick his wounds with his family, before deciding to try his luck next in Los Angeles. After three years he had his green card; after ten he had earned enough to pay his creditors and raised the funds to open Matsuhisa in Beverly Hills. Just two years later the prestigious *Food and Wine* magazine named Nobu one of the US's ten best new chefs. In 1993 the *New York Times* went one better, naming Matsuhisa one of the ten best restaurants in the world.

Now the world can't get enough of the chef-turned-stellar-restaurateur. Last year he spent only two months at his home in Beverly Hills: the rest he was travelling, opening new restaurants or visiting existing members of what he describes as his 'family', such as the Australian branch of Nobu, launched with Robert de Niro at Crown in Melbourne last year. 'One day I will stop … but so far it feels like it is endless … the family keeps on growing!' he smiles.

This frenetic life means that meals at home, catching up with his wife and two adult daughters, are treasured. 'My wife is a very good cook. She'll make grilled fish, tempura, noodles. In winter, hot pots with chicken, beef or seafood with vegetables.'

Sounds like next time we should also be asking Mrs Matsuhisa for a lesson!

Originally published in delicious, *2008*

MARIO BATALI: THE MOST
FAMOUS ITALIAN CHEF

Mario Batali is famous. Think Jamie, Gordon and Nigella all rolled into one ... and then some. With his cookbooks, four TV series on constant rotation on a US food network that reaches 80 million homes and his seven New York restaurants, Batali is now probably the world's best-known Italian chef. In fact, last year business magazine *Forbes* ranked him amongst the 50 most bankable celebrities in the US, just behind Tiger Woods but in front of Jennifer Lopez and David Letterman. But while most chefs who reach this level of fame often lose the respect of their peers, Batali also won the prestigious title of 'America's Best Chef' in 2005 after being shortlisted the previous two years.

This 46-year-old Seattle boy has come a long way from his early jobs washing dishes through college and cooking at the Stuff Yer Face pizzeria – and by a route that was at best circuitous. Born in Seattle, he spent part of his childhood in Spain, studied Spanish theatre at university, dropped out of a culinary course in the UK and then ended up cooking food in a pub with an equally unknown Marco Pierre White. He cooked on yachts in the Mediterranean and for three years in a tiny Italian village of 200 inhabitants. He only came to New York by accident. He was actually on his way to cook in Bahia, Brazil, when he stopped off in Florida and was persuaded to help a friend open a restaurant in the Big Apple instead.

Po, his first restaurant of his own, was a speedy success, building Batali's reputation for generous rustic Italian food that wasn't scared of peasant ingredients. Now Batali is a familiar sight nipping between his myriad New York kitchens; a big man on a scooter with his trademark ponytail and orange Crocs.

Sitting on a tall stool at the bar of Otto, his pizzeria near Washington Square, with a Diet Coke in hand, he holds forth on what makes great Italian food with a frenetic hailstorm of words that marks him now as a true New Yorker.

Mario's maternal great-grandfather, Angelo Merlino, opened Seattle's first Italian deli, but his father, Armandino, worked as an executive for Boeing. When it came to a formative Italian culinary influence on his life it was left up to Armandino's mother, Leonetta. 'I don't think we'd lost that Italian heritage. I just think we'd modified it, like so many Italian Americans, to take into account the readily available local ingredients,' he says now. 'My Grandma, however, still held on to it. We celebrated that by going to her house.'

This slow erosion of heritage was something that Batali also noticed when living in Italy. 'The kids my age didn't want to learn how to make tortellini. Even over there. American pop culture has so invaded Italy that they want curry with their risotto because they are tired of the same thing, not realising that when they are 55 all they are going to think about for the rest of their lives are those tortellini.'

Batali feels that this means that Italy is slowly homogenising, and it worries him, because it is the huge regional variations in how to cook dishes (and use ingredients) that make Italian food such a rich cuisine. 'When a French person wants to make *béarnaise* sauce it's the same in Cannes as it is in Paris. When you talk about *ragù bolognese* it's not even the same between neighbours. They relish that distinction!' he snorts.

For Batali the single most telling revelation while living in the tiny village of Borgo Capanne outside Bologna was understanding how the sparseness – the nearly emptiness of a dish – made Italian food so good. 'There's no white noise. There are no superfluous ingredients. There're no strings. It's a single violin and it's so magnificent. That's what woke me up. I worked there three and a half years to break me of the habit of putting smoked eggplant on my peas and pappardelle!'

He also came to understand the Italians' almost obsessive connection with, and reverence for, family home cooking. 'I've always reckoned that for an Italian the best thing he could ever taste is something that smelled like his mom's skirt when he was six and standing next to her in the kitchen,' he suggests, only half joking.

The other big realisation about great Italian food was that when it comes to pasta or other carbs, it is all about them and not the sauce. 'In Italy a pasta sauce is referred as *condimento*. It's a condiment,' he says. 'It's like the mustard we put on our sausage. The sausage is the main event and so in Italy the noodles (or the farro or the beans) are the main event. The Italians want to taste the way the wind smells on a Thursday when it's blowing through the wheat field. They are more interested in pasta tasting like baked bread rather than tomato sauce with a bunch of shit in it.'

Understand these simple lessons and Batali suggests creating great Italian food at home is as easy as buying well. He feels there is no substitute for essentials like real sea salt, great extra virgin olive oil, salted capers, salted anchovies, real parmigiano reggiano, pancetta and prosciutto di Parma or San Daniele. And when it comes to the right meat or fowl, Batali suggests buying the best you can afford. 'If you have a great sauce you can hide adequate protein behind it but Italians don't even know what sauce is. Olive oil is their sauce!'

Mario's own Italian cooking is autographed by the way he loves the flavours 'tuned up' as he calls it. The flamboyant use of acid and chilli are two signature traits. 'I like to take my food close to the edge. It's more exciting. What I like about Italian cooking in its capriciousness and whimsy. Latin culture would throw hot sauce like Tabasco over a plate of linguini with clams and then every mouthful would be ubiquitously hot. The Italians like one bite to be hot … one bite nothing … one bite only clam. It's a ride, like an opera, and so much more intriguing.' As he says this, he bounces in his perch as if he actually tastes each of those mouthfuls, his volume see-sawing with the drama of the ride.

Batali sees an appreciation of acidity as a sign of a more evolved culinary culture and likes to splash some acid – vinegar or lemon juice maybe – at the very last second to tweak a dish. 'It adds brightness,' he enthuses. 'After eating a lot of conservative food I find it to be a little more high-wire. I want acid or pepper or lots of herbs added at the very last second. Herbs in slow-cooked dishes have a lovely muted roundness but if you add a little of them raw at the very end you get this exploding spectrum from the muted to the raw. It's far more interesting.'

When you find out that he's also a fan of food that's crispy and salty, it's perhaps less of a surprise to find out that alongside Italian he rates Vietnamese as one of the world's greatest cuisines. 'I love the way that in South-east Asia the food explodes with flavour, isn't filled with fat and is so light.'

While everything Italian that Batali touches seems to turn to gold it was a shock when the French restaurant he opened faltered. As Batali sees it, the problem was two-fold: he was too hands-off and it was a pre-theatre restaurant unable to get main courses on the table by 7 pm! 'It was a good lesson and I got off lightly for such a monumental fuck-up!' he now manfully admits. 'But it's an interesting time because a lot of people are watching me to see if I am slipping up ...'

This very public examination was exacerbated last year by the publication of Bill Buford's warts and all book about working in the kitchens of Mario Batali's flagship restaurant, Babbo. It's an experience that Batali likens to 'standing naked for five days on stage in a bright room with mirrors and lights'.

The book largely paints Batali as a man whose appetites and ambitions are as boundless as his girth. Tales of Bacchanalian behaviour abound. 'The myth of Mario – he built it,' suggests Batali. 'People still come up to me and say "Can you still drink a case of wine?" I say "Fuck yeah, Thursday afternoons!" The one thing I learnt from this book experience is a thing called "limited access" ... but I suppose it's like being on the gossip pages in this town. Once you realise it is merely a yarn based loosely in reality, it's not so intimating anymore.'

While Batali admits that this Belushi-esque 'myth of Mario' hardly harms his image as a party animal, he claims that is seldom him anymore. In fact, in the short time I'm in New York two people tell me how they regularly see him walking his boys to school at 7.30 am. 'I have modified my lifestyle since Leo and Benno came along,' he admits. 'I cook breakfast for them every morning from a little menu of about 12 items. Sure, every now and then I'm still out until five in the morning but it's not every night. It's not even every week, but I am not going to tell anyone that! That way I look like a superman when I turn up at the gym at 7 am.

'I concentrate my intensity into short weekend bursts outside of town. It's never anything dangerous. We don't do any drugs and people don't die instantly of wine, they die instantly of heroin and cocaine mixed together. Our *speedball* is a little brandy and maybe an espresso – we're not "going down" to that!'

What could have killed him, however, was the brain aneurism that doctors discovered seven years ago. It's something that Batali says made him appreciate the less intense moments more but still look for the intense moments as often. 'Look, it's something you're born with and it either pops or it doesn't. It wasn't a question of lifestyle – that I'd overrun the engine – and quite frankly my hubris problem meant that I never felt like I was going to die.'

With restaurants opening in Las Vegas and Los Angeles this year, Batali has opportunities for those 'weekend bursts' but one wonders if he'll have time. There's a third series of *Iron Chef USA* to be filmed, his own kitchenware range to sell and his partnership with NASCAR racing to promote. This latest move is smart as it takes Batali deep into the heart (and hearts) of the American heartland to discover America's own peasant food.

He's also writing two more books. One is a mum-to-be cookbook; the other, *The Art of Eating in Italy*, will tell you what you should eat when you are in Italy, rather than where to eat. 'It's all, "If you are in the Veneto in the fall you should be looking for radicchio, baby. And here's a recipe you should get someone to cook for you"!' is how Batali describes it.

If only that someone was Batali. He'd probably wrap that radicchio in pancetta to pan-fry it and then, just before serving, slather it with loads of black pepper and raw red onion soaked in red wine vinegar. Because when it comes to Mario Batali's food, it's Italian – just not quite how Nonna made it!

Originally published in delicious, *2007*

KAREN MARTINI: THE ARRIVAL

It's rare to find a chef who can woo the palates of both Sydneysiders and Melbournians. It's even rarer when they reject the glitz, glam and adoration of the Harbour City to come back to Bayside to open a pizza joint. But that's just what über-chef Karen Martini has done.

Two years ago Martini was lured by Maurice Terzini to leave The Melbourne Wine Room, the restaurant they co-owned in St Kilda, to head the kitchens at a spectacular new place he was planning to open on the cliffs above Bondi Beach.

It was an instant success. Martini's big-flavoured but unfiddly food combined with the location and crisp Melbourne-style service saw Icebergs Dining Room named best new restaurant by Sydney's *Good Food Guide* last year. But it was not an easy gig. 'It was a monster. I had 18 chefs. At the Wine Room I'd had six. I was on the pans 60 hours each week and it took it out of me physically,' she recalls.

The Sydney dining market was also different from Melbourne: both less adventurous and more used to seeing food tricked up. 'I was forever knocking the garnishes off the top of dishes,' she remembers.

'Sydneysiders also like to be seen in the right spot. What they are eating is generally secondary. I'd often hear them say "Oh, it's a great place – and the food's good too".'

Even though she came back to Melbourne for a couple of days every two weeks or so, the hardest thing about the two years was the separation from her partner in both business and life, Michael Sapountsis. 'It is hard to maintain that intimacy after a while and I can't cook if I am not happy,' she says.

Martini and Sapountsis met eight years ago. He was the head barman and she was the head chef at the Wine Room. 'He had impeccable style. He seduced me over caviar and champagne, late night sushi at Kenzan or dessert at est est est,' she recalls.

He employed similar tactics to help lure her back to live in Melbourne: 'I would ring her and tell her I was at Kenzan or Victoria Street. Or it might be four in the afternoon and I'd ring up and tell her that I was having *carpaccio* and a glass of wine in the Wine Room and that the sunlight was coming through the glass. Stuff that couldn't be done up there.'

With tactics like that it's no surprise that when her two-year agreement with Terzini was up the woman Michael describes as 'beautiful, uncompromising and dreamlike' was coming home.

Ask Martini what the best thing about being back in Melbourne is and the answer is one word: 'Michael'. Although the chance to find that one-off pair of shoes at the Luisa warehouse in Murrumbeena also played its part. 'I love shoes and handbags. In fact I love shopping,' she admits a little guiltily.

'I missed the familiarity of St Kilda. It really feels like home. I've lived here for ten years and it's just nice to toddle down to the newsagents. I also missed the markets, the coffee and buying wholewheat bread from Danny at Baker D. Chirico.'

'The water and the weather in Sydney was beautiful but down here we thrive on eating beautiful food and enjoying wine indoors and out – even if it is under heaters.'

The prospect of opening a casual pizza restaurant with Michael and a couple of friends also helped draw her back. Mr Wolf opened a month ago in an Inkerman Road site that has associations for her so strong that she even dreamed they'd open there. 'It used to be Luxe,' she explains. 'Back then it was like our lounge room. We'd come down for a cheeky terrine on a Sunday night and always bump into loads of friends.'

While it's good to be back, her new life in St Kilda is hardly less busy than the Sydney spell. Martini is initially overseeing the food at Mr Wolf. She's also looking at spending two days a week in the kitchen at The Melbourne Wine Room, the other St Kilda restaurant they still co-own. She maintained a watching brief over the kitchen there during her time in Sydney but a more hands-on presence will mean a menu renovation in the near future. She's also maintaining what she calls a 'guest chef' role at Icebergs and is writing a column for *Sunday Life*, the colour supplement that runs in *The Sunday Age* in Melbourne and *The Sun Herald* in Sydney.

'It's nice she is back but it still doesn't feel like she is because the house is in disarray. We are both so busy,' says Sapountsis.

The future seems no less packed. Sapountsis talks of opening a fancy restaurant in Melbourne 'that showcases Karen's food better'. Karen talks of a Greek restaurant in a seaside resort only open six months of the year. They both mention the idea of a steak restaurant, Mike's Bar and Grill, and there is the talk of children — maybe next year. 'I keep bringing home the station wagon brochures,' jokes Karen.

Originally published in Melbourne Weekly Bayside, *2004*

HESTON BLUMENTHAL:
THE MAGICIAN

In the rarefied air of the world's best restaurants, Heston Blumenthal is the Sundance Kid to Ferran Adria's Butch Cassidy. These two modernist chefs are widely regarded as among the very best in the world, but if Adria is the technical innovator behind a raft of new culinary techniques and ideas, then Blumenthal is the magician. The compact Englishman with the shaved head has the instincts of a showman. At his restaurant, The Fat Duck, in Bray, about 40 minutes' drive west of London (which has earned three stars from Michelin for the last four years), he heartily embraces the notion that the new-style cuisine to which he subscribes should make you laugh as much as being provocative.

I catch up with Blumenthal in Milan, where he is presenting at *Identità Golose,* Italy's four-day celebration of culinary technique and ideas. From the dour pictures that dot the internet I'm expect a serious and quite imposing character, and while there is no doubting that he's got an incredibly sharp mind, away from his kitchens he is a surprisingly open and likeable chap. He's also shorter than I expected.

For an hour we sit in a Milanese bar and over a couple of beers discuss his latest obsessions, which have little to do with the kitchen but everything to do with creating a happy customer.

Earlier that day, discussing his notion of the perfect Christmas meal, he had stood on stage wreathed in dry ice loaded with the aromas of Christmas (wood-smoke, pipe tobacco, leather) while the PA played the sound of a crackling fire and declared, 'Context is so important for eating anything.'

While the demonstration explored the impact of engaging all the senses when eating, Blumenthal is even more focused on the emotional impact this can have: how to engage his customers at a deeper level both while they are in the restaurant, and even before they arrive.

Getting customers in the right mental state is something about which Blumenthal is quite passionate, and with good cause, when you hear him citing research published in *Neuroscience Magazine*. 'The research found that in stressed people the ability to taste flavour is reduced by up to 50 per cent. If we are excited, however, then we'll actually be more receptive to tastes and smells!' he explains, unintentionally providing the answer to one of life's great conundrums: why wine that tasted magnificent in the vineyard's cellar on holiday often seems disappointing when you try it back home.

This area of taste perception has been further explored by a PhD student at Nottingham University whose research is funded by Blumenthal's restaurant. She has found that perception of taste (i.e. salty and sweet) changes on a daily basis. To put it simply: a happy customer will get more out of the food than a stressed one. Similarly, a stressed chef is likely to have less acuity when it comes to adding salt or sugar, which could lead to over-seasoning of dishes.

For Blumenthal, though, it is in the dining room that he is directing his current thinking about taste perception. Perhaps the most celebrated example of this is his dish 'Sound of the Sea', which comes with an iPod playing a soundtrack of gull cries and lapping waves for the diner to listen to while they eat this dish of seaweeds, shavings of sea creature, a briny oyster foam and tapioca 'sand' set on glass above a box of real sand.

The dish was inspired by research conducted by Charles Spence at Oxford University, further exploring the notion that sound can enhance taste. Spence discovered, for example, that hearing 'crisp' sounds before eating chips will make them taste crispier, and '62 per cent of people tested who listened to the sound of the sea while eating an oyster found it more salty with the soundtrack, and 87 per cent found it more pleasurable,' Blumenthal explains. 'Sixty-three per cent found it less pleasurable when eaten listening to barnyard sounds and only 8 per cent found the oyster more salty. We did the same test with our bacon and egg ice-cream. With the sound of sizzling bacon it tasted more bacony to people; eggier with the sound of clucking!'

'Sounds of the Sea' was once even more complex, I learn. 'Initially for that seaside dish we looked at fans to simulate a sea breeze and even had maritime cutlery especially commissioned. Then we stripped it back to find what really pulls the sensory triggers in the most universal way. Almost always I do the most complicated process before pulling it back,' Blumenthal laughs.

Much of what Blumenthal talks about revolves around setting the scene for the dining experience: how to create that ideal and most receptive of guests. In his eyes this is a customer who has developed a childlike excitement about coming to the restaurant before they eat.

This is the reason he's employed a magician to train his floor staff in some basic tricks or sleight of hand that can be used to create the wow factor to help achieve that state in customers.

The vision is that your waiter conjures an egg (surreptiously blown and filled with ice-cream mix before service) from behind a customer's ear. The egg is then cracked and turned into ice-cream at the table through the wonders of liquid nitrogen. A more grandiose deception that Blumenthal's trying to find a way to achieve is pouring both still and sparkling mineral water from the same bottle at the table.

This desire to 'fill people with excitement and fun' also has him talking about working in the future with everyone from scriptwriters and novelists to hologram designers, box manufacturers and lighting engineers to create the right mood in the restaurant.

His grandest plans, however, are built around working out ways to engage the customer before they reach the restaurant. 'People book two months in advance, so we've looked at how to build their excitement over that time. I want them rubbing their hands with anticipation on arrival rather than arriving with their noses in the air looking for faults,' he explains.

'To get them into the right frame of mind – to get that "kid in the candy store" feeling – we thought we'd send them a paper lolly bag and in it is an atomiser and a web address. When they open the page they'll hear an old-fashioned shop bell tinkle and they will walk into a candy store. The atomiser contains a spray that smells like a candy store and then we'd rub the same smell on the frame of the restaurant's front door. We might even put visual clues from the website on the menu or around the village to trigger those feelings as well. After they pay the bill they'll get a paper bag of lollies.

'The trouble is that this is 1600 sweets a week, which means four new chefs, a new room and we haven't even costed in the admin yet. At least we found the right smells to put into the atomiser. The challenge we had was that when I went to an old-fashioned candy store none of them actually smelt like my metaphor ...'

At this point Blumenthal lets out a little guffaw. You get the distinct impression that he's fully aware of how pretentious some of this sounds – and he's more than happy to laugh at himself. Interestingly, however, his own boyish enthusiasm for these more unconventional ideas is so infectious it sweeps you along, and I find myself thinking, 'Well, why not?' And suspecting that Blumenthal is more Willy Wonka than a Silly Wanker.

Parts of this piece originally published in Restaurant *magazine, 2008*

DOES HESTON
BLUMENTHAL SMELL
OF CARAMEL?

No, this is wrong. I'm ambling up the Paris end of Bourke Street and there's Antonio Carluccio drinking coffee outside Grossi Florentino, while fellow Londoner and the only Australian chef to hold two Michelin stars, Shane Osborn, has his photo taken outside the Cellar Bar. Add a pack of Bassett hounds in tutus smoking cheroots outside Pellegrini's and it's the sort of dream I usually have after a night of far too much cheese-board action.

There are no dogs in pink tulle; instead, standing outside Pellegrini's is the world's great English-speaking chef, Heston Blumenthal. Now that's really, really weird.

It shouldn't be a surprise, because in my role as creative director at the Food & Wine Festival I've worked with Rockpool's Neil Perry so Blumenthal and the US's greatest chef, Thomas Keller, can come to Melbourne before Perry's big Sydney charity dinner, which is the ostensible reason for their visit. So, like, I know Blumenthal's coming.

But after five years of pursuing him for the festival it's still just plain odd to find him milling around somewhere so familiar. But then, overall, this third weekend in March is bound to be pretty strange affair, with so many chefs we'd courted for so long finally arriving.

Each embraces the city in different ways. The garrulous giant UK chef Sat Bains flies in at 1 am and promptly heads to the casino for a beer; while the almost monastically-focused Philip Howard from London two-star The Square arrives at 8 am and by 9 is in the kitchen at The Point (with his old sous chef Scott Pickett) prepping for an industry dinner for Melbourne chefs that night.

While Howard and Shane Osborn win gold stars for their pro-fessionalism, Iñaki Aizpitarte and his offsiders from über-hip Parisian bistro Le Châteaubriand are far more free-form. While here they develop a taste for Madame Brussels, and one suspects that they also would have liked to have drunk beer and smoked in the Langham kitchens while prepping their tastings for MasterClass. They come in for a ribbing from the English contingent, led by Bains, and Osborn chews toothpicks (taken after their meal at Flower Drum) to mimic Iñaki's penchant for rolling one in his mouth in a typically lugubrious Parisian fashion.

Italy's hottest chef, Carlo Cracco, has been the hardest to get over the line, with many long late-night calls to Milan, including one where he suggested he'd 'ride off into the sunset on the back of a kangaroo' if his stipulations weren't met. This just confirmed to us why we had to have him here. He arrives, however, all debonair charm and does more with a partially dehydrated egg yolk than you'd ever dream possible. He is one of a posse of international visitors who enjoy The Press Club. Cumulus Inc. and MoVida also attract much praise from those chefs who go.

If Cracco is far nicer than you might imagine, then Blumenthal is somewhat shorter (and, consequentially, Thomas Keller is far taller). Blumenthal also has an easy manner, which is a bit at odds with his status as one of the three best chefs in the world. Yet basking in the warm March sun outside Pellegrini's, he is chatty and openly relieved to be on the other side of the world from the media firestorm surrounding the closure, and subsequent re-opening, of his restaurant. He admits to having never looked forward to a long-distance flight more than the one that brought him here.

For Blumenthal, his visit is a blur of media commitments, dinners at

Rockpool and Vue de monde, racketball games (he's a bit of a demon, as Vue de monde's Shannon Bennett finds out in a 4–0 drubbing), and his two MasterClass appearances. I catch up with him and Keller to discuss their session, which Neil Perry will moderate. Blumenthal acts mock-hurt at the suggestion from his PR that the issue will be shutting him up rather than drawing him out, but it's impressive how without complaint he signs over 350 copies of the chefs' statement that he wrote with Keller to be given to all the attendees at his sessions – even though Keller teases him about his inability to keep his signature to the same place on each statement.

Twelve hours later and I'm standing in a tiny darkening airlock with Keller, Perry and Blumenthal, waiting to introduce their session. I had butterflies meeting Keller the day before but, strangely, with the three of them there these subside. Blumenthal makes up some ridiculous story about how he invented underarm bowling in cricket after a freak fielding accident, tripping over the boundary rope playing for the Sussex under-16 team. Then he and Keller discuss whether twisting the top of your ear sharply clockwise is the best way of staying awake when jet-lagged, and Blumenthal jokes about how they are both going to storm out in mock-disgust at Perry's first question.

Suddenly it's time to step out into the Melbourne Recital Hall and two things hit me. The first is that I'm about to introduce the two greatest chefs in the English-speaking world (which immediately means those butterflies return wearing size-12 hobnail boots and bring along all their friends and relations) and that this is a pretty cool way to conclude my four-and-a-half year tenure at the Food & Wine Festival. The second is that there seems to be the faintest smell of pine forest, wood smoke and leather in this enclosed little space. Sneakily I lean close to Blumenthal. It's him.

For some reason I always thought Heston Blumenthal would smell of caramel – like a moreish salty Caramac bar, probably – but actually he smells like Christmas. Maybe even like Santa Claus, fresh from the chimney. And frankly he's not a bad gift to present to the assembled chefs, media and fans waiting out there in that darkened auditorium.

Originally published in 'A2', The Age, 2009

MORO: THE SAMS

In the UK, Moro has done for Spanish food what the River Café has done for Italian, or so says no less an authority than Nigella Lawson. 'That's very flattering. We'd love to think so,' says chef Samuel Clark a little shyly.

He's the male Sam in the successful husband and wife partnership that opened London's Moro ten years ago to a flurry of critical acclaim. Back then the true flavours of Spain were a rarity in the city; now London is alive with a wave of little tapas bars and more formal *comidores*, as the Spanish call their restaurants. 'Spanish is definitely the buzzword in town at the moment,' says his wife and fellow chef Samantha.

'I suppose we did get people excited about Spanish food in this country, although about half of our menu is actually Muslim-Mediterranean, which can put some Spanish people out when they come here!' laughs Sam.

Ask the couple why there is this global interest in Spanish food, and Samuel puts it down to the fact that Spanish food is underpinned by great ingredients like *mohama* (wind-dried tuna), *jamón pata negra* (a sweet, prosciutto-like ham made from semi-wild black-foot pigs that live off foraged acorns) and fantastic vinegars, which are all still prepared in an artisanal way. 'These are a fantastic basis for cooking great food.

The Spanish flavours are familiar because they are in the European or Mediterranean tradition, but different because they do taste particularly of the country. When you eat something that's been marinated in smoked paprika you just think, "That tastes Spanish",' says Samuel.

The Sams are proud that they've never done clichéd Spanish dishes but have instead concentrated on finding what Samuel calls 'those really sexy little numbers that are done in small villages and that most people wouldn't even recognise as Spanish food'.

Finding those dishes in Spain and North Africa requires a fair amount of legwork and the two of them travel extensively. They've got plans to go to Egypt and Lebanon later this year, and they even spent their honeymoon in a beaten-up Kombi bought from an Aussie guy (naturally) that they drove through Spain and Morocco and on to the edge of the Sahara. 'We immersed ourselves in the whole feel of those countries and those amazing places like the High Atlas mountains and the Sahara. It really helps us approach food in an authentic way – to capture the evocation of a dish when we get home,' says Samuel.

'Yes,' agrees Samantha. 'The way we cook it is very much with the heart. It has to be: ingredients change. The garlic might be stronger one week, weaker the next.'

The couple fell in love with Spanish and Moorish flavours independently before they met. For Samuel it was thanks to spending time with Muslim friends: he loved the sharing of meals around the table; that wonderful use of sweet and savoury; the very un-English liberation of eating with your hands. For Samantha, who spent summers with a grandmother who lived in southern France and time in Italy when studying Italian, her first visit to Spain was a revelation. She was bowled over by the whole lifestyle as much as the food. 'Compared to France and Italy, Spain was much more me. I immediately loved it,' she recalls.

It's a love affair that the Clarks continue through their own little holiday home up in the hills of Andalucia, where Sam and Sam retire to immerse themselves in the Latin way of life with their children Luke (6) and Eve (4).

While Samuel had wanted to be a chef for as long as he could remember, for Samantha it was never a conscious decision. 'I fell into it,' she says. It was a lucky tumble, because it was at her first job in the kitchens of pioneering gastro-pub The Eagle (coincidently round the corner from where Moro is now) that the couple worked together and fell in love.

Samuel, who grew up in the South London suburb of Battersea, had already spent five years cooking at the River Café when it first opened. Although Samantha also worked at the River Café after The Eagle, it is a common misconception that they worked there together.

Working with Rose Gray and Ruth Rogers was very influential on both the young chefs, as Samantha explains: 'Our approach is not dissimilar to that of the River Café and their whole ethos of relying on top-quality ingredients from Italy and letting the food speak for itself.'

Just like Rose and Ruth, it's their complementing strengths that make the Sams such a strong team. He admits to being obsessed with flavour, while acknowledging that Samantha is far better at teaching people the Moro way. She praises his skills with rice dishes and suggests that about the only time they argue in the kitchen is over footling little things like whether a particular salad should or shouldn't contain egg.

'We want them to be able to shut their eyes and imagine they are in that country,' he says. 'It seems you Australians have been much quicker than the Brits to embrace those Moorish flavours,' Samuel says excitedly.

Originally published in delicious, *2007*

ANTHONY BOURDAIN:
THE TERROR

The strange thing about proximity to fame is how quickly the halo spreads. No sooner has *Epicure* mentioned in an off-hand manner that I'm one of a bevy of people looking after US chef and author Anthony Bourdain while he's in town to film a episode of his cable show *No Reservations*, than suddenly chefs and bar owners who would seldom talk to me usually are making chummy contact and suggesting that their venue would be the perfect place to drop in with him. Many of these offers are suffixed with breathless-teen fan requests to just meet the great man …

Bourdain's fame is built on his reputation as a sort of Chandler-esque figure of the American kitchen, sodden in a life of guns, crazy Puerto Rican chefs and class A drugs – an image formed by his book *Kitchen Confidential*. It's the sort of rep that has him, while we are together, hailed by everyone from kebab shop owners to blokes driving hotted-up Fords, as well as foodies.

The tall debonair bloke I meet all these years on is far and away a more clean-cut Tony Bourdain. The constant cigarette is no longer dangling from his lip and *Coyote Ugly* bar antics are limited to a small flurry of different araks and Efes beers over dinner. He says he likes to keep himself nice while he's filming, but I suspect that the birth of a daughter a couple of years ago has helped anchor him. His wife's prodigious judo skills might also have something to do with it!

I've met Bourdain a couple of times before – once sharing pizza at Ladro, when he professed love for Rita Macali for the lateral chef burns on her inner forearms. At another dinner, his unrestrained views on vegetarians surfaced with the sort of volcanic force that's funny but also a little menacing if you've got tofu and alfalfa sprouts in the fridge back at home.

On this trip his schedule has been especially full. Bourdain is a self-confessed chef groupie and lover of new food experiences, so there was dinner at the Half Moon in Brighton with the O'Connell brothers, Pearl's Geoff Lindsay and Greg Malouf from Momo; beasts cooked on a spit barbecue on the rooftop of the Melbourne Supper Club; spicy boiled fish and some incendiary Sichuan food with Tony Tan at the inappropriately named Dainty Sichuan ('better than most in Sichuan', apparently); and road trips with host and trip-fixer Paul Wilson to meet David Blackmore's wagyu cattle and discover Dan Hunter's food at the Royal Mail. The latter was a highlight.

Bourdain's people have specified to me that he is interested in looking at Melbourne's street food. So after he whoops my arse at Trugo (that peculiarly Melbourne game invented by railway workers, with a passing resemblance to croquet in the same way that I have a passing resemblance to George Clooney) we head to Sydney Road. There we eat Lebanese pizza at A1 and Tabet's, a couple of kebabs, taste the bastourma and sujuk sausage at the wonderful Istanbul Butchers – and discuss the many incarnations of savoury bread that line this culinary artery, from the Iraqi cheese triangles at Amir to Singaporean Indian *murtabak* and Turkish *gozleme*. One thing not on the menu is sweet pastries from Balha, as Bourdain has no sweet tooth. I take a childish Alpha-male pride in the fact that he has to break for a lie-down after all this. He claims jet lag; I suspect inferior capacity.

We reconvene for a night planned to capture the essence of the changing face of eating out in Melbourne. Gin and tonics in the back garden of The Alderman are followed by dinner next door at Rumi. Naturally Joe Abboud's modern Lebanese-cum-Persian place sums up the notion of classically trained local chefs bringing their training to bear on the food of their cultural background – a bit of a trend these days with George Calombaris' Hellenic Republic, Ismail Tosun's Gigibaba et al.

Bourdain is the perfect dining companion – irreverent, hungry, loquacious, and obscenely well-travelled. The conversation darts from the political situation in Lebanon (where he's filmed) and buying a house outside Hoi An (where of course he's also filmed) to the issue of old lady fans who try to French-kiss him and where to bury a body on the New Jersey turnpike.

Conversation stops, however, for a plate of perfectly crisp but tender quail served with grape molasses. It's that sort of a dish. And the type of tucker so good he orders it again without looking up. The same thing happens with skewered ribs served with an intense garlic sauce called *toum* that stops him in his tracks. He's not had it before and the new experience seems to energise him – so much so that he leaves railing about why more people don't fly to Melbourne to eat when the food is this good. Maybe the fact he's travelling with a film crew might change that!

Originally published in 'A2', The Age, 2009

JOHN BURTON RACE:
THE BAD BOY

John Burton Race has disappeared. The mercurial chef and grumpy old man of the ABC TV series *French Leave* has hopped into his sleek black Porsche and sped away from me and the summer tourists that choke the lanes and quays around his new restaurant in the painfully picturesque Devonshire fishing town of Dartmouth.

It's a slight concern, not just because we've come to the time allotted to chat and take his portrait, but also because his assistant seems to have no idea where he's gone. But then one gets the feeling that John Burton Race is not the sort of boss to try to tie down or question too closely. He has quite a reputation for a savage temper. A reputation won, along with two Michelin stars, at his L'Ortolan restaurant in Berkshire.

That was back before the fearsomely driven chef's surprising decision – not least to his family – to up sticks from his new London restaurant and move to south-west France for a year.

Two hours later we have travelled down impossibly green lanes to his new family home, assured he'll be there. It's a large rambling farmhouse the Burton Races are in the process of moving into. John's long-suffering wife, Kim, has no idea where he is either. Or who we are. She adopts that familiar demeanour that made her such a sympathetic character in *French Leave*. We make small talk until we hear the sound of fat, low-profile tyres crunching gravel. It's the return of the chef, in his crumpled pink polo shirt with a mischievous grin and a story of poor mobile coverage and flat tyres.

For all the stories of bullying and excesses, John Burton Race is a surprisingly likeable bloke. He pulls out cold beers. He's tall, smokes incessantly and talks with intensity and humour in that slightly smart, old-colonial accent of his, soaking his conversation with very English self-deprecation.

'To be perfectly honest I didn't want to come back at all,' he says, pulling on the ever-present cigarette and talking wistfully about his time in Montferrand, which formed the basis for *French Leave*.

'I would have loved to stay but three of the girls were coming up to their important exams and there had been enough disruption. Everybody had given up everything to come with me to do this. I had my fun and that was the end of it.'

The question was, what were John and the family coming back to? The London restaurant had been sold and their house in Oxfordshire was still let out. The ferry home from Europe to England dropped them in the West Country, and while looking to buy a small country house hotel in the region, John and Kim fell in love with the Devon countryside. With property prices skyrocketing and their first choice, a place called the Horn of Plenty in the Tamar Valley, falling through, they decided to settle on a restaurant instead.

Under Joyce Molyneux and Tom Jaine, Dartmouth's Carved Angel had been one of the best regional restaurants in the UK, but things had slipped. When John heard it was for sale it was the perfect opportunity – especially when the TV company that had shot *French Leave* said they'd like to film John and Kim's new adventure. The result was *Return of the Chef*, the series currently screening on the ABC.

'We got on with our business of opening the restaurant and they got on with filming the trials and tribulations of all that,' explains John. And there were a few. Problems with the builders; some embarrassing issues with the budget; and Burton Race's attempts at exposing a few suppliers who falsely claimed their produce was free-range or organic. All of this caused ripples, but it was nothing compared to the furore over his treatment of his staff. 'I was adamant that I was going to only employ local people,' he says. 'It was a complete, utter disaster. I soon realised – in the manager's case after a day, in the case of the local girls about three weeks – that they were going to send me bust. They had no idea about service at all. So I got rid of them and bought in some of the French guys who had worked with me before. That pissed a few locals off.'

Dartmouth is proudly insular. The county flag of Devon flies on many houses. Visitors are dismissed as 'grockels' and while John's Porsche got daily parking tickets, the locals at the restaurant who survived the purge would get a tip-off, sometimes even from the parking inspectors themselves!

Now some of those unfriendly local attitudes have softened slightly, not least because John has become a passionate advocate and supporter of the local produce. 'Ninety-five per cent of my produce comes from Devon,' he claims. 'It's brilliant. Dartmouth has the best crab in England and great lobster, thanks to the way fresh water from the River Dart meets the sea. This gives them this really sweet flesh. There's salmon and sea trout. You've got sea bass running off the Gulf Stream. You've got red mullet. We've got brill, turbot, mackerel, bream, various types of sole.

'Then I have a guy near Tavistock making my butter. He's churning it just for me. I have people in Blackawton, Muddiford and Modbury growing for me. Carl, who you see in the series, still brings me my lobsters and the crab are pulled up from the boats that tie up at the quay outside the restaurant. I'm in touch through my little butcher with the farms. If I wanted to I could get the name of that cow you're eating!'

This has been vital to Burton Race's radical change in his approach to food. 'Going to France taught me that the emphasis should be on the ingredients, getting it fresh and not doing too much to it. My whole style of food has gone about-turn. It's gone simple,' he says.

'For 13 years I was a two-Michelin-star cook with all the comp-lications, trappings and trimmings that go with that. I had a wine list that was 800 bins. That's about 350,000 quid [A$900,000] sitting in the cellar. The table settings cost hundreds of pounds before anyone even sat down to eat a piece of bread. I had guys making five different canapés for before you'd even started the meal and they'd only work on those canapés. It got to the point that it was so expensive to eat in my gaff that I couldn't afford it!'

What Burton Race wanted with the New Angel was somewhere relaxed, unpretentious and family-friendly. 'I wanted it to be the sort of place I wanted to eat. I don't want them to walk into a temple. In my previous places it was so quiet that if you dropped a fork it blew the windows out!' he jokes.

That's certainly not the case at the New Angel. There are no table-cloths and no silver: it's all stainless cutlery and very simple glassware. There's no carpet, no curtains and no finery at all. When we're there almost every table has a child at it. The small smoking room he set up as somewhere to indulge his chain-smoking habit is clogged, not with cigarette smoke, but with parked strollers. In spite of all this, the inspectors gave the New Angel a Michelin star just six months after opening.

Welcoming kids is part of Burton Race's personal battle to encourage children to be more adventurous and try things they've never had before. 'I tell every parent that we'll do a half portion of anything on the menu and I'll charge them half-price,' he says.

It's a battle that he seems to have already lost with his own kids. 'Listen, half my kids are hopeless. I find it very frustrating,' he says. 'Charles would just eat chocolate. Our youngest, Amelia, would eat you if you stood still because she is very much like me and she'll go for it. Eliza's cool. Martha's nowhere. She just eats fat shit and it makes her fat. Olivia's a bit picky. Mum's anti-fish because she's allergic to it, so that has spread down the line a little bit. In France they'd live on junk and I was just trying to get them off it. I think I have got a bit further now but I definitely haven't won that battle.' Having said that, Burton Race hardly helped his cause: before France he'd never actually cooked for his children.

The move to France and the subsequent return to England was supposed to signal a change in emphasis for John Burton Race. He even went so far as to promise his family that he'd make time for them and not get totally get sucked up into the new restaurant. 'Sure, coming here has allowed me to spend a little bit more time with them, but mostly I lied,' he now admits with a cheeky smile.

'Whatever standard you set, you need a certain level of commitment. And let's face it, you can talk it up as much as you like but they are shit hours being a chef. When everyone's working, we're working. When everyone is on holiday, we're sweating. When it's Christmas and you are opening the presents, I'm cooking the lunch.

'What can you do? You don't ever get the balance right, but I am a lot more relaxed now. If I want to go drinking with my friends, I will. Prior to going to France I never did – I'd rather die than miss a service in the restaurant. My wife would say, "If you don't take the night off, John, we are getting divorced." I'd say, "Send me the papers." That's what I was like.

'That is absolutely true because that's what happened to my first marriage. I called her bluff but she wasn't bluffing! Don't ever get divorced. It took me about five years to get the money. Do you know how broke I was? It was terrible!'

John has two children from this first marriage. He also has two with Kim, and they, along with Kim's other four children, live with them. So what kind of a dad is he? Burton Race's self-assessment is pretty brutal. 'Oh, I'm rude, honest, direct and all of them know there is a certain line you can't cross. But more or less they get what they want. I give them more time now that I have ever done – which isn't difficult because I used not to give them any!' he laughs – more at his own shortcomings than with cruelty.

Burton Race is the first to admit that he deserves some of his reputation for not being very nice. 'I have always been the antisocial bastard who would rather not say hello,' he admits. 'My reputation isn't terribly good because I have always been rude; especially when I was younger. I had my own ideas and everyone else could go and fuck themselves.'

He talks of literally flinging back plates of food at young chefs that didn't meet his exacting standards in his old kitchens. 'Sometimes things do still piss me off, but I *used* to bash people. I don't do any of that anymore.'

He's also described himself as a 'loud-mouthed arrogant git and a totally mad bastard'. That's something that he admits is still there, even if it is more buried now. 'I've just got older, my hair's falling out, I'm grey, a bit fatter than I used to be but I've still got the brain of an 18-year-old … my wife says 12.'

While age may have mellowed him, being exposed on television has also been a complete eye-opener and helped force a change in his demeanour. 'It's everything that I didn't want and everything that I absolutely despised. People stop you in the street and shake your hand, or criticise the way you treat your family. Or say they had a really nice meal or that I'm too expensive. They think they know me. And they think they own me. Actually 90 per cent of the time I really like it but 10 per cent of the time I wish I had kept it all a big secret.'

With the fame has come some pluses – like financial security. He now has consultancies paying him more than he used to earn as a chef. In fact, he hasn't even taken a salary from the restaurant.

'Security' is, however, a fleeting concept in the Burton Race household. John talks of the tough years and risks he's had to take to get where he is now. 'I had to find my way – the house was on the line, heck, even the kids' dinner was on the line – to get where I wanted to get. I've had setbacks. Huge highs and great lows. I've gone bust and made money. And that's life. But then I want "He had a go at most things" on my tombstone.'

Now that things look secure at last, Singapore-born Burton Race talks of his one big fear – getting stuck in a rut. Does this mean the family lives in dread that he will uproot them again? 'Of course they are worried. And so they should be,' he admits. 'I am having the time of my life but if you ask me what I am going to do next year I don't know. I don't wanna get bored. When I change my mind, I just go boom! But for now I'm happy. We're opening this place where we'll have a few bedrooms in town, then there's a cooking school that is going in on the top floor of the restaurant. Also a place has come up in Exeter and some of my old boys are coming back to work with me down here, so that gives me some options for expanding. And I really want to have a pub around here that does great, simple food ...'

A pub is on the agenda for tonight as well. Kim has frocked up to go out and John's got no intention of working. That's one lesson he's learned. 'Right, we're gonna get mullered. End of. That's why I've got a taxi,' he says, pushing back from the table in the waning sunshine. And as suddenly as he appeared, John Burton Race is gone; a full ashtray and the slight aftershock of his manic energy the only signs he was once here.

Originally published in delicious, *2007*

JIMMY SHU:
THE HANU MAN

When you arrive at Alice Springs airport there's a quarantine bin that boldly declares that tomatoes, capsicums and chillies are absolutely forbidden.

It's a mystery, then, how Jimmy Shu managed to smuggle his restaurant Hanuman into The Alice. For here the food sings with the fiery heat of bird's-eye chillies and the fragrance of herbs that would never grow among these red, rocky desert hills.

But then, the chef-cum-restaurateur behind Melbourne restaurants such as Shakahari and Isthmus of Kra (and who subsequently blazed a trail for Australian fusion cookery at Monsoon and Near East) has always been adept at getting his hands on hard-to-find ingredients. Whether it was helping Asian food importer Jerry Lee start out in the early eighties – when few knew what star anise was, let alone torch ginger – tracking down hidden growers of lemongrass, or even less kosher methods. In the eighties he was nabbed by Customs trying to sneak in a couple of galangal roots hidden in his sandshoes and given a serious dressing down. 'But they never found the kaffir lime leaves in my wife's bra,' he whispers.

This love of exotic ingredients has found a perfect home in The Alice and in Darwin, where the first Hanuman opened. 'Darwin sometimes feels more like Asia than Australia,' he says.

While his long-suffering wife, Selena, and his two daughters still live in Melbourne, Jimmy has become a de facto Territorian over the past five years. 'I spend more time in Darwin but I love Melbourne. It's like being torn between two lovers,' he explains. 'But Melbourne is a very tough market for a restaurant and I got turned off doing business there.'

Jimmy arrived in Melbourne from Malaysia in 1974, the day before Cyclone Tracey hit Darwin, with $50 in his pocket. Love brought him to Australia: he was following a woman of whom his domineering father didn't approve, but he told the Customs official that he wanted to open a restaurant. The officer gave him a valuable tip – work for others to learn the business first. So when the relationship withered, Jimmy worked three jobs to learn, and earn, what he could. The worst was putting jam in doughnuts at the Croydon market. 'The doughnuts were straight from the boiling oil so you are supposed to dust your hand with sugar to provide some insulation. The trouble is that the hot oil from the doughnuts melts the sugar and you'd get these awful caramel burns all over your hands,' he says.

It was washing dishes at a hotel, however, where he learnt the most. Jimmy was constantly looking over his shoulder to see what he could pick up … 'but I'm still washing dishes,' he jokes.

In spite of a serious addiction to LPs by everyone from ELO to Creedence Clearwater Revival, he had earned enough by 1980 to purchase Tony Tan's share in Shakahari – a vegetarian restaurant in Carlton co-owned by Kim Beh Un and Ma Kim Poay.

'I worked with that partnership for 11 years and it was fantastic but it ended badly – the male spouses got involved. I think I opened my mouth too much. A taxidriver asked me about working in a long-term partnership and I told him how good it was; then the next week all the problems started!'

Since then Shu has tried his hand at everything. He opened Monsoon and Near East in Melbourne, where he met his wife, Selena. 'She is a brilliant cook of Nonya background – half Indonesian, half Chinese – and a wonderfully supportive woman,' he says. He also opened the first conveyor-belt sushi restaurant in Kuala Lumpur (Kaitan) and an elegant bistro there called Zigi's, which served Italian and Thai food. 'This was the mid-nineties: we had pizza with Thai toppings and a roti pizza,' he remembers.

He's even had a noodle bar in Brisbane, called Gado Gado, but now he is best known for his Hanuman restaurants in Darwin and Alice Springs, where he serves a menu that champions what he sees as the true flavours of Thai and Indian, rather than fusion styling.

Shu's seduction by the Northern Territory happened on a trip to Darwin to source barramundi. The combination of eating the best chilli bugs he'd ever tasted and a distinct lack of competition in the town sealed his decision to open a restaurant there. Hanuman proved to be no little success; his fame meant he was even invited back to Melbourne to take a lead role at the Commonwealth Games Athletes' Village kitchens in 2006. There could have been few better people to feed so many cultures at once, because Shu was actually born and raised in Sri Lanka. 'I'm the Chinese boy that grew up eating *chapattis*,' he laughs. 'I am a bit of a hotch-potch. A mixed bag.'

Back in Sri Lanka, his father was an entrepreneurial Chinese restaurateur who made his own soy sauce and purchased the island's first noodle-making machine from a closing Chinese trade exhibition. As the oldest of four children, Jimmy's job was to make the noodles and the soy sauce. The wonderful aroma of that fresh soy stays with him still: 'It's unforgettable; so mellow.'

It was hard yakka though and his father a very tough, determined man. When the restaurant was starting out and money non-existent, his father would spend his days on a bicycle following the coal delivery truck 'like a piranha', picking up fallen coal to fuel the stoves.

Jimmy was the black sheep. 'Being the oldest put a lot of pressure on me,' he says. 'I hated my father because he got away with murder. But even though he cooked bastardised Chinese, I now realise that I learnt a lot from him.'

One thing is clear: Shu sees himself as much more of an ideas man than a hard-nosed businessman. 'I don't think you can be a ruthless businessman as well as a romantic food lover,' he says. 'I just love food. It is such a great way to experience other cultures. I love the way the Thais cook with the heart and with their palate. I keep telling our chefs you have to cook with your palate and not from a recipe because ingredients can differ in intensity and pungency so much between here and there. Take lemongrass. Here we fertilise it a lot. Back there they can't afford fertiliser so it is virtually growing wild, so it's very potent. One lemongrass stalk there has the equivalent flavour of four or five here.'

So when it comes to cooking Thai food like his, take Jimmy's advice and add flavourings bit by bit, tasting as you go until you find that elusive balance that is the secret of great Thai food.

Originally published in delicious, *2006*

GILBERT LAU: THE WAITER

The slight little boy, he must be about six, is standing up to his knees in the thick black mud of the emptied pond, smiling. He reaches down into the ooze. And then deeper still. To where the biggest ones always hide. His fingers search, pry and snake until they feel a familiar cold muscular smoothness. The hands dart and then, in a spray of ooze, emerge triumphantly brandishing a wriggling strap of fury. A long, fat eel.

It's a memory a world away from the polished elegance of Melbourne's Flower Drum restaurant, but the beatific smile of the little boy is more than a little familiar. It's the same smile that is an almost permanent fixture on the face of Gilbert Lau – the restaurateur, waiter and now reluctant retiree whose calm presence is still synonymous with Melbourne's most critically acclaimed restaurant.

For decades that smile has masked the trials, sacrifices and sheer hard work that have gone into building 'the Drum' into one of the world's great Chinese restaurants.

Lau has seen a lot in his 62 years. He was born in a village in Toi Shan – a region of what was then Canton in China's south. It was fundamentally an agrarian existence. The village would harvest their fishpond every six months for carp and eels, and his recent return for the first time in 55 years brought back vivid memories of the vegetable gardens and the taste of peanuts 'pulled straight from the ground'. 'The family still has a restaurant in the village and our old family home was still there, but the village has faded,' he says.

Lau recalls that early family life with his five younger brothers was happy. They were relatively well off. Lau's grandfather owned a three-storey eating house and opera theatre, the Wing Hing Lau (the name 'lau' means 'house'), where the extended family also worked.

The postwar upheaval that culminated in the 1949 declaration of a communist government in China, however, left many families like the Laus scrambling to emigrate. 'Everybody is trying to run away and we are no exception,' recalls Lau. 'Hong Kong basically became my home for nine years. We stayed there until we were processed to come to Melbourne.'

Melbourne was the logical destination for the Lau family, as Gilbert's grandfather and great-grandfather had come to Australia in the 1850s, lured by the gold rush. They landed at Robe to avoid the ten-pound head tax imposed on Chinese gold workers in Victoria and walked to 'new gold mountain', as the Chinese diggers had dubbed Bendigo. ('Old gold mountain' was San Francisco.) 'In those days they never had industry in Toi Shan. So people sold themselves as labour. That's why Toi Shan villagers are scattered over the New World,' says Lau.

Lau's own father had also lived in Victoria for a while, in 1929, and he returned here to earn money to support the family in Hong Kong. But the Laus' life there was still lean compared to Canton, with no money for a telephone or a record player. The one consolation was food. Any spare money that Lau could muster was spent on tidbits from Hong Kong's Hakka street vendors. It was at these stalls that his love of food was ignited.

His first food memory might be of a pork bun in the family restaurant in Toi Shan, but Lau's eyes light up when he talks of pig skin deep-fried 'until it is fluffy', served with turnips and fish balls. A prawn soup with prawn roe has him rolling his eyes in reverie. 'This is basically food to me. My fast food,' he says.

Though he was keen to move to Melbourne, his father insisted he stay in Hong Kong for a Chinese education, despite the fact that Lau says he was a 'very average student'. Only Chinese poetry and history engaged him.

At last in 1957, aged 15 and a half, Lau sailed on the *Cheung Sha* to join his father in Melbourne. 'It was like coming home,' he recalls with joy. 'Father is here. My uncles are here. Half the village is here. I have about 20 restaurants to choose from to work in!'

Lau lived above his grandfather's shop in Little Bourke Street – where the Mask of China now stands. He went to school at St Mary's Boys in North Melbourne and would wander the nearby Victoria Market in awe. With his first pounds he purchased grapes – a luxury he could only afford to savour once a year back in Hong Kong. He bought a case. 'I couldn't eat them all. I just looked at them and thought "This shows how rich I am",' he now remembers.

Young Lau needed a job, but it was his uncle who decided that he should work on the floor of his restaurant, rather than in the kitchen. 'He dictated what we all did. He sent my brother to the kitchen and he's been a chef for the last 30 years. He still cooks at the Flower Drum, so uncle obviously picked the right area for both of us!'

The food of Chinese restaurants in fifties Melbourne horrified Lau. That US invention, chop suey, dominated menus. 'We'd soak the cabbage overnight because it cost too much to cook it from raw. Then we'd serve it on fried noodles with cold chicken on top. I asked, "Do people eat that?" Uncle said, "Of course they do." From that day onward I say to myself, "I have to make this a little bit better."'

As he says this he dabs his rheumy eyes with a tissue, something he does all through our two and a half hours together. This has the strange effect of amplifying his apparent amusement at some stories and the poignancy of others.

They might well be tears of laughter when he tells of how they used to make their own 'soy sauce' back then from no more than sugar, MSG, a touch of salt and black food colouring. 'People used to drink it and say it was very tasty because it wasn't too salty,' laughs Lau, dabbing his eyes.

After seven years in Melbourne the old Lau family wanderlust resurfaced. Gilbert Lau returned to Hong Kong, working in reservations for Cathay

Pacific and selling menswear for Lane Crawford. Here he first set eyes on Alice, the woman who would later become his wife. She was working in the department store's Oriental gallery. Yet Gilbert didn't talk to her for 12 months. Was he shy? 'No, maybe too busy making a living,' he counters.

In 1967 he travelled again, to Canada and the US. The restaurants he worked in there were hugely different from Hong Kong and Melbourne. He learnt how to make cocktails, organise rosters for 400-seat restaurants and how to survive living only on tips. This taught him the right professional attitude to 'earn gratitude'. In San Francisco he discovered smart Chinese restaurants like The Empress of China, taking a shine to both the concept and the name.

In 1969 Lau returned to Melbourne, and was joined by his mother, Alice and the rest of the family. 'I'd come back with all these ideas I'd picked up while travelling. I wanted a place of my own,' he says.

It was a dream shared by an old colleague from the fifties' Bourke Street scene, Ken Louey. Together they hatched a plan to buy the ailing Lymco restaurant – a plan that came to fruition in 1971 when they reopened it as The Empress of China.

Ask Lau what made his first restaurant unique and he ponders for a second. It wasn't just the presence of real soy sauce. He reckons it was delivering the food to the table one dish at a time rather than all at once. 'I said to Ken, if they have everything on the table in front of them they might eat it quickly because they don't want it to get cold, and we may be able to fit in a second sitting but people will never come back.'

He also sought out ingredients others weren't using, like barramundi and banana prawns from Queensland, and served eye fillet when others would use skirt. 'Food is ingredients. Ingredients are what make people remember you,' he says.

The problem was that after a few years Gilbert felt the Empress was too small and Ken felt Gilbert's new plans were too big. They went their separate ways. On Monday 26 May 1975, Gilbert Lau opened the 150-seat Flower Drum in a converted car park at 103 Little Bourke Street. The name came from *Flower Drum Song*, a movie about the overseas Chinese and their life in America.

Here Lau pushed his attitude towards service even further. He concentrated on planning customers' meals for them in an effort to make everything simple for the diner. Success, however, was not instant: it took three years for the Flower Drum to gain popularity. 'We weren't running to the bank to borrow money, but we weren't sure if we were a success,' says Lau.

Those early years as a restaurateur were extremely demanding. Lau worked up to 90 hours a week and, for the first seven months, without a day off. And for a period there were two Flowers Drums to run during the protracted transition to the current location.

His sacrifices back then were amplified by the fact that he had married Alice in 1969. They lost their first baby, but in February 1972 Jason came into the world, followed in December 1973 by Michael. Lau admits he hardly ever saw the young boys and that Alice raised the kids by herself. 'Alice was fantastic. She looked after the house and two boys. I did whatever I could on the financial side,' he says.

He now regrets that he wasn't there for the family more, but acknowledges that, 'You do what you have to do to support the family … there are so many bills to pay.' I point out that there's more than an echo of his father here and he agrees: 'He did not know the family for years and years and years.'

Now there's more time. Four years ago he started working only a six-day week – but if this was meant to help him gear up for retirement, it's not working. He still finds it impossible to relax. Even though he sold the Flower Drum to three of his long-serving employees 18 months ago, Gilbert has stayed on as a consultant. I suspect that his new contract probably doesn't specify that he comes in as much as he does. But then, here is a man who admits to being 'very particular', with an obsession that 'things need to be right'. He also admits to being very stubborn.

Enter the warren of offices in back of house at the Flower Drum and little seems to have changed. Lau still has his chaotic little office lined with cases of wine. There's a small list of favoured customers stuck to the wall. The desk is piled with papers but no computer – he claims not to understand them – and there's an ever-present tissue box. It's a total contrast with the neat calm of the dining room. 'You'd think after 18 months I'd no longer have the vibe but maybe it is just so addictive … maybe in another year and a half it will go,' he suggests hopefully.

The very idea of him taking up outside interests, however, has Lau laughing almost to the point of breathlessness about his inability to embrace the golf course or a bowls club. 'Terrible. I am absolutely terrible. Surely you'd think there must be something else equally as exciting as restaurants, but for 18 months now I am still searching.'

He has started to listening to Chinese opera again, which he describes as 'all this shouting like "aarrrg"'. He still enjoys fine wine, but after 40 years he no longer smokes. 'You couldn't smoke anywhere so I stopped. It was hard to give up but when you have to you can,' he says, although admitting that there have been more than a few lapses. 'I still want a cigarette,' he admits.

He has, he says, seriously cut back on his involvement in racing, too – a passion that is often whispered to be his most notorious vice. Lau says he now only follows the horses during the Spring Carnival, but it's clear that racing is still one of his real passions. 'I loved racing. It's the only thing that would really relax me on a Saturday, but I haven't been to the races for nearly 15 years now,' he claims.

It should be noted that for Lau the Spring Carnival runs for about six weeks and includes all the lead-up races, the Caulfield Cup, the Kyneton Cup, the Sandown Cup, the week at Flemington – and even the Eclipse Stakes. 'I only really love the Spring,' he says with a beaming smile. 'I like the long-distance races like the Caulfield, the Mackinnon, the Melbourne Cup, the Wakeful. You really have to follow and watch how it goes.'

He actually sighs with pleasure after mentioning the Wakeful and then talks excitedly about how he loves to unwind by watching tapes of old races like the Melbourne Cup, rejoicing in the grace of Phar Lap and the power of the majestic Bernborough.

'Oh Christ, Bernborough,' Gilbert gulps, as if remembering a long-lost love rather than the Queensland horse whose run of 15 straight wins was broken in front of 108,213 people by the Caulfield Cup handicapper's 68-kilogram load.

He even pulls out, from the jumble in the shelves behind his desk, 10-year-old pictures of Market Lane, a horse he part-owned that won five races straight but made him no money.

If not golf or racing, what does the future hold for Gilbert Lau? One thing is for sure: Lau is denying he'll dive back into restaurant ownership. He claims it was only a search for culinary inspiration and a chance to revisit his roots that he was seeking when he journeyed to China this year, and poo-poos the rumour that he is about to open a restaurant in Shanghai. He suggests Hong Kong as a much more likely location. 'Not that I have any plans at the moment,' he quickly adds.

It would surely be a fitting end, should the culinary adventure of the little boy from Toi Shan come full circle. Suggest this, however, and Gilbert's response is predictable. He smiles. 'No, Melbourne is the place to open a restaurant,' he says with finality.

SOME OF GILBERT'S RULES OF SERVICE

'A waiter is supposed to act however they like but this is how I prefer to act.'

- If people don't feel like talking then do your job and leave nicely. You are not there to debate.
- Never stay there too long.
- Never interrupt when people are conducting their party. Go in at the right moment.
- Ask things very directly, very politely, very quickly. Then leave very quickly.
- Don't embarrass the hosts.
- My attitude is that I am like your servant. I am a waiter. There is nothing wrong with that.
- Every restaurant is an orchestra. The front of house and the kitchen must play harmoniously. The head waiter has to perform equally as well as everyone else. If one little thing is unsatisfactory then the evening has a mark.

Originally published in 'Epicure', The Age, 2004

SHANE OSBORN: THE BEST

There were five fire engines outside his restaurant when Shane Osborn arrived on Monday 15 November 2004, but that isn't the sight that sticks in the 34-year-old chef's memory. It's the homeless man walking along the street drinking a charred bottle of vintage Krug Champagne that was still hot from the fire. The bottle was one of many that had spilt from the blackened fridges firemen had pulled from the smouldering restaurant. It was a sobering moment.

The day before, Shane Osborn had been a chef on top of the world. In January that year he had become the first Australian to win a second coveted Michelin star, and thus confirmed the status of his intimate 49-seat restaurant, Pied à Terre, as one of London's five best. His first book, *Starters* (Quadrille, 2005), had just been published to good reaction and, best of all, his partner, Julia Miller, was expecting their first child.

It was only when Perth-born Shane got inside that he saw how total the damage was. 'It was totally heart-wrenching. The fire had destroyed the top floor and the roof, but it was the water [used for putting out the fire and from burst pipes] that did the most damage. Only a year before the place had been given a half-a-million-dollar refurb.'

The ceilings had collapsed, the walls too, and both Pied à Terre's rotating collection of artwork and much of its extensive cellar was history. At least his hand-written collection of recipes in the basement was largely unharmed.

It was a sickening blow, but the real challenge was then trying to keep his team of 33 staff together while they rebuilt. With an annual wages bill of $1.3 million and monthly rent of another $25,000, time is money. A lot of money. It was a very nervous few months until the insurance assessor agreed to pay their $8 million claim and pick up these on-going costs and the cost of rebuilding the restaurant. 'I had more than a few sleepless nights,' recalls Shane.

Those sleepless nights were probably good training. In January this year Julia gave birth to Rose, and one of the few positives to come from the fire is that he now has time to spend with her, as the restaurant won't reopen until August. He is totally smitten. 'She was born by Caesarean so I got to hold her first. It blew me away. Out of all the things I have ever done, nothing comes close. The realisation that this little person is so dependent on Julia and me; that everything we do is going to affect her for the rest of our lives. It's amazing.'

Ironically it was thanks to a fire next door to Pied à Terre two years earlier that Shane first met Julia. 'The fire alarms were all going off and then this beautiful blonde Irish girl came running in. She's a carpenter so she had on one of those belts with all the tools hanging off it. I was standing in the restaurant and she told us we had to get everyone out. 'I turned around and said, "Who the *!@# are you?" She said "There's a fire, you @!*# dipstick, get out!" She's a bit fiery. After evacuating we were stuck outside for seven hours and we just got talking.'

While some top UK chefs drive around in red Ferraris and live in swank houses, Shane and Julia's home life is reassuringly down to earth. The couple lives in a rented flat in the London suburb of Queen's Park and although he owns a little VW car, Shane cycles to and from work. His only expense, other than travelling and eating out, is the house music he buys for the DJ decks at home that are his hobby.

'We are trying to buy a place but it's so expensive here,' he says. 'You see a one bedroom flat for £260,000. It's ridiculous compared to Australia. Also, London is not a great place to bring up kids. There's an idea that we'll move out when we have more. I want them to have space to run around. I want them to know what an apple tree looks like and what rhubarb looks like growing out of the ground.'

Returning to live in Perth, however, is not an option. After over ten years living in London he now feels it's home. 'I like the humour here. People say it is a cold place, and I'll admit that the first two years were tough, but now I've met some fantastic people that I know I'll have as friends forever.'

When it came to cooking, Shane started young. His godparents ran a catering company and his mum, Pat, was a caterer. From the age of twelve Shane had been helping her at weddings and twenty-firsts, peeling carrots and arranging food on platters.

At home Pat cooked simple food for Shane, his dad, Tony, and his elder brother and sister: lasagnes, pastas and homemade hamburgers. 'It was never extravagant but it was good and simple,' he recalls almost wistfully.

In fact, along with the beach and the big skies, the lazy mornings reading the newspaper in cafés and the nights with the boys eating searing Thai salads washed down with a half slab of VB, it is his mum's tuna pasta casserole that he misses most about Australia. 'It's fantastic. It's topped with melted cheese and broken-up potato chips.'

His childhood might have been surrounded by food, but it still didn't prepare him for his first day as an apprentice at Perth's Highlight 33 restaurant. This revolving restaurant was *the* place in town back in 1985. 'The first time I walked into that kitchen there was food everywhere and just the wonderful smells blew me away. I'd go to the dry stores and there'd be these 25-kilo bags of white and dark chocolate buttons. I'm fifteen years old. Of course every time I'd go to that fridge I'd be munching away!'

Shane loved his four-year apprenticeship there. Then he moved on to Pierre's, also in Perth. There the predominantly French and English brigade of chefs filled his head with stories of cooking in London and Paris. On his first visit to London he fell in love with the place, yet he returned to Perth 18 months later to work for Jonathan Alston at the

Captain Snelling Hotel in Claremont. 'I am where I am today in a good part because of the role Jonathan played in pointing me in the right direction,' he says of his good friend, who currently runs the kitchens at Melbourne's Scusami.

Then after two years in Sweden, Alston – now working in London – encouraged Shane to come and try his hand there. The rest is, as they say, history.

He worked with a succession of London's top chefs – Marcus Wearing at L'Oranger, Philip Howard at The Square, and the mercurial Tom Aikens at Pied à Terre. He helped them win their stars and picked up knowledge, skills and experience that shape the look and taste of his food today.

When Aikens resigned from Pied à Terre after an alleged incident of kitchen abuse two weeks before Christmas 2000, his young sous was asked to step into the breach. At first Shane said no, but he relented, won his own star that year – making him the first Australian to win one – and last year regained the restaurant's coveted second star. This January Michelin reconfirmed that honour.

While he credits the influence of other English chefs he has worked with, there is also a strong Australian sense to his food. The flavours are big yet his dishes are praised for their lightness. 'That lightness has a lot to do with my upbringing,' he reckons.

He eschews those heavy reductions of veal *jus* loved by Francophile English chefs and admits to a very Australian love of 'tang', seeing dishes like his ceviche of scallops (featured in *Starters*) as the perfect combination of sweetness from the scallops and sourness from the lime marinade's acidity. 'This is the sort of dish that I learnt in Australia,' he says.

There is a love of simplicity that underpins much of Shane's food. 'It's like Marco Pierre White's great quote: "You know a chef's great when he can leave things alone." That's an art,' he says.

That is, dare one say it, another rather Australian approach, but then even after ten years it's easy to see Shane's Aussie roots. 'I'm a little bit laid-back,' he says. 'I've never been afraid to ask questions and I'm not afraid to go up to people and shake their hand. That's an Australian thing.'

That's also one of the reasons why you won't see him at those self-congratulatory awards ceremonies that London's restaurant scene seems to love. 'I stay in the kitchen,' he says. 'London can be a very bitchy atmosphere. It's sour. It's this group against that group and that all depends on with whom you trained. Me, I'm independent.'

Independence and a certain relaxed Australian swagger also underpin Osborn's approach to winning his Michelin stars. Not for him the bow ties and white gloves of some of Europe's pompous gastro-temples. 'We have always been outside the normal radar of the Michelin stars,' Shane explains. 'We don't use silver cutlery. We don't want a Champagne trolley. And I don't have my name on my jacket. I've even been told I ought to wear black trousers not chef's checks! But I wear them because I cook every service. If anyone wants to know who's in charge in the kitchen, it's me, the one screaming and shouting!'

A totally refitted Pied à Terre will open in August 2005, while further on the horizon are plans for a second restaurant (now opened, holding its own star, and called L'Autre Pied). Something bigger, simpler and a fair bit cheaper. And maybe too a range of fresh baby food – a reaction to his shock at seeing some commercial UK baby food that had enough preservatives in them to keep them 'right' for four years!

Then there is the looming spectre of another book, but this will be something else simple rather than a coffee-table magnus opus detailing his body of work. 'I won't be ready to write that for at least five years; until I have taken my food to the place I want it to be. It is still progressing and it's got quite a long way,' he says ominously, promising a lot more to come.

Originally published in delicious, *2005*

DAN HUNTER:
THE GARDENER

In the kitchen of the Royal Mail Hotel in the tiny Victorian hamlet of Dunkeld, 18-year-old apprentice Damien Naylon is sifting through a bunch of wild sorrel. 'Try a leaf,' encourages head chef Dan Hunter, who picked it that morning on his walk to work. 'It's lemony, isn't it?'

Stand watching the kitchen at what has been described as Australia's most exciting regional restaurant and you'll see Hunter constantly encouraging his team of six to try, to taste, to smell. To see how gently smoking leeks makes them smell sweeter; to learn what the leaves of Mexican marigold taste like, or the deep blue flowers of the hyssop.

At 34, Dan Hunter might be too young to match most people's image of a mentor. But his young team will tell you they have all come to this sleepy corner of Victoria, over three hours from Melbourne, lured from such luminary restaurants such as The Court House in Melbourne or Quay in Sydney, to work with him.

Read Hunter's CV and it all starts to make sense. There are the years with Jeremy Strode at Langtons, at Verge with Karen White and at Caelis in Barcelona, but his time as head chef of Mugaritz, a rural two-star restaurant outside Bilbao, that is the big drawcard. For the past three years Mugaritz, run by Spain's most exciting young chef, Adoni Luis

Aduriz, has been named among the world's top ten places to dine in San Pellegrino's 'World's 50 Best Restaurants' list.

Discussing how he runs his kitchen, Hunter acknowledges that Andoni was a huge influence. 'You don't keep secrets and you involve the team,' he says of the philosophy he's carried over at the Royal Mail.

As in Spain, the chefs here pick herbs, flowers and vegetables from the restaurant's gardens and hothouse each day. The calm of the main garden, with its fruit trees, yabbie-filled lake and views of Mount Sturgeon, is a marked contrast from the crucible of service. Spending time there also allows the kitchen team to develop a deeper understanding of the produce they are using. 'This job is a lot of hours doing something mechanical; I want them to get inside it a bit,' says Hunter.

'When we first planted the garden, chives were the first herbs to flower. There was a three-week build up of the bud, and waiting for it to open. Nurturing the plant and the anticipation of it flowering meant when it was ready for use in the kitchen you treated it with the utmost respect. It also makes it far easier to marvel in the beauty of its raw state. Even at Mugaritz it was not like this. Here the herbs can have been cut just two hours before you eat them – everything is pristine.'

This freshness is vital to Hunter's food, which is built around a purity of flavours: 'My food is becoming cleaner, but the dishes are always built around accentuating the [flavour of the] central element of a dish.'

'You're not going find this opportunity anywhere else in Australia,' says Joel Alderson, who at 26 is the next-oldest in the kitchen after Dan. 'I like the idea of a destination restaurant and one with its own gardens growing herbs and produce for the menu is hard to find. Dan also asks us for our opinions – we're always discussing the food. You don't find that in many places.'

Joel and fellow Royal Mail chef Will Wallace (22) worked together at Sydney's Bistro Balzac. They both say the atmosphere here is different to many big-name kitchens. 'Dan is quiet, clean, precise. There's no room for error but it is calm and focused here. There's no yelling, shouting or throwing things,' explains Will. 'The village is quiet too – we go to Melbourne every couple of weeks to stay in touch with the outside world – but I grew up in Scone in New South Wales, so coming here is a bit like going home.'

Joel also describes the culture shock of coming from Sydney to a village of 600, but he reckons there are positives. 'I'll go off and climb a mountain and have a look,' he says with a smile.

Interestingly, most of the team was raised in small country towns and Dan explains that's comforting to know. 'I know they can handle living here. Working here is all-consuming, but otherwise there is not much else to do. I was a teenager in Bairnsdale and I hated it. The moment I turned 18 I ran for my life, but now I can see the beauty of it.'

At least there were no such acclimatisation issues for young sorrel-picking apprentice Damien. He was brought up in nearby Hamilton. Dan knew he had to give him a job when he heard that he had a waterbath installed in his bedroom at the shared house where he lives. 'He'd been cooking Ferran Adria recipes there!' laughs Dan.

Originally published in Vogue Entertaining + Travel, *2008*

DAMIEN PIGNOLET:
THE FRANK

It's a mark of the parochial nature of this country that most people down in Melbourne don't know Damien Pignolet. Yet even at 1000 kilometres' distance he has had a profound influence on what and how we eat out. When Pignolet opened Bistro Moncur at Sydney's Woollahra Hotel in 1993, he started the craze for gastro-pubs and joined Anders Ousbeck's push towards affordable casual dining, as opposed to all the pomp and ceremony of fine dining. Previously Pignolet and his late first wife Josephine had, in the wake of two other Melbourne refugees, Tony and Gay Bilson, helped developed a restaurant culture in the harbour city where previously the best restaurants were, by his own admission, in hotels and more about being seen than the food.

After 26 years there, Damien Pignolet is most certainly a Sydneysider (although he admits to loving coming back to Melbourne to stay with close friend Stephanie Alexander), but it was in Victoria that this confirmed Francophile was brought up, first discovered French food and was trained at one of William Angliss's earliest four-year hospitality and catering courses.

Pignolet was born and raised in Caulfield, the youngest of four children in a very conservative middle-class home. While his parents had been battlers, marrying on the day of the Wall Street crash, by the time Damien arrived there was a motor car and a weekender in the hills at Belgrave.

While food was a major part of the family's daily ritual, culminating in the Sunday roast with endless vegetables, not a lot of money was spent on what they ate. 'The market gardens were just out in Oakleigh,' Pignolet says, 'and I can remember the horse-drawn carts in the streets selling fruit and vegetables. Everything was so fresh. And there were some great bakeries all around Caulfield.'

The Pignolets kept ducks and chooks in the backyard but these were only killed on special occasions and Damien remembers it as hugely efficient cookery. Nothing was wasted. His mother, Elsa, cooked but it was his father who insisted on hot soup being served at every meal, regardless of the weather. And there was always dessert. 'I remember my mother's lemon meringue pie, which was very special. Lemon delicious and steamed puddings were the order of the day and these were properly made – not out of a packet.'

While he admits that his mother was not so modern as to have served the lamb pink, all his memories are delicious. 'She had a palate, my mother. The bulk of people who cook professionally do not have a palate. Too often even the simplest things like scrambled eggs are under- or over-seasoned.'

Elsa even tried to learn recipes from Papa Pignolet – Damien's grandfather, who had run a girls' finishing school called L'Avenir in a grand St Kilda mansion – but met with mixed success, including a potato omelette that always stuck and would get her in a state.

The young Damien was besotted by cookery and feeding people – setting up a toy mobile kitchen with pots, pans and crockery in a trailer behind his pedal car. Even though life for the Pignolets' class in those days was certainly not about restaurants, there were occasional visits to the local Chinese and Damien vividly remembers travelling into town with his mother to have lunch with his father at a venerable Russell Street restaurant. 'I was about four,' he recalls. 'There were wood panels on the wall and lots of banquette seating. I remember eating Weiner schnitzel. It must have been a very special occasion.'

These were all influences, but none were perhaps as profound as the impact of a run-in with a twelve-year-old street bully who threw five-year-old Damien against a brick wall, damaging his leg. At first he was placed in a leg-splint but later Perthes, a bone-wasting disease, was diagnosed. The only cure then was time in a full-body splint.

For almost four years Damien lay in a hospital bed, unable to move anything but his hands and his legs. Ask him about the memories of food from those dark days and he admits to a lasting horror of mashed swede. He also recalls a day when, still in the splint, he lay in the sunshine and smelled grilled lamb chops with peas. 'It is a magical memory,' he says. 'The perfect marriage of flavours, as common and simple as it may be. It was crucified, not pink, but the fat was all crunchy. No wonder my father died at 63!'

His other memories of those days are of developing a whole town of imaginary rich friends and dreaming of becoming an architect. 'It was a sheltered life. I had books and my mother collected magazines like *Home Beautiful* for me. There was a mirror above the bed which reflected whatever I was doing, as I couldn't sit up, but I could not do very much. I drew. I loved drawing to fill in the time.'

When he eventually left hospital, aged eight and a half, the family was living in East Brighton. His was not an easy re-entry into society. One leg was still in a sling and he needed crutches, but it was the psychological damage that was almost more debilitating. 'What do I remember about coming home? Fear; I was frightened of being hurt again. I was tyrannical, so anyone who came my way got smacked with my crutch.'

His education had also been severely affected, so he started in grade one at the local Brighton primary school, where he was four years older than all the other kids. 'I was very quickly promoted to the class where I should have been, but then I had to battle,' he says. 'I was different and, yes, I was bullied. They relished picking on someone who was different but the crutch is a power tool and I did quite a bit of damage. I got through it because I had the support of my family, friends and teachers and if you could believe in yourself you are halfway there. If you spend all that time lying on your back and you cannot move you develop extraordinary focus.'

Even when his leg got better, the young Pignolet didn't fit in and it seems that he started to relish 'being different'. While as the youngest he had helped his mother a little in the kitchen before his hospitalisation, he started cooking seriously some time after coming out of hospital. He discovered food outside his family's meat and three veg both through the *Women's Weekly* – the first dinner party he cooked was *Sauerbraten* from one of their recipes for this sweet–sour marinated pot roast – and through a poor Dutch family he knew, whose repertoire of soups and rye bread with chocolate sprinkles the young Pignolet found 'mystical and exciting'.

He also had a Hungarian friend whose lunch of radishes, salami and rye he copied when everyone else was eating Vegemite, peanut butter and cold cuts. 'I was yet again different – very important,' he admits.

Seeking inspiration, more than could be found in the *Weekly*, Pignolet headed to the library where he discovered Auguste Escoffier, and his love affair with French food began. 'I thought it was the most extraordinary thing I had seen in my life. There were no photographs but it was just an extraordinary, romantic approach to food and incredibly formal in the way the recipes are written. He described the stock cooking as "dispumating", which is basically dispersing all the crap, and that really created both a stimulus and excitement about French food.'

Pignolet's future course was set when he realised that he didn't have the necessary aptitude for maths to become an architect and that interior design was just 'too woozy' as he calls it now – or 'too poofy' as he called it then. A friend's father got him an audience with the general manager of the Ress Oriental Hotel, which stood on the site of Collins Place, and it sounds like Pignolet was seduced by glamour of hospitality.

'The manager's office was all Louis XV, with this incredible furniture and there was this elegant man with this fabulously cut suit in pale grey. I had never seen tailoring or someone behaving in such an elegant manner. Plus he was really nice. Said I had to go to Switzerland to study but I hadn't the money – and my father had reacted to my career choice with a "No son of mine is going to be a chef" – but he also mentioned a course that had started two years earlier at William Angliss in hotel management and catering.' Pignolet was one of the 150 who applied and one of the 20 who were accepted.

The course, and his first of many visits to France in 1976, confirmed his Francophilia. Then he was lured to work in Sydney in 1979 by Mogens Bay Esbensen and never looked back.

Today Pignolet is executive chef and co-proprietor of Sydney's Bellevue Hotel and Dining Room. He lives alone in the gritty but glamorous Sydney suburb Potts Point, having divorced his second wife and never having had children.

He has just released his first book, *French* (Lantern, 2005), which is a hefty handbook to the techniques of the French kitchen woven into an epic collection of recipes for French classics, but written with Australian ingredients in mind. As you might expect, given Damien's childhood love of design, it is also a very good-looking book. 'I hate indexes that need a magnifying glass. I hate cluttered layouts and recipes. I wanted it to look sumptuous. The way I cook and approach life is by no means scanty. I love to do it with a lot of style. I love to live well,' he explains.

At home this stretches to eating at a table properly laid with linen and napery even if he's dining alone. 'I may only be eating for twelve minutes, and I could stand up and eat and shovel it in and save the linen, but where is the pleasure in that? It is lovely having something formal about life.'

The quality of the food is also vital to him. As he puts it: 'I prefer not to eat than eat shit.'

Originally published in Melbourne Weekly Bayside*, 2005*

GABRIELLE HAMILTON: THE GODDESS

The US media is more than a little in love with Gabrielle Hamilton. Prune, her 30-seat bistro in New York's East Village, has been hailed by *New York* magazine as 'great' for dinner, 'famous' for brunch *and* the 'best place for lunch' in the Big Apple. Even the *New York Times'* hard-nosed restaurant critic, Frank Bruni, praises it as 'wildly popular ... highly influential'.

Forty-two-year-old Hamilton puts this down to the impact her simple neighbourhood restaurant had when it opened eight years ago. 'Back then every New York restaurant was the same,' she remembers. 'All the food was highly conceived, each dish had a paragraph-long menu description, and everywhere was playing the Gypsy Kings. We were a big pin in that balloon.'

'Honest', 'unpretentious' and 'darling' were words bandied about as the city rushed to embrace a restaurant where BYO was welcomed, the décor was mismatched *Les Puces* flea-market chic, and Michelle Shocked whispered from the speakers. The attitude was one Hamilton describes as, 'Hey, kids, let's just put a show on in the barn!'

She explains that Prune was a direct response to everything she'd been subjected to – and been forced to subject food to – for twenty years as a cook with mid-level catering companies. 'It was opening my own restaurant that made me love the work,' she says. 'With Prune I wanted to make food only touched by one or two people. It needed to be cooked *à la minute* (to order) and nothing like those awful steaks seared at 2 pm and then reheated to order later that night. It also had to be food from a root source that I knew well.'

This manifesto delivered Prune a modern but homespun menu that reflects an edgy Americana as a culinary melting pot. It draws on influences from her French-born mother to an apple-pie upbringing in then-rural New Jersey. Recipes like the lamb roast from when she was eight, her mother's vinaigrette and a *pâté* she learnt from a French farmer's wife have joined everything from late-night stoner combos such as sardines and spicy mustard on Nabisco supermarket crackers to butter and white sugar sandwiches dunked in heavy cream – a favourite after-school snack that became a Prune signature. 'It is personal food – not taught or invented by a chef in a stainless steel kitchen,' Hamilton explains.

The name Prune is also drawn from her roots – a childhood nickname from her years growing up as one of five children. Now, with partner Michele, who teaches medicine at Cornell University, she has two boys of her own, Marco and Leone, and admits to eating poorly at home now because of them. 'The older one is already anti-vegetables – I don't know how that happened – and I always seem to be running out of time. I seem to be always just boiling pasta and buttering it. I probably look forward to being at work more now just to have some complexity in what I cook!' she laughs.

Another of Gabrielle's self-proclaimed 'rules of cooking' at Prune was to banish expensive ingredients such as lobster and fillet steak in favour of more frugal peasant delicacies like sweetbreads, monkfish liver or secondary cuts. 'Prune has become known for its use of offcuts and offal,' she explains.

While she is proud to champion secondary cuts, one thing you won't hear her talking about is that American *leitmotif*, apple pie. Even though she wryly describes hers as the greatest apple pie in the world, 'I feel I need to work against the image that homely and comfort is the only food that female chefs can do, which seems to be an obsession of the media,' she says.

Ironically, this might have helped Hamilton's elevation to media darling a tad – although nothing like as much as being a pioneering poster girl for artisan food. Prune's success has inevitably led to imitators but Hamilton is sanguine about this. 'You get knock-offs in fashion, music and literature as well. We have an in-joke here that whenever we hear somewhere new has opened someone will always say, "Let me guess: small plates, well-crafted cocktails, artisan, local and seasonal produce",' she says, reciting a virtual blueprint of her restaurant.

While she's delighted that more chefs are seeking out great artisan produce, she's a little concerned at all the pretension that goes with it. 'Look, this rise of using seasonal local produce was something that needed to come – I mean people used to go out into the garden and eat – but now it's got crazy with these co-ops and boutiques that commodify artisan produce. It's become a lifestyle with its own magazines attached, as if nowadays people need to be told what to do and think. What's funny and fucked up is when you see places making claims like that in March their peas are local. I just want to shout "liar" at them.'

The one place you won't find lies is Hamilton's CV, even though she will happily tell you that it is the 'shittiest résumé of all time'. It's dominated by twenty years in bad catering kitchens and a job on the side as a stripper. 'My aim was to make money and write "the novel",' she says of this other job. 'I'd walk past high-end restaurants and look at their skinny hostesses in their short skirts and I'd chuckle. Just for wearing one thing less I was getting paid so much more, and my staff meal was so much better than theirs because we'd order in!'

This dream of writing, which pre-dates her time in the kitchen, reaches its ultimate fulfilment this June with the publication of her first book. *Blood, Bones and Butter* will focus on Hamilton's trials and tribulations at all those places on that dodgy CV of hers, and it promises to be another reason for Gabrielle Hamilton's loyal acolytes to love her.

Originally published in Vogue Entertaining + Travel, *2008*

PART IV

TRAVEL

NEW NORDIC CUISINE

For many, the phrase 'Nordic cuisine' is inextricably linked to images of horny-helmeted Vikings in furs tearing at roast meat with their bare hands. This, however, rather flies in the face of the current facts. Today Copenhagen restaurants hold as many Michelin stars as their counterparts in Rome or Madrid, and the winners' podium of the world's finest culinary competition, the Bocuse d'Or, is dominated by young Swedes, Norwegians, Danes and even the occasional Icelander.

The crowning moment for the emerging cult of New Nordic cuisine came this year when Copenhagen's Noma was named in the world's ten best restaurants. Noma's chef/owner René Redzepi explains that until recently the culinary traditions of Scandanavian countries had all but disappeared from the restaurant world, given the desire of the rich for imported French chefs.

'When I was starting out it was unheard of to open a Danish place,' he recalls. 'The problem is we had a venerable culinary tradition but few countries have as little self-esteem for their own cuisine. In Denmark everything of our tradition is a joke – we sell mead with a cartoon Viking on the label.'

New Nordic chefs seek to use local ingredients and traditional culinary ideas to distil a modern version of the region's food, and it is with the same clarity that Redzepi remembers the cruel jibes from his peers when he returned from working at El Bulli in 1999 determined to open a restaurant dedicated to Danish food. 'They asked if the restaurant would be called the Seal Fucker and serve whale penis! They thought we would be a mayfly. Now others have realised that they can find their own voice. Most restaurants that open here nowadays are New Nordic [rather than French].'

'We have woken up from a French dream,' agrees Magnus Ek of Sweden's idyllic rustic restaurant, Oaxen Skärgårdskrog. 'It just used to be easier to use imported products than local products, but on the tiny island south of Stockholm where the restaurant is I can collect sixteen wild herbs when I am walking the dog!'

With few established local suppliers, the sourcing of great local produce is still hard. As Redzepi explains, 'We get our sea urchins from the Faroe Islands. There's no industry there: I just call a bloke. If I want biodynamic pigs I have to wait until the farmer feels the mother is ready to let piglets go!

'Our cuisine is extremely seasonal and extremely local but you can find seven different types of urchin, razor clams by the bucket and scallops of all sizes along with a huge variety of wild plants. We have twenty-five million people but a huge land mass and lots of wilderness.'

In Helsinki, Chez Dominique chef Hans Välimäki has roasted zander on the menu, while in Copenhagen, émigré Englishman Paul Cunningham champions fjord shrimps and Danish oysters at The Paul. The 2005 Bocuse d' Or bronze winner, Rasmus Kofoed, might marinate pumpkin in sea buckthorn juice at Geranium, his pretty restaurant in the king's herb garden at the Danish Royal palace.

Some of these young chefs, like Redzepi and Ek, might look to Spain for technical inspiration, but it is the use of core ingredients like salt, vinegar and sugar (to balance flavours or for the traditional skills of preserving) that more closely unites them.

Most also share a belief that New Nordic cuisine should be as close to nature as possible. As the 1997 Bocuse d'Or winner, Sweden's Mathias

Dahlgren, puts it, 'We are after natural tastes so we must use things from nature.'

High on Dahlgren's natural order is fat – in fact meals at his eponymous restaurant in Stockholm's venerable Grand Hotel might start with a dish of 'sourdough bread with three fats' – milk fat in the form of cheese, rape seed oil, and animal fat, which might be fried smoked pork. 'We use the natural acidity of milk to balance fat food,' he explains.

'In fat we trust' might be Dahlgren's motto, but equally important to international acceptance of these restaurants is their gorgeous design, built on the Scandinavian design aesthetic pioneered by the likes of Alvar Aalto and Arne Jacobsen, whose original 'blondewood and ply' thinking still shapes the look of many Australian cafés today.

Dahlgren picked up this year's *Wallpaper** Design Award for best new restaurant and the interior of Noma's converted 19th-century warehouse beside the harbour in Christianshavn is no less schmick. Restaurant Paustian – 2007 *Michelin Guide* rising star Bo Bech's temple of wonderfully simple food like salt-roasted local celery or local shrimp cooked wrapped in spruce – is actually part of a glitzy homewares store.

So it seems that while New Nordic might champion traditional produce and flavours, when it comes to the design of both the dishes and the restaurants that they are served in, the look and the ideas are thoroughly, and most alluringly, modern.

Originally published in Vogue Entertaining + Travel*, 2008*

IN SEARCH OF SAMPURU

Y̲ou may think you've seen plastic food displays before, but their secret breeding ground is the Tokyo suburb of Asakusa. Here on Kappabashi Dori (street) is the epicentre of plastic food. Amongst 170 kitchenware stores selling everything from bento boxes to bain maries is an enclave of shops selling nothing but those plastic and wax models of food and drink.

At emporia like Tokyo Sample or Sample Shop Maiduru, you'll find glistening bowls of *katsudon*, crispy-looking *tempura* prawns and plump *tekka maki*, ice-cream cones, foaming brewskis and spaghetti bolognese – all frozen in spookily accurate representations.

Prices for these fakes, known as *sampuru* or *mokei* in Japan, range from US$15 for a small piece of nigiri sushi to over US$100 for something more lavish like a bowl of *ramen shoyu*. This one does come complete with a pair of chopsticks invisibly suspended in mid-air above the bowl, supported only by the strands of plastic noodles that trail up from the solid soup beneath.

The use of replica food by Japanese restaurants to illustrate their menus was in common practice eighty years ago and may have even started up to twenty years earlier. Then it was seen as the perfect way of introducing Japanese customers to the influx of new and

312

unfamiliar dishes that arrived on Japan's shores as the country relaxed its isolationist stance.

The trouble was that the models, made of wax, tended to melt on hot days. The popularisation of plastic after World War II provided a better alternative. This, combined with the influx of non-Japanese speaking *gaijin* through the Allied Occupation (1945–1952), who wanted to know what was on offer without deciphering a Japanese menu, secured the role of faux food. By the time the first US servicemen arrived for R 'n' R from the Korean War, plastic food had taken over the windows of Tokyo restaurants.

The best of these modern replicas are still hand-finished and hand-painted. This accounts for their cost and, with over 80 per cent of Japanese restaurants displaying faux food, helps make *sampuru* a $150 million a year industry in Japan.

Sampuru's kitsch mundanity has also given them a Jeff Koons-like status as art objects or quirky tourist souvenirs, with Kappabashi increasingly a stop on tourist itineraries alongside the Sensoji Temple and the Tsukiji fish market.

So bear that in mind when you are contemplating the sting of the bill or how little Tokyo menus change over the year. A full display can cost a restaurant a couple of thousand dollars, and that's without the extra cost of casting their unique signature dishes. It's a persuasive argument against weekly menu changes or too much innovation from the kitchen.

Originally published in Saveur, *2003*

HYDERABAD

Extreme sports come in many forms, but in the Indian city of Hyderabad what really gets the heart rate racing is travelling along one of their newly opened traffic flyovers – after being told that it only reopened that morning after a major collapse.

But the risk of plummeting to one's death under a shower of concrete and steel seems worth it if you can avoid the traffic chaos below. The tedium of gridlock in this city of 5,700,000 people is only lifted by uncomfortable encounters with tragically deformed beggars and bands of foul-talking, cross-dressing eunuchs, who make everyone in this superstitious city nervous by threatening to curse those who don't give them alms – or even worse, lift their saris and flash them.

Recently in the news as the temporary home of Aussie cricketers Adam Gilchrist and Andrew Symonds, and for the opening of its new international airport, Hyderabad is one of those wonderful contradictions at which India excels. It is a city with a strong Muslim presence in the centre of a Hindu world. An IT powerhouse where, in the last ten years, a black burqa has become as common a sight on its crowded streets as a shiny SUV.

It's also a different Indian city. There's a proud history of peaceful religious co-existence and it's cleaner than most, thanks to a nightly rubbish-clearing program. And they are at least trying to attack the traffic problems that throttle every major Indian city – even if the flyovers appear wobblier than three jellies on stilts. Or maybe it was just me that was shaking.

We drive out west past grand colonial buildings and along the River Musi, which divides the old city from the new. Here, verdant meadows are dotted with grazing water buffalo, *ghats* full of flailing laundrymen, discarded plastic bags and the occasional slightly deranged-looking holy man flinging rocks at the kids tormenting him.

We push on, out through the city's bustling suburbs to one of the sleepy villages that they've almost enveloped. Here you'll find Golkonda fort and more than the occasional inquisitive glance from the doorways of the homes. Built in 1512 by the young sultan who named Hyderabad for the dancer he loved, its ten kilometres of ramparts once housed an army of 10,000 and the famous Koh-i-noor diamond. The ruins are still one of India's great sights.

I climb to the top of the highest crag at Golkonda's heart and crowning it I find the durbar pavilion, where Hyderabad's once fabulously wealthy rulers held court. While it might be sweltering on the plains, up here a gentle breeze ruffles the blue proto-turbans of young Sikhs and flutters the butterfly-colours of the saris and kameezes of other Indian tourists.

Beneath me, Hyderabad reclines in the midday heat. To the east is the old city – the four scrawny fingers of Charminar's minarets scratch up through the misty horizon. To the north, beyond the stuccoed granite domes of the Qutub Shahi tombs of Hyderabad's 16th- and 17th-century rulers, glitter the modern gems of Hyderabad. There, the glass and steel edifices of HiTech City glisten.

The decision of former Andhra Pradesh chief minister N. Chandra-babu Naidu to entice the world's technology companies to Hyderabad has been so successful that IT companies, and the BPO and KPO (business and knowledge process outsourcing) companies that followed, now employ more than 200,000 people across the HiTech City precinct. It's earned the city the nickname of Cyberabad.

HiTech City is a bit like a big version of those faceless business parks on the outskirts of Brisbane or Sydney, but it's fun to visit to shout abuse at the call centres, or just to see the familiar Indian scenes of crowds jostling rough street carts for cups of sweet spiced tea, but with everyone wearing a 'dog collar', as the status-enhancing swinging photo security passes have been dubbed.

A modern attraction that's far more obviously intriguing is the 1666-acre Ramoji Film City. As well as being a bit of an amusement park, it claims to be the largest film production complex in the world. It is known as Tollywood, as many of the movies are made in the Telugu language common in South India.

To really understand Hyderabad, however, you'll also need to visit some rather older edifices. The succession of Muslim dynasties boasted of their power here by building grand monuments and palaces. Besides Golkonda fort and the Qutub Shahi tombs – unique because they house a whole dynasty buried together – there is the graceful 17th-century Mecca Masjid (mosque) and, just up the road, the 16th-century Charminar. Named for its four minarets (*char*), this stands at the hub of the old city like an Indian precursor to the Arc de Triomphe, but with crazier traffic and way more hawkers. Climb the 149 steps of one of the minarets for a great aerial view of the old city and the local bazaar, as well as to escape the incessant and insistent spruiking, which is a bit like going one-on-one with the most persistent late-night infomercial you've seen, with the TV volume turned up to full.

It's also worth visiting the palaces of the most recent rulers, the Nizams, such as Chowmahalla Palace or Purani Haveli (which houses the Nizam Museum). There's a bizarre Aussie connection in that the last Nizam, Mukarram Jah, spent much of his life on the Western Australian sheep station he bought outside Geraldton, before ending up broke in a two-bedroom apartment in Turkey.

Whether in the alleys of the Begum Bazar around the Charminar, with its medieval butchers, overstuffed stalls and charcoal-filthy blacksmiths working on the street, or the flash Western stores that line the choked roads of Begumpet and Banjara Hills, people in Hyderabad love to shop. The comparative affluence of the young IT workers in what is one of India's fastest-growing cities helps explain the explosion of malls where you'll find Western brands, and the number of fascinating and very bling-heavy wedding stores.

In India, the wedding is a huge deal, with the most expensive on record costing a steel magnate more than $65 million, and these stores sell everything for the big week, from ornate saris and richly embroidered tunics to jewellery and all manner of wedding accessories.

Hyderabad also has a long history of pearl trading, but the pearl's soft lustre is rather at odds with the other crafts for which the city is famous. These tend to be gaudier than a Gold Coast seventies night – whether enamel-inlaid bangles or garish local fabrics that are often strangely fringed and shot with metallic threads.

The main local handicrafts are silver-inlaid and engraved bidriware ornaments. Originating in the town of Bidar, north of Hyderabad, a process of oxidising this zinc and copper alloy turns it black but leaves the silver gleaming.

But the real reason to come here – other than to cheer on the Deccan Chargers – is the food. Hyderabad's political history and geographic position make it one of India's most fascinating culinary cities. Influences from the south mesh with the chilli-hot cuisines from the three regions of Andhra Pradesh (Rayalaseema, Telangana and Andhra) and dishes of Hyderabad's Islamic rulers and the Muslim population.

A visit to Rythu Bazar is a great way to get a sense of the quality and range of the ingredients local cooks can access. The same chief minister who enticed the IT guys also set up this farmers' market to ensure local smallholders got a fair price for their produce. And the produce is gorgeous – glossy eggplants, piles of garnet-seeded pomegranates, and huge mounds of green chillies, which are usually used fresh (red chillies are used dried). Then there is the less familiar – stalls selling thirty different dried pulses, small round zucchini-like *parval*, a fruit called *bear*, which has a crabapple-like astringency, or piles of *gongoora* (Indian sorrel leaf).

People don't seem to get up too early here – a legacy of the late-rising Nizams, some say – so there's no need to rush for breakfast.

First try Chutneys, a popular spot owned by an Indian movie star that serves a menu that displays Hyderabadi food's connection with South Indian cuisine. Skip through the metal detector and you enter a space full of middle-class businessmen; one hand clasping a mobile to an ear, the other tearing off mouthfuls of the house special – a fat puffy *dosa* steamed between banana leaves. Equally delicious are warm *vada* doughnuts. These are all served on metal plates with bowls of fresh wet chutneys, including a rocking sweet ginger one. To drink, there's sweet milky South Indian coffee, which has been 'pulled' (poured back and forth from height) to make it creamier.

Less formal – in the way that bare feet are less formal than thongs – is the dingy vegetarian hole-in-the-wall Sandimar, with its fascinating open kitchen. Buy tickets for what you want from the man at the door to exchange for soft fluffy cakes called *idli*, served with a thin, tangy curry soup, or lightly fermented batters set as *dosai*, perhaps cooked as an expanse of crispiness broken by nuggets of fresh coconut, onion and chilli. The oddest entry on the menu? Horlicks!

A quintessentially local activity is having a leisurely chat over a cup of Irani tea, a combination of strong reduced tea and a reduction of milk and sugar. Try the Embassy Hotel at Basheerbagh Crossing or Alpha near Secunderabad station, which first started serving Irani tea in 1950. Make like a local and order a tea split between two to share – to order it, ask for it 'one by two'. You'll also find good Irani tea and a legendary flaky egg roll at Paradise, which is generally well regarded for its *biryani* as well.

Biryani is one of the iconic Indian dishes that originated in Hyderabad. Over tea at her garden compound home, local Islamic food expert Mumtaz Khan explains that the perfect Hyderabadi *biryani* should be light and slowly cooked. This combination of light fluffy rice cooked over and under coals in a dough-sealed cauldron can come with lamb or chicken, and it's the former that poses the bigger challenge. Khan explains that it's harder to get lamb right; it needs to be pink, neither overcooked nor undercooked and never black, which shows it hasn't been properly soaked before cooking.

Other classic local dishes from this heritage include lamb griddled on local black stone laid on coals, and *haleem*. Originally prepared for Ramadan, and reminiscent of Jewish *cholent*, this is a rich, slow-cooked stew of meat and wheat that is pounded and braised to a rich creamy consistency.

While you'll find *haleem* sellers across the town, the most impeccable and richly creamy version is found at Kebab e Bahar at the Taj Banjara. This terrace restaurant is one of the city's must-do culinary experiences, not least for a ten-course degustation menu featuring iconic local dishes such as marinated lamb cooked on a stone griddle (*pathar ka gosht*), potatoes cooked in almond paste, very Persian stewed apricots (*qubani ka meetha*), and a fine luxurious *biryani*. Supremely fluffy, it comes well garnished with fried onions and herbs, served with a very 'correct' smooth nut and pepper sauce (confusingly known as 'salad') and those ubiquitous curds. Mrs Khan would especially approve of the perfectly cooked lamb.

By contrast, as an introduction to the more earthy Andhra food, try the bustling Amaravathi. Dishes to try include the delicious rich *gongura mamsam*, local lamb cooked in a rich gravy with lemony broad leaf, salty chicken pepper fry, and *lachha paratha*, a flaky roti. However, locals will tell you that the chilli heat of these Andhra classics has been softened to a dull roar to appease the softer palates of HiTech City.

Once you've handled that, dare to seek the even less fancy Rayalaseema Ruchulu, another spot definitely not on the tourist trail. In this warren of small rooms you'll be eating a meal of some intense heat at laminex tables next to the local cricket team. This is rough, rustic food – lamb cooked with cinnamon in a thinner gravy that's typical of Rayalaseema cuisine, liver curry, fried brains, scrawny chooks going by the warning of 'country chicken'. The egg *pakora* (egg in batter) is shockingly, hiccup-inducingly hot. Far easier is the Apollo fish, a dish of fried river fish with green chillies, cashews and curry leaf that hums rather than screams with heat.

After all the capsaicin you'll need to stop at the old Mozamjahi marketplace. The ice-cream here is a 65-year-old family institution.

There are now two rival stands run by brothers – pick a side by sitting at the red-seated tables if you favour Famous, and blue if you're rooting for Shah's. Choose from flavours such as mango or sitaphal. Other street foods to search for include squiggly fried and sugar-syrup-soaked *jaleebi*, battered green chilli fritters, and fruit salad sold under a sort of reduced or condensed milk topping.

Hyderabad was once a dry city, though since this ban was lifted a bar culture has grown up, fuelled by all those cashed-up HiTech City workers. However, some morally protective restrictions remain, such as some bars and clubs restricting entry to mixed-sex groups or couples.

Fitting in with Hyderabad's bar culture – even if you aren't wearing one of those dog collars – is easy. They love to abbreviate everything. So pubs like 10 Downing Street and Bottles & Chimney go by the shorthand of 10D and B&C.

Despite its mall location, the sprawling 10D has a British pub feel right down to the carriage lamps and chesterfield sofas. There's beer by the pint, shepherd's pie and ubiquitous skewers of *tandoori paneer*. B&C, popular with the Indian IT crowd, has more of a nightclub feel.

Hyderabad's first real bar was the dark and moody Underdeck – known as UD, obviously – at the Taj Banjara. Here you'll find an older crowd, lethal cocktails and a big screen for sports. Again the pubs of London are the inspiration for the décor.

Other design-driven bars worth a look are Fashion (F Bar) and Touch, although by the time you read this the city will have a few more places. The owners of both B&C and Liquids are planning to open second bars closer to HiTech city to serve the expected influx of 200,000 new tech workers over the next five years.

To contemplate the future growth of HiTech, we end our time here with drinks at Liquids. There's something very 21st-century Melbourne about ducking down a lane and into a deserted car park under an office block looking for the lift that will haul you up to the top floor. The heavy doors swing slowly open to reveal a large, sleek, modern space lit by floor-to-ceiling windows, with plush white sofas and soft blue light. The cool air-conned room hums with ambient music and the murmur of tech-speak from affluent young Indians and expats.

Outside those huge windows, the dusk turns to night and the rope lights on houses start to blink. Once again, the pandemonium of the city stretches out before us, while in the distance the outline of Golkonda is all but a fading blur on the western horizon.

Originally published in Vogue Entertaining + Travel, *2008*

FIJI FOOD

The sea is an impossible blue, the island rustles with palm trees and the bays that pare the coast are crescents of soft white sand. Every three months these idyllic surroundings become 'the office' for top Melbourne chef Jacques Reymond.

For twelve years Jacques has been the consultant chef for Turtle Island, 500 acres of paradise nestled in the Fijian island chain of the Yasawas. Working with Turtle Island's owner Richard Evanson, over the years Reymond has created a five-star resort kitchen built strongly around local produce and the talent of the islanders who make up his kitchen brigade.

'I do it because I love the people. They are the biggest asset that we have over here,' says the urbane 49-year-old Frenchman.

Jacques speaks warmly about the relaxed village atmosphere compared to the highly charged surroundings of his own eponymous restaurant's kitchen. In both places he is as much a teacher as a leader, but out here he is usually training up people who have little culinary experience outside their traditional ways.

In Yasawan society women handle the cooking chores, with fish and root vegetables like taro and cassava as the staples. 'When Laite, our pastry chef, joined us 12 years ago she had never touched a bag of flour.

Now she makes all the croissants, brioche, viennoiserie, ice-creams and three types of bread a day!' It is an achievement of which both seem shyly proud.

Just as Jacques has given to these smiling islanders, so they have given to him. The resort's menu is peppered with dishes that hint at the inspiration that Jacques and his team have taken from the traditional ways. Fijian curries, marrying coconut milk with a simple masala of fennel seed, cumin and other Indian spices, and *kokoda* are both regulars on the menu. *Kokoda*, pronounced 'kokonda', is like a Fijian ceviche, where raw fish is 'cooked' by the acid in lemon or lime juice.

Every Thursday night the resort hosts a traditional *lovo* – a feast slowly cooked in a covered pit lined with hot rocks and palm fronds. For five hours a menu of pumpkins, sweet potatoes, cassava, taro, whole fish wrapped in banana leaves and even a suckling pig are slowly, slowly cooked to a succulent conclusion. Just as it has been for generations, this spread is followed by the dancing and singing of the *meke*, which celebrates the Fijians' warrior past. 'It's a chance for us to celebrate and respect the culture of the people who surround us,' Jacques explains.

One thing that underpins all the meals here is the magnificent organic and hydroponic garden that stretches up the hillside behind the resort. 'The island is about 70 per cent self-sufficient in terms of fruit and vegetables,' Jacques explains as he snaps a finger of baby corn that's so juicy it oozes white milk.

Five full-time gardeners tend the four acres of garden, and they don't just grow for the 30 guests but also the 180 locals who work on the island.

The garden resembles somewhere from the book of Genesis. There are huge bananas, three types of melon, papaya, limes, mangoes, soursop, pandanus, pineapple, lemongrass, taro, okra, eggplants, carrots, capsicums, tomatoes, four types of lettuce, five types of beans – from little native Fijian bean to French – basil, coriander, chives, mint, baby fennel. The list is almost endless – there's even a little row of asparagus.

It's easier to cook here, Jacques reckons. 'I just go to the garden and pick when I want and what is ripe,' he says.

There are also less familiar names in the garden. *Bele* – a local spinach – a large cooking banana called *wondi* that the kitchen bakes stuffed with crayfish, and *rourou*. It was these taro leaves that almost ended Jacques' time here before it had even started. 'I was walking through the garden and tore off a handful of these big green leaves and started munching on them,' he remembers now.

'I choked, fainted and nearly suffocated. The leaves are poisonous raw but cooked they are fine. They are wonderful wrapped around fish you are baking or chopped, cooked and blended with bug meat and coconut milk.'

Now if Jacques wants to know anything about the local flora he consults venerable local man Bill, who's been on the island for 22 years. It was he who introduced Jacques to a rare Fijian tree whose leaves have a citrus flavour not unlike kaffir lime leaves, but stronger. 'It makes a wonderful refreshing tea,' Jacques explains.

The sea and local fishermen provide much of the rest of the supplies for the resort. 'We regularly get local *walu* [Spanish mackerel], crayfish, tuna, white snapper, trevally, coral trout and huge octopus,' he says. Ordering mud crabs is just a matter of sending a message to a village on a nearby island – Jacques has now learnt how to drum this out for himself.

The kitchen smokes its own fish using a red hardwood sawdust from the local *noconoco* tree. This imparts a delicate flavour and red lustre to the fish. 'That's another skill that the kitchen team have brought from their villages,' Jacques explains.

Regular seaplane visits and boats from Fiji's main island of Viti Levu bring the supplies that the local environment can't provide. Most of the meat is brought in from Australia or New Zealand. One thing they never need to order is honey: the island has fifty hives of its own.

Turtle Island is also pretty unusual for a world class resort in that, other than during Jacques' quarterly visits, the locals run the kitchen. Day to day there's no European-trained chef telling them what to do. 'Three years ago we decided to dispense with an Australian head chef as I felt the kitchen team had built up the necessary skills to do the job.

I also felt that this would make them stronger as a team. Now Benny, who comes from a neighbouring island, runs the kitchen and it's working wonderfully, although a little differently. A Fijian would never order another Fijian to do something but they still manage to sort out what has to be done,' Jacques says.

And it's a pretty hectic schedule for the kitchen team of fourteen. It starts with sumptuous breakfast. Then there's a vast buffet to prepare for lunch and a weekly revolving selection of different communal dinners in dramatic island locations. There's also the challenge of meeting the demands of guests, who each have their own idea of what comprises the ideal picnic to take for a day frolicking at their own secluded cove. Crayfish, a roast chicken or just a simple club sandwich – Benny and his team are there to make it happen. The resort also offers guests the chance to dine out under the stars *à deux*, another variation in the routine that the kitchen has to take in their stride. Then there are the locally inspired little appetisers to be made to accompany cocktails every night – perhaps *rou rou* balls or freshly steamed baby clams served on the shell. It seems never-ending.

There are some perks. A couple of times a year one of the team gets to visit Melbourne as a guest to see for themselves how things happen in Jacques' 'other restaurant'.

'They are pretty shy and don't ask many questions but they love it. They see an efficiency and discipline that they've probably never seen before.'

And there are more positive benefits for the local islanders than the occasional trip to Oz and the employment the resort provides. Every year Turtle Island brings in eye specialists from Australia and the US, who take over the resort and operate a free eye clinic for all Fijians. The resort also hopes to build a hospital and high school on the far side of the island.

A month later and we are sitting in Jacques' Melbourne office. There's a thin mist of drizzle outside and the only humming is not of cicadas but of a vacuum cleaner and the fax machine. While Jacques is in Melbourne this fax is his main contact with his team in the kitchen at Turtle Island. He tears the page from its jaws. It's Benny. He's after a good recipe for a flourless chocolate cake for one of the guests. Jacques gazes out of the window and then starts writing: 'In a double boiler first melt 400 grams of plain chocolate …'

Originally published in delicious, *2003*

THOONA OR LATER

Thoona? Where the hell is Thoona? It's a fair enough question when you are bumping along through the featureless paddock country between Mulwala and the Hume, heading somewhere none of us have been before, to be greeted by who knows what.

Apparently Darryl, the ex-copper driving the Thoona pub's 'courtesy' bus, knows – although he's already made everyone a little bit nervous by leaving the engine running when he picks us up from some share-cropper's shack outside Benalla. Isn't that what bank robbers do on a job? I think someone also said they heard banjo music.

The answer is that Thoona (population 65 – according to Darryl) is in the country north of Lake Mokoan, in between Benalla and Wangaratta, Victoria. It's not the sort of place you'd pass through unless you had some pressing business in Bungeet West, Boweya or Almonds. Well, unless you photograph cute old country general stores for a hobby, or have a yen for a bit of top-grade wheelie bin racing.

Besides the remains of the first cooperative butter factory in the north-east of Victoria – feel free to take a break and a few deep breaths if the heady excitement of all this is getting too much for you – Thoona does have three churches. Standing equidistant from St Brigid's Roman Catholic Church (which looks like it was bought from a Cold War

Russian bunker catalogue) and the primary school is the Thoona Hotel, bestriding Thoona's two main thoroughfares like the Colossus of Rhodes – only far better because it serves beer.

The Thoona pub is one of the reasons why I like drinking beer. It's unpretentious, has a covered courtyard so kiddies can be seen playing through very thick glass, and a veranda where you can lean against a mud-crusted old Land Cruiser, smoke and listen to a mate crap on about such big business terms as 'plausible deniability' and the 'firepower model'. These seem especially ridiculous when you are pouring the second jug of 'jackaroo juice' as the last rays of the sun kiss Mount Meg. (You know, I still don't really understand what he was talking about, but apparently they are: a) a sort of alibi international businessmen use to cover a potential client's aberrant sexual behaviour while business entertaining; and b) a way of persuading that client you'll make him loads of money – without resorting to debunking that client's 'plausible deniability' to his wife.)

They also serve a classic selection of pub meals, which might never get them in the *Good Food Guide* but are perfect with beer – or that aforementioned jug of Bundy and Coke. As well as offering ice-cream with sprinkles and chocolate sauce (which is always a big plus as far as I'm concerned), their handy wipe-clean laminated menu also uses such words as 'scrumptious' which, quite frankly, is not seen enough on the leather-bound *cartes* of Australia's three-hat gastro-temples.

To start we pick French fries smothered in gravy, calamari rings and crumbed prawns, which are good in a risk-friendships-and-nick-the-last-one-when-everyone-has-their-eyes-on-the-dartboard sort of a way. Yes, they probably come out of a pack from the freezer but there's more to life than beers and skittles you know – there's also the crunchy pleasure of salty deep-fried frozen stuff eaten with beer or candy-sweetened spirits.

With this in mind, a hefty chicken parma comes easy and proves that too often some of us (okay, I) forget that eating out is more about the people we are with, the atmosphere in the place and simple tucker than the quality of the glassware or the provenance of the micro herbs.

Add a bottle or two of honest Kelly Country red from a local list that includes drops from Baileys (where Ned reputedly once held an honest job fencing), Taminick Cellars and Auldstone and I'm happy. Although not as happy as the buck when he finds out his future bride has rung ahead and arranged with Daniel the barman to buy him a couple of bottles. That's smart on so very many levels. And it's another sign that while the Thoona pub might be 'just a pub', it understands more about the essence of hospitality than some of its far glitzier cousins.

You can see why the bright lights of Benalla – even with its bowls club, shimmering rooms of pokies and several restaurants – fade once you're in this typical country pub. Oh, and they even drove us back, despite – or perhaps because of – the catchphrase-spouting business tyro deciding that he'd bait the blokes in the pub bar drinking bourbon and Coke. I have a belated piece of advice for him to go with his knowledge of 'plausible deniability': if they're drinking 'bikie juice', leave 'em well alone.

Originally published in 'A2', The Age, 2009

THE WORST FOOD
IN THE WORLD?

As the perpetually new notches in my belt attest, I am a man who is moderately fond of my food. Most food. Along the way, though, I have encountered aberrations that have left culinary scars on my psyche.

There was a Caesar salad at a Echuca golf course where the cheese oozed sweat like a fat man on a crowded Sydney bus and the anchovies had a two-week growth and still maintained the finger-marks where they'd been grabbed as a bundle from the catering jar.

Then, at a bush barbecue in Finke, I burnt my fingers on a rancid kangaroo tail that had a stench that clung like an angry pitbull.

These are but fleeting moments, however, and none that could equate with the sheer palate-numbing terror of four days in Düsseldorf. My first sense that things were going to get ugly was at the airport. A TV was showing a German cooking show in which the finished offerings were grey and sludgy enough to be Düsseldorf's suburbs.

Deep in the heart of Germany's industrial north-west, Düsseldorf is not a pretty town. Everywhere there is that depressing postwar reparation architecture, reminders of the seven-week bombardment in the spring of 1945 when half the city was destroyed.

Today Düsseldorf's only claims to fame appear to be that Goethe once stayed there, that they do a brisk business in sensible shoes and that there's an endless, soul-sapping drizzle.

It's also home to one of the world's premier meat shows, Intermeat, a show dominated by German visitors obsessed with meats both 'sausage' and 'red'. When they say 'red' round here they really mean pig. The Germans love their pork – minced, pounded, salted, smoked, boiled, roasted or forced into tubes of skin – and it is always served in portions that say 'piggy', not 'pork'.

Way back when the Egyptians banned swineherds from the temples for fear that their pigs carried leprosy, German tribes fêted the porker. She was the 'Great Pig', a sort of Mother Earth character, valued for her fecundity.

While Paris was chasing porkers from its streets at night for their habit of eating babies, pigs here in Westphalia roamed free in the forests, much prized for their flesh. Then, when the Rhine–Rhur axis became the industrial heart of Germany, how suitable that the pig should become one of the first animals to be grown as 'industrial meat' to sustain the workers. In fact, the per capita consumption of pork in Germany leapt from 14.5 pounds in 1850 to 99 pounds by 1975. This consumption growth outstripped that of other meats by over 100 per cent.

Now, this isn't the lean 'new-fashioned' pork we are talking about here, but great wobbling wedges of white. Germans actually deserted pork after leaner piggies were introduced following World War II. Consumption had dropped to 44 pounds per head by 1950 and only started to climb back when Mr Piggy stopped going to the gym and took up eating pizza again.

Now, I have nothing against eating some oink when it's good. In the last twelve months I've rhapsodised about a suckling piglet whose skin gave with the same soft, sweet crack as the top of a crème brûlée. I have paid a week's wages just for a plate of Sanchez Romero Jabugo ham (JJJJJ reserva especial) and relished those organic black-foot pigs fed exclusively on acorns. But that was Spain and this is Düsseldorf – the sort of city where 'organic' is more likely to mean something made of organs.

From Düsseldorf's favourite beer halls to the restaurants, it was as if a porcine Henry Ford was planning the menus – 'anything so long as it is pork' seemingly their motto. This German food was monochromatic. The veg matched the washed-out colour of the meat. Endless potatoes and sauerkraut cured me of my kinder-kid horror of eating green things. I kept wanting to reach for the remote control to turn up the colour controls on my meals.

My first meal was emblematic. They say that pork is the meat that tastes most like human flesh and there was something about the sloppiness of the fat and the pallid hairy skin of that first boiled hock that had me lifting my trouser leg to check it wasn't my own flaccid calf I was picking at. This was the second chapter in a meal that started with raw minced pig spread thick on a bit of bread – in Berlin this is a delicacy called *Hackepeter*. On top there was a layer of onions almost spread thick enough to stop my mind wandering over past warnings about the dangers of eating uncooked pork and the recent discovery of foot and mouth at a nearby piggery.

The mistake was letting slip my profession. Increasingly I grew to dread any sentence that started with the words 'You must try ...' Especially when followed by '*Pfälzer Saumagen*'. Pig's stomach is an acquired taste that I hope I never ever have to eat enough of to acquire.

Lard omelettes, 'hacked' pork steak, congealed black pudding and pickled upper pork shank and hooves were just some of the delicacies I was too polite and pig-shocked to refuse. Perhaps surprisingly, the lard omelette turned out to be rather nice, with lots of streaky bits of speck seamed with crisped fat.

Unappetising porky dishes aren't just the speciality of Düsseldorf, of course. My sister lived in Hamburg, lost three stone and will now never eat red meat thanks to her first warming plate of *Schlachtplatte*, literally a 'slaughter dish' stew containing every bit of the pig bar the oink. Just down the Rhine in Koln they serve *Kölsch Kaviar* (sliced and fried blood pudding), while in Bavaria their bottom-fermented beer goes well with a plate of lung, heart and spleen (*Beuscherl*).

Some have suggested that the prime aim of German food is actually to create a thirst that'll allow you to drink more. The French have long commented on the saltiness of German food and in the 16th and 17th centuries there were travellers' tales of Germans sprinkling salt on their bread to drive their thirst. If that's the excuse for German cuisine, then after evenings sampling Koln's Kolsch or Düsseldorf's top fermented Alt beers, it deserves some sneaking admiration. But couldn't someone just tell them about pork scratchings?

Originally published in 'Epicure', The Age, 2002

THE FOOD OF LATIN AMERICA

Shannon Bennett is serving tacos at Vue de monde, Guy Grossi has turned his back on prosciutto in favour of hand-carved *jamón* from Salamanca and Melbourne's cocktail of choice has moved from a Brazilian caipirinha to a Cuban mojito. Oh, and the world's most famous chef is Spanish.

Australia's understanding of this cuisine has come a long way since the Franco years, when Spanish food was too often stodgy paella served with chips and a soundtrack of 'Una Paloma Blanca', and the best known food of Latin America was frozen margueritas at Taco Bill's. Now from Sydney's Bodega to Melbourne's MoVida, Ausralia boasts an ever-increasing array of Spanish and Latin American restaurants trying to showcase the 'real food' of their regions, and getting the more esoteric Latin American ingredients has become as easy as a trip to Johnson Street, Tullamarine or Springvale.

It is the true food of Latin America that is still quite new to the palates of Australia. Leonardo Cuce opened Inkari restaurant a couple of years back with a desire to showcase the food of Latin America and even in that time he's noticed how much easier it is to find ingredients. '*Yuca* [cassava] is easy to find now – we use it in casseroles or fried – before it would turn up sporadically in ones or twos. You'll even find *jicama* down at the market these days. In some cases they are being imported from Chile or, as garlic is, from Mexico, but also there are a lot more people growing them here and in Asia,' he says.

Choosing what to put on a Latin American-inspired menu can be quite a challenge given the broad range of dishes. It is a choice that becomes even wider, as Gardenias' chef/owner Aldo Riquelme explains, for often dishes in South America can have the same name but differ quite substantially – something that is also common back in Spain. 'Given the size, remoteness and climatic variations of the country, local ingredients are often substituted, whether it's for the stuffing of an *empanada*, which becomes unique to a region – let alone a country – just by changing a technique or ingredient, or the way a chicken broth in Chile uses potato while up in Colombia they'll use cassava,' he says.

It's a theme that Leonardo Cuce's partner, Silvia, expands on. 'For example, each country has their own tamales,' she explains. 'Maybe they use a cornmeal dough or maybe it's made out of potato or mashed plantain; maybe they stuff the dough with chicken and a pepita sauce or with sweet pork, cinnamon and sugar – or even sultanas and prawns like they do in Guatemala or El Salvador. Even what the tamales are wrapped in for steaming differs. Most places use a corn husk, but in Colombia they are more likely to use a banana leaf.'

The food on show at Australia's Latin American and Spanish restaurants would have been radically different if Columbus and his successors hadn't stumbled on that part of the world. In 1519 Hernando Cortés reported on a native diet in Central America of peanuts, tortillas and sweet potatoes, while tales from Pizarro's trip deep into South America in 1525 tell of the locals living on maize, ducks and rabbits. The stories told by *conquistadores* in the Spanish court two years later were rather more lurid, speaking of an opportunistic diet that included game, beans, algae, iguana, guinea pigs, frogs and insects of all forms, including a rather special worm tortilla.

So before we go any further, let's just tally up who got what in the culinary exchange between the New World and Old World.

The Old World got tomatoes, chillies, capsicums, cashew nuts, avocados, tomatillos, vanilla, chocolate, chokos, coriander, achiote oil, allspice, many beans and pulses (including green, haricot, kidney, borlotti, cannellini, lupin and pinto). Then there were some pumpkins and squashes like zucchini, and papayas, pineapple, guava, passionfruit, tamarillo, feijoa, 700 varieties of maize (and thus sweetcorn, polenta, etc.), a whole spectrum of root vegetables including sweet potatoes, cassava, potatoes and jicama, plus the barbecue and cereals like quinoa and amaranth. We also got access to some exotic meats like turkeys, although neither guinea pig nor llama ever really took off in Europe. Even without them, some scholars estimate that more than half the food eaten around the world originated on the American continents.

The Spanish and Portuguese spread these crops, including the chilli, cashew and maize, to their colonies and trading partners around the world. By 1523 maize was being grown in Crete and the Philippines, and peanuts, sweet potatoes and maize were introduced to China and sub-Saharan Africa by the middle of the 16th century. Overall, the impact was immense and it could be argued that this was more of a reverse takeover – that the foods of the Americas were actually more influential in shaping the rest of the world's cuisine than Spanish- and Portuguese-introduced ideas and ingredients were on shaping the Latino kitchen.

The reciprocation of the European invaders was equally impressive. They introduced sugar cane, wheat, coffee, chickens, pork, beef, sheep, goats, sausages, onions, rice, bananas, possibly plantains, apples, pears, wine, vinegar, olives, capers, mint, lemons, limes, apricots, peaches, oranges, grapes and dried fruits, basil, garlic, cumin, cinnamon, oregano, tamarind, pastry, frying, salt-cod, slavery and syphilis – although the New World paid us back for that last one by giving us tobacco.

Mexico

Tom Stevens, a leading Australian expert in Mexican cuisine, sees the influence of the Spanish kitchen on Mexican food as patchy at best, likening it to the way the indigenous peoples adopted the invaders' religion but adapted it on their own terms. 'Frying was the biggest impact that the Spanish brought because before that food was usually boiled or steamed, like *tamales*,' he says, although roasting, grilling and pit-baking were also employed in pre-Columbian times.

'There's also Spanish impact through ingredients such as almonds, wine and cinnamon, of which Mexico is now the biggest consumer. Almonds pop up in those regionally diverse, ground chilli pastes called *moles* [pronounced 'molay' and meaning 'concoction'], which are used in Mexican cooking as sauces. These produce influences pop up in dishes like *pescado a la Veracruz*, which is basically a tomato-based sauce with strips of local jalapeños and imported bay leaves and capers, and it is even claimed the presence of bitter chocolate in *mole poblano* was an invention of Spanish nuns, pointing to another influence of Spain. Traditional flavourings include a dizzying array of dried, fresh and smoked chillies, supported by dried leaves such as *epazote*, spicy *hoja santa* and avocado.'

A lot of seafood is eaten all over Mexico and in general vegetables are consumed as salsas. In fact, given the long expanses of coastline, seafood is important throughout the Americas, whether it's the raw but acid-cooked ceviches of Peru or the claypot fish stews of Chile. If you travel through Mexico, the wheat-flour tortillas and beef of the north, which are both Spanish introductions, give way to corn-based baking further south.

Cuba, Puerto Rico and the Dominican Republic

The food of the islands of the Caribbean bears the influences of a dizzying number of colonial powers, from the British and the Dutch to the Danes and the French, all of whom followed the Spanish into the region. It is islands like Cuba, Puerto Rico and the Dominican Republic, however, that show the most marked Spanish traits in their cuisine. Puerto Rico has a version of Madrid's famous *cocido* made with chickpeas, pig's feet and chorizo.

In Cuba, favourite dishes include oxtail, *ropa vieja* (shredded beef), *brazo gitano* (which is named after a similarly rolled Spanish cake but is made with salt beef, tomatoes and cassava pastry) and *caldo gallego* – a take on Galicia's famous greens, beans and pork soup.

They also make a version of Valencia's *Moros y Cristianos* – a combination of black beans with rice first cooked to celebrate the end of Moorish rule. This dish pops up in Mexico, and 'rice and peas' are a common combination across the Caribbean and Central America, too.

These three islands also indulge in a little pit cookery with their *lechon asado* – this slow-cooked suckling pig is traditionally served with *Moros y Cristianos*.

Colombia and Venezuela

Maize is important from Mexico through to Colombia and down the Andes. A flour made from white corn makes Colombia's signature tortillas, *arepas*. These plump discs are as far removed as the flatbread of Mexico or the omelettes of Spain as they could be. *Arepas* are one of the popular street foods of Bogota, according to Frank Torres, who cooked his native Colombian food at his restaurant-cum-bar, Eldorado. 'You'll also find corn flour used to make tamales stuffed with chicken and pork, or *empanadas*,' he explains. 'In Colombia these pastries will usually be filled with beef, potato, spring onion, garlic and cumin. In Cuba it could be guava paste and cheese.'

Colombians love their pork. Witness the way they guzzle those little crisp-fried bits of bacon called *chicharron* – also known as *chicharrones* in Mexico – with a beer. And in fact, those same Spanish flavourings of cumin and garlic are present in the popular Colombian dish *lechona*, where they are mixed with dried peas, rice and pork, stuffed into a boned-out suckling pig and roasted.

Colombia's tropical location also impacts on their food so those tamales are likely to be wrapped in banana leaves rather than corn husks and the country is one of the largest producers – and consumers – of plantains in the world. These starchy bananas are used ripe or green, and in everything – fried, in soups or even mixed with pork as deep-fried balls.

They appear in Colombia's famous *sancocho* beef stew with *yuca*, squash and fresh corn, too. This is often made with a *sofrito* base. The fried combination of capsicum, onions, tomatoes and garlic bears more than a passing resemblance to a Catalan *sofregit* or *samfaina*. *Sancocho* also pops up on the tables of Trinidad and the Dominican Republic.

The banana and the plantain can be seen alongside other African influences across the Caribbean and through the north-east coast of South America down to Brazil. 'All that region love plantains, but then the food in Venezuela tends to be similar to Colombia,' says Frank. 'For other starches, just like the Mexicans, Brazilians and French Guyana, we love *frijole* beans. *Yuca* also features a lot, while a meal without rice is not considered a meal in Colombia. However, when it comes to chilli we tend to be chickens and have it on the side!' says Frank.

Colombia also has a chorizo sausage but it's very different from the Spanish version, as it is usually eaten fresh rather than dried and features veggies like spring onion, onions or garlic, rather than just pig and paprika.

Bolivia and Equador

'Corn … tortillas … chilli sauces' that's how Gardenias' Aldo Riquelme sums up the food of Bolivia, while Silvia Cuce explains you'll also find quinoa boiled to use like couscous as a salad, gratinated with capsicum or even made into tamales.

Kristine Becker, who co-owns both the Hairy Canary and the Canary Club, largely agrees. 'Although they are separated by Peru, Bolivia and Equador both use more ingenious ingredients – loads of maize, game and legumes. Bolivia has all these chillis growing on the hillside so their food has loads of heat. Theirs is also a fatty style of cooking – they use loads of pork belly fat – and there's a shortage of healthy veg,' she says.

Chile

Becker says that, for her, the food of Latin America is always indigenous mixed with Spanish influences. 'In Chile, where my family is from, we love to cook things wrapped in leaves, like *humitas*, which are baked parcels of corn, beef mince and perhaps sweet onions, olives and even currants, which shows that Moorish–Spanish influence.'

One dish that Riquelme says Chileans like to claim as their own is *curanto*, which he says is similar to a NZ hungi: 'We just cut up a pig and throw it in there to cook,' he says.

Like most countries in South America, Chile also makes its own *empanadas*, but as the name just means 'baked in pastry', as you would expect, there are regional differences. Otherwise potatoes are the starch of choice, whether served on the side or baked as a crispy pie layered with sweet potato, sliced hard-boiled egg, minced pork or tuna and sprinkled with sugar. 'That must always be eaten with *mojo* paste and dunk bread into it,' says Kristine.

Mojo, also known as *pavre*, is a Chilean condiment of that is more herb-based in the south and more pepper- or chilli-driven in the north, although each family prizes their own recipe. 'My grandmother gave me the family recipe on my twenty-first,' remembers Kristine. (Mexico also prizes *mojo* but there it tends to be a garlic- and coriander-heavy oil and lime juice sauce. It is also similar to Peruvian *aji* or *aji verde*, which might be more herby.)

While there is some debate about whether Chileans love their food hot, Becker is in no doubt. 'You are not a man until you can eat a chilli on its own without any assistance. You should sit there and chomp on the chilli – fork one hand, chilli in the other.'

Peru

You expect rivalry between neighbours and so it is between Chile and Peru. Both claim *pisco* – a local brandy – as their national drink but the Peruvian kitchen is markedly different. Audrey de Groot is from Suriname, where the cuisine is tropical produce mixed with Dutch-Indonesian, Indian and African slave influences (the national dish *pon* is oven-baked chicken with cassava and bitter orange peel). With Pedro Ochiniano, her Peruvian partner in Boomerang Global Trading, she imports everything a homesick Peruvian might yearn for, from the tiny grains of quinoa, a millet-like cereal which is soaked and cooked in stews, to the hard amber-like chips of dried yellow potatoes (*papas seca amarilla*), which also need soaking. Potatoes are central to the Peruvian kitchen and de Groot explains they claim to have 1000 varieties, along with a number of different chillies. In Peru those potatoes may come served with a fetta-like cheese sauce that is green from a traditional Peruvian mint paste.

Other Peruvian delicacies besides those ceviches include peppery *ajis*; thinly sliced, marinated and grilled ox heart (*anticuchos*), served unsurprisingly with grilled potato and corn; and *arroz con pollo*, a very Spanish-sounding dish of chicken and rice. 'Peruvians always seem to use garlic and lots of green herbs like coriander, parsley and basil. Their food has lots of influences from other countries, including from Japan and Thailand, but rather than being spicy it tends to be tasty thanks to lots of marinating.'

Greg Turner has travelled all over South American and for him Peru was a country where the food was characterised by a simplicity born of poverty, yet he still gets excited about the memory of a potato dish with a boiled-egg and spicy cheese sauce. For the spelling of this dish he has to call to Peruvian ambassador as we talk. It's *papa a la huancaina*.

Argentina

Greg owns Richmond's long-running restaurant Enris, which serves Argentine dishes, not Peruvian, and he'll happily tell you that when it comes to eating, Argentina is all about beef. From his very first visit he remembers 'people grilling meat everywhere, even on the median strip of the freeway. I went to lunch and ate a month's worth of meat in one sitting – and then we did it again for dinner!'

The Argentineans use the same word for roasting as the Spanish, but their rich grasslands provide a feast of meat for the traditional char-grill or barbecue that is far less common in Spain. 'Besides slow-roasted beef ribs there will be blood sausage; maybe some pork, chicken and homemade chorizo. There could be some goat or some rabbit and probably *matambre*, which is a thin cut like skirt that is rolled, stuffed, boiled and broiled very slowly. It would be served with a herby chimichurri sauce made with oil, vinegar and cayenne pepper, which is as ubiquitous as tomato sauce at a backyard barbecue here, or perhaps a Chilean salsa of onion, tomato, capsicum and lemon, possibly mixed with coriander and chilli. The pan-European influence post–World War II means the meal might be accompanied by a creamy mayo-based salad like a waldorf or Russian salad.'

The Argentineans also have a ferociously sweet tooth, whether it's for spoonfuls of that sickly sweet caramel called *dulce de leche* (also known as *carretja* in Mexico, *mangrar* in Chile, and something totally different again in Colombia) or submarines, which are glasses of hot milk with a hunk of chocolate melting in them. They also love their ice-cream – part of the Italian influence on the country's palate. 'It's the only country I know where they have home-delivered ice-cream,' laughs Greg.

Brazil and Uruguay

Over the border in Uruguay the food is similar but with lots of German and Middle European influences, Greg explains. In Brazil, their version of the *asado* is the *churrascaria*. The title of Brazil's national dish, however, should probably go to *feijoada*, which is a heavy stew of black turtle beans, pork extremities, salted and smoked pork cuts or sausages and jerked beef. It has distinct similarities to the pepper-pot stews of those Caribbean islands colonised by the English, like Jamaica, Antigua and Trinidad, as well as to the haricot-based or kidney bean-based *feijoadas* of north-east Portugal and the *fabadas* of Asturia. The presence of turtle beans in this dish – and of *piri piri* seasoning on other dishes – is a clue to the influence of Africa on the food of Brazil.

Tradition says *feijoada* was originally a slave dish and the fact that these black beans come from the African continent supports the premise. However, it was recorded as a dish favoured by the colonists as early as 1569, which throws some doubt on this romantic notion – and the Portuguese name is a sign of that country's colonial domination over Brazil. *Feijoada* is usually served with orange slices and *farofa*, the lightly roasted and almost flaky cassava flour that's a staple of the Brazilian kitchen. The same dish pops up in other Portuguese colonies around the world, like Angola.

I suspect that everyone I've talked to finds themselves browsing aisles of Latin-flavoured favourites at the wonderful Casa Iberica once in a while, so I ask the Johnson Street grocery's matriarch, Alicia de Sousa, whether she can spot where people come from by what they buy. 'Oh yes,' she says, smiling. 'If they pick up black peas and guava paste they must be from Cuba; Colombians will be looking for the pre-cooked fine white corn flour for their *arepas* and the coarser flour for their tortillas. The Peruvians will leave with quinoa and *papa seca* (dried potatoes). Venezuelans could be looking for black beans or flour for *arepas*. El Salvadorans will buy that cashew juice cordial. Chileans will buy dried peaches and a type of barley (*trigo*) to make a cold drink in summer, while the Argentineans only want apricots that have been dried back home in Argentina, as they're prepared with acid and have a sharper taste and less chemicals used on them. Even which *horchata* they choose tells me something about them. The Spanish like this refreshing drink made with the extract of tiger nuts, the Italians make it with almonds, the Mexicans with corn and in El Salvador they make it with rice and *morro* seeds.'

It's a beautiful summation, so I am almost scared to ask if there are any common products that will be bought by both Spaniards and Latin Americans. This is surely the acid test of how closely related the food of the Americas is to its so-called inspiration.

Alicia's is a fascinating, and short, list. Coffee, olives, possibly chorizo and, if it's Easter, some Latin Americans might join the Spanish and the Portuguese in buying salt cod. This leads me to think that the Spanish influence on the Latin American kitchen is one of two things: either overblown or so deeply embedded that it is no longer noticeable.

Originally published in 'Epicure', The Age, 2007

FILMING WITH A STUDD

When I think of what America has given the world, space travel, ballpoint pens and four-wheel drives pale compared to the 1950 invention of the cheese slice by Kraft and Nabisco's inspired idea of putting cheese in a can so that you can spray it into your mouth.

It's funny, then, to be standing in the university town of Ann Arbor, Michigan, about to embark on an artisan cheese odyssey with Australia's most famous cheese wrangler, Will Studd, as he films an episode of his latest, and for once aptly named, *Cheese Slices* TV series.

A lot has happened to the US cheese industry since the cheese slice and EzyCheese – not all of it is bad. In fact, while the numbers of raw milk farmhouse cheese producers is declining in France and the UK, in the US there has been an explosion of artisan cheese production.

Will and his crew have already been shooting for over two weeks straight and the mood is tense and flighty, the way it can be when a small group has been living closely together for too long.

They have flown in from lactose-intolerant Japan, where Tetsuya Wakuda introduced them to such culinary delights as an abalone and cheese dish so beautiful it made people cry. In fact, 'you should have been with us in Japan' becomes the motto of this stultifyingly dull trip across seven Midwestern states from Ann Arbor to Charlotte, Virginia, visiting two rather fine cheese-makers and the best cheese deli in the US along the way.

Ann Arbor is famous for three things – the university of Michigan, Iggy Pop and Zingerman's Deli. Zingerman's founder, Ari Weinzweig, is one of Studd's heroes and he's been dreaming of coming here for 20 years. It's a small, narrow shop but the groaning cheese counter is like an inventory of the US's best artisan cheese. The gems range from the gruyère-style Mountain Cheese and Pleasant Ridge's nutty three-year-old Reserve, which are both from Wisconsin, to rather good creamy but bitey raw cow's milk blues from California's Point Reyes and Bayley Hazen in Vermont, where they milk a herd of just twenty-five Ayrshires for the cheese.

It's beautiful stuff, but that's not to say there aren't still abominations in the world of US artisan cheese: as Zingerman's monumental cheese buyer Carlos Souffrant points out, Badger Cheese produce a wax-sealed processed cheese in the shape of – you guessed it – a badger.

'Over the last twenty years more and more people have been going back to making cheese,' explains Souffrant, 'but processed cheese is a fundamentally American product. Kraft Cheese Slices were revolutionary because mixing cheese with hydrogenated oil meant it could be poured into a mould.'

Understandably unimpressed with the original cheese slice, Will does still find the US experience fascinating: 'There are lots of parallels with cheese-making in our country, but we've stalled. The artisan cheese movement here started ten years after us, but they are now way ahead.'

Unlike Australians, the US cheese-makers can use raw milk to make cheeses to be sold after they have been aged sixty days. Frustration at this disparity burns brightly inside Studd. His arguments to move to the US system are persuasive and he talks passionately about young Australian cheese-makers working overseas who want to come home to make cheese but won't, because they can't make the cheese they want there.

What makes the US unique is that while the number of cheese-makers using raw milk is growing in the US, in Europe the traditional farmhouse producers are dying out. 'When I started in cheese there were a dozen farmhouse cheddars and twenty producers of raw milk camembert: now those numbers respectively are three and nine,' says Studd.

From humble beginnings, Zingerman's has grown into a little empire with a bakery, creamery and a roadhouse where we dine on lumpy grits. It is the first of a litany of dreadful meals, in which the overall highlight is a plate of battered deep-fried gherkin slices. The cheese might be good, but we struggle to find a decent meal on this tour of the heartland of America.

As if to grind this in, when I get back to my hotel room the local channel plays an advert 'introducing Kraft natural cheese' (which seems about fifty-eight years too late) and one for a junk-food product that proudly proclaims in a huge star splash, 'Now made with real cheese!' This begs the question, 'What was in it before?'

From Ann Arbor we drive south, south, south over the Ohio River, heading to Louisville in Kentucky. To alleviate boredom I try to subvert the crew by igniting a passion in them for aerosol cheese piped into Bugles – a teeny corn cornet that has impeccable sweet–salty junk food credentials. The sound guy isn't the only one who comes back for seconds. Studd catches me and gives me a look that could curdle milk – but later he admits to sharing an early childhood passion for sucking Primula cream cheese from its metal tube.

Elegant Louisville is the birthplace of Cassius Clay and the home of Thomas Edison, bourbon and the Kentucky Derby. Here Will meets debonair blueblood goat-cheese matron Judy Schad, from Capriole Farms, for a bourbon tasting. All goes well until her goat's cheese wrapped in bourbon-soaked chestnut leaves is pulled out of vacuum-packed plastic for tasting.

I should have seen the storm clouds gathering then.

That night over dinner, a fired-up and bourbon-fuelled Studd argues with Schad – first passionately about using *penicillium candidum* to promote rind growth rather than the more elegant *geotrychum,* which produces a more yeasty and less rubbery crust for the cheeses with which it comes in contact. Then he argues more pointedly about the suitability of wrapping her goat's cheese in plastic, which she says she does to arrest its ageing and help the cheese better acquire the flavours of bourbon. 'I don't think petrochemicals have a place in maturing cheese' is one of the more inflammatory comments Studd makes in response to this.

When Schad shoots back, 'I do it the way I want to get the result I want,' the whole shoot looks to be in danger of falling over – after a 842-kilometre drive. Luckily Schad calms quicker than Studd, and the next day, filming at her Indiana property amongst some of her 550 goats, Studd looks a little sheepish in his trademark white shirt. Look closely at those scenes and you'll see the tension. I like Schad immensely.

The next day, a long drive east across three states is punctuated by gigantic fireworks stores that bring out the ten-year-old pyromaniac in me, towns you've only heard of in *The Simpsons* – 'so *there's* Shelbyville' – and the depressingly jaunty plastic fascias of junk-food chains. The traditional family roadhouse that Zingerman's seeks to ape has been largely lost under a kaleidoscope of Subways, Maccas, Arby's, Waffle Houses – chains, chains, chains – that now feed the Midwest.

We stop at a Burger King in the terrifyingly named Nitro, West Virginia, for a root beer. The summer heat lies like a sweat-sodden shearer's singlet across the car park. By the trash cans, two teenage workers on smoko share scares about gunpoint hold-ups in this dirt-poor town. Studd and I both get too nervous to go in – instead we get the hell out of Nitro.

Driving, we talk about the show. Studd largely funds the making of *Cheese Slices* himself, using TV as a medium to educate and inform people about how important artisan and farmhouse cheeses are by visiting benchmark producers. His hope is that this will encourage their survival for future generations. It's a lofty goal, but after having met a young cheesemonger in Ann Arbor whose interest in cheese was solely sparked by an earlier series of Studd's show, it seems as if his plan is working. This, however, may be the last series, as Studd wrestles with challenge of what stories are left untold about the world's fine cheeses. 'There are a few left, but I don't want the next one just to be wacky.'

This definitely *would* have been the last series if Studd had continued accelerating his SUV towards the back of a braking truck on this road to Virginia. He's concentrating on duelling with the crew's car when my screams of 'Stop, STOP, STOP!' alert him to the brakelights of the semi that is eighty … sixty … twenty … three yards ahead. There's a sickly smell of rubber and terror as the anchors finally bite and the SUV almost pirouettes on its front wheels. The next fifty miles are sombre as we both contemplate what might have happened if Will had been in the car by himself.

We crisscross rivers on steel box bridges to a soundtrack of angry banjos, finally reaching the strange nowhere town of Galax in the Blue Ridge Mountains, which is famous as a home of bluegrass music. It feels like a set from *Deliverance*. Perhaps that's why Studd's decision to visit the local Wal-Mart in a pink floral shirt has the crew (and me) distancing ourselves so quickly. Heck, this is the sort of scary white-trash store that has its own gun department; the slogans on the rear windows of the huge utilities in the car park are largely not pro-Harvey Milk, or even pro-Obama.

There's nowhere to eat that's open and the bluegrass clubs are closed, so dinner is junk food from the local supermarket, where slack-jawed teenage yokels cash their welfare cheques to buy beer from a bottle-o section brimming with cheap Aussie critter wines.

As we sit on the wide verandah of the B&B, picking through corn chips flavoured with Monterey Jack dipped in a jar of microwave-melty orange cheese that defies description, the crew's thoughts turn back to Japan – again: 'We feasted of yakitori made by Japan's best chef there, you know,' they tell me. 'You should have been there, Matt!'

Not even lighting enough fireworks to supply a Sydney New Year can cheer me up. Things reach a new low when a firework proudly called 'POW Rescue' fails to conjure up a bedraggled, stubbled and bound US Ranger from a Baathist basement, instead just fizzing to a sparky conclusion. I'd complain, but it's too far to drive back to Indiana and I'm a little too scared even to walk to the car now that it's dark in Galax.

The next day Studd is back in his trademark white shirt to film this episode's opener in a field of the Jersey cows responsible for Meadow Creek cheese. He mutters as he prepares, 'White shirt on, white shirt off,

11 times a day.' His crew mutters as he stumbles over his lines. Everyone needs a break.

Later, over a farmhouse lunch, Studd and Meadow Creek owners Rick and Helen Feete discuss everything from the corrosive nature of whey and the negative impact of locavorism on remote producers like themselves, to the difference between industrial and artisan cheese judges in the US. The former, according to our new banjo-playing friends, apparently look for cheese with bags of flavour up front but no length to its finish. That's so you'll want to pop another piece in your mouth immediately after the first to maintain the flavour.

The Feetes are 'back to the landers' who make one of US über-chef Thomas Keller's favourite American cheeses. We try an aged version of their taleggio-style Grayson and it is the best thing I eat in the US. It has a length that carries on from their Virginia Highlands property almost to the airport in Raleigh, North Carolina. Just when I felt the trip had been in vain, Meadow Creek produces a cheese that justifies the hype about the boom in US artisan cheese. But I still reckon it was more fun in Japan.

Originally published in 'Epicure', The Age, 2008

WHAT A WHINER!

For some men it is fast cars, for others it's fast women, but my fatal weakness has always been dairy. At an early age I understood that those holes in a crumpet were intended solely to transport more melted butter to my mouth, and I was lucky enough to spend summers with a sheltered country grandmother who believed me when I told her that Coco Pops were meant to be served for breakfast not with milk, but with nothing more than a huge dollop of whipped cream. I wasn't a svelte child.

Today my dairy cravings are slightly more mature, and I get listless without regular fixes of Strzelecki (the blue, not Sharon), Ironstone and goat's cheese from Tongola or Holy Goat. The real Holy Grail, however, is on the other side of the world in the great artisan cheese shops of Europe. These are my Louvre, my Tate and Prado – singular places full of earnest young cheesemongers in smocks or white pork-pie hats, willing to have a long and serious conversation, without yawning, about the emergence of the first fine English soft cheese (such as the camembert-like Tunworth) or the comparative the grading of gruyère into *mi-salé*, *salé* or *douce* strengths.

My holiday is defined by different cheeseboards. In London, it is hard cheeses like Wensleydale, Caerphilly, real Montgomery Cheddar and

Cornish Yarg (which always sounds like it was named by West Country pirates). Paris is all about three-year-old comté, five-year-old gruyère and anything gooey made in a farmhouse. Switzerland is the romance and heady excitement of buying five different gruyères made on five different little farms – all of whose mountain pastures I can see from the door of the little village *laiterie*. Oh, and Switzerland is also about the fights we have over the Époisses that I carry round Europe for both succour and defence – I swear it is so stinky it can sting your eyes worse than a shot of mace. This is a cheese so ornery it demands its own fridge unless you want everything to smell like the Parisian sewers in summer. This means emptying the minibar.

After three weeks of dairy degustation, I fear that if you bled me only curds would seep from my veins. After four, however, I'm starting to have food dreams about 'back home'. My palate is clogging up from all this cheese and a succession of meals in fine diners where technique is dominated by classical French culinary thinking and sauces loaded with cream or butter. Also those fondues and nights of raclette don't help either.

It all makes me realise that those cream, cheese and butter sauces of French invention are now almost extinct in Melbourne's better restaurants, thanks to our demands for lighter food and our embracing of influences from South-east Asia, Spain, the Middle East and, most importantly, the olive-oiled part of Italy.

Instead of cheese I start craving the fresh, wet crunch of a Granny Smith apple and the brilliant, eye-popping zing of freshly squeezed lime. My teeth keep demanding the sensation of chomping through salads of iceberg lettuce, cucumber or watermelon, dressed with little more than a squeeze of lemon. My tastebuds dream about fresh pineapple, berries and stone fruit, but when I go to a UK supermarket to buy the vegetables for Christmas lunch everything seems to come ready-peeled, tired and in neat plastic bags. I want to buy fresh herbs, but apart from parsley and basil the only other choices comes in tube form.

From that day forward I check my fingernails each morning to see if they are loose, worried that this obsession with greenery and acidity might be a sign of the onset of scurvy.

Look, this overseas travel business is all very well, but on the flight home I write a note in my dairy diary about how there are only so many cheese shops bulging with raw milk cheese that you can frequent before you start to think about the joys of how we eat in Australia today – with a table set with food that is vibrant, clean and fresh, dishes loaded with crunch and acidity.

It's just strange that I have to travel to the other side of the world to have this Damascene revelation about the essence of what makes our food here so special. Strange, but not at all unpleasant ... if I hadn't I'd never have discovered that smooth, nutty gruyère from the alpine pastures that nestle under the ski slopes of Isenau. Now that's the sort cheese that's perfect for breakfast, lunch or dinner.

Four of Europe's Best Cheese Shops

Laurent Dubois, 2, rue de Lourmel, 75015 Paris. 01 4578 7058
La Laiterie du Petit Diable, rue du Bourdier, 1865 Les Diablerets. 024 492 31 87
La Fromagerie, 2–6 Moxon Street, London W1. 020 7935 0341
Neal's Yard Dairy, 17 Shorts Gardens, London WC2. 020 7240 5700

Originally published in 'A2', The Age, 2009

PART V

MASTERCHEF

MASTERCHEF AUSTRALIA

TV has a funny effect on people. The first sign I had that I was in danger of becoming typical spoilt TV talent was when I got into the lift in an Adelaide hotel and, after a couple of minutes, wondered why it wasn't moving. I hadn't pushed the floor button. I realised that within three days I'd become so used to having someone from the production office opening doors, arranging cars, pushing lift buttons and generally ministering to my needs, that I'd lost touch with reality.

But my early experience filming the Australian version of the hit UK show *MasterChef* hasn't all been about being fussed over and the regular on-set delivery of Snickers at 4 pm. There was also the ominous realisation on the first day that the big bloke who followed my fellow judges and me into the urinals was an ex-SAS bodyguard employed to keep us safe.

If that was freaky, it was nothing compared to the first 17-hour day of shooting. What little TV I had done was with a small crew of three and just one camera. When I walk into the Perth audition studio where we will start the search for Australia's first *MasterChef*, there are seven cameras and the size of crew that you'd see on a big budget movie.

I think all three of us judges on the show – myself, and chef/owners Gary Mehigan (Fenix and The Boathouse) and George Calombaris

(Hellenic Republic and The Press Club) – feel a slight sense of unreality about being chosen for what is arguably the biggest food show ever made. We joke about the fact that Gary has been picked for the sentimental streak that will definitely see him cry in the first few shows, George for his Joe Pesci-like use of the English language and myself – well, they didn't cast me, they cast my cravats, and I'm along for the ride as their wrangler.

There is no doubt that having known both Mehigan and Calombaris professionally for over half a dozen years in Melbourne makes the whole thing a little less weird, even though there have been no rehearsals or 'getting to know you' sessions before the many cameras start rolling at the Perth auditions. The notion of a critic working alongside two chefs is a bit like a mongoose dancing with two cobras, but within the first couple of tastings it becomes clear that on either side of the pass is the same appreciation of what makes a good dish.

We agree on other things as well. Like the fine of a slab of beer for any of us who utters such overused reality TV words as 'journey' and 'passion'. 'Yummy' and 'kernel' are also banned. So far I owe two slabs, Gary one, and George a mighty six.

It's also not long before our various performance peccadillos are identified by the crew – like Gary's inspiring Churchillian speeches and George's little skips, or my involuntarily tapping of the tasting table, when we find a dish that delivers big time. Then there are my too-lingering looks when I'm tasting, which have been dubbed – rather cruelly and, okay, I admit, accurately – my *Bold and the Beautiful* moments.

We also all have to learn that words like 'dick', 'suck', 'lick', 'balls', 'bong', 'disco biscuit' and 'wanker' are not suitable for the show – although apparently 'wanky' is.

Tasting the dishes presented by the hopefuls keen to collect one of the coveted *MasterChef* aprons, which are the ticket through to the final fifty in Sydney, is a skill all of its own. We are all trying not to be too soul-destroying; 'Give them loads of love,' exhorts the team of producers. The last thing any of us want to do is turn someone off cooking at home. That means trying to control the gag reflex induced by tasting papaya soup that smells strongly of vomit, and attempting to find something – anything – positive to say about a pile of severely overcooked fettuccini with a creamy sauce spiked, unfortunately, with sweet chilli sauce.

The contestants who have been put through by the show's producers to the final round of audition tastings seem to fall into two categories: those who can actually cook and those who might make good TV. These include people in fancy dress, a bearded submariner, a dumpster-diving freegan who likes to cook road kill, an ex golf pro who once beat Tiger Woods and a bloke who's been banned from his local bar for nuding up and who then proceeds to get his kit off on set after he doesn't get through. Occasionally one of these will shock us, and the producers too, one suspects, by actually being able to cook. For example, golfer Lucas Parsons' marvellous Singapore crab could hold its head high in any of the joints along the East Coast Parkway.

The dirty, the arrogant, and the wannabe TV chefs are the ones who get short shrift in the judging. It is after one such towelling that I receive my first piece of hate-mail. It's from an old boss whose son-in-law I have, in her words, 'torn a new arsehole'. This disagreement is resolved when I ask her how she would have treated me if I'd turned up for a job interview covered in blood and kitchen grime.

The TV chef thing is fascinating, as the majority of people with this dream tend to have neither the knowledge and skill, nor the unique idea that would make a network pick them up. They largely don't make it, but then, with over 7000 applicants we see a lot of very good home cooks whose love of food and cooking is so palpable that they tear up when asked to describe how important food is to them. Emotion is the currency of the new brand of reality TV, but no matter how much they cry, how cute they are, or how quirky they act, they're not getting through unless their food knowledge, their skills or their dish warrants it.

The thing is, when it comes to *MasterChef* 'good' really isn't good enough for a dish. The question most often asked by the judges is 'Is this a *MasterChef* dish?' The answer too often is 'no', but then we are also smitten with pillow-soft gnocchi, satiny tortellini, an ethereal sponge cake, a crumble filled with passionfruit, mango and custard, and a daube of beef so perfect that it has Gary almost refusing to let anyone else taste it. All these get their cooks through to Sydney, where a series of challenges will quickly whittle down the fifty contestants to the final twenty who'll battle it out to take the title of Australia's first *MasterChef* – and the associated book deal, training package and $100,000 cheque that will help the winner fulfill their culinary dream.

Things get a lot more serious once we've culled the contestants down to the top fifty. Then we are finally united with the show's host, Sarah Wilson, who has previously been filming with the contestants while we tasted at the auditions. We shoot the series of challenges that will winnow them down to just twenty in a huge series of old Redfern railway sheds, where we can line up fifty cooking stations in one hundred-metre-long rank. They chop two tonnes of onions (and some fingers) to display knife skills. They are made to identify the seventeen ingredients in a spaghetti bolognese. They are given $50, two hours and a lift to Sydney Fish Market to buy ingredients and return to the makeshift warehouse studio to cook a two-course seafood menu. Those who survive those challenges get to lift up a mystery box, and then I get to taste and comment on their cooking of thirty-nine pork chops. Now that's a real challenge! Only the prospect of George doing his famous koala impression and one extraordinary dish can lift our spirits after that.

This is TV, and moments of stress, excitement and challenge are followed by large tracts of time when we stand around like cattle, or 'warm props' as the brutal cameramen dub their on-air 'talent'. In these interminable minutes we bicker over which of the three of us is going to be Kyle – we all want to be Marcia Hines, naturally. I start getting paranoid it's going to be me when host Sarah Wilson keeps introducing me, somewhat fancifully I think, as a 'feared food critic'. In the long days of auditions to get 175 hopefuls down to the final twenty, the only other thing we disagree on is whether mashed potato should taste primarily of potato or cream and/or butter.

In spite of all those hours of work, when we see the final cut of the first six shows we find that fourteen hours of filming can be reduced to eight minutes of screen time. But then, a show like *MasterChef* should always be about the aspiring contestants rather than the judges. It will be you, the viewers, who will have to decide over the next week of TV whether the hundreds of hours the judges put in getting to the final twenty was worth it. We reckon it probably was. And hopefully by then you'll want to stay and watch how that final twenty will fare in the head-spinning challenges that follow.

Originally published in 'Epicure', The Age, 2009

STATES' EATING HABITS

Over the last five years I have spent a fair amount of time travelling this great land from sea to shining sea, doing little more than eating. It's a horrid job but, as those sanction-busting French armaments companies always say when they are caught supplying electrodes and high-powered machine guns to unsavoury dictatorships, if I didn't do it someone else would.

The experience has led me to the slow-dawning realisation that certain dishes, ingredients and techniques seem to cluster in each of the states. Three days in Canberra left me with the distinct impression that it wasn't really a meal if it didn't include a smoked lamb chop and end with a little lemon tart with a thin, crunchy, caramelised sugar topping like a crème brûlée.

This half-baked theory became somewhat more obvious recently when I got to taste 121 home-cooked meals in five capitals over seven days as part for the audition tour for the first series of *MasterChef*.

With this in mind I would like to propose that, just as each state has its state flower, state animal and state flag, so they should also each have a state dinner or dish.

While the numbat and black swan might claim the status as Western Australia's state animal and bird, Perth declares its English roots and, one suspects, its isolation, through its love affair with the lamb chop. Often accompanying it is a mash of some form, whether it be humble potato or more exotic sweet potato. Sumac may also feature as a rub and in Perth they further express exoticism by placing skinned orange segments in their salads.

In Adelaide, in spite of South Australia's reputation for fine local produce, it seemed that it was chicken breast – perhaps stuffed with cheese or crusted with parmesan and served with a creamy sauce – that first leapt to mind as a sure-fire dinner dish to impress. Naturally, it should be made with one of Saskia Beer's chooks and all elements of the dish must be sourced from Adelaide's Central Market, which has a spiritual importance in South Australia to rival how Victorians feel about Queen Vic, South Melbourne or Prahran combined. A large number of desserts I saw there, however, seemed to take inspiration from the tiramisù and the Cherry Ripe. Now marry those together and you create a dish worthy of national – not just state – status … a Cherry Ripe tiramisù!

In Melbourne things seem a little more complex, but certain ingredients and dishes surfaced with a surprising regularity. Risotto, most regularly in a 'wild' mushroom version, appeared more than was statistically probable (or dietarily desirable), and zucchini flowers arrived fried and stuffed with everything from cheese or eggplant puree to nothing. But it was beetroot – sliced, roasted, as a sauce or even as a foam – that arose as the most popular element in any dish. Make a beetroot risotto and top it with a zucchini flower filled with goat's curd and you'd have the dish to slot alongside our existing emblems like Leadbeater's Possum, the Helmeted Honeyeater and the Weedy Seadragon.

New South Wales likes its state emblems to be punchy and obvious. They've got the platypus, the waratah, the kookaburra and the blue groper (which perhaps explains the sordid performances of some of their politicians last year). So when it comes to a state dish you'd expect them to go the same way. They seem to love South-east Asian salads with chilli, lime and palm sugar dressings, while homemade sweet chilli jam is the condiment of choice. As for protein, lamb made a flurry of appearances but scallops, prawns or salmon were the most popular ingredients. Given this love of seafood (and the job rationalisations in New South Wales caused by the economic problems up there) they could probably save a few bob by getting the blue groper to do a double shift as both emblematic state marine inhabitant and state dish. Perhaps served whole, deep-fried with chilli jam and a Thai herb salad.

Chefs in Tasmania and Queensland restaurants seem to have a desire to express their creativity by offering oysters gussied up in a dozen outfits, from Kilpatrick to tempura battered with mirin. A far more home-cooked expression of the Sunshine State would be a big simple plate of Morton Bay bugs (served with a Champagne and salmon roe sauce if presented on the Gold Coast or in Noosa). Naturally you couldn't serve that with a glass of Bundy and Coke on the side – everyone knows up there that Bundy and dry is the proper accompaniment to seafood!

Originally published in 'A2', The Age, 2009

JOHN TORODE:
THE OTHER
MASTERCHEF JUDGE

Australian chefs have underpinned the rebirth of London's culinary credentials in the last decade. Skye Gyngell and Bill Granger introduced the UK to the lighter, simple flavours of the Antipodes' café culture though Skye's Petersham Nurseries and their books; Shane Osborn and Brett Galvin were flag bearers for a whole brigade of Australian fine-dining chefs who have played a vital role in the establishment of the country's Michelin-starred credentials.

The most unlikely – and quite possibly the most influential – of these culinary missionaries, who has reshaped the way the British approach food both in restaurants and the home, is Melbourne bayside-raised John Torode. For it is Torode who has become the face of hit BBC program *MasterChef.*

Arriving in the UK in 1990, Torode helped introduce modern, fast-cooked but sophisticatedly simple Australian-brasserie-style cooking to the UK through his stints at Terence Conran's huge but critically acclaimed gastrobarns Quaglino's and Mezzo. He had previously attracted attention at La Pont de la Tour for his introduction of Asian flavours in specials on the solidly Francophile menu.

While Torode is a still a fan of that fast-cooking style, he's less sure about its viability for a restaurant like his – especially as so many of those sorts of simple brasserie dishes are achievable at home. 'I think there should be a massive difference in restaurant food and home cooking,' he says. 'If we served two lamb chops and mash we wouldn't survive here, but whole belly pork that takes three days to do; Chinese roast duck; Thai duck salad that takes two days to get ready – those are things people are unlikely to do at home but will come out for.'

Most recently, Torode has become a reluctant superstar through his role as one of the two judges on nine series of BBC's *MasterChef*, a televised culinary cook-off that attracts up to five million viewers each week.

To use the vernacular of the reality-TV medium, Torode's forty-two-year 'journey' has been an interesting one, to say the least. Early years moving between Sydney, Melbourne and Maitland were marked by the death of Torode's mother when he was just four. The family eventually settled back by the bay in a house on the beach at Edithvale when Torode was ten. He went to St Bede's college in Mentone and at seventeen became an apprentice at a fifty-seat Beaumaris BYO restaurant called Jean Pierre. 'If I was lucky, on Saturday they'd give me a kitchen porter; otherwise I washed my own pots and pans,' he remembers with a shudder.

He cooked at Melbourne's influential Tsindos Bistro and at twenty opened his own place in Bentleigh East called Pasta Connection, which crashed. 'It went bankrupt. I was 21,' he reveals.

After this he 'wandered around aimlessly', working as a barman in Brisbane and Surfers until he ended up overseeing the catering contract for the Sydney Football Stadium and the Showground. 'It was the hardest thing I ever did. I got pneumonia twice,' he tells me as he sips coffee on the top floor of Smiths, his four-storey London dining destination overlooking the fine lines of Smithfield meat market.

The catering job taught him about the logistical side of running a food business, but when the travel bug bit and he headed to London, he soon got bored of wearing a suit. 'I hated it,' he says of his first UK job.

'I wanted to cook, so I went back into the kitchen. I was paid $12 less than my rent – I survived by buying a bicycle and nicking food from the fridge at work!'

Today Torode is one of the UK's most familiar food faces, though he claims that these days he doesn't do parties or what he calls the 'social circle stuff'. 'Most people don't know I have a family,' he says with a smile — even though he has two young teenage children with his first wife (who lives in Penzance) and two more with his current partner. 'No wonder I'm tired,' he laughs.

Four years ago Torode decided it was time to get out of the kitchen, claiming he was bored of having a 'sweaty arse for twenty years'. 'Cooking is a young man's game. When I was eighteen or nineteen I could do double shifts and then go out for beers, but now I have hangovers and feel like shit. Most young chefs don't know what a hangover is!'

Recently he's also vowed to spend more time with his young family — even taking his first Christmas break for twenty years — by concentrating solely on the TV show and Smiths. Given how hot the show is in the UK, naturally there is talk about more series and he also lets slip a dream of a new place in London's east that the financial crisis might put the brakes on.

Ask Torode about how the English culinary culture has changed while he's been living there and he suggests that London has moved with the times, pointing out everything from extraordinarily designed restaurant spaces like Hakkasan to the rising interest in weekend breakfast that is a more recent phenomenon for London. He still believes however that Australia is far more open to new ideas and willing to take risks, 'I think about this a lot,' he tells us. 'In Oz we are used to being exposed — we go round in shorts and a vest; in Oz the doors always open. Here everyone is wrapped in overcoats so we tend to be much more positive.'

Listen to those words and you can see one thing remains constant — unlike some expats who now see themselves as Brits, Torode is still proud to call himself an Aussie. He even promises to be suitably combative with his English staff come this summer's Ashes series!

Originally published in Melbourne Weekly Bayside, *2009*

A HONG KONG TALE OF
THREE DUMPLINGS

So, eight days filming in Hong Kong, that crazy amalgam of rampant consumerism and grunge which feels like *Blade Runner* hosting a Jackie Chan chase scene … a frantic, fecund, tumbling, bubbling mass of humanity.

Eating there was a similar assault on the senses – a tottering procession of *har gow*, *shu mai*, suckling pig – all crispy skin and melting fat – truffles, Chinese egg tarts, hidden-away private dining dens, and odd street food served from rough-and-tumble holes in the wall.

It is the abiding memory of three dumplings, however, that remains most vivid.

No, those dumplings are not me and the other two *MasterChef* judges, although there is something distinctly dumpling-like about our little trio, but three pieces of dim sum so jaw-droppingly, mouth-wateringly delicious that they rate as three of the best things I've eaten this year.

The surroundings where we found ourselves eating gave no clue to the oncoming seismic experience. Lost in a little side street in an unfashionable Hong Kong suburb stands this tiny, grungy dumpling shopfront; its windows steamed up, its small interior a sardine-squeeze maze of packed tables where dumpling fans cram.

Bizarrely, for a city obsessed with global luxury brands, this rather rough spot is the hottest place to eat in Hong Kong. But then, chef Piu was the dumpling chef at Lung King Heen, the only Hong Kong restaurant with the peak rating of three Michelin stars. He has turned his back on that Hong Kong island glamour to cross Victoria Harbor and head up to edgy Mong Kok to open his own thirty-eight-seat place. It's an area best known for night markets full of illegal knock-offs, allegedly Triad-run mahjong parlours, and knocking shops where the price on the door is set by the country of origin of your chosen companion. It's not synonymous with great food!

Piu's Tim Ho Wun is changing that, so much so that you'll need to take a number and queue for ages to get a seat. While we wait, I get someone to translate the Cantonese order form for me. Needless to say, we over-order, ticking too many boxes, scared that we might miss some gem through the vagaries of this impromptu translation. We order a couple of serves of the *char siu bao*, as we are all piggily intrigued by the promise of a crunchy glaze made from pork fat and sugar.

After forty minutes, two seats become free. Forget reality TV eliminations, this is where the real drama happens. George is quicker off the mark behind me and wedges himself between the wall and a couple of Cantonese students. Outside, Gary presses his nose to the window like a sad puppy at a pet shop New Year's sale.

George waves laden steamer baskets him as a cruel taunt. I think I might have seen a tear, although it might have been a drop of rain rolling down Gary's cheek. The skies have opened with the sort of torrential downpour that drenches the city regularly at this time of year.

The room is eerily silent. We don't understand why until the arrival of a little basket of small golden baked buns about the size of airline bread rolls. These are not your usual puffy white pork buns. We tear the incredibly short pastry open to find a filling of sweet, smoky *char siu* pork floating in velvet-smooth hoisin gravy. Its delicious sweet saltiness echoes the flavours of the bun's crumbly pastry, which I suspect has been made with lots of sugar, salt and lard, hence its decadence. (The Flower Drum sometimes serves a similarly decadent pastry made with foie gras, which has the same lightness of texture, if not of taste.)

It is an OMG moment when pastry and filling marry in my mouth. Pig fat loves sugar, and with the dark richness of the sauce and that ridiculously light pastry, it's like tasting with a full orchestral backing. This is a *char siu bao* to spoil me for every other version I have had, or that I will ever have. The crust of baked sugar and lard is the perfect finishing touch – a further textured expression of sweet saltiness. Now I understand that the silence was out of respect for the food.

Our reaction is slightly more barbarian. We both start talking loudly and excitedly so the students leave and Gary can take his place alongside us. We've saved two buns for Gary and we both take immense vicarious pleasure in watching his face dissolve as he loses himself in his own pork bun epiphany. It is best thing any of us have eaten this year; this status marked by the greediest of our number repeating the double bun order immediately.

No wonder, then, that we were scared we'd be busted for dumpling smuggling when we left the country; that Customs' X-ray would find our insides lined with a procession of pork buns. I was doubly worried, because after a final night that ended with me dancing to a Chinese heavy metal band in a shady Wan Chai dive, I went back secretly the next day to double-check that those buns really were that good. Even with the joyous revelation of that first bite now passed, the baked *char siu bao* still conducted a choir of angels with full trumpet and harp accompaniment in my head. As is so often the case, it is the simplest things well done that give one the most soul-shaking feelings of pleasure.

There was more, obviously … Earthy parcels of glutinous rice with the dark stickiness of gravied pork at their centres and the tea-smoky tannic flavour of the lotus-leaf wrapping clings to the sticky grains. Prawn dumplings of a delicate purity, those little, slightly chewy-skinned footballs filled with mince; and chunky-hearted *shu mai* dumplings.

Among the blizzard of bamboo boxes I remember beef balls so large they made us think twice about the significance of the name, dumplings filled with amaranth and garlic, spring rolls, sticky-skinned translucent *chiu chow* dumplings and the seeming incongruousness of a wonderful square of springy sponge cake.

There were also silky rice rolls served with both a filling of *char siu* pork and prawns, as well as little plates of feet, guts and knuckly bits of bones that seem to be more gristle than meat.

We never got to try the braised lettuce, for some reason. I suspect that Gary sent it back for being too green. At any time during the meal we had enough bamboo steamers on the table to knock up quite a functional life-size representation of Richard Nixon's metaphorical 'Bamboo Curtain. In fact, the amount of food that did arrive at the table was so embarrassing huge that while most average bills here are for about HK$60 ($10) we managed to rack up a HK$240 bill!

Originally published in 'A2', The Age, 2009

SOME IMPORTANT THINGS I LEARNT DOING MASTERCHEF

1. Garnish is the devil. The rule is that if you can't eat it then it doesn't belong on the plate. If it's not an integral part of the dish, then nix it.
2. More effort in prep makes it easier and more enjoyable to cook.
3. Somewhat surprisingly, fetta tastes rather nice topped with sour cherries in syrup and a few pine nuts. This became my impromptu green room (ours is called green because it resembles a swamp, complete with mouldy carpet) canapé for Bill Granger, Donna Hay and Luke Mangan when they came to visit. I think they were a) impressed; b) threatened; c) polite.
4. Simple home food can be plated up far more stylishly if you leave the carbs off the plate. Add the carbs and it looks home-style or peasant. Not that there's anything wrong with that.
5. If you make a pie, make sure the crust is cooked, otherwise you'll look very silly.
6. The more innocuous the title of a dish featured in a challenge, the more devilish it will be. Witness the friendly-sounding 'Chocolate Mousse Cake' challenge, which would have tried the patience of Job.

7. If you have a good palate and oodles of patience, you can achieve amazing dishes with the right recipe. You must, however, follow the recipe.

8. Cooking is now cool with pre-teens. This is very good news.

9. When tasting food, gaze wistfully into the middle distance. This makes people believe you are thinking deeply rather than just trying to recall where you left the car keys.

10. Having people watch you eat – and then commenting on it – is very weird. Stop staring, you peeping toms!

11. A great dish comprises balanced layers of flavour and texture. Acidity and crispiness are the most important factors in a great dish.

12. You can drink a soy chai tea without wearing a kaftan … although it helps.

13. Cook from your heart.

14. Food and feeding people is a beautiful thing.

15. Gary likes beer and puddings. George hates chilli but loves a story. I love weird stuff I haven't seen before and anything foreign.

16. My most used word was 'unctuous'; George's was 'yummy'; Gary's were 'nice' and 'yielding'.

17. The judges argued about three things in the course of the competition: about the nature of great mashed potato; about whether Australia's first *MasterChef* needs to go on to do an apprenticeship; and about whether five or seven dishes was the right number for a sneaky lunch in the middle of filming. Gary and I'd say seven; George would say five – and then insist on ordering double desserts.

18. The last five cooks in this series were the best five cooks we saw in the competition, thus vindicating the judges' (and producers') decision to pick winners based first and foremost on the best dishes cooked.

19. Learn from your elders in the family – don't loose those cherished family recipes.

20. Cook with your children or grandchildren – but realise that it will get messy, very messy. Cooking teaches them about maths, planning,

science and where they come from. This makes cooking the sort of curricular stream that should be central to all education.

21. Apparently butter makes everything better. That's why I've sent a case of Western Star to Beirut.

22. Cooking for one is no fun.

23. People love beetroot because you can beat an egg but you can't beat a root.

24. Six am isn't early; 4.35 am is early.

25. In the end I lost eight kilos while making *MasterChef*. I am not sure why. Perhaps standing around burns calories. I predict big things for my book outlining the 'Dawdle Diet'.

26. Even great chefs can crumble in the kitchen under pressure. So when cooking for friends, reduce the stress as much as possible by using familiar recipes and familiar ingredients. Oh, and always practice anything new on your family first.

27. Good TV revolves around jeopardy. Great TV revolves about people you care about placed in that jeopardy. Oh, and lots of expensive cameras – ideally mounted on helicopters or on a Chapman, which is like a very, very expensive billy-cart with padded suede seats.

28. Always expect the unexpected.

29. It is possible to stand still for long periods of time if you run through all the cheesy male catalogue model poses you can think of, from the cuff pop to the thumbs in pocket. Although after twelve hours of that, you'll understand why polar bears go mad in the zoos and swing from side to side.

30. Smart brunettes are hot. *MasterChef* judges are not – unless they are in Hong Kong and it's 33 degrees.

31. According to the make-up artist who does us both, Kyle Sandilands is more professional than me. Should this concern me?

32. It is impossible to go to Hong Kong for a week without putting on three kilos.

33. There is a small group of people who watch TV with a magnifying glass. For the record, at no time during the show was I a) a freemason; b) sacked; c) dead; d) having marriage difficulties; e) wearing a

hearing aid; f) a walrus or g) snide. If I put my hand in my jacket it was because I was pretending to be Napoleon during the French challenge. If I wasn't on the show it was because I was working at the Melbourne or Noosa Food & Wine Festivals. If I wasn't wearing my wedding ring it's because I'd taken it off to do the gardening and then forgotten to put it back on. Okay, maybe I was occasionally walrussy or snide. And that wire coming out of my ear was for an earpiece so that a very clever woman called Caroline Spencer could tell me what was for lunch and that yes, there was a dynasty of French kings called the Merovingians.

34. Melbourne people are cool – and a bit aloof.

35. Always try to dress like you are either a serve of several colourful scoops of gelati (perhaps vanilla, watermelon and chocolate), or the most lurid eighties cocktail at Studio 54. This will entertain you in quieter moments.

36. If you are a good cook you don't have to follow a recipe word for word. Be brave, stop and think about what you've got and how confident you are you can improve it.

37. If an FM breakfast radio presenter asks you to taste something – don't. It is unlikely to be nice.

38. Always be nice to the director, but it is the first assistant director who you really need to suck up to.

39. Never ego-search the web. Some people can be quite hurtful and cruel. And that's just George Calombaris.

40. Never touch a pan taken from the oven with your lip to see if it's hot.

41. Don't do anything that you find uncomfortable unless you are scared of it. It is uncomfortable to find yourself on the same TV show as the PM or Julia Gillard, because you obviously know you aren't worthy – and feel a bit embarrassed that you are lowering the tone.

42. When undertaking a mystery box challenge – or as I like to call it back at home, a spot of 'fridge shaking' – remember that you don't have to use everything on offer in the box or the fridge. Just pick three or four ingredients that you know will work together. Like a

marriage, the fewer people in it, the easier it is for everyone to get along.

43. If you twirl your wedding ring while the cameras are rolling your wife will know you love her.

44. Food writers have the best job in the world. Being a chef is far tougher.

45. If you want to employ someone to 'whoop' with genuine exhilaration when you pull something out the oven – employ a Queenslander. Queenslanders give the best whoop, followed by Sydneysiders, but Queenslanders are willing to do it while wearing fancy-dress.

46. 'MCK' is how the cast and crew referred to *MasterChef* Kitchen – the Sydney warehouse fitted out to be out home for the four months of filming.

47. Tired people are more likely to cry.

48. Don't cut anything while holding the knife around the base of the blade with your fingers curled under the cutting edge. If you slip you will slice off your fingertips.

49. Never, ever, eat off your knife or hunch over your food.

50. Make-up artists touch up people all through the day and never get in trouble for it.

51. Julia returned to MCK for the final week a far better cook and with vastly improved plating skills. If only she hadn't overcooked that goat – along with the duck that she beat Peter Evans with, it was the best dish she cooked in MCK. Had she earned the advantage going into the pie challenge she could have won.

52. Justine was the queen of flavour on the show. She managed to get the most intense flavour out of the simplest of ingredients. She also behaved with a dignity and maturity far greater than her years. Justine had so many highlights, but the dish of celeriac puree, carrots and duck that wowed Jacques Reymond at my Legends Dinner Party also wowed me. It was arguably the best dish of the whole competition and poor old Gary and George didn't get to taste it!

53. The first time we saw Chris we knew he'd be a contender. He was a good leader, meticulously clean and always true to his vision,

presenting a litany of great honest food. Eggs in Hell was an inspired idea but it was the pig's head that was his dish of the tournament. If it hadn't been for the tough beef cheek and the failure of the *brik* pig's trotter parcel he could have gone on to win.

54. Always remember to shave any stubbly bristles from your pig's trotter before cooking it.

55. When I put her through as the last of our Top 20, I predicted that Poh would bring us dishes of disaster and dishes of genius. After her return, the dishes of genius dominated. If only she'd learn to read the recipe! From those Abacus beans that were like a taro gnocchi to the crazy congee, via those amazing deep-fried jaffa-filled meringue balls, she cooked some of the competition's most exciting food.

56. Julie was the most improved cook, handled the pressure best and constantly surprised us with her ability to master the scariest challenges with no little skill. Her performance in the two final pressure tests was nothing short of miraculous. This is why she stayed the longest and won. Her best dish? Well, the pigeon breast she cooked in Hong Kong was actually even better than Pak's and a match for Donovan's! Tasting that, I knew she was a serious chance to become Australia's first MasterChef.

57. And finally, don't ever try to look intelligent and pensive by striking a pose like Rodin's Thinker, pressing your fist to your chin. Too many viewers will think that you are just smelling your fingers or picking your nose.

Much of this piece originally published in 'A2', The Age, 2009

A CRAVAT STORY

If a disproportionate amount of time was spent during *MasterChef* watching us all eat and discussing it, then 'inordinate' would be the only word to describe the column inches devoted to my cravats. Who would have thought that a few humble strips of cloth could excite or appall so many viewers?

Sure, the joke was always that the producers cast my cravats, not me. Having said that, the reaction to my neckwear choice was both immediate and, initially, perplexing, justifying this decision. Some loved it as a way of injecting a little colour into a monochrome world, while others' dislike and anger over the scarves perhaps speaks about Australians' innate distrust of authority and flamboyance. Both are values that the humble cravat seems to project into the eyes of some people.

For while the necktie is the perfect mark of sobriety and middle-class conservatism, there has always been something a little louche about the cravat, jabot or ascot. Like white shoes, they mark the wearer as someone who should be watched; someone with the propensity to be a cad, imperious, trouble or all three. A cursory glance down the list of names of the great cravat-wearers of history confirms this. They include Louis XIV of France; Regency dandy and royal confidant Beau Brummell; that style maven the Duke of Windsor, who abdicated the

British throne to marry a divorcee; Lord Byron; Bonnie Prince Charlie; all the bounders in any book by the Brontës or Austen; Noel Coward; and most of the Kelly Gang (Dan, Ned, Steve Hart, even Aaron Sheritt). All were pictured wearing neck scarves or cravats.

In art, too, the cravat has been used to denote that someone was 'NQR' (not quite right). It has been sported in different forms by several generations of Count Dracula; other vampires, including Tom Cruise as Lestat in *Interview with a Vampire*; Oliver Reed as Bill Sykes in *Oliver*; Basil Fawlty; gangsters like Al Pacino in *The Godfather II* and Andy Garcia as Terry Benedict in *Oceans Eleven* – and even Austin Powers wears a lacy jabot.

I started wearing scarves and cravats aged eighteen, influenced by my three main style icons – the dandified Brian Jones, who was the coolest of the Rolling Stones; Fred Jones from the carton *Scooby-Doo*, who sported a natty orange scarf; and Harry H. Corbett, who played Harold in *Steptoe and Son*. Corbett added a grungy edge to the loosely-tied op shop scarf, in contrast to his father's tattered neckerchief.

I didn't think much about it. I just thought they all looked a little dashing in their own ways. After all, both Clark Kent and Cary Grant were noted fans of the ascot – as the Americans call their cravats.

Now, after thirty years and several false starts, the cravat looks like it's making a comeback – if only in elite circles. Ashton Kutcher, David Beckham, George Clooney and Jeremy Piven have sported them and even Brad Pitt has been seen wearing an ascot loosely draped around his neck. And about time too – the cravat has a long and illustrious history that needs a new chapter.

The name 'cravat' is actually claimed to be a bastardisation of *croat* (or *Hrvatska*, to be more linguistically accurate). It is believed that in a time before uniforms, Croatian military units in the German Thirty Years War (1618–1648) wore scarves so they could identify who was on their side during battle. The cravat crossed over and earned its name when a Croatian military unit went to serve with the French in Paris several years later. Their officers' flashy neck gear came to the notice of the most stylish ruler in Europe, France's King Louis XIV. After the death of his mother in 1666 and the subsequent relaxation of official court dress codes, the Sun King appointed a court *cravatier* to ensure that he had a choice of new cravats to wear each morning. Charles II introduced the cravat to England a few years after his Restoration in 1660, where it became a raging fashion for a while.

Not that the Croatians were the first to wear a scarf tied around their necks. There are reports of scarves used as a fashion accessory in 221 BC China, and some of the terracotta warriors, which date from 210 BC, also sport a knotted cravat of sorts. In classical Rome, senators wore *fascalia* or scarves wound round their necks. Originally these were supposed to keep the vocal cords warmed up for orations, however some historians have hypothesised that later they became a mark of status. It is rare, though, to find any sculpture from ancient Rome that is cravatted. What is easier to substantiate is that some Roman legionaries used to wear a scarf (*focale*) knotted around the neck, in part to stop their armour or tunics chaffing.

But the acceptance of the cravat in royal circles can be laid at the Croatians' door, though in part this was due to luck. For within a year of Croatian poet Ivan Gundulic posing, in 1622, for the first portrait of a man in a cravat, Phillip IV of Spain (and the rulers of other Catholic countries) banned the ruff in a campaign against fashionable excess. This resulted in the birth of the soft collar and left space for the cravat and its brothers – the *steinkirk*, the solitaire and the stock – to thrive. In fact, the neck scarf became such a sartorial craze that in 1688 Randle Holme commented in his treatise *Academy of Armory and Blazon* that 'a cravatte is another kind of adornment for the neck being nothing else but a long towel put about the Collar, and so tyed before with a Bow Knott. This is the original of all such Wearings but now by the Art and Inventions of the seamsters, there is so many new ways of making them, that it would be a task to name, much more to describe them.'

The cravat found renewed popularity in England with a group of 18th-century dandies called 'the macaronis', who adopted the foppish ways and fashions spied on their Grand Tours around Europe. (In researching this story I discovered that one of my ancestors, the gentleman gardener Uvedale Price, was a macaroni – so the wearing of cravats obviously runs in the family.) But the lacy froth of a cravat favoured by the macaronis was replaced at the end of the 18th century by a sleeker strip of white linen, as the English – inspired by the likes of the Regency king of fashion and royal confidante George Beau Brummell (1778–1840) – adopted a simpler cravat. It was this that passed into popular dress for the affluent – or for those who wanted to be seen as such.

In Brummell's day, cravats were always white, at least until he left England in disgrace and deeply in debt in 1816. By 1818 colours started to make an appearance.

The mania over the different tying styles that Brummell and his ilk had fuelled reached such a fever pitch that in 1828 H. Le Blanc Esq. published *The Art of Tying the Cravat; Demonstrated in Sixteen Lessons, Including Thirty-Two Different Styles*. This was basically a handbook for the lesser classes, aimed at polishing up their cravat-tying skills so they might be mistaken for being from a higher station in society than they actually were. It was a handbook in social climbing by way of the cravat. In fact, in 1818 a satirical pamphlet called *The Neckclothitania* had been published, skewering the obsession with intricate cravat knots. (Yes, it does sound like people had too much time on their hands after the Napoleonic War.)

It wasn't until the start of the 20th century that the cravat, or its looser cousin the ascot, started to lose its grip on society's throats. The final death knell sounded in the late 1920s with Jesse Langsdorf's formal invention of the necktie that could be made by machine.

Strangely, across all these centuries of cravat-dominance I can find no record of dandies inter-twining different coloured or patterned cravats for the resulting endless combination of colour-ways. Sure, Beau Brummell might have worn at least three cravats in a day, but they were always worn separately.

Nor can I find any record of Brummell, Louis XIV or even Brian Jones naming their cravats. Admittedly, as Brummell only wore white ones, his need for names was less pressing – although a surprising richness of language did grow up over the different tying styles. There were knots with names as exotic as the Four-In-Hand, the Cravate Americaine or even the Cravat en Cascade.

The naming of my scarves and cravats is based on a very sound principle. To whit: when you have ninety different scarves or cravats, you have to have a clear code to define which cravats we are talking about when *MasterChef*'s stylist, Clare Bridgeman, and I are planning the wardrobe for the next day. Just saying 'the red cravat' is not good enough when there are half a dozen red cravats in the cupboard. For example, there is 'Mia', which is a long skinny red cravat with a sparse but stylish green and yellow paisley-patterned edging. Then there are the two Michelles. Both are red with white polka dots. 'Long Michelle' is an un-waisted ascot and long (obviously); 'Short Michelle' is a waisted cravat but now known as 'Slutty Michelle' because she kept misbehaving and popping out of the shirt to flap around. She also ran away to the Logies with my fellow judge George Calombaris and was seen in his breast pocket at TV's Night of Nights. Then we have 'Danielle', 'Alison' and 'Marieke'. The first two are twenty-year-old companions in different shades of burgundy sourced from the Harrods sale in London; the latter is pale yellow with a saucy pattern of little red rectangles.

Many of these cravats and scarves have been donated by friends and are accordingly named in their honour; hence why the name 'Marina' pops up quite often in the cravat inventory. It's my way of thanking them for the time they have spent scouring op shops on my behalf.

Then there are cravats that have come from deceased relations of friends and colleagues and which are named after the original owner. There is 'Racing Phillip', which is a natty royal blue with small white spots, and 'Country Phillip' which is brown with a repeated pattern of delicate sky-blue paisley eye.

As for my favourites, I am quite fond of 'Hermes' and 'Versace' which are top scarves with correspondingly suitable patterns – the former is all golden bridles and bits on a white and blue background, while the latter is a gaudy orange sun on a background of green, yellow and deepest blue. It is, however, the combination of 'Ros', which is a pale cream linen cravat with a fine brown–grey paisley outline, with the fine floral pattern of 'Lilac Leona' that is perhaps my 'go to' combination – especially when I am wearing a dark blue shirt. As a matter of interest I am wearing 'Ros' and 'Danielle' on the front cover of this book; 'Alison' is in my pocket and on the plate are 'Long Michelle', 'Lilac Leona', 'Jessica' (which is a pure pink scarf), 'Myf' (the short, fascinating white and purple), '*Tenugui*', and 'Nathan', which is the shiny scarf at the back. You see, not all my scarves are named after glamorous women.

Of course, if you want to find out more about my cravats and what they are really thinking, you can follow them at MattsCravat on Twitter. True cravat fans can join the Facebook group We (Heart) Matt's Cravats.

ADDENDA: CITY TIPS

I can't help myself, I love making lists and in the process of chatting to people about this book it seemed evident that what the first draft lacked was some restaurant suggestions. Old reviews are pretty worthless, but luckily I've spent a fair bit of time in Adelaide, Melbourne and Sydney this year doing other stories and filming *MasterChef*, so it seemed logical to cobble together a few hit lists that might prove diverting – always with the proviso that time is the enemy and things, owners and chefs can all change in the ensuing months! Oh, and so no one is left out I've also lobbed in a few personal suggestions for where to eat in Brisbane, Perth, Noosa, Tasmania and Darwin, as I've also had a few feeds there this year.

I should note that these aren't my favourite little holes in walls, burger joints and rough and tumble ethnic canteens, but the sort of places where you want to lavish yourself when you have limited leisure in a strange town. Like they annoyingly say in bad hotel restaurants where the floor staff all wear name tags: 'Enjoy!'

Melbourne

I'm a bloke. As I've said, I like to make lists. It's what we do. Not the sort of useful lists that remind us what to buy at the supermarket – it is far more fun to try to remember what you need and then do that whole, 'How could I forget we need milk, loo paper and washing-up liquid?' thing – but the sort of fanciful lists on such pressing subjects as the Best Shepherds in a Grand Final, Top 10 Rock Songs to Slam Dance To or the far shorter Hollywood Actresses Almost as Hot as my Wife.

Needless to say, the majority of my lists relate to Melbourne's restaurants, which is useful, as this is what friends, family and strangers at parties most frequently ask me. Well, that and whether I think it is 'appropriate for a grown man to be wearing that'.

It seems everyone is hungry for a selection of approved places to eat out, based on a selection of specified criteria. My usual knee-jerk reaction to these questions is just to answer 'Cumulus Inc.', whether it's a request for somewhere 'hip', 'for breakfast', 'romantic', 'good value', 'with cutting-edge food', 'in the CBD', or just 'where I can eat anchovies straight from the tin'.

Now, in a vain effort to circumvent this and also to organise my thinking into neat little packages, I feel it is time to answer these most-asked questions.

I'll resist revealing the most controversial of my lists, which remain locked in my bottom drawer strictly marked for my personal amusement only. These number such gems as the Six Best Waiters in Melbourne – Male and Female, the Five Big-Name Chefs in Melbourne who are Clumsy Cooks and the Six Big-Name Restaurants that Melbourne Could Live Without.

Far safer, and far less likely to be dragged through the courts, are my most requested lists. The most common demand is for my favourites, but that's a request that can't be answered, as these answers depend on who I am with, who's paying, how hungry or how rich I am.

The next most requested is my list of Six Favourite Places to Send Overseas or Interstate Visitors, which is far easier to construct. This usually includes **Donovan's**, **Vue de monde**, **Cumulus Inc.**, **Attica**, **Bella Vedere** in the Yarra Valley and the **Royal Mail** in Dunkeld, as together these provide a good sense of why Victoria is such a unique place to live. Needless to say, if whoever's asking is over twenty-five I'd also be forced to add my list of Six Unmissable City Bars, which currently includes **Spice Market**, **Cookie**, **Madame Brussels**, **Sweatshop at Seamstress**, **Siglo** and **Match**.

If they are young foodies then I'd be also giving them my list of the Eight Best Places to Eat at the Bar around Town, because counter dining is so hot right now. This would revolve around **Bar Lourinhã**, **Coda, Gigibaba**, **Von Haus**, **Longrain**, **MoVida Next Door**, **Cumulus Inc.** (again) and a trip out to **Shira Nui** in Glen Waverley for the sushi bar. If that was too much of a hike, I'd suggest lunch at the sushi bar at **Shoya** in the CBD because chef Shigeo Nonaka is a master of elegant presentation. Or, if they hate raw fish, sitting at the shelf looking down the laneway at **Journal Canteen** on the corner of Degraves Street and Flinders Lane.

If they are in love, then they will get my Nine Favourite Places for a Romantic Meal, which, needless to say, is solely motivated by the places where I've romanced the one I love. So it's **Jacques Reymond**, **Da Noi**, a window table at the **Stokehouse**, the enforced proximity of **Ocha**, the warm, dark, woody womb that is **The European**, the intimacy and elegance of the counter at sushi bar **Aka Tombo** in Prahran, breakfast at **The Lake House** (because, let's face it, you'll need to stay over the night before) in Daylesford, the moody lighting and sexy food of **Cutler & Co**, and the back room at **Pellegrini's** in the city. The last one is the most important, as there is nothing more romantic than being lost so deep in the eyes of the one you're with that you lose track of time and are oblivious to the fact that you are surrounded by the rush-hour-train-station hustle and bustle of the communal table here.

Then there's my Five Best Tips from Taxi Drivers: Richmond's **Daawat** for the biryani, Malvern's **Indian Harvest** for the lamb chops, **Jaipur Curry Bar** for the prices and the goat, **Woodapple** in Hampton for the Sri Lankan food and **Madras Banyan Tree** down the Nepean for the dosai.

Then there are those places that always make me feel good and at one with the world. This is an eclectic list but each carries with it a little story and slice of personal history that helps make it special to me. There's **Abla's**, the modern Lebanese and Persian ideas at **Rumi**, the cellar bar at **Grossi Florentino**, **Afghan Village** in Camberwell, **Happy Cook** in Nunawading for their wonderful Peking duck you order in advance, **Giuseppe Arnaldo & Sons**, Richmond's **Koutouki Coffee Shop** for the simple home-style community Greek in the most basic of surroundings, Carnegie's **Siam 1** for their attack of sweet, salty, hot flavours, and **Cafe di Stasio** because it always ends badly (in the best possible way). Having worked on the telly show with Messrs Mehigan and Calombaris, their places – even though I can never again review them, having worked so closely with the guys, or even mention them here by name – have now been added to that list.

Sydney

Set adrift for six months in Sydney with a promise to behave myself, there's little else to do other than improve my guitar picking and get to grips with the city's restaurant culture. For the irony is that although I travel extensively around this wide brown land looking at producers and places to eat, the Harbour City is the state capital where I seem to have spent the least time eating.

So I've spent the last six months rather deliciously playing catch up. In doing this, it has certainly helped having the mobile numbers of those twin colossi of Sydney reviewing, the *Sydney Good Food Guide* editors Joanna Savill and Simon Thomsen, for advice.

I ate out over one hundred times over this period but I won't mention here places that I feel we do better down south. Somewhat unsurprisingly, cool, cheap places thus do not feature heavily in this round-up!

It is normal in these types of pieces to build to a crescendo as the writer finally names their favourite restaurant/tropical beach/brand of nail gun – so I won't.

The place in Sydney at which I spent the most time (after home and 'the office') was not the gym, a cabana by the pool at The Ivy with Channel 7 starlets (helloooo, Todd McKenney), or even the Opera House. In a rather telling assessment of my diary, it was the casual, airy first-floor retreat known as **Sopra** that occupied most real estate in my Sydney calendar.

Sopra sits above a fruiterer and Italian deli called **Fratelli Fresh** in the suburb of Waterloo, on the way to the airport, and it serves the sort of simple but deliciously elegant food you'd like to eat every day. Crunchy polenta chips topped with a rich but subtle mushroom and blue cheese sauce; salads of perfect tomatoes and spun curds; braised quail; fat meatballs; tightly curled little fists of pasta dough tossed with chilli and springy prawn meat; and chef Andy Bunn's finest moment: a salad of little more than shredded savoy cabbage turned with good balsamic and some shavings of parmesan, which manages to be fresh and crisp yet decadent at the same time. It's a triumph everyone should try.

The other big favourite was **Bodega**, for both their bar with its high stools and high little tables, and the compact dining room where – like Sopra – bookings aren't taken. Bodega is oft compared to Melbourne's wonderful MoVida (and its little brother next door) but Bodega's look is slightly more technicolour and its flavours push far more towards Latin America rather than the Iberian peninsula, although you'll also find some adventurous modern takes that refine dishes like scallops and blood pudding or crème Catalan. Their 'fish fingers' – a sort of ceviche bruschetta – are a must.

When it comes to pushing the boat out, it has to be faced that Sydney has far more places to spend a lot of money than Melbourne. Occasionally it's even worth it. Currently **Tetsuya's** seems to have hit a particularly rich vein of form. While the room might be simple, despite its serene garden view, the multi-course menu that marries Japanese and modernist European ideas with a bright Sydney confidence is exciting people again. And the lack of tourists in Sydney means it's now far easier to get a table here.

If you are looking for somewhere a little sexier, try **Marque**, where Mark Best's food is also singing at perfect pitch at the moment; his sauternes custard is like slipping liquid satin in your mouth, while an equally sensuous mix of warm crab and frozen foie gras arrives smoking provocatively.

If you want a similarly delicious and cutting-edge menu, but with a tourist-friendly view, then a window table at **Quay** is highly recommended. Just check when you book that there won't be a gigantic ocean liner moored next to the restaurant when you go. This can mar the view of the harbour and Opera House somewhat – but on the table you'll be able to see why Peter Gilmore's delicate dishes won Quay every available restaurant award in the last twelve months.

For the fish lover I'd also single out Greg Doyle's **Pier**, because it's a little more laid-back, also on the water and boasts Katrina Kanetani's funky desserts. If I was rash enough to state that she was one of the three best pastry chefs in the country I don't think too many people would fight me about it. It's also not a bad place for a more relaxed business lunch.

For a more formal business lunch location, try **Becasse**, **Est.** or **Sepia**. With its grand dining room Est. is the more spectacular room – especially if you book one of the tables by the tall windows – but Sepia is the new kid on the block and boasts two of Sydney's most innovative chefs united in the kitchen. Martin Benn became a Sydney star cooking at Tetsuya's and Daniel Puskas made a table at the teeny suburban **Oscillate Wildly** as hard to snare. Go for interesting food and a noted strength in seafood.

If you are a fan of **Rockpool Bar and Grill** in Melbourne, you should also make note of its new Sydney home which opened a few months back. With its soaring Art Deco interior, dominated by dramatic green marble columns, I'd suggest that it is the grandest looking dining room in Australia. This makes it the sort of place a competitive Sydneyside business associate might take you to show off. Instead, make like a smart-ass Melbournian and suggest you meet in the restaurant's bar for the same wagyu burger that the Melbourne original made famous, and then make sure you've booked a table downstairs at Neil Perry's other new place, **Spice Temple,** for dessert. I developed a serious craving for the watermelon granita spiked with ginger and chrysanthemum wine, and their delicious mocha ice, here at this dark and moody modern Chinese restaurant that is not a bad place to go and hold hands – if you are so inclined.

If romance is on the cards, then try Champagne and dessert at **Aria** after watching something garment-rendingly dramatic at the Opera House. It stays open suitably late and *MasterChef* tragics (like me) can get a photo with Matt Moran and try the dessert he made Poh and Julie cook in the show's finale. If you are looking for something a little less uptown, then **Restaurant Assiette** is a far more intimate fine diner that seemed to be largely frequented by hand-holding couples on the night Mr Calombaris and I went. Please note that at no time did we hold hands just to 'fit in'. On a warm night **Universal** is also rather special, not least because Christine Manfield is cooking some riotously good food at the moment – intricate, intense but above all supremely harmonious, whether marrying Asian or sub-continental flavour notes. I also like the relaxed mood and cheek by jowl stool seating of **Billy Kwong**. The modern Chinese menu is fab – especially the crispy eggs, and the pork dishes.

For a daytime assignation, a ferry from Circular Quay to Manly and a short taxi ride to **Pilu at Freshwater** is a fine way to wile away a sunny day. Get a seat on the enclosed terrace with a great view of the surf and enjoy rather refined Sardinian food – think of a less rustic Da Noi. Then walk up over the headland and back along Manly beach to get the ferry home. If you hate the water then try the casual elegance of **Lucio's** or **Buon Ricordo,** which are like Café di Stasio's far better behaved (but as deliciously entertaining) elder sisters in pretty Sydney frocks. Their delicate and highly finessed takes on regional Italian gems ensure the plates sing like a Puccini duet.

There are three other names you should have in your mobile for that Sydney trip. If you are a serious foodie you could do a lot worse than grab a seat at the bar at the **Bentley** in Surry Hills for Brent Savage's somewhat 'out there' culinary expressions that are far more bullseye than miss. The bar at **Icebergs**, perched as it is overlooking the generous curve of Bondi Beach, is another favourite with Robert Marchetti's stylish Italian menu as sleek as the décor and the clientele. For a similarly finessed approach to the Italian kitchen but with more of a Sydney pub feel, then the flashly renovated **Beresford Hotel** has a fine beer garden and Danny Russo's excellent modern Italian menu. His squid ink tortellini stuffed with crab meat are a thing of legend.

Adelaide

Adelaide is criminally under-valued by some eastern-states foodies as a culinary destination, but take this list below for a burl round the city of churches and you'll have a fine, and filling, time! These nine are ordered from the smartest to the most casual and mark the sites of my most recent 'good meals' in Adelaide.

For a big night out it has to be **The Manse**. Ayhan Erkoc's menu shows a grasp of modern ideas honed working with Peter Gilmore at Quay and Mark Best at Marque in Sydney. Technique, however, is never allowed to overpower flavour, as a rich chicken liver parfait with the flavours of madeira, hazelnut and beetroot shows clearly. The dining room with its lushly dressed tables, matt and gloss detailed black feature walls and judicious use of white leather, silver and glass, looks remarkably fresh in spite of being over three years old and gives the old mansion a decidedly contemporary edge.

Georges on Waymouth has always been a popular Adelaide business lunch haunt but the arrival of chef Sandor Palmai now means there is a menu to match the very professional service, solid wine list and the relaxed ambience for which Georges has long been known. Palmai seems far more comfortable here than in some previous gigs such as at The Melting Pot (deceased) and this shows on the plate with excellent dishes like confit duck and lentil tortellini with Persian feta, radicchio and caramelised pear, or a white chocolate crème brûlée with dark chocolate *zeppoli* (Sicilian doughnuts) and a lime and hazelnut sorbet.

The Melting Pot attracted some good chefs and one of Adelaide's most exciting young chefs came to my attention first when cooking there. Now Adam Liston has found a new home in the re-built basement wine lodge that is **The Wine Underground.** Liston has culinary ambition to burn and is happy pushing the food envelope – crab congee with yabby essence and an intense garlic emulsion, anyone? – but at this wine-centric and rather comfortable cellar he has found matching enthusiasm and professionalism front of house in the form of Genevieve Prior.

One of the hottest new arrivals in Adelaide has been the resurrection of the fine North Adelaide site (previously Cibo) by Matthew and Olivia

Trim, the enterprising couple behind Adelaide's Farina and The Manse. **Sparrow** has proved to be a roaring success. This sprawling modern space aims to have something for everyone, with a herb-pot-fringed terrace for warmer days, a smarter dining area inside and counter seating for more casual assignations. Talented young chef Matthew Goodlet's menu is equally flexible, ranging from good pizzas (try the roast pork and apple) and charcuterie to more formal offerings like gossamer-thin carpaccio of octopus combined with the flavours of potato and paprika. Breakfast might be smoked kingfish with a poached egg and brioche, or blood sausages with poached egg and hollandaise.

Another fine addition to Adelaide's menu has been the morphing of of the old Melting Pot into a far more casual guise as **The Pot**. Its open kitchen, scrawled brown paper specials and woody interior is matched with a very contemporary menu from young chef Ashley Brandom, which skips from charcuterie – like terrines, a parfait and rabbit rillettes – and slow roasted lamb or suckling pig, to surprisingly chic but ballsy salads that might pair wedges of iceberg lettuce hearts topped with aioli and an anchovy with soft boiled eggs, slices of gherkin, capers and the occasional frizz of fine lemon zest. It is well-priced and there's also an interesting short list of wines by the glass.

Panacea is funky café with restaurant-quality food that manages to capture the laid-back, friendly atmosphere that Andy Currens and Adam Nero nurtured when they had the Cibo in Hyde Park. That glam *femme* crowd has followed them to this modern space with its bold pendants lights and cute decking courtyard with its Chinese elm and tables set with comfortable and stylish Italian 'Caprice' chairs from JR Richards. The menu from Dioni Pike (ex Wine Underground) is loaded with honest food like vine-wrapped stuffed sardines, slow-cooked pork belly with saffron aioli, and a caramel-glazed baked apple filled with crème Catalan. The wine lists nods to well-priced local South Australian heroes like SC Pannell, Cascabel and Majella, but start with a Gin and Pink – an elegantly tart cocktail that marries homegrown organic ruby grapefruit juice with Tanqueray Ten gin and a splash of Cointreau for impressive results. Breakfast on Saturdays is manic and more freeform.

Amy Hage has been putting up some of Adelaide's most interesting food for over five years. People still flock to **The Food Business** for a lunch of the signature leek and oyster pies or pheasant rillettes, but now carpeting and a chocolate padded chesterfield wall makes The Food Business an attractive dinner option at the weekends as well. Come for Hay Valley lamb rack with labne and lentils or Barossa chook with grapes and roast garlic. For breakfast, take one of the umbrella-shaded tables and revive with brioche French toast with buttered apple and a Brekkytini. This decadent blend of Cointreau and gin is spiked with lemon juice and the tang of marmalade – naturally it is served with toast!

With its stylish pressed metal wainscoting, **Bistro Dom's** long narrow room has the feel of a French train station bistro – the sort of place you can start the day with a good coffee and a buttery croissant or baked eggs and then return to step up for a lunch of pan-fried lambs' brains with potato salad and bitter greens or a leek and blue cheese tart, for the less carnivorous. Check with them for dinner opening, which used to only be on Friday nights.

Queen Street could be Adelaide's coolest suburban strip, with designers and vintage furniture shops all nuzzling up against a stylishly retro café of old polished boards, old Sunday school chairs at pavement tables, and a huge blackboard. Here you'll find the **Queen Street Café**, offering some great café dishes with a restaurant's attention to detail. Chef Bill Petropoulos puts up elegantly simple dishes like avocado on dark rye toast – the bread especially sourced from a small-batch artisan baker – for breakfast or a grilled chicken salad with kipfler potatoes, green beans and egg.

Ohhh, and where to drink afterwards? While Adelaide may not have the same booming bar culture as Brisbane, those good places it does have are gems by any measure. **Dragonfly** has a slightly grungy feel, but look closely and you'll see no little thought has gone into sourcing some rather fine pieces of modern furniture to set against the quirky interior. Drink longnecks of Coopers or get festive with their Lychee Rose – a saucy mix of Plymouth gin, lychee liqueur and fresh lime with pink grapefruit juice. Still hungry? Then there's a good selection of perfect bar food, from calamari fritti with aioli to salty chilli soy beans in their pods to pop into your mouth. The location, set away from the hurly burly of Rundle Street, is another plus. For something a trifle more zhooshy, then try **Botanic** or **The 1878 Apothecary,** which are both great examples of stylish, grown-up bars full of clubby furniture and adult wine lists. I am a very big fan of the latter so if you see me there misbehaving, do say hello – and do forget anything that I might be doing. The bar at the **Richmond Hotel** can also be a good bet.

Brisbane and Noosa

Brisbane is quite the bustling culinary hub these days, even if Queensland is still the only state to be able to boast as many fine restaurants in the regions as there are in the state capital.

For me, **E'cco** is the quintessential new egalitarian Australian restaurant. Casual enough for you to spot cricketer Matthew Hayden slipping off his shoes under a table in the bar, but smart enough that in the dining room ladies who lunch can dissect one of über-chef Philip Johnson's bright, light dishes. His light, approachable but clever food is loaded with textures and a heady mix of acidity, sweetness and savour.

For a slightly plusher experience it's hard to go past Kym Machin's menu at **Urbane.** While this young chef enjoys playing with cutting-edge ideas and techniques in his food, it is never at the expense of the true flavours of the ingredients. Professional service and some interesting wine options helps complete the picture. Not a place for those that value volume over finesse though…

Machin's predecessor at Urbane was Ryan Squires and his return to Brisbane has made for one of Australia's most interesting restaurant openings in 2009. His **Buffalo Club** is the sort of uncompromising modernist place where sometimes it feels like someone is playing with your head – or painting abstract works on the plates with food. I mean, who else would pair toasted marshmallow with foie gras or the plump, firm flesh of freshly caught 'crevette' – yes, obviously anyone who describes big shrimp like that to a 'crevette'-wearer like me wins extra points – with the flavours of mandarin, coriander, eggplant and soy and then add the spindly little legs for crunch? Beautiful, clever and unusual.

The next big coming is the launch of the northern outpost of Matt Moran's **Aria,** which promises to bring the same sleek modern food that its Sydney big brother is loved for. Instead of a harbour view, Moran's new Brisbane home has river views from the old Pier Nine site. A perfect spot for a languid Friday lunch.

When it comes to drinking, the Sixties citrus-lounge-cool of **Sky Room** above the Buffalo Club in Fortitude Valley and its sister, **The Bowery**, offer edgy adult drinking options and some interesting cocktails that aren't all about sugary sweetness. If you are looking for a slightly earthier but still cool experience, try the **The Lark**, in an 1888 Paddington cottage. Fashion types should head for the smooth upstairs lounge while it is slightly more rough and tumble in the courtyard and main bar – although just as enjoyable. Good cocktails, floor staff with good wine knowledge and chips with a blue cheese sauce await!

Noosa

I am hard-pressed to think of a beach town that has quite the depth of great food as Noosa. Melbournians seem to view Noosa as a bit like Far North Brighton, such is the concentration of Pru and Trudes up there during the Victorian school holidays. The north-facing beach is one attraction but the restaurants are almost as important. The big news in 2009 was the move of **Wasabi** from its simple Sunshine Beach digs. A stylish but stark room makes the most the Noosa River view, and in Danielle Gjestland Wasabi has a notable maitre d' who seems to have blossomed at their new home, as has the Japanese food of Shinichi Maeda. Always one of Australia's more interesting sushi chefs, he's made Wasabi one of the country's destination restaurants. Afterwards, drop in to **Parque Mexico** over the way for just a little play with some of the forty-four tequillas on offer in this eccentrically designed bar.

Two other Noosa stayers, **Berardo's** and **Humid**, should also be on your intinerary. In Berardo's Hampton-white interior, complete with matching baby grand, chef Shane Bailey is proving that similarly clean, simple food driven by peak local produce is a crowd-pleaser. While the combination of Mary Morrison's intelligent wine list and Michelle

Gordon-Smith's focused, honest food at Humid makes it a bit of a foodie favourite. The rabbit, leek and macadamia pies are a stayer but my recent winter memories are of spatchcock on celeriac puree with Brussels sprouts, poppy-plump sugar-snap peas and a tangy, sweet pine nut and currant glaze.

If you are reading this in 2010, check out the online reports on how the new young head chefs at two other top-end attractions – Nathan Nichols at **River House** in Noosaville and Ben Beirtei at **Spirit House** in the hinterland at Yandina – are faring. Early signs – and their pedigrees; Ben was with Marty Boetz at Longrain – certainly promise good things.

For breakfast or brunch, book somewhere beachside like **Bistro C**, **Seasons** or **Sails**, although you'll be seen by more people sitting on the Parisian-like pavement seating at **Aroma**. Good coffee helps justify that scene.

For something a whole heap less intensely laid-back, try the far daggier township of Sunshine Beach round the headland. Here you'll find two rather delicious and very eclectic cafés that do the whole retro, found-object thing with a distinctly sub-tropical feel. Try **Fratellini** for coffee, pizza and a darn good paper read, or the op-art colourful **Mooshka** for Damian Roberts' modern internationalist café food.

Perth and the Hills

While places like Jackson's, Frasers, Must and Clarke's of North Beach are all proven performers, if I only had two meals in Perth I'd be chasing the more casual offerings of two of the city's other icon chefs, Kate Lamont and David Coomer. Lamont's **Cottlesloe Wine Store** is a great relaxed spot to unwind away from the bustle of the CBD, with a tight menu of small-plate dishes like confit duck salad with mandarin oil or artichoke and fennel gratin. Closer in at Nedlands is Coomer's **Pata Negra**, which also opened in 2009. This moody, split-level space is attracting a lot of positive critical heat for the modern tapas menu that is more Iberian and Moorish inspired – think platters of *jamóns*, *arroz negro* (rice cooked with squid ink) or fennel, orange, date and radicchio salad. Not a surprise, when you discover that the kitchen team is ex-Star Anise sous chef Matt Stone and Kurt Sampson. Sampson was Greg Malouf's right-hand man at Momo for several years and also ran some well-respected and less high falutin' places of his own. **Star Anise** is Coomer's glossier big brother and a pick for the full-on fancy pants dining experience.

If you are looking for classic fine dining and don't mind a bit of a ramble, head up to **The Loose Box**, where Alain Fabrègues draws on classical French technique and local produce, including Western Australian truffles, of which he is a passionate supporter, to conjure up elegant fine dining. Add old-school ambience and you'll find this a refined and detailed journey for the palate. If you stay over in one of the cottages, finish off the Francophile experience by dropping into Franck Maurice's marvellous old-school patisserie. **Le Croissant Du Moulin** has been running for over twenty-five years and will sate your early-morning hunger with croissants of suitable lightness and the sort of pastries that make you wish you had two mouths and four stomachs.

Tasmania and Darwin

I went to Tassie three times last year but I haven't eaten there extensively enough this year to make full suggestions given the number of changes down there recently. **Stillwater** would remain my go-to place in Launceston, while what I love about further south are the cafés of Hobart and the produce you'll find down that way. The oysters around Coles Bay and Bruny Island, Bicheno crays, Domaine A's pinot and merlot, Alistair Wise's macaroons, Yves Ginat's Miellerie honey, the octopus from Pirates Bay, Roger Scales' smoked ocean trout and the goats' cheese from Tongola – which probably makes the **Wursthaus** deli in Hobart my favourite place to eat, although as guzzling while standing in the store is not great manners, maybe go there to shop for the perfect picnic! Either they've got it or they will know where to find it!

It's the same thing in the Alice and Darwin, but when I go back, on the cards are a Thai dinner at Jimmy Shu's **Hanuman** restaurant or hunkering down for a monster crab feast at **Char** – John Kilroy's steak restaurant which is a monte for a long liquid and tropical lunch in Darwin.

MATT'S ADDRESS BOOK

Victoria

Donovan's, 40 Jacka Boulevard, St Kilda. (03) 9534 8221.

Vue de Monde, 430 Little Collins Street, Melbourne. (03) 9691 3888.

Cumulus Inc., 45 Flinders Lane, Melbourne. (03) 9650 1445.

Attica, 74 Glen Eira Road, Ripponlea. (03) 9530 0111.

Bella Vedere, 874 Maroondah Highway, Coldstream. (03) 5962 6161.

Royal Mail Hotel, 98 Parker Street, Dunkeld. (03) 5577 2241.

Spice Market, Beaney Lane, Melbourne. (03) 9660 3777.

Cookie, Level 1, 252 Swanston Street, Melbourne. (03) 9663 7660.

Madame Brussels, Level 3, 59–63 Bourke Street, Melbourne. (03) 9662 2775.

Sweatshop at Seamstress, 113 Lonsdale Street, Melbourne. (03) 9663 6363.

Siglo, Level 2, 161 Spring Street, Melbourne. (03) 9654 6300.

Match Bar and Grill, 249 Little Lonsdale Street, Melbourne. (03) 9654 6522.

Bar Lourinhã, 37 Little Collins Street, Melbourne. (03) 9663 7890.

Coda Bar and Restaurant, Basement, 141 Flinders Lane, Melbourne. (03) 9650 3155.

Gigibaba, 102 Smith Street, Collingwood. (03) 9486 0345.

Von Haus, 1a Crossley Street, Melbourne. (03) 9662 2756.

Longrain, 44 Little Bourke Street, Melbourne. (03) 9671 3151.

MoVida Next Door, 1 Hosier Lane, Melbourne. (03) 9663 3038.

Shira Nui, 247 Springvale Road, Glen Waverley. (03) 9886 7755.

Shoya, 25 Market Lane, Melbourne. (03) 9650 0848.

Journal Canteen, 253 Flinders Lane, Melbourne. (03) 9650 4399.

Jacques Reymond, 78 Williams Road, Prahran. (03) 9525 2178.

Da Noi, 95 Toorak Road, South Yarra. (03) 98665975.

Stokehouse, 30 Jacka Boulevard, St Kilda. (03) 9525 5555.

Ocha, 156 Pakington Street, Kew. (03) 9853 6002.

The European, 161 Spring Street, Melbourne. (03) 9654 0811.

Aka Tombo, 205 Greville Street, Prahran. (03) 9510 0577.

The Lake House, King Street, Daylesford. (03) 5348 3329.

Cutler & Co., 55–57 Gerturde Street, Fitzroy. (03) 9419 4888.

Pellegrini's, 66 Bourke Street, Melbourne. (03) 9662 1885.

Daawat, 358 Victoria Street, Richmond. (03) 9429 1857.

Indian Harvest, 111 Waverley Road, Malvern. (03) 9571 0472.

Jaipur Curry Bar, 16 Bourke Street, Melbourne. (03) 9663 3848.

Woodapple, Shop 1/ 427 Hampton Street, Hampton. (03) 9598 7800.

Madras Banyan Tree, 924 Nepean Highway, Hampton East. (03) 9555 7170.

Abla's, 109 Elgin Street, Carlton. (03) 9347 0006.

Rumi, 132 Lygon Street, Brunswick East. (03) 9388 8255.

Happy Cook, 156 Springvale Road, Nunawading. (03) 9894 1663.

Giuseppe Arnaldo & Sons, Shop 25/ 8 Whiteman Street, Southbank. (03) 9694 7400.

Koutouki Coffee Shop, 402 Burnley Street, Richmond. (03) 9425 9488.

Siam 1, 65 Koornang Road, Carnegie. (03) 9571 7334.

Café di Stasio. 31 Fitzroy Street, St Kilda. (03) 9525 3999.

New South Wales

Sopra, 7 Danks Street, Waterloo. 1300 552 119.

Bodega, Shop 1/ 216 Commonwealth Street, Surry Hills. (02) 9212 7766.

Tetsuya's Restaurant, 529 Kent Street, Sydney. (02) 9267 2900.

Marque, Shop 4/ 355 Crown Street, Surry Hills. (02) 9332 2225.

Quay, Overseas Passenger Terminal, George Street, The Rocks. (02) 9251 5600.

Pier, 594 New South Head Road, Rose Bay. (02) 9327 6561.

Bécasse, 204 Clarence Street, Sydney. (02) 9283 3440.

Est, Level 1, 252 George Street, Sydney. (02) 9240 3000.

Sepia, 201 Sussex Stret, Darling Park, Sydney. (02) 9283 1990.

Rockpool Bar and Grill, 66 Hunter Street, Sydney. (02) 8078 1900.

Spice Temple,10 Bligh Street, Sydney. (02) 8078 1888.

Billy Kwong, Shop 3/ 355 Crown Street, Surry Hills. (02) 9332 3300.

Aria, 1 Macquarie Street, Circular Quay. (02) 9252 2555.

Restaurant Assiette, 48 Albion Street, Surry Hills. (02) 9212 7979.

Universal, Shop 105/ 46 Burton Street, Darlinghurst. (02) 9331 0709.

Pilu at Freshwater, On The Beach, Moore Road, Harbord. (02) 9938 3331.

Lucio's, 47 Windsor Street, Paddington. (02) 9380 5996.

Buon Ricordo, 108 Boundary Road, Paddington. (02) 9380 8955.

The Beresford Hotel, 354 Bourke Street, Darlinghurst. (02) 9357 1111.

Bentley Restaurant and Bar, 320 Crown Street, Surry Hills. (02) 9332 2344.

Icebergs Dining Room and Bar, 1 Notts Avenue, Bondi Beach. (02) 9365 9000.

South Australia

The Manse, 142 Tynte Street, North Adelaide. (08) 8267 4636.

Georges On Waymouth, 20 Waymouth Street. (08) 8211 6960.

The Wine Underground, 121 Pirie Street. (08) 8232 1222.

Sparrow, 10 O'Connell Street, North Adelaide. (08) 8267 2444.

The Pot Food & Wine, 160 King William Road, Hyde Park. (08) 8373 2044.

Panacea, 72–72 Halifax Street, Adelaide. (08) 8232 3523.

Food Business, 4 Linden Avenue, Hazelwood Park. (08) 8379 8699.

Bistro Dom, 24 Waymouth Street, Adelaide. (08) 8231 7000.

Queen Street Café, 12 Elizabeth Street, Croydon. (08) 8340 0708.

Dragonfly, 193 Victoria Square, Adelaide. (08) 8212 5661.

Botanic, 309 North Terrace, Adelaide. (08) 8227 0799.

The 1878 Apothecary, 118 Hindley Street, Adelaide. (08) 8212 9099.

Richmond Hotel. 128 Rundle Mall, Adelaide. (08) 8215 4444.

Queensland

E'cco, 100 Boundary Street, Brisbane. (07) 3831 8344.

Urbane, 179 Mary Street, Brisbane. (07) 3229 2271.

Buffalo Club, Level 1, 234 Wickham Street, Fortitude Valley. (07) 3216 1323.

Aria, 1 Eagle Street Pier, Brisbane. (07) 3233 2555.

Sky Room, Level 2, 234 Wickham Street, Fortitude Valley. (07) 3852 4718.

The Bowery Bar, 676 Ann Street, Fortitude Valley. (07) 3252 0202.

The Lark, Shop 1, 267 Given Terrace, Paddington. (07) 3369 1299.

Wasabi, 2 Quamby Place, Noosa Sound. (07) 5449 2443.

Berardo's, 50 Hastings Street, Noosa Heads. (07) 5447 5666.

Humid, 195 Weyba Road, Noosaville. (07) 5449 9755.

River House, 301 Weyba Road, Noosaville. (07) 5449 7441.

Spirit House, 20 Nindery Road, Yandina. (07) 5446 8977.

Fratellini, 36 Duke Street, Sunshine Beach. (07) 5474 8080.

Mooshka, Shop 6, 46 Duke Street, Sunshine Beach. (07) 5474 5571.

Western Australia

Lamont's Cottesloe Wine Store, 12 Station Street, Cottesloe. (08) 9385 0666.

Pata Negra, 26 Stirling Highway, *Nedlands*. (08) 9389 5517.

Star Anise, 225 Onslow Road, Shenton Park. (08) 9381 9811.

The Loose Box, 6825 Great Eastern Highway, Mundaring. (08) 9295 1787.

Le Croissant Du Moulin, 169 Railway Road, Gooseberry Hill. (08) 9293 4345.

Tasmania

Stillwater, Ritchie's Mill, Patterson Street, Launceston. (03) 6331 4153.

Wursthaus Kitchen, 1 Montpelier Retreat, Battery Point, Hobart. (03) 6224 0644.

Northern Territory

Hanuman, 93 Mitchell Street, Darwin. (08) 8941 3500.

Hanuman, Crowne Plaza Hotel, 82 Barrett Drive, Alice Springs. (08) 8953 7188.

Char Restaurant, corner of The Esplanade and Knuckey Street, Darwin. (08) 8981 4544.

ACKNOWLEDGEMENTS

This book really should have about fifty names on the front cover, because its publication is thanks to the efforts of a huge number of people.

Firstly, the wonderful publisher Alison Urquhart, who seems to know instinctively that what she wants is what I want, and who shares a similarly nerdy love of history and all its wonders with me. Oh, and her boss, Nikki Christer, who helped convince me that Random House Australia was home ... something that I truly realised when I met all the very fine staff there.

Jessica Dettmann edited all the copy and didn't get too angry with me – even when I probably deserved it. She even let me keep some of the crapper jokes in. Needless to say I just repaid her by ensuring the deadlines were kept punishingly short.

Rosie Manion, Brett Osmond and the marketing team; Gavin Schwarz and the national and regional sales teams; Linda Watchorn and the production team; Christa Moffitt, the designer, and Midland Typesetters (gotta love Bembo 11/16); all of whom have probably put in far more effort than this book really warrants. Thanks, too, to my favourite reader, Anni Hayes, for picking up so many of my errors.

And last but not least at Random House Australia, Karen Reid and the publicity team – especially the marvellous Kate Taperell, who drew the short straw and had to look after me and my addiction to doing radio, and keep my ridiculous ego in check. And all while juggling a mobile phone and piccolo latte in the other hand.

Of course, this book wouldn't have been possible if it wasn't for all those who saw a glimmer of hope in my writing and fanned it with their warm advice and offers of work over the years. Without them these pages would have been blank. Caroline Roessler gave me my first restaurant column and, like Pandora, loosed me on the world. Without her I'd be still writing about *Neighbours* and *Home & Away*.

John Lethlean brought me onto the 'Epicure' section of *The Age* and there really was no better place to write about food. Over the years I have developed a strong respect and friendship for all my 'Epicure' editors. Both Kylie Walker and her deputy, Necia Wilden, and Veronica Ridge and her deputy, Jane Willson, have shown sometimes reckless faith in my abilities (perhaps knowing that their skills as editors could always tame my copy into something readable). Together we have won many awards both for the section and me – yippee. More recently, my writing has come under the wing of Sally Heath, editor of *The Age*'s 'A2' section, and I have found her both wise and funny; accordingly, my writing has benefited, because without great editors you don't get good writing from average hacks.

If *The Age* has been my yin, then *delicious* magazine and *Vogue Entertaining + Travel* have been my yang. Editor-in-chief Trudi Jenkins has been an inspiration for as long as I have known her and a rare visionary in Australian publishing (she'll hate me saying that, because it's true). She has also surrounded herself with two of the best food magazine editors in the world, Sarah Nicolson and Kylie Walker, each supported by two teams that I am very proud to be a part of, specifically Danielle Opperman, Valli Little, Sarah, Alison, Amanda, Scott and Simon at *delicious* and Sally Feldman, Sophia Young, Selma and Jacqui at *VE+T*. No wonder, with unrivalled talent like that, that both magazines have won so many major awards here and overseas in the last seven years. It also helps to have a very smart management team led by Sandra Hook and Fiona Nilsson. Oh, and who could forget my favourite event team of Fiona Westall, Tobi and Fran. Then there are the photographers who do the bulk of the travelling with me on stories. You'd be hard-pressed to find two more enjoyable travelling companions – or better, quicker, more patient snappers – than Mark Roper and Catherine Sutherland. Mark also did the cover shots for the book and all the publicity shots too, because he's a decent fellow.

There are many more who've had the misfortune of trying to turn my gibberish into presentable copy. To all of those subs and editors I'd like to say sorry, and thank you. Especially to Alison Dean and Dan Stock at *Melbourne Weekly Bayside*, along with their previous compadres Richard Conrad and Peter Waters. And others like Donna Reeves, Kym Wilson, Susannah Walker, Lucy Tumanow West, Rebecca Cox, Roslyn Grundy, Carrie Hutchinson, the tennis boys and Tracey Platt, whose professional advice, editing, eating and friendship I have cherished.

There are others whose influence is less direct but no less important. Henrie Stride, Mark Klemens and all the team at Profile Management; George, Gary and Sarah, whose countless story ideas and suggestions have made writing in the *MasterChef* green room such a joy; David Mott, Cathie Scott, Brooke Burns, Sandy Paterson, Jennifer Lenne, Sam Hastie, and Anthony McCarthy at Network Ten; Carl and Mark Fennessy, Paul Franklin, Judy Smart and Jono Summerhayes at Fremantle Media. And of course the team at the Melbourne Food & Wine Festival, including my 'other wife' Natalie O'Brien, Sharlee, Rachella, Ute, Lara, Ellie, Sally, Sara, Zoe, Ian and a most supportive network of chefs and restaurateurs, producers, politicians and wine-makers. I am very proud that together we brought some truly inspiring chefs to Australia and put together some amazing events. And finally Charlotte James, who is my online guru.

Isn't it strange how it seems to be mainly women that I've worked with?

Then there is also the great fraternity of food writers, a network that means that whatever city you're in there is always someone who is ready to share their knowledge of where's best to eat. This generosity never ceases to amaze me. So stand up and take a bow: Tony Love,

ACKNOWLEDGEMENTS

Lizzie Loel, Bob Hart, Dani Valent, Michael Harden, Simon Thomsen, Simon Plant, Joanna Savill, Janne Apelgren, Nina Rousseau, Cherry Ripe, Benedict Beauge, Jen A. Murphy, Barbara Atkinson and William Sitwell.

ABOUT THE AUTHOR

In the real world, *MasterChef* judge and critic Matt Preston writes about food for *delicious* magazine, *The Age*, *Vogue Entertaining + Travel* and *Food and Wine* in the States. He's still a bit amazed that such a job exists.

London-raised but Australia-based, Matt has dedicated the last ten years of his life – and about twenty kilos – to tracking down some of the more interesting stories behind the food we eat and the people who cook it.

Matt lives in Melbourne with his saint of a wife, Emma, their three children, a dog, four ovens and a number of trophies for his food writing, including a very nice gold ladle that is inscribed with the immortal words *Le Cordon Bleu World Food Media Awards – World's Best Food Journalist – Matt Preston*.

Just please don't tell him that you can buy these in Hanoi's markets for five bucks a dozen.

Become a friend at Matt Preston's official Facebook page or check out the website www.mattpreston.com.au.